Cultural Criminology

Advisor in Criminal Justice to Northeastern University Press
Gilbert Geis

CULTURAL

JEFF FERRELL
&
CLINTON R. SANDERS

CRIMINOLOGY

Northeastern University Press
BOSTON

Northeastern University Press

Copyright 1995 by Northeastern University Press

Library of Congress Cataloging-in-Publication Data

Cultural criminology / Jeff Ferrell, Clinton Sanders [editors].
    p.   cm.
    Includes bibliographical references and index.
    ISBN 1–55553–235–7 (cloth : acid-free paper).
    —ISBN 1–55553–236–5 (pbk. : acid-free paper)
    1. Crime—United States.   2. Popular culture—United States.
3. Crime in mass media—United States.   4. Social control—United
States.   5. United States—Social conditions.   I. Ferrell, Jeff.
II. Sanders, Clinton
HV6030.T69   1995
364.973—dc20   95–11501
                    Rev.

Designed by Diane Levy

Printed and bound by Thomson-Shore, Inc., in Dexter, Michigan. The paper is Glatfelter, an acid-free sheet.

MANUFACTURED IN THE UNITED STATES OF AMERICA

99 98 97 96 95 5 4 3 2 1

To Zoot

Contents

Acknowledgments

Cultural Criminology reflects an emerging, collective conversation among its contributors, an ongoing exploration of (and disagreement over) the many ways in which cultural and criminal processes come together. In this sense, were it not a bit redundant, it would be appropriate to acknowledge the book's contributors here. But this collective inquiry has of course involved many others as well. Among those, we thank and acknowledge especially Howie Becker, Sue Caulfield, Donna Hale, Christina Johns, Stephanie Kane, Peter Kraska, Marilyn McShane, Tony Platt, Jeffrey Ian Ross, Marty Schwartz, Margaret Smith, and Trey Williams for invaluable insights, information, and perspective. We also hope that this book serves as an invitation to those beyond this brief listing whose research, reflections, or experiences have likewise taken them inside the intersections of culture and crime. As with the rest of life, this work is less a finished project than an open road, and we invite you to join us along it.

Other friends and colleagues have also contributed directly and indirectly to this work. At Regis University, we thank Alice Reich, Jamie Roth, and Steve Doty; Rochelle Hannon, who with the help of Colleen Warrens, worked tirelessly on the book's comprehensive reference section; and librarians Marcia Schipper, Richard Hansen, Kathleen Lance, and Nancy Gorman, whose dedication to the scholarly enterprise makes possible this and other projects. At Northeastern University Press, William Frohlich, Director, and Scott Brassart, Editor, have provided the sort of support, enthusiasm, and professionalism essential to the completion of this undertaking.

Finally, we note some debts that can best be acknowledged individually. Clint Sanders thanks especially Eleanor Lyon. Jeff Ferrell thanks especially Gil Ferrell and Dorris Ferrell, for decades of love and support; Joel Ferrell, for a sense of subculture and style; and Karen Lang-Ferrell, for everything.

PART ONE...
INTRODUCTION

1 ...

Culture, Crime, and Criminology

JEFF FERRELL AND CLINTON R. SANDERS

This book explores the common ground between cultural and criminal practices in contemporary social life—that is, between collective behavior organized around imagery, style, and symbolic meaning, and that categorized by legal and political authorities as criminal. As the essays collected here show, intersections of culture and crime have defined the evolution of public controversies past and present and increasingly shape the experience and perception of everyday life. Zoot suiters and gangbangers, Robert Mapplethorpe and rap music, mediated muggings and televised anticrime campaigns—all demonstrate that cultural and criminal processes continually interweave along a continuum of marginality, illegality, and public display.

The many contemporary confluences of cultural and criminal dynamics force us to reconsider traditionally discrete categories of culture and crime in our research and analysis. Many social groups and events traditionally conceptualized as criminal are in fact defined in their everyday operations by subcultural meaning and style. At the same time, various groups and events conventionally placed under the heading of culture regularly suffer criminalization at the hands of moral entrepreneurs, legal and political authorities, and others.[1] Further, the criminalization campaigns launched against various subcultures and subcultural activities themselves operate not only by constructing legal statutes and enforcement procedures but by deploying mediated symbols and mobilizing powerful cultural references. To account for the culture and subcultures of crime, the criminalization of cultural and subcultural activities, and the politics of these processes, then, we must move toward an integration of cultural and criminological analysis— that is, toward a cultural criminology.

Crime as Culture

Anyway, I got in a lot of trouble with the police over the motorsickles and my involvement with gangs. . . . So the people that interested me were the real hardened criminals, who were always dragging me into trouble. But they had style.

—artist Robt. Williams[2]

Criminal behavior is, more often than not, subcultural behavior. From the interactionist criminology of the Chicago School and Edwin Sutherland to the subcultural theories of Cohen, Cloward and Ohlin, and others, criminologists have long acknowledged that actions and identities labeled criminal are typically generated within the boundaries of deviant and criminal subcultures.[3] In this sense much of what we take to be crime is essentially collective behavior; whether carried out by one person or many, particular criminal acts are often organized within and instigated by subcultural groups. Though the boundaries may remain ill-defined, and the membership may shift in gross numbers and level of commitment, these subcultures constitute definitive human associations for those who participate in them. Biker, hustler, Blood and Crip, pimp and prostitute—all name subcultural networks as much as individual identities.

As Sutherland and the Chicago School knew a half century ago, and as innumerable case studies have since confirmed, though, criminal subcultures incorporate far more than simple proximities of personal association. To speak of a criminal subculture is to recognize not only an association of people but a network of symbols, meaning, and knowledge. Members of a criminal subculture learn and negotiate "motives, drives, rationalizations, and attitudes"; develop elaborate conventions of language, appearance, and presentation of self; and in so doing participate, to greater or lesser degrees, in a sub*culture*, a collective way of life.[4] In turn these often intensely emotionalized subcultures shape the ways in which their members come to understand and value themselves. Intimate participation in a collective way of life demonstrates and displays, to oneself and to others, personal attributes that make one worthy of belonging, being accepted, and—potentially—becoming important.

Much of this subcultural meaning, action, identity, and status is organized around style—that is, around the shared aesthetic of the subculture's members. As earlier researchers have found, and as many of the essays collected here demonstrate, subtleties of collective style define the meaning of crime and deviance for subcultural participants, agents of legal control, consumers of mediated crime images, and others.[5] If we are to understand both the terror and the appeal of skinheads, Bloods and Crips, graffiti writers, zoot suiters, rude boys, drug users, and others, we must be able to make sense not only of their criminal acts but of their collective aesthetics as well.

Katz's research, for example, has linked criminal acts and aesthetics by examining the styles and symbolic meanings that emerge inside the everyday dynamics of criminal events and criminal subcultures.[6] By paying attention to dark sunglasses and white undershirts, to precise styles of walking, talking, and otherwise presenting one's criminal identity, Katz has sketched the "alternative deviant culture," the "coherent deviant [a]esthetic" in which bad asses, cholos, punks, youth gang members, and others participate.[7] In these cases, as in other forms of crime on and off the street, the meaning of criminality is anchored in the style of its collective practice. As the essays included here demonstrate, the biker's ritually reconstructed motorcycle, the gang member's sports clothing and tattoos, the graffiti writer's mysterious street images, and the skinhead's music constitute the essential cultural and subcultural materials out of which criminal projects and criminal identities are constructed and displayed. Once again, participation in a criminal subculture, or in the "culture of crime," means participation in the symbolism and style, the collective aesthetic environment, of criminality.[8]

From early work within the British cultural studies tradition to Katz and other contemporary criminologists, though, research has shown that symbolism and style shape not only criminal subcultures but the broader social and legal relations in which these subcultures are caught.[9] And as the essays collected here demonstrate, both criminal subcultures and their styles grow out of class, age, gender, and ethnic inequalities, and by turns reproduce and resist these social fault lines.

As we will see, guardians of the moral status quo regularly focus their efforts at social and legal control on the cohesive symbols adopted and displayed by members of youthful, insubordinate "taste publics."[10] And while this criminalization of group style may, in essence, constitute a simple-minded attempt to stamp out dissenting groups and acts by denying the display of membership symbols, its ironic consequence is often the amplification of these symbols' stylistic power, and in turn, enhanced commitment among the group members that have constructed them.

This interplay of subcultural style and legal authority reminds us of Becker's classic criminological injunction, that we must examine not only criminal subcultures but the legal and political authorities who construct these subcultures as criminal.[11] When we do we find these authorities both reacting to subcultural styles and employing symbolic and stylistic strategies of their own against them. The criminalization efforts of legal and political campaigners display again the power of cultural forces; in criminalizing cultural and subcultural activities and campaigning for public support, moral entrepreneurs and legal authorities manipulate legal and political structures, but perhaps more so structures of mass symbolism and perception.

To understand the reality of crime and criminalization, then, cultural criminology must account not only for the dynamics of criminal subcultures but for the dynamics of the mass media as well. The following essays will explore mediated images of drug violence, surveillance, serial killing, and sexual assault, and the effects of these images on contemporary public perceptions and policies in regard to crime. But of course these contemporary cases build on earlier mediated constructions of crime and control. The criminalization of marijuana in the United States a half century ago was predicated on "an effort to arouse the public to the danger confronting it by means of 'an educational campaign describing the drug, its identification, and evil effects.' "[12] Aggressive mob behavior and police assaults on zoot suiters in the 1940s were "preceded by the development of an unambiguously unfavorable symbol" in Los Angeles newspapers.[13] In the mid-1960s lurid media accounts of rape and assault set the context for a legal campaign against the Hell's Angels; at almost the same time, legal attacks on British mods and rockers were legitimated through the media's deployment of "emotive symbols."[14] In the 1970s the "reciprocal relations" between the British mass media and criminal justice system produced a perception that mugging was "a frightening new strain of crime."[15] And during the 1980s and early 1990s, mediated horror stories have legitimated "wars" on drugs, gangs, and graffiti in the United States and have produced moments of mediated "moral panic" over child abuse and child pornography in Great Britain.[16]

Clearly, then, both the everyday collective practice of criminality and the criminalization of everyday life by the powerful are *cultural enterprises* and must be investigated as such. This being the case, effective criminological research and analysis must incorporate understandings of media, language, symbolism, and style—that is, an appreciation of cultural processes and subcultural dynamics. Put more simply: making sense of crime and criminalization means paying close attention to culture.

Culture as Crime

Further, Mapplethorpe's controversial *Honey, 1976*, is said to portray a nude child "just as thousands of other child molesters/pornographers before and after him. . . . The photo advertises the availability of the child (and, by extension, all children) for photographic assault and rape."

—*Richard Bolton, quoting a* Washington Times *editorial*[17]

In the same way that everyday crime and criminalization operate as cultural enterprises, everyday popular cultural undertakings—those social activities organized around art, music, and fashion—are regularly recast as crime. Certainly much in the worlds of art, music, and fashion gets caught up in controversies over "good taste," public decency, and the alleged influences of popular culture. In some cases the producers of art or music themselves stoke these controversies to promote consumption of their cultural commodities; in other cases, right-wing interest groups, religious fundamentalists, and others promote these cultural conflicts as part of their theo-political agendas. Frequently, these two dynamics intertwine in ironic, symbiotic relationships of mutual amplification. Of interest here, though, are the many cases in which such conflicts not only promote controversy, but also reconstruct cultural production, distribution, and consumption as both criminal and criminogenic.

The recent history of Western popular music provides an ongoing array of such cases. The emergence of punk music in Great Britain during the 1970s, for example, incorporated both controversy and criminalization. When London underground designer and shop owner Malcolm McLaren recruited singer John Lydon (Johnny Rotten) and helped organize the definitive punk band, the Sex Pistols, he was also assembling an intentionally confrontational and disturbing style. Drawing on the violently confused imagery of sadomasochism, bondage, fascism, and anarchy, McLaren, Lydon, and the Sex Pistols produced a predictable public reaction. The British media condemned the band, and the larger punk movement, as violent threats to British society. British politicians and allied moral entrepreneurs, responding to the media-generated furor, raged against this perceived threat to civil order and morality. The Sex Pistols, who themselves each carried prior criminal records, now came under violent attack (for example, stabbings, beatings), and were forced to hire bodyguards and to begin playing club dates under assumed names. In addition, British authorities ruled the band's promotional displays to be obscene; local authorities prosecuted record shops carrying Sex Pistols albums and related materials; and legal authorities fined the head of Virgin Records, the Sex Pistols' record company at the time, for violating obscenity statutes. Subsequently, U.S. customs officials delayed a U.S. tour by denying the Sex Pistols entry visas, purportedly because of their criminal records; and throughout the 1980s, British police continued to raid record shops and confiscate "obscene" punk and alternative records.[18]

Contemporary popular music controversies in the United States mirror the British punk experience. During the early 1990s, for example, Florida's governor urged the state prosecutor to indict the black rap group 2 Live Crew under racketeering statutes. Failing this, a local sheriff took the band to civil court over obscenity charges, sent his deputies and other undercover officers into record shops, and ultimately arrested black record shop owner Charles Freeman on obscenity charges. (Freeman was subsequently convicted of obscenity by an all-white jury.) Florida authorities also conducted a highly publicized arrest of 2 Live Crew's members on obscenity charges following a live performance by the band.[19]

Meanwhile, back in the United Kingdom, legal authorities confiscated 24,000 copies of an album by rap group N.W.A.; and in the U.S.,

Nebraska authorities clamped down on five businesses for selling rap music.[20] Local, state, and national associations of police officers—with the support of then Vice President Dan Quayle and others—attempted to interrupt both distribution and performances of rapper Ice-T's song "Cop Killer," arguing in the mass media that "the publication of such vile trash is unconscionable. This song does nothing but arouse the passions of the criminal element."[21] Virginia authorities responded by arresting a record store owner for selling Ice-T's album "Body Count," and large record store chains reacted by removing the album from their shelves.[22]

But if the "low culture" worlds of punk and rap have not escaped criminalization, neither have the "high culture" echelons of gallery and museum art. During 1990 San Francisco police and the FBI raided the studio of Jock Sturges, a photographer whose works hang in the Metropolitan Museum of Art, the Museum of Modern Art, and other acclaimed galleries and museums. Police also seized Sturges' associate Joe Semien, interrogating him for two days before his release. On the basis of a series of casual photographs that Sturges had taken of friends while on a nude beach in France, federal prosecutors accused both men of involvement with child pornography.[23]

In Cincinnati, the Contemporary Arts Center (CAC) faced similar legal problems in relation to an exhibit of (gay) photographer Robert Mapplethorpe's works. Anticipating such problems, the CAC restricted admissions to the exhibit, developed voluntary disclaimers, and even filed a preemptive lawsuit requesting legal protection. Nonetheless, a local grand jury indicted the CAC and its director, Dennis Barrie, on charges of "pandering obscenity and for the use of a minor in materials related to the nude." Though a county court jury later found Barrie and the CAC not guilty, a number of similar cases have emerged and been publicized in the United States over the past few years.[24]

From punk and rap to fine art photography, these cases embody not only the criminalization of popular culture but the politics of culture and the dynamics of the mass media as well. Significantly, the criminalization of popular culture is both a politicized attack on particular media forms like popular music and itself a form of media. Like those who work publicly to criminalize the lives of drug users, zoot suiters, bikers, and other members of insubordinate groups, those who campaign to criminalize the worlds of music and art do so by mobilizing powerful cultural resources in the construction of mediated morality plays. When Jesse Helms and Patrick Buchanan publicly declare "cultural war" on the National Endowment for the Arts and gay and lesbian artists; when Tipper Gore and her Parents' Music Resource Center, and the Reverend Donald Wildmon and his American Family Association (AFA), decry the criminogenic effects of "obscene" words and images; when Cincinnati's Citizens for Community Values, and local sheriffs and politicians, attempt to outlaw alternative art and music, all employ their political and media networks to disseminate select images and precise cultural references.[25]

In this redefined cultural context, popular music becomes an obscene and seditious catalyst for youthful disobedience and social decay; and visual art is transformed into a lascivious crime against social decency, a kind of high-toned pornography. Thus, in the Cincinnati case, for example, Citizens for Community Values mailed almost 18,000 letters to "Cincinnati leaders"—letters that called for "action to prevent this pornographic art from being shown in our city."[26] The *Washington Times* argued that Mapplethorpe portrayed nude children "just as thousands of other child molesters/pornographers before and after him." And more generally, Wildmon's AFA continues to utilize an annual budget of $5 million to print in national newspapers full-page advertisements alleging the criminogenic influence of popular music and television and to send its newsletter to 400,000 subscribers.[27]

These criminalization campaigns of course incorporate not only media dynamics but the reactionary politics of cultural control. And in criminalizing popular culture, they at the same time promote the moral agendas and political careers of those who design them. The simplistic criminogenic models at the core of these constructed moral panics over art and music deflect attention from larger and more complex political problems like economic and ethnic inequality, and the alienation of young people and creative workers from confining institutions. In turn these crude causal equations of art and music with crime proffer the general public a false and demagogic hope that insubordination can be banished without a reworking of the structures of authority that, ironically, give rise both to insubordination and to the moral entrepreneurs who wish to suppress it. And the construction of moral panic around unconventional symbolic expression further works to the advantage of key political and moral leaders in that it grants them status as public spokespersons who offer "practical" remedies for the causes of contemporary criminality and moral decline out of their ostensible concern with the welfare of society.

Not surprisingly, then, these criminalization campaigns, like those seen previously, disproportionately target ethnic minorities, gays and lesbians, young people, and other outsiders. It is certainly no accident that, historically, marijuana users, black and Latino/Latina zoot suiters and gang members, and working-class bikers in the United States and Great Britain have been the focus of highly publicized criminalization campaigns; and it is no accident that, among all the varieties of contemporary artistic and musical production, radical punk bands, black rap groups, and gay visual artists have been most aggressively recast as criminals. In all these cases, the marginality of these groups—and the audacious styles through which they celebrate and confront their marginality—threatens the caretakers of moral and legal control.[28]

Clearly, both the collective production of art and music and the mediated responses to cultural production by legal and moral authorities incorporate the ongoing politics of crime, criminalization, and legal control. That being the case, research into art, music, and culture must incorporate a critical understanding of mediated criminalization campaigns, legal procedures, and even criminological theory. Put more simply: making sense of culture means paying close attention to crime and criminalization.

Collisions of Culture and Crime: Toward a Cultural Criminology

So far we have examined three broad categories of social and cultural experience: criminal identities and events that incorporate dimensions of cultural meaning and style, artistic and musical worlds caught up in the dynamics of crime and criminalization, and the mediated processes by which both subcultural and popular cultural worlds are criminalized. But precisely where are the boundaries between these categories of everyday life? What, for example, of the elegant, elaborate manifestations of Latino/Latina street life? The stylishly criminal zoot suiters of the 1940s; the handcrafted low riders of today, whose slow cruising attracts the attention of both pedestrians and police—are these manifestations of ethnic heritage and ethnic inequality primarily cultural or criminal?

And what of the Sex Pistols? Are they best understood as convicted criminals or cutting-edge musicians, as purveyors of obscenity or performance artists? Answers to these questions are, of course, as ambiguous as are the boundaries between culture and crime—boundaries that are in turn shaped and blurred by the power and prestige of those involved. When the U.S. Supreme Court ruled in 1991 to uphold a legal ban on nude barroom dancing, for example, it offered a "venue sensitive" definition stressing that nude dancing in other cultural contexts—such as "an opera at Lincoln Center"—would not be banned, but protected as art.[29]

These sorts of politically charged confusions of culture and crime—and thus the need for a critical cultural criminology—are strikingly documented in the following essays. And it is in fact our wish that these essays will hopelessly confound the categories of "culture" and "crime"—but at the same time begin to sketch a model for making sense of the confusion.

A first group of essays examines the complex dynamic by which media institutions, mediated representations of crime, and the day-to-day experience and perception of crime collide and interweave. In "Repetitive Retribution: Media Images and the Cultural Construction of Criminal Justice" (chap. 2), Clinton Sanders and Eleanor Lyon show how media institutions and criminal justice institutions collude in the construction of politically useful images of crime and crime control. In "The Media and the Construction of Random Drug Violence" (chap. 3), Henry Brownstein presents a remarkable case study in just this sort of dynamic, as he reveals the process by which images of random drug violence in New York City were both constructed by the media and in turn utilized to support a movement of politics and policies to the right. Su Epstein and Kenneth Tunnell likewise document particular constellations of crime imagery, and analyze the ways in which such images both reflect and reproduce larger social circumstances. In "The New Mythic Monster" (chap. 4), Epstein explores the presentation of serial killers in popular film and the often blurred boundaries between these "mythic monsters" and the serial killers who inhabit contemporary headlines. In "A Cultural Approach to Crime and Punishment, Bluegrass Style" (chap. 5), Kenneth Tunnell provides a rich description of murder and other crime themes found in bluegrass music and grounds these themes in broader structures of social and cultural life. Gary

Marx, in "Electric Eye in the Sky: Some Reflections on the New Surveillance and Popular Culture" (chap. 6), next records the remarkable range of surveillance imagery that populates contemporary popular media, and explores the implications of this imagery for understanding new forms of social control and social conflict. In conclusion, Gregg Barak offers in "Media, Crime, and Justice: A Case for Constitutive Criminology" (chap. 7) both an analysis of mass-mediated understandings of crime and control, and a model for deconstructing and ultimately reconstructing these understandings.

A second group of essays explores the particular styles of criminality that emerge within criminal(ized) subcultures and the broader interplay of these styles with collective perception, criminalization, and social and legal control. Jeff Ferrell's "Style Matters: Criminal Identity and Social Control" (chap. 8) examines the role of subcultural style in constructing collective identity and interaction and in shaping the complex dynamic between criminalized subcultures and legal authorities. In "Hammer of the Gods Revisited: Neo-Nazi Skinheads, Domestic Terrorism, and the Rise of the New Protest Music" (chap. 9), Mark Hamm demonstrates that, within particular social and cultural contexts, distinct forms of subcultural music and style have underwritten the development of skinhead associations and skinhead violence. "Struggles Over the Symbolic: Gang Style and the Meanings of Social Control" (chap. 10) likewise presents Jody Miller's remarkable account of the ways in which legal authorities come to understand and evaluate gang style in their exercise of legal control. In "Squaring the One Percent: Biker Style and the Selling of Cultural Resistance" (chap. 11), Stephen Lyng and Mitchell Bracey richly document not only the subtleties of biker style and the role of legal and media institutions in its evolution but the ultimate exhaustion of this style in the postmodern marketplace. And in "The World Politics of Wall Painting" (chap. 12), Jeff Ferrell concludes by analyzing illegal art and graffiti worldwide in terms of subcultural style, cultural production, and legal control.

As these essays examine media institutions, mediated images of crime and criminality, and the complex relationship between subcultural style, media dynamics, and legal authority, they begin to uncover the many entanglements of culture and crime in contemporary life. They also show that all those caught up in this mix—bikers and street gang members, but also legal authorities and media crusaders and consumers—interact inside the ambiguous intersections of symbolic production, situated meaning, and criminality; and that in so doing, these social actors and actresses experience culture and crime not as categorical abstractions nor as distinct arenas of social existence but as emergent processes twisted together in the texture of everyday life. If we are to make sense of their experience, then, we as criminologists and sociologists must also move beyond the duality of culture and crime to examine the many ways in which culture and crime not only collide but coproduce one another.

As this introductory essay already demonstrates, and as these collected essays emphasize, a number of fundamental themes run through this integration of cultural and criminological concerns. First is the essential role of the *media* in shaping the intersections of culture and crime. It is not simply that the mass media report in certain ways on criminal events or provide fashionable fodder out of which criminal subcultures construct collective styles. For good or bad, postmodern society exists well beyond such discrete, linear patterns of action and reaction. Rather, it is that criminal events, identities, and styles take life within a media-saturated environment, and thus exist from the start as moments in a mediated spiral of presentation and representation. Criminal events and perceptions of criminality are reported on by the media less than they are constructed within the media; their existence is inevitably measured more by ratings points than by rates of crime. Criminal subcultures reinvent mediated images as situated styles, but are at the same time themselves reinvented time and again as they are displayed within the daily swarm of mediated presentations. In every case, as cultural criminologists we study not only images but images of images, an infinite hall of mediated mirrors.

This notion of collective imagery, and the collective production of shared symbolism and meaning, points to a second theme woven into cultural criminology: *style*. As artists and musicians run afoul of obscenity statutes and those who choose to enforce them, as street cops find fault with the sagging pants or shaved heads of gang members, they collectively engage in "crimes of style"—crimes that reveal the power of shared styles in shaping not only criminal identity but legal authority and the boundaries of social control.[30] This essay and those that follow demonstrate the importance of style in the construction of criminal and subcultural identities. But when legal authorities, moral crusaders, and others push for new legal sanctions and more aggressive enforcement to deal with these identities, their perceptions, emotional responses, and controlling reactions are in turn shaped by their own stylistic imperatives. Legal and moral authorities operate within an "aesthetics of authority"; from within a set of aesthetic assumptions and legal controls that define the beauty and desirability of "decent" public art, "clean" cities, and "appropriate" personal style, these authorities condemn and criminalize controversial art, street graffiti, homeless populations, and "tough-looking" kids.[31] And they do so not only because these identities and styles threaten legal or moral control as such, but because they undermine the stylistic certainty and aesthetic precision essential to the functioning of legal authority and social control. In this process of condemnation and criminalization, as we have seen, authorities are moreover able to mobilize their own powerful stylistic resources to reshape the public meaning of tough kids or disputed art.

Style in this sense constitutes the turf over which young punks and old authorities, street corner toughs and street-wise cops, alternative artists and anti-obscenity campaigners battle. And as they engage in these aesthetic turf wars, the combatants continually negotiate the boundaries of culture and crime.

To speak of "turf wars" is, of course, to point to a third theme sewn into the fabric of cultural criminology: the need to take into account power, conflict, subordination, and insubordination, and thus to develop a *critical* cultural criminology. These essays demonstrate time and again that the connections between culture and crime are crafted out of social inequality. As we have already seen, powerful political-economic, legal, religious, and media forces shape the campaigns to criminalize popular culture and particular subcultures and direct these campaigns at outsiders of all sorts. These outsiders—whether gang members, punk musicians, or gallery artists—in turn construct alternative subcultures and styles that provide collective identity and demonstrate resistance to the very powers that criminalize them.[32] Subordination and insubordination define the interplay between culture and crime; and it is through this interplay that power is both enforced and resisted.

As the essays collected here show, though, this interplay operates on many levels beyond the obvious. The criminalization of insubordinate cultural styles and products, for example, regularly works both for and against the interests of legal and other authorities. Ironically, criminalization and mediated cultural denunciation frequently act to generate around the targeted people and products an aura of uniqueness, creativity, and romantic resistance that in turn provides emotional power and pleasure. At the same time, as countercultural products and activities are condemned by authorities and gain the appeal derived from their symbolization of resistance, they frequently come to be seen within circles of mainstream cultural production as having enhanced commercial potential. Because of this, the dominant culture industry regularly co-opts criminalized styles and products and markets homogenized versions for mass consumption. Subversive culture, then, commonly constitutes a key source of the innovation essential to the continued commercial success of the dominant cultural production apparatus. In short, the mainstream cultural system absconds with, and mass markets, what began as the criminal seeds of its own destruction.[33]

This critical focus on the complex interplay of power, inequality, and insubordination also means that cultural criminologists must pay close attention to the particular characteristics of authorities and outsiders alike. Young people, and especially minority youth, for example, seem to be regularly entangled in the intersections of culture and crime. Punk and rap musicians, graffiti writers, bad asses and gang members—most come from backgrounds of ethnic discrimination and poverty, and almost all are young. As will be discussed in subsequent essays, this correlation between youth, culture, and crime points us down two related lines of inquiry. First, we must investigate youth cultures as primary settings for the production of alternative style and meaning, and therefore as the primary targets of legal, political, and moral authorities threatened by the audacity of these cultural alternatives. Second, and more generally, we must critically explore youth as a category of social, cultural, and criminal stratification intertwined with the more established stratification categories of social class, ethnicity, and gender.[34]

The development of the sort of cultural criminology imagined here—a criminology that accounts for subcultural styles, media dynamics, aesthetic orientations, social and cultural inequalities, and more—will necessitate journeys beyond the conventional boundaries of contemporary criminology. If we are to examine the many intersections of culture and crime, we will need a variety of analytic and methodological resources. As we will discuss in the closing essay, this will likely involve both resurrecting and reinventing a number of theoretical strands within criminology and at the same time drawing on exterior fields of inquiry like cultural studies and the sociology of culture.[35]

As we will also discuss there, this movement beyond disciplinary frontiers, this synthesis of divergent intellectual perspectives, and this focus on situated cultural dynamics point to possibilities not only for a critical cultural criminology but a postmodern cultural criminology as well. Contemporary social, feminist, and cultural theories are all moving rapidly beyond disciplinary constraints to create synthetic, postmodern perspectives on social and cultural life. Though marked by their eclectic and divergent components, these perspectives share some fundamental ideas, the most significant for our purposes being that the everyday culture of individuals and groups incorporates powerful and conflicting dimensions of style and meaning. The symbolism and style of social interaction—the culture of everyday life—in this way forms a contested political terrain, embodying patterns of inequality, power, and privilege. And these patterns are in turn intertwined with larger structures of mediated information and entertainment, cultural production and consumption, and legal and political authority. An adequate understanding of everyday life, and of everyday experiences and perceptions of criminality, must therefore be sufficiently synthetic and multidisciplinary—and sufficiently attuned to symbolism and style—to account for these many dimensions of meaning.

Cultural criminology thus provides criminologists the opportunity to enhance their own perspectives on crime with insights from other fields, while at the same time providing for their colleagues in cultural studies, the sociology of culture, media studies, and elsewhere invaluable perspectives on crime, criminalization, and their relationship to cultural and political processes. Bending or breaking the boundaries of criminology to construct a cultural criminology in this sense does not undermine contemporary criminology as much as it expands and enlivens it. Cultural criminology widens criminology's domain to include worlds conventionally considered exterior to it: gallery art, popular music, media operations and texts, style. In the same way, it introduces criminology into contemporary debates over these worlds, and defines criminological perspectives as essential to them. The specific relationships between culture and crime, and the broader relationship between criminology and contemporary social and cultural life, are illuminated within cultural criminology.

Notes

An earlier version of this chapter was published by Jeff Ferrell in the *Journal of Criminal Justice and Popular Culture* (1995) and is reprinted here by permission.

1. Howard S. Becker, *Outsiders: Studies in the Sociology of Deviance* (New York: The Free Press, 1963), 147–63.

2. Quoted in Michelle Delio, "Robt. Williams: Esthetician of the Preposterous," *Art?Alternatives* 1 (April 1992): 45.

3. Edwin Sutherland and Donald Cressey, *Criminology*, 10th ed. (Philadelphia: Lippincott, 1978); Albert Cohen, *Delinquent Boys: The Culture of the Gang* (New York: The Free Press, 1955); Richard Cloward and Lloyd Ohlin, *Delinquency and Opportunity: A Theory of Delinquent Gangs* (New York: The Free Press, 1960); see Walter Miller, "Lower Class Culture as a Generating Milieu of Gang Delinquency," *Journal of Social Issues* 14 (1958): 5–19; Marvin E. Wolfgang and Franco Ferracuti, *The Subculture of Violence* (Beverly Hills: Sage, 1982); Lynn Curtis, *Violence, Race, and Culture* (Lexington, MA: Heath, 1975).

4. Sutherland and Cressey, 80. Of course, social learning, strain, and other criminological theories also incorporate various perspectives on the cultures and subcultures of crime. And see similarly Jeff Ferrell, "The Brotherhood of Timber Workers and the Culture of Conflict," *Journal of Folklore Research* 28 (1991): 163–77, for an application of this argument to labor and union subcultures.

5. Among earlier works, see, for example, Harold Finestone, "Cats, Kicks, and Color," in *The Other Side: Perspectives on Deviance*, ed. Howard S. Becker (New York: The Free Press, 1964), 281–97; Stuart Hall and Tony Jefferson, eds., *Resistance Through Rituals* (London: Hutchinson, 1976); Dick Hebdige, *Subculture: The Meaning of Style* (London: Methuen, 1979); Stuart Cosgrove, "The Zoot-Suit and Style Warfare," *Radical America* 18 (1984): 38–51. See also William Sanders, *Gangbangs and Drive-bys: Grounded Culture and Juvenile Gang Violence* (Hawthorne, NY: Aldine de Gruyter, 1994); and "Style Matters" (chap. 8) and the following essays in this collection.

6. Jack Katz, *Seductions of Crime: Moral and Sensual Attractions in Doing Evil* (New York: Basic Books, 1988).

7. Katz, *Seductions*, p. 90.

8. See Jeff Ferrell, "Making Sense of Crime," *Social Justice* 19 (1992): 110–23; Jeff Ferrell, *Crimes of Style: Urban Graffiti and the Politics of Criminality* (New York: Garland, 1993).

9. Among early British cultural studies, see, for example, Hall and Jefferson, *Resistance*; Paul Willis, *Learning to Labor* (New York: Columbia University Press, 1977); Hebdige, *Subculture*. For more on these works, and on contemporary work in these areas, see "Style Matters" (chap. 8) and the other essays that follow in this collection.

10. Herbert Gans, *Popular Culture and High Culture* (New York: Basic Books, 1974).

11. Becker, *Outsiders*, 163.

12. Becker, *Outsiders*, 140.

13. Ralph H. Turner and Samuel Surace, "Zoot-Suiters and Mexicans: Symbols in Crowd Behavior," *American Journal of Sociology* 62 (1956): 14–20.

14. Hunter S. Thompson, *Hell's Angels: A Strange and Terrible Saga* (New York: Ballantine, 1967); Stanley Cohen, *Folk Devils and Moral Panics* (London: MacGibbon and Kee, 1972), 31, 54.

15. Stuart Hall et al., *Policing the Crisis: Mugging, the State, and Law and Order* (London: Macmillan, 1978), 71, 74.

16. See, for example, Cohen, *Folk Devils*; Simon Watney, *Policing Desire: Pornography, AIDS, and the Media* (Minneapolis: University of Minnesota Press, 1987); Philip Jenkins, *Intimate Enemies: Moral Panics in Contemporary Great Britain* (Hawthorne, NY: Aldine de Gruyter, 1992); Victor Kappeler, Mark Blumberg, and Gary Potter, *The Mythology of Crime and Criminal Justice* (Prospect Heights, IL: Waveland, 1993); Philip Jenkins, *Using Murder: The Social Construction of Serial Homicide* (Hawthorne, NY: Aldine de Gruyter, 1994); Philip Jenkins, " 'The Ice Age': The Social Construction of a Drug Panic," *Justice Quarterly* 11 (1994): 7–31; Erich Goode and Nachman Ben-Yehuda, *Moral Panics* (Cambridge, MA: Blackwell, 1994); and for more on contemporary media constructions of crime and deviance, the various essays collected here. Interestingly, an examination of the "drug courier profiles" incorporated in the U.S. war on drugs indicates that these profiles target alleged "couriers" as much on the basis of personal style as on ethnicity—and that in many cases they target personal style as a lived manifestation of ethnicity; see the following "Style Matters" essay here (chap. 8).

17. Richard Bolton, "The Cultural Contradictions of Conservatism," *New Art Examiner* 17 (June 1990): 24–29, 72.

18. See Tricia Henry, *Break All Rules! Punk Rock and the Making of a Style* (Ann Arbor: UMI Research Press, 1989); Hebdige, *Subculture*; Catherine McDermott, *Street Style: British Design in the 80s* (New York: Rizzoli, 1987); David Holden, "Pop Go the Censors," *Index on Censorship* 22 (1993): 11–14.

19. See "Do the Rights Thing," *Entertainment Weekly*, 30 March 1990, 38–39; Holden, "Pop"; "Shop Owner Takes Rap on Rap Album," *Rocky Mountain News*, 4 October 1990, 2; Gene Santoro, "How 2 B Nasty," *The Nation* 251 (July 2,

1990): 4–5. Perhaps significantly, Steven Dubin, *Arresting Images: Impolitic Art and Uncivil Actions* (London: Routledge, 1992), 10, reports that an assistant state attorney involved in prosecuting the 2 Live Crew case was upset that a retired sociology professor was included on the jury!

20. See Adam Dawtrey and Jeffrey Jolson-Colburn, "Scotland Yard Confiscates Rap Album," *Rocky Mountain News*, 7 June 1991, 111; American Civil Liberties Union, "The Arts Censorship Project" (New York: ACLU, 1992, pamphlet).

21. *Rocky Mountain News*, "Police Look to Stop 'Cop Killer,'" 18 June 1992, 86; see Mark S. Hamm and Jeff Ferrell, "Rap, Cops, and Crime: Clarifying the 'Cop Killer' Controversy," *ACJS Today* 13 (1994): 1, 3, 29.

22. See Arts Censorship Project Newsletter, "Attacks on Rap Music Continue as Paris and ACLU Launch Affirmative Free-Music Campaign" (New York: ACLU, Winter 1993), 4. Punk musician Jello Biafra and his Alternative Tentacles label, rocker Ozzy Osbourne, singer Bobby Brown, and numerous other popular musicians have also recently come under legal attack; mediated campaigns have increasingly laid criminogenic blame on rap music, film and television images, and other popular cultural forms. For more on these and related issues, see Jeff Ferrell, "Criminalizing Popular Culture," in *Criminal Justice and Popular Culture*, ed. Donna Hale and Frankie Bailey (forthcoming).

23. See Bruce Shapiro, "The Art Cops," *The Nation* 251 (9 July 1990): 40–41, 57; Robert Atkins, "A Censorship Time Line," *The Art Journal* (Fall 1991): 33–37.

24. Steven Mannheimer, "Cincinnati Joins the Censorship Circus," *New Art Examiner* 17 (June 1990): 33–35; "CAC, Barrie Win in Court," *New Art Examiner* 18 (November 1990): 13; David Lyman, "Post-Mapplethorpe Blues in Cincinnati," *New Art Examiner* 18 (January 1991): 56; see Ferrell, "Criminalizing Popular Culture."

25. See, for example, "2,000 Christian Conservatives Cheer Anti-Abortion Speech," *Rocky Mountain News*, 12 September 1993, 34A; Carole Vance, "The War on Culture," *Art in America* 77 (1989): 39, 41, 43; Tipper Gore, *Raising PG Kids in an X-Rated Society* (Nashville: Abingdon, 1987).

26. Mannheimer, 34.

27. Bolton, "Cultural Contradictions," 25, 26.

28. Nadine Strossen, "Academic and Artistic Freedom," *Academe* 78 (November/December 1992): 8–15, likewise notes the social class bias of recent Supreme Court rulings on obscenity and free speech. See also Michael Bronski, "It's Not the Flesh, It's the Flowers: The 'Art Wars' Rage On," *Radical America* 23 (1989): 47–55, on Mapplethorpe's "out" gay sexuality; Hall and Jefferson, *Resistance*; and Ferrell, "Criminalizing Popular Culture."

29. Strossen, 15.

30. See Ferrell, *Crimes of Style*.

31. See Ferrell, *Crimes of Style*.

32. See, for example, Hall and Jefferson, *Resistance*; James Scott, *Domination and the Arts of Resistance* (New Haven: Yale University Press, 1990); Ferrell, *Crimes of Style*; and the essays in this collection.

33. See, for example, Sarah Thornton, "Moral Panic, the Media and British Rave Culture," in *Microphone Fiends: Youth Music and Youth Culture*, ed. Andrew Ross and Tricia Rose (New York: Routledge, 1994), 176–92; and Stephen Lyng and Mitchell Bracey's essay in this collection (chap. 11).

34. Among classic works on youth, culture, and crime, see, for example, Cohen, *Folk Devils*; Hall and Jefferson, *Resistance*; David Greenberg, "Delinquency and the Age Structure of Society," *Contemporary Crises* 1 (1977): 189–223; Hebdige, *Subculture*; Dick Hebdige, *Hiding in the Light* (London: Routledge, 1988); Mike Brake, *The Sociology of Youth Culture and Youth Subcultures* (London: Routledge and Kegan Paul, 1980); Herman Schwendinger and Julia Schwendinger, *Adolescent Subcultures and Delinquency* (New York: Praeger, 1985).

35. In other words, as criminologists we may wish to make use not only of Becker's *Outsiders* but of his *Art Worlds* (Berkeley: University of California Press, 1982) as well.

PART TWO . . .

MEDIA, REPRESENTATION, AND CRIME

2...

Repetitive Retribution: Media Images and the Cultural Construction of Criminal Justice

CLINTON R. SANDERS AND ELEANOR LYON

Introduction: The Mediated Reality of Misbehavior

Media not only act as symbolic goods or marks of distinction, but as institutions. They are crucial to the creation, classification and distribution of cultural knowledge.[1]

The mass media are a pervasive feature of the environment in which we play out our lives. The messages and information we receive through the media have extensive impact, from influencing our choice of deodorant to—as we will see here—affecting our understanding and treatment of crime and criminal actors and actresses. The media are powerful, and often ubiquitous, technological tools for "reality engineering."[2] As such, they typically are employed, both subtly and overtly, to serve the interests of the powerful, complex, bureaucratic structures that determine the form and content of messages and the larger apparatus of social control, of which the media are an integral part.

The transitory and public messages that the media disseminate to a large and heterogeneous audience tend to offer an image of the world that is unrealistically clear-cut and understandable. Media messages are selected and editorially shaped so that they offer an identifiable portrayal of established values, interests, and normative expectations. In presenting an "authorized" cultural image, the media confer and enhance the social status of certain actors, actresses, and groups. In this way media images are central to the establishment of what Howard, Becker has referred to in a more limited context as the "hierarchy of credibility."[3] The social, economic, and cultural interests/perspectives of those in positions of authority are persuasively offered as the "way things really are" (or ought to be).

Central to this simplified cultural portrayal are the linked issues of who misbehaves, why they do it, and what happens as the consequence of bad behavior. Given the dominance of crime and other forms of rule breaking as a theme in media representations of reality, a variety of perspectives has been employed to judge the social repercussions of these mediated images of crime and deviance. Various "effects models" have enjoyed considerable general popularity. For the most part, these appealing perspectives offer a view of the audience as collectively involved in accepting, more or less uncritically, the media's portrayals as factual presentations of reality. Depictions of violence or other troublesome behaviors are viewed as offering at least some members of the audience dangerous models, or as arousing emotional responses that may give rise to potentially destructive actions.[4] In simplified form these sociopsychological views of the consequence of media depictions of rule breaking are central to the popular "quasi-theory" to which various "claims makers" concerned with real-life misbehavior refer in constructing moral panics about the apparent decline of contemporary society.[5]

A contrasting view of the societal impact of media representations argues that routine portrayals of violence, crime, and deviance enhance the power of those with a vested interest in the status quo rather than effecting a breakdown in social order. From this perspective media images of misbehavior "cultivate" in members of the audience a belief that the larger social environment is dangerous and frightening. In this view social control is enhanced because frightened citizens are more easily manipulated and are willing to trade away civil freedoms for the safety offered by established authorities and the institutions of which they are a part.[6]

A related orientation toward the controlling effects of media representations is offered by those who espouse a "dominant ideology" view. At base this orientation presents media content as reinforcing class divisions since media messages are "saturated with official ideology and bourgeois sensibilities."[7] A somewhat more subtle version of this approach is seen in what Jock Young terms the "consensual model." According to this perspective the media consistently act to reinforce the conventional beliefs that society is essentially orderly and that most people agree on what is right and wrong. "Normal" people voluntarily choose to abide by the accepted social rules and expectations. Within this context crime and deviance are presented as unearned pleasures that threaten the social order.

The media focus on events that media gatekeepers deem to be "newsworthy." Since the audience has little interest in routine or everyday happenings, the commonly superficial and summary portrayal of crime and other matters of current public concern displays a strong tendency to focus on atypical events, actors, and actresses. These stereotypical media images are juxtaposed against an overtypical depiction of a social world where—in contrast to a few sick, immoral, or misguided deviants—most people are hardworking, orderly, and law-abiding.[8]

Proponents of the consensual model persuasively maintain that the media are controlled by people who have a vested interest in perpetuating the status quo and, consequently, in fostering the impression that society is predominantly orderly and only occasionally threatened by deviants. While rule-breaking behavior is interesting and titillating media fare, the media managers are careful not to make it appear too appealing to the audience. The purpose of the presentation of deviance is to arouse moral indignation rather than to create a desire to participate in the hedonistic pleasure that deviance can bring. Consequently, media portrayals of the deviant stress that deviants eventually suffer pain—death, arrest, or loss of property and status—as a result of their rule breaking. Deviance is presented as arising from sickness, irrationality, lack of moral training, or weakness.

According to those who employ the consensus perspective, one of the ironic results of this biased presentation is that deviance is "amplified." Simplistic presentations of norm violation increase negative perceptions of and reactions to criminals and other deviants, thereby further isolating them and increasing the probability that they will act more deviantly in the future. In addition, the popularity of deviance as a media topic amplifies perceptions of deviance when members of the audience, accepting the "reality" of the media presentations, come to define serious and socially disruptive rule breaking to be more widespread and threatening than it actually is.[9]

It is impossible to reject an understanding of media representations as having significant social impact. However, most conventional orientations tend to present an overly monolithic view of media organizations and the level of their leaders' shared interests with other powerful social actors and actresses. Further, these models tend to discount the selectivity exercised by members of the media audience. Ignoring the interpretive creativity of the audience members and their selective fashioning of definitions of reality based on their pre-existing perspectives, interpersonal relationships, and unique experiences leads to an excessively deterministic view of the media as the dominant item of cultural capital for those in positions of power.[10]

Although people's understandings are shaped significantly by their real-life experiences with crime, media messages are key to how the public comes to perceive criminal behavior and other forms of insubordination as constituting social problems. Most generally, the various media interact as a cultural system that offers a portrayal of social reality and the troubles contained therein. In this light, media messages *construct* issues so that they provide an effective core for organizing "moral crusades." Constructed and exaggerated portrayals of misbehavior, through focusing on certain issues and ignoring others, identify those political and social issues of central significance. Consequently, the media influence the "agenda" of public concern and fuel public agitation directed at those institutions and individuals deemed responsible for maintaining social order.

This public agenda typically is mounted in conventional "frames." These thematic packages help to symbolically define the focal issues and the possible positions one could take relative to them. The proffered positions are commonly simple and routine. In our ostensibly democratic culture, media representations of such matters as crime, problematic drug use, troublesome behaviors of young people, and so forth tend to be shaped by a "balance norm." Officially sanctioned etiological and ameliorative orientations tend to be framed between competing views. This typically involves established spokespersons presenting and debating "opposing" perspectives that, upon examination, are different only in the most minimal and cosmetic ways.[11]

The position we take here is that media presentations of crime and other forms of insubordination have definite social, cultural, and—most importantly—policy impacts. In offering misbehavior in the simple, dramatic, episodic, and minimally contextualized style designed to capture the interest of the largest audience, media managers construct the conflict between rule-breaking and rule-abiding behavior so as to highlight and reinforce public allegiance to conventionality and its guardians. But media images of crime and criminals act as more than simply contemporary Durkheimian rituals impelling normative consensus.[12] They also have identifiable impacts on the structure and content of criminal justice agencies and policies.

The media and criminal justice agencies are linked in a reciprocal relationship. Media attention is directed at certain atypical, but dramatic, criminal acts. These portrayals generate and direct public concerns while shaping the steps taken by criminal justice agencies to appear responsive to these concerns. Agencies then devote major resources to cases that typify the forms of crime that have come to be central to the public agenda. This intensified focus tends to result in successful "solutions" to highly publicized crimes. Working with the media, agencies consequently present these successes as indicating their interest in the public welfare and their general effectiveness as guardians of the social order.

This complex and reciprocally reinforcing relationship between the mass media and criminal justice programs is the primary focus of this discussion. Following a brief overview of media representations of crime and its control, we will examine specific examples of the ways criminal justice perspectives and practices are influenced by media constructions. Given their central place in the current agenda of public concern, we will focus on the media portrayal of homicide and drug-related crime and the ways in which official agencies of social control respond to cases that typify these sorts of criminal events.

Media, Crime, and Social Control

Criminal deviance and other forms of misbehavior are central themes in a variety of media, from comics and cartoons to television and film.[13]

Deviance is a central media theme primarily because it interests and titillates the wide variety of heterogeneous groups and individuals that make up media audiences. Employing the tried-and-true deviance theme helps to decrease the uncertainty that the media managers feel when confronted with the ongoing problem of deciding what kind of programs will be commercially successful. Further, as noted previously, media presentations of deviance instruct the audience about the normative boundaries of society and thus facilitate social control. The simplistic and stereotyped presentation of deviants encountered in the media provides the audience with a vivid object lesson about the causes and consequences of violating conventional norms.

In his oft-cited content analysis of prime-time TV programming, Joseph Dominick found that at least one crime was portrayed in two out of every three programs studied. Forty percent of the offerings of the three major networks he analyzed consisted of programs dealing with crime and law enforcement. While the media's preoccupation with crime has obvious economic and status-quo-enhancing utility, the depiction is very much unlike the picture derived from official crime statistics. In "real" life most "official" crime is against property; the media emphasize serious interpersonal crime (in Dominick's study over half of the violations portrayed were murder or assault).[14]

Another way in which the media misrepresent illegal behavior is by focusing on crimes as simple and direct individual acts rather than as sophisticated activities engaged in by established groups.[15] This is understandable, given the media's immediate, show business requirements. Individual crime is simple to locate, provides dramatic action and striking visuals, is easily comprehended by the audience, and generates uncomplicated emotional responses.

This simplistic, media-derived "understanding" of the character of criminal deviance has clear implications for devising mechanisms of official social control. Most basically, individualistic images of marauding "bad guys"—to use that wonderfully simple and popular category current in law enforcement circles—make it easier to justify the establishment of harsh modes of retribution. As Gerbner says:

> You call a group "barbarians" if you want to be brutal toward them. You call people "criminals" if you want to suspend normal laws of decency and behave toward them in what would otherwise be considered a crimi-

nal way. You call a group "insane" if you want to suspend the rules of rationality and reason in managing them. That is not to say that there are no real criminals or insane people, but [the media] use these terms as a projective cultural apparatus to encourage isolating newly identified deviants from "normal people." This has the social function of coping with threats, for it justifies both dismissing and brutalizing these groups.[16]

Drawing on emotionalized issues like drugs, gangs, or serial killers, on which currently popular moral panics focus, the media portray dangerous individuals tenuously held in check by exemplary agents of social control. The media offer a frightening present juxtaposed against a romanticized past. As such, images of deviance and the deviant are central elements in the marketing of moral outrage.[17] This outrage, in turn, is employed as cultural capital by political figures and key actors and actresses within criminal justice organizations.

Although courtroom dramas, from *Perry Mason* to *L.A. Law*, are perennially popular as television and other media fare, the activities of police (and private detectives, their typically more effective entrepreneurial competitors) provide the most frequently employed thematic focus.[18] As Frank Price, the producer of such popular programs as *Kojak, Columbo,* and *Quincy,* once put it: "It's self evident that the cop show is a proven staple. . . . You're always experimenting, or should be, with other forms. . . . [Programming] is like drilling for oil . . . but you always know the cop show is there."[19]

Like most occupations, police work is overwhelmingly routine and commonly rather boring. The action requirements of media fare, however, mean that the routine realities of police activities cannot be accurately presented in film and on television. Each weekly TV episode, for example, must include the standard elements that the audience expects: high-speed car chases, shoot-outs, verbal and physical violence, and the apprehension of the criminals just before the program concludes. These dramatic requirements structure fictional presentations so that police work appears far more adventuresome and successful than it is in reality.[20] While the majority of actual crimes are not cleared by arrest, and solutions to real crime generally come about through extensive, undramatic conversations with informers, media police nearly always "get their man (or woman)," usually through the discovery and analysis of physical evidence. As screenwriter and former Los

Angeles police officer Joseph Wambaugh has observed: "All the emphasis on physical evidence is ridiculous. . . . Most finger prints are smudged and most bullets are smashed. Police work in a free society is like police work in Moscow or Hitler's Germany. It's all about informers."[21]

Another problem with the fictional portrayal of law enforcement is that programs leave the impression that the solution to crime lies in the apprehension of a suspect. Rarely do cop shows present the extensive and messy legal process subsequent to the capture of the (presumed) criminal.[22] When it is presented, however, the post-arrest legal process is portrayed in film or on TV as unrealistically as are the activities of police and criminals. In an early analysis of TV courtroom dramas, Charles Winick found significant distortions of the image of legal work and procedure.[23] Crusading attorneys were always successful in defending their clients, often coercing an admission of guilt from a witness during cross-examination. Rarely, if ever, was there any presentation of such messy features of the legal process as arraignments, hearings, plea bargaining, jury selection, and deliberation.

Another obvious feature of the media presentation of law enforcement is that police officers are consistently portrayed as committing civil rights violations. This illegality appears justifiable within the context of the plot because it is an effective means of achieving the socially desirable goal of apprehending a dangerous deviant. The major illegal acts perpetrated by fictional police are warrantless searches and seizures, failure to advise suspects of their constitutional rights, and use of physical violence or harassment against citizens.[24] Given the mediated reality of crime as a clear threat to the society and its members, violence and other illegal police tactics appear to be justified. Police are the foot soldiers in the "war on crime," and the practicalities of their work often require bending or breaking "unrealistic" official constraints.[25]

The repetitive, ambivalent, messy, and distorted media portrayal of official agents and agencies of social control has various implications for the public's constructed view of criminal justice, as well as for the orientations and activities of criminal justice personnel.[26] Though occasionally troubled by the personally aggrandizing illegal behavior of the "bad apple" in the organizational barrel, media representations generally reflect an effective, if chaotic and beleaguered, social control apparatus. Official violence (both sanctioned and unsanctioned) is necessary and productive because the public is confronted routinely by violent, insane, or drug-crazed evildoers. While it is likely that such constructions of reality have only marginal effects on the daily behavior of individual members of society, the organizational and policy effects are considerable. "Solutions" are devised and implemented that focus the attention and efforts of criminal justice personnel on the atypical cases accentuated in the media; individualistic etiological explanations are dominant and often become the foundation for agency approaches; and criminal justice efforts and resources are devoted to phenomena that are the current focus of moral panic rather than those that are most threatening, and for which practical ameliorative approaches could be reasonably implemented.

This symbiotic interconnectedness between media organizations, media workers, and social control agencies and agents is strikingly demonstrated in Mark Fishman's field study of crime reporters in New York City.[27] He found that the police clearly tended to offer information that would generate organizationally advantageous news reports. Police provided stories about extreme cases of crime that were "newsworthy," in the sense that they fit into currently popular "crime waves" being emphasized in the press. In turn reporters constructed stories that demonstrated the police concern for and avid attempts to deal with threats to public safety. News reports were, then, advantageous to both organizations. They acted as effective sources of positive public relations for the police and, since they focused on criminal threats that were of considerable concern to the public, they increased the sale of newspapers. As Fishman summarizes his analysis of the effects of this cooperative relationship:

> The system of unusual reports provides media newsrooms with a steady diet of the most extreme examples of street crime. . . . Because they rely on the police for raw materials, journalists convey an image of crime wholly in accord with the police department's notion of serious crime and social disorder. . . . Because their criteria for newsworthiness are inferred from media coverage, the police continue to provide the press with the same types of incidents that have been reported in the past. . . . Crime news is mutually determined by journalists, whose image of crime is shaped by police concerns, and by police, whose concerns with crime are influenced by media practices.[28]

This construction of media images of crime on the basis of agency interests and the related structuring of agency practice in line with media representations is not only apparent in the relationship between police and news organizations. Media portrayals of criminal deviance also affect the views and activities of programs at other levels of the criminal justice system. We now examine how media images shape the selection, definition, and prosecution of criminal cases further along the formal social control process.

Media Images and Criminal Justice Agency Practices

Homicides typically receive maximum media attention, especially if the circumstances of the offense are dramatic and involve victims who are "innocent" and/or members of the middle or upper class. The most obvious implication of this pattern is that the police are presented as effective guardians of the safety of "worthwhile" people. The reciprocal relationship between the media and agents of social control is especially notable here. Coverage of a dramatic killing generates attention focused on the investigation, which, in turn, fuels additional effort to find a perpetrator. If the murder victim is a child, media attention and the public outcry are especially strong, and agency efforts at identifying the perpetrator are especially vigorous.[29] For criminal justice agencies, homicides offer significant public relations advantages since they have the highest rates of clearance by arrest. In part this is because of the typical relationship of the parties—they are commonly known to each other, so the perpetrator is easily identified. Because of the heinous nature of the offense, extra investigational resources are often devoted to the case, supported by media attention and public outcry. The eventual solution is then offered by the criminal justice system as a prime example of its effectiveness.

While common, this pattern of media and criminal justice focus on homicide is not uniform. Interviews with families of homicide victims have shown that poor, urban African American and Latino/Latina families do not receive extensive media publicity and law enforcement attention. Minority families in which a member has been murdered commonly complain of being "ignored" by the media, and that investigations are not pursued actively. These suspicions that the police may not take these types of victimizations as seriously have at times been substantiated. Police officers routinely label homicides that occur on the streets of particular poor neighborhoods, because of their location, as "DDGBs" ("drug deal gone bad") or as gang killings. In contrast, middle-class families of murder victims often complain about the ongoing intrusiveness of the intensive media publicity focusing on the victim and the family in the aftermath of a homicide.[30]

A series of unsolved homicides of minority women in the East Coast state where the second author did research provides another striking example of this typical pattern of selective media portrayal and the related directing of law enforcement efforts. The women's bodies were commonly found after being dumped on city streets. Limited media attention described the women as prostitutes (thereby discounting them as "victims")[31] and treated their deaths as individual incidents, despite prominent patterns privately acknowledged by the police. Families of the victims were outraged and pressed for further investigation of the crimes as the work of a serial killer. After substantial agitation by the families and leaders of the minority community, an investigative task force was appointed. However, the task force was provided with few personnel and woefully inadequate resources, and a perpetrator was never apprehended.

The so-called war on drugs generated by the Reagan-era identification of drug crimes as a major issue offers another example of the reciprocal relationship between media images of crime and criminal justice activities. The declaration of the war on drugs was followed by vast increases in both the funding of street enforcement and the media coverage of drug busts. Soon this ongoing publicity constructed, both for the public and criminal justice agents, the view that drugs were *the* major driving force of crime. Drug crimes came to be seen as "normal crimes."[32] Court and correctional professionals began to describe virtually all people they processed as having "drug problems," and sentencing assessments increasingly began to focus on the presumed drug problems of convicted defendants. Assessments for individualized, community-based sentencing in many state jurisdictions have come routinely to include drug treatment, monitoring, and urinalysis, regardless of the type of offense or evidence of a substance abuse problem.

Enhanced and extended by media portrayals of both fictional and "real" criminal events, the drug interpretation of crime has now become so pervasive that criminal justice professionals see court dockets as filled with little else. In the criminal justice system studied by Lyon, during case- and policy-related conversations, court personnel typically came to define the vast majority of assaults and public disturbances as resulting from fights over drugs. Further, criminal justice workers began to assume that family fights, as well as much child abuse and neglect, were now more likely to be caused by "crack" cocaine and other illegal drugs than by the effects of alcohol or non-drug-related factors.

While there is, of course, a relationship between illegal drugs and many criminal acts,[33] the simplistic presentation of this connection by conservative political leaders and its essentially uncritical acceptance by the mass media have been largely responsible for creating a moral panic in which "drugs = crime" is the key equation. As consumers of media-generated constructions, criminal justice personnel also come to accept the validity of this portrayal even when the specific cases they encounter routinely fail to adequately support this appealingly uncomplicated etiological view.[34] In turn criminal justice professionals structure agency procedures and shape policy on the basis of their beliefs that the crime problem they are responsible for solving is, most elementally, a drug problem.

The media-generated image of serious crime as the handiwork of a group of violent, drug-crazed, gang-associated individuals from minority backgrounds has significant repercussions in the complex, multifaceted interplay between the public, political policy makers, commercial interests, criminal justice managers and workers, and the media. A fearful public is likely to support punitive policies that it believes ideally will offer solutions to the crime problem or, at least, decrease public vulnerability. Individualistic explanations contribute to conservative and punitive responses, as seen in the current popularity of the "three strikes and you're out" criminal justice fad, which is premised on the notion that most crime is caused by a relatively few nasty people who should be locked up forever. While it is certainly the case that there are some rather nasty people and that some of them contribute disproportionately to crime, the individual "bad-seed" view pushed by the media has become the driving model for public concern and for punitive criminal justice approaches. Individualistic explanations lead to the position that people should be given just "a few bites of the apple" and then nothing. During the debates associated with the enactment of federal crime legislation in 1994, for example, massive public animosity was generated by news reports of "midnight basketball" as an element of crime prevention and by the provision of health care services in prison that were presented as superior to those available to private citizens. The stereotypic "individual monster" model of crime accepted by a large proportion of the public and criminal justice policy makers leads naturally to the position that the criminal does not deserve the care we accord to full human beings.

Conclusion

The cultural creation of social reality is a political act.[35] In contemporary society the mass media are available and effective political tools to be fought for and wielded as various social problems claims-makers work to construct the meanings upon which political decisions and social policies are based. Concerned with corporate profits, beset by uncertainties about the form media products should take to prove successful, and continually involved in competition with those who control other media outlets and forms, media managers work to identify, create, and present those issues of most public concern. Given the conventional restraints of the media, gatekeepers consistently aid in the generation of moral panics by constructing stereotypic images of problems (e.g., crime), presumably generated by simple factors (e.g., the decline of the traditional family), which call for direct and uncomplicated solutions (e.g., "three strikes and you're out"). This imagery spotlights individual evildoers as the focus of concern, though sometimes they join together in gangs, "drug posses," bands of "wilding" teens, or other dangerous subcultural groups to wreak havoc on a generally orderly and law-abiding citizenry.

It is not necessary to posit a manipulative cabal of media managers conspiring with power-hungry political leaders to cynically construct such a portrayal to recognize the existence of such imagery and the advantage some groups and individuals enjoy when it is widely accepted as "fact." Stereotypical notions of problems are as likely to be believed by, and emotionally resonate with, media managers as they are by those who are active in constructing social problems and by members of the general public. In addition—and most importantly for our discussion here—as the mediated image of criminal deviance as a social problem marketed by the media comes to be regarded as generally factual, it is employed routinely by key actors in the criminal justice apparatus to shape programs and focus organizational practices.

Within the complex interplay of the media and the criminal justice system, considerable selectivity is exercised in constructing depictions of or responses to crime. This selectivity yields clear advantages for both institutions. For the media, stereotypical portrayals provide a more salable product that resonates[36] with what the public "knows." For the criminal justice system, simplistic notions of crime and criminals speed the processing of cases and increase local resources. Focusing on cases that embody current public concern increases the likelihood that the local criminal justice system will acquire augmented federal funding. The media and the criminal justice system work hand-in-hand with policy makers to support particular—though changeable—definitions of "the crime problem." Within this complex web of images, interests, and policy decisions, dramatic media depictions of crime generate public fear and calls for punitive solutions. In response, policy makers devise policy shifts and offer increased funding directed at those criminal acts, actors, and actresses at the core of the current moral panic. The criminal justice system responds, in turn, by redirecting enforcement activities in line with its institutional interests as well as in response to its media-promoted perceptions of the "real" crime problem. Increased enforcement efforts yield documented evidence that "we have a lot of that." In short, criminal justice procedures premised on the presumed validity of the media/public/legislative image of the crime problem reinforce the image, since now more of "that" is going through the system.

The public is, then, composed of "consumers" of media representations of crime, and of the ostensible solutions offered by the criminal justice system.[37] As concerned consumers, members of the public put various forms of pressure on "outlets" for the criminal justice "product," so as to ensure that it is, within the boundaries imposed by their media-generated understanding, an adequate and effective social commodity. To the extent that the justice system can meet—or, more properly, shape media coverage so that it appears to meet—public expectations, the system's legitimacy is enhanced.[38] An important feature of this legitimation is the reinforcement of the cultural "hierarchy of credibility" or the increased control exercised by those Tuchman[39] refers to as "authorized knowers." The social identity of those in positions of authority—in media organizations, the criminal justice system, and politics—is reinforced as those in charge are consistently presented as knowing the most effective solutions, being competent to implement ameliorative policies, and having the best interests of the public at heart. This constructed reputation is particularly advantageous to agency directors who can convert the legitimacy founded on media constructions into increased funding, added personnel, and other organizational resources.

In closing, however, it is important to note that there is an ironic consequence to the media's representation of crime and other forms of insubordination. Mediated moral denunciations also create cultural capital for those individuals and groups so denounced. In that presentational conventions often simplistically romanticize misbehavior, youth gangs, punk rockers, drug users, and other insubordinate subcultures can transform ostensibly negative images into definedly positive and cohesive ones. Symbols of subcultural style that help to focus the public's moral indignation—clothing, forms of body alteration, argot, music, and so forth—gain power as representing resistance to conventionality. But of course these symbolic "marks of mischief" are then co-opted by established producers of popular culture and marketed through the very same media sources that played a key role in originally establishing their dark power.[40]

Notes

1. Sarah Thornton, "Moral Panic, the Media and British Rave Culture," in *Microphone Fiends: Youth Music and Youth Culture*, ed. Andrew Ross and Tricia Rose (New York: Routledge, 1994), 176–92.

2. Michael Solomon and Basil Englis, "Reality Engineering: Blurring the Boundaries Between Commercial Signification and Popular Culture," *Journal of Current Issues and Research in Advertising* (forthcoming).

3. Howard S. Becker, *Sociological Work* (Chicago: Aldine, 1970), 126–28.

4. Media (especially televised) presentations are claimed to be associated with a wide variety of disvalued activities, from airplane crashes (David Phillips, "Airplane Accidents, Murder, and the Mass Media: Towards a Theory of Imitation and Suggestion," *Social Forces* 58 [1980]: 1001–24) and teen suicide (David Phillips and Lundie Carstensen, "The Effects of Suicide Stories on Various Demographic Groups 1968–1985," in *The Media and Criminal Justice Policy: Recent Research and Social Effects*, ed. Ray Surette [Springfield, IL: Thomas, 1990],

63–72) to criminal violence (Steven F. Messner, "Television Violence and Violent Crime: An Aggregate Analysis," *Social Problems* 33 [1986]: 218–35). Such studies—especially those purporting to find a causal relationship between media depictions of violence and interpersonal violence—have been the focus of considerable debate. It now appears most likely that the dominant connection between media presentations and problematic behaviors in real settings is that the former have some "priming" effect on the latter; media images act to precipitate the behaviors in those who are most "at risk."

5. For discussions of these key features of the constructionist perspective on social problems see Joel Best, ed., *Images of Issues: Typifying Contemporary Social Problems* (Hawthorne, NY: Aldine de Gruyter, 1989); Malcolm Spector and John Kitsuse, *Constructing Social Problems* (Hawthorne, NY: Aldine de Gruyter, 1987); and Stephen Markson, "Claims-making, Quasi-theories, and the Social Construction of the Rock 'n' Roll Menace," in *Marginal Conventions: Popular Culture, Mass Media, and Social Deviance*, ed. Clinton R. Sanders (Bowling Green, OH: The Popular Press, 1990), 29–40.

6. George Gerbner et al., "The Demonstration of Power: Violence Profile No. 10," *Journal of Communication* 29 (1979): 177–96. For overviews see Richard Ericson, "Mass Media, Crime, Law, and Justice: An Institutional Approach," *The British Journal of Criminology* 31 (1991): 219–49; Ray Surette, "Criminal Justice Policy and the Media," in *The Media and Criminal Justice Policy*, ed. Ray Surette (Springfield, IL: Thomas, 1990), 3–17; and Eleanor Lyon, "Media Murder and Mayhem: Violence on Network Television," in *Marginal Conventions*, 144–54.

7. Ericson, 221.

8. See Jock Young, "Mass Media, Drugs, and Deviance," in *Deviance and Social Control*, ed. Paul Rock and Mary McIntosh (London: Tavistock, 1974), 229–59; and Joseph Shelley and Cindy Ashkins "Crime, Crime News, and Crime Views," *Public Opinion Quarterly* 45 (1989): 492–501. In his discussion of the process by which moral panics surrounding the use of illegal drugs are generated, Reinarman (Craig Reinarman, "The Social Construction of Drug Scares," in *Constructions of Deviance*, ed. Patricia Adler and Peter Adler [Belmont, CA: Wadsworth, 1994], 96) refers to this rhetorical "recrafting (of) worst cases into typical cases and the episodic into the epidemic" as the "routinization of caricature."

9. Jock Young, "The Amplification of Drug Use," in *The Manufacture of News*, ed. Stanley Cohen and Jock Young (Beverly Hills, CA: Sage, 1973), 50–59; and Leslie Wilkins, "Information and the Definition of Deviance," 22–27, in the same volume.

10. This "limited effects" view of media messages is a key element of what Cohen and Young ("Introduction," in *The Manufacture of News*, 15–21) refer to

as the "commercial laissez-faire" orientation favored by media gatekeepers. This perspective presents the media (especially the news media) as offering an essentially objective portrayal of reality. Because audience members are selective in exposing themselves to and interpreting mediated messages based on their pre-existing beliefs, these portrayals have, therefore, little impact other than simply reinforcing the picture of the world already carried by the audience.

11. See William Gamson, "A Constructionist Approach to Mass Media and Public Opinion," *Symbolic Interaction* 11 (1988): 161–74.

12. See Graeme Newman, "Popular Culture and Criminal Justice: A Preliminary Analysis," *Journal of Criminal Justice* 18 (1990): 261–74. Schattenberg (Gus Schattenberg, "Social Control Functions of Mass Media Depictions of Crime," *Sociological Inquiry* 51 [1981]: 75) emphasizes the Durkheimian function of media presentations of crime, succinctly observing that "depictions of crime are like the parade of the convicted felon through the village streets to the block or the scaffold."

13. One-third of the programs studied by Gerbner and his students in the classic examinations of televised violence involved some form of criminal deviance. Berman (Ronald Berman, *How Television Sees Its Audience* [Beverly Hills, CA: Sage, 1987]) estimates that during the 1980s 80 percent of prime-time programming focused on the general issue of crime and its control.

14. Joseph Dominick, "Crime and Law Enforcement in the Mass Media," in *Deviance and Mass Media*, ed. Charles Winick (Beverly Hills, CA: Sage, 1978), 105–28.

15. Some researchers (e.g., Robert Cirino, *Don't Blame the People* [New York: Vintage, 1972]) have noted that greedy, middle-class, middle-aged males seem to be overrepresented as individual perpetrators of interpersonal violence. While right-wing analysts such as the Lichters (Linda Lichter and Robert S. Lichter, *Prime Time Crime* [Washington, D.C.: The Media Institute, 1983]) interpret this as indicating the anti-capitalist, liberal bias of the media, another explanation is far more persuasive. Minorities are simply underrepresented in the media. However, when they *are* portrayed, minority characters are disproportionately likely to be presented as criminals. See Lyon, "Media Murder"; Jack Katz, "What Makes Crime 'News'?" *Media, Culture, and Society* 9 (1987): 47–75; and Helen Benedict, *Virgin or Vamp: How the Press Covers Sex Crimes* (New York: Oxford University Press, 1992).

16. George Gerbner, "The Dynamics of Cultural Resistance," in *Hearth and Home: Images of Women in the Mass Media*, ed. Gaye Tuchman, Arlene Kaplan Daniels, and James Benet (New York: Oxford, 1978), 46–50.

17. In general, criminal deviants are portrayed as exemplifying evil. Driven by innate immorality, greed, madness, or—more recently—the effects of illegal drugs or the criminogenic "peer pressure" inherent in youth gang subcultures,

criminal deviants not only act bad, they also appear evil. While those who abide by or protect the social norms typically display a normal or attractive appearance, deviants are portrayed conventionally as Lombrosian throw-backs—ugly, deformed, and frightening. As Needleman and Weiner (Bert Needleman and Norman Weiner, "Heroes and Villains in Art," *Society* 14 [1976]: 35) maintain in their study of the relationship between appearance and moral status in the arts:

> [The media] have consistently presented moral transgressors in forms recogniz-ably distinct from the forms associated with the moral masses and moral champi-ons. In this convention, the scale of moral status is made roughly parallel to the socially prevailing scale of personal attractiveness: in fine, the moral champions are associated with attractiveness and beauty, while transgressors are made to appear recognizably unattractive or ugly.

For further discussion of the relationship between villainy and physical appear-ance, see also Donald Shoemaker, "Facial Stereotypes of Deviants and Judge-ments of Guilt or Innocence," *Social Forces* 51 (1973): 427–33; and Priscilla Warner, "Fantastic Outsiders: Villains and Deviants in Animated Cartoons," in *Marginal Conventions*, 117–30.

18. During any given period, social-control-oriented themes comprise from 20 percent to 80 percent of prime-time TV programming. See Schattenberg, "Social Control"; Newman, "Popular Culture"; and B. Keith Crew, "Acting Like Cops: The Social Reality of Crime and Law on TV Police Dramas," in *Marginal Conventions*, 131–43.

19. Quoted in E. Zuckerman, "The Year of the Cop," *Rolling Stone* 237 (1977): 57–63.

20. Given the commercial importance and extensive availability of programs dealing with police work, the major issues are how faithfully these shows re-flect actual law enforcement practices and what impact these stylized presenta-tions have upon the average viewers. A number of studies have been conducted that focus on these issues. These studies (e.g., Stephen Arons and Ethan Katsh, "How TV Cops Flout the Law," *Saturday Review* [19 March 1977], 11–18; Crew, "Acting Like Cops") and statements by police officers (see Connie Fletcher, *What Cops Know* [New York: Simon and Schuster, 1990]) clearly indicate that cop shows distort the reality of law enforcement as severely as they misrepre-sent the deviant behavior the police are supposed to control.

21. Quoted in Zuckerman, 63.

22. This neglect of the legal process is also found in news reports of crime. One study of newspaper reports (Sanford Sherizen, "Social Construction of Crime News: All the News Fitted to Print," in *Deviance and Mass Media*, ed. Charles Winick [Beverly Hills, CA: Sage, 1978], 203–24) found that over two-

thirds of the newspaper articles analyzed did not deal with the post-arrest stages of the criminal justice process.

23. Charles Winick and M. Winick, "Courtroom Drama on Television," *Journal of Communication* 24 (1974): 67–73. For a more recent discussion see David Meyer and William Hoynes, " 'Shannon's Deal': Competing Images of the Legal System on Primetime Television," *Journal of Popular Culture* 27 (1994): 31–42.

24. Arons and Katsh, "TV Cops"; Zuckerman, "Year"; and Crew, "Acting Like Cops."

25. In his analysis of British police dramas, Clarke (Alan Clarke, " 'This Is Not the Boy Scouts': Television Police Series and the Definitions of Law and Order," in *Popular Culture and Social Relations*, ed. Tony Bennett, Colin Mercer, and Janet Woollacott [Philadelphia: Open University, 1986], 219–32) refers to the media portrayal of police (and their practical use of violence) as central to the "humanizing of authoritarianism."

26. For a recent and critical discussion of the relationship between media portrayals of street crime and criminal justice policy, see Stuart A. Scheingold, *The Politics of Street Crime: Criminal Process and Cultural Obsession* (Philadelphia: Temple University Press, 1991).

27. Mark Fishman, "Police News: Constructing an Image of Crime," *Urban Life* 9 (1981): 371–94.

28. Fishman, "Police News," 387–88.

29. At this writing (Fall 1995) the case of Susan Smith, the young South Carolina mother who initially maintained that her two young children were kidnapped by an African American car-jacker and who eventually confessed to having drowned them, is generating considerable public concern and media attention. This case provides a prime example of how murders of young, "innocent" victims have significant media appeal, precipitate massive public interest, and result in extensive criminal justice effort to apprehend and punish perpetrators who are capable of such "inhuman" acts. The highly controversial, but typical, spin being put on the Smith case is that the murder was a consequence of her insanity since, presumably, only a deranged mother could perpetrate such a heinous act.

30. Eleanor Lyon, "Services to Families of Homicide Victims" (Report submitted to the Connecticut Commission on Victim Services, 1987).

31. See Eleanor Lyon, "Deserving Victims: The Moral Assessment of Victims of Crime" (Paper presented at the annual meetings of the Society for the Study of Social Problems, Miami, FL, August 1993).

32. David Sudnow, "Normal Crimes: Sociological Features of the Penal Code in a Public Defender Office," *Social Problems* 12 (1965): 255–76.

33. For recent discussions of the complex relationship between illegal drugs and criminal behavior, see Elliott Currie, *Reckoning: Drugs, the Cities, and the*

American Future (New York: Hill and Wang, 1993), 148–212; and David Nurco, Timothy Kinlok, and Thomas Hanlon, "The Drugs-Crime Connection," in *Handbook of Drug Control in the United States*, ed. James Inciardi (Westport, CT: Greenwood, 1991), 71–90.

34. The media focus on the linked issues of drug-related and violent crime has clear impact on the perceptions of judges and other central players in the criminal justice system. For example, Lyon routinely provides data from the court's information system on the dispositions of criminal cases handled by the state's courts to court personnel. When she notes the high proportion of misdemeanor public order and property crimes, court professionals commonly question the accuracy of the statistics provided. They also maintain that the majority of the property crimes are drug-related or must involve substitution of charges. These perceptions are not supported by the available data.

35. While hardly a novel idea, this view is presented and expanded with regard to criminal justice most ably by Foucault. See Michel Foucault, *Discipline and Punish: The Birth of the Prison* (New York: Pantheon, 1977).

36. Gamson, "Constructionist."

37. See Leslie Wilkins, *Consumerist Criminology* (New York: Academic Press, 1985).

38. This point is expanded in Ericson, "Mass Media."

39. Gaye Tuchman, *Making News* (New York: Free Press, 1978).

40. For specific examples of this phenomenon see Clinton R. Sanders, "Marks of Mischief: Becoming and Being Tattooed," in *Constructions of Deviance*, 511–29; Jeff Ferrell, *Crimes of Style: Urban Graffiti and the Politics of Criminality* (New York: Garland, 1993); Kathryn Fox, "Real Punks and Pretenders: The Social Organization of a Counterculture," *Journal of Contemporary Ethnography* 16 (1987): 344–70; and Thornton, "Moral Panic."

3 ◂ ◂ ◂
The Media and the Construction of Random Drug Violence

HENRY H. BROWNSTEIN

Introduction

From 1986 to 1990, the news media in New York City constructed a compelling picture of reality in which drug-related violence was spreading and becoming random in its selection of victims. In so doing, it encouraged a belief in the growing vulnerability of white, middle-class people in the face of such violence. This case is an example of how the media, operating in a particular political context, effectively supported the movement of government policies toward the right. The relationship of that construction to public policy is discussed, as is its grounding in erroneous premises and its potential for harmful social consequences.

The Media and the Construction of Reality

The reality of everyday life is a social construction.[1] When the news media report stories as news, they objectify reality.[2] Naturally, then, the newsmaking process is subject to some measure of distortion.[3]

The process of making news inevitably is value-based.[4] Robert S. Lichter and his associates interviewed 240 journalists and concluded that those people whom they call the "media elite" distort the news in a liberal direction.[5] Others have argued that the news is actually constructed in a particularly conservative direction.[6] The case of news about drugs in New York City in the second half of the 1980s supports the latter conclusion.

The Context of Newsmaking

The contemporary American news media are both an institution designed to inform the public and a business—the primary purpose of which is to make a profit.[7] Thus, news reporting is as likely to sensationalize events as it is to report them, as likely to serve as an instrument of propaganda as a source of information, and as likely to be a creator of myth as a purveyor of truth.[8]

To obtain the information needed to make news, the media rely on experts and public officials whose control over knowledge makes them the gatekeepers of that information. To construct news that is not favorable to those with power and authority over knowledge is to risk being cut off from the information that is needed to be able to construct news at all. Consequently, news is necessarily constructed in a political context.

Reinarman and Levine demonstrate how the current drug crisis in America is a construction of the news media within a conservative political context.[9] After establishing that official claims about "a pandemic [crack] 'crisis' endangering the lives of 'a whole generation' of youth are at odds with the best official data," they suggest that "the crack 'crisis,' like previous drug scares, is in part the product of the association of 'dangerous drugs' with a 'dangerous class' [of people] and of the peculiarly fertile features of politics in the current context."[10] Specifically, they argue that in the 1980s, the New Right and Ronald Reagan used drugs as an "all-purpose scapegoat with which they could blame an array of problems [that had been exacerbated by social and fiscal policies of the Reagan administration] on the deviance of the individuals who suffered them."[11] Further, they argue that normally liberal Democrats responded to the political pressure created by the drug "crisis" and accordingly moved to the Right on social issues.[12] Notably, the prominence of drugs as an issue "dropped sharply in both political speeches and media coverage after the 1986 [congressional] election, only to return during the 1988 [presidential] primaries."[13]

In New York State, the political context in relation to drugs was shaped in 1986 by the growing concern about crack, a refined and smokable form of cocaine.[14] In his annual address to the New York State legislature in January 1987, just after his election to a second term, Governor Mario Cuomo told the legislators:

This year, we must intensify our efforts as never before in the face of the emergence of crack—the extraordinarily potent, highly addictive and relatively inexpensive cocaine derivative. The lightning speed with which this lethal drug has spread through society is evident in substantial increases in drug-related deaths and demands for treatment by drug users. Crack has also been accompanied by rising incidents of violent crime, including robberies and murders. We must attack this new menace by enacting stiffer penalties for its sale and possession.[15]

With this statement the governor identified the major themes of a campaign against crack and other drugs as follows:

1. Crack is a particularly lethal and addictive drug.
2. The use of drugs, especially crack, has reached epidemic proportions.
3. Drugs, especially crack, are largely responsible for the increasing rates of crime and violence.
4. The proper response to the crack menace is enhanced enforcement of drug laws.

In a press release dated 5 May 1986, the governor identified a fifth theme: drug education or prevention and treatment programs are also important responses to the crack problem.

By January 1989 the "Campaign Against Drug Abuse" was the highlight of the governor's annual address to the state legislature. He opened his remarks by telling the legislators that New York's three most serious problems were "drugs, drugs and drugs."[16] He then announced the formation of an anti-drug abuse council that would coordinate statewide efforts through the office of the lieutenant governor.

A major function of the council was to develop a statewide drug strategy. The first "State of New York Anti-Drug Abuse Strategy Report" was issued at the end of 1989. Of 110 recommendations, 41 were enforcement-oriented, 38 were in the area of prevention, and 31 in the area of treatment.[17]

The drug strategy in New York tried to balance conservative and liberal elements. But given the belief in a drug crisis brought on by the introduction of crack, both the government and the public showed greatest interest in law-and-order responses to "dangerous" drugs. The news media supported this reactionary position and added its own theme: drug-related violence as random violence. The random violence theme mobilized the white middle class against drugs and thereby invited an even more repressive response than might otherwise have been possible.

Making the Case for Random Drug Violence

Between 1986 and 1990, countless news stories about crack, other drugs, and drug-related criminal violence were generated. A review of printed news stories about these phenomena during this period in New York City reveals how the media, operating within a predominantly conservative political context, took the government's notions about crack, pursued these themes, and constructed a "reality" in which drugs—crack, in particular—were identified as responsible for widespread and random drug-related street violence.[18]

Given its reliance on public officials for information, from the beginning the news media took its cues from state government in its campaign against crack and drugs. There were few articles about either the accuracy or validity of the assumptions on which the government themes were based, or about their appropriateness. Discussions of alternative strategies, such as legalization, when they were reported at all, were left to the editorial columns.

Shortly after the governor's 5 May 1986 press release, the news media in New York began to report on the problem of crack. On 18 May 1986 the *New York Times* published an article called "Opium Dens for the Crack Era" on page one. The article described the "scene" at a particular crack house, highlighting the experience of a "17-year-old girl from Queens who, together with two friends, brought $200 to a Manhattan base [crack] house and smoked it in less than an hour. To get more crack, she said, she had sex with the operators of the base house and the customers."[19] The themes of the article—the growing use of crack and its pernicious and addictive qualities—were grounded in quotes from "officials."

On 31 July 1986 the *New York Times* published an article about a meeting between state and city government officials at which they jointly issued a number of proposals calling for more state judges, more court-room space, more federal judges to handle drug cases, the deportation of illegal aliens convicted of drug offenses, mandatory jail sentences for repeat misdemeanor drug offenders, and increased state penalties for possession or sale of crack. The following day they published another article, which was headlined "Rise in Major Crimes in City Continues, the Police Report." The article provided statistics to support the argument that crime was increasing and reported on the deployment of a special unit of the New York City Police Department to help in precincts with soaring homicide rates. The author wrote, "Police officials yesterday attributed many of the increases in reported murders, robberies, and other crimes to drugs, particularly the rapid proliferation over the past several months of crack, a potent cocaine derivative."

In 1986 there were congressional elections in the U.S. and a gubernatorial election in New York. In 1987, not an election year, there was considerably less media emphasis on drugs.[20] Still, the media kept the reactionary drug themes alive, maintaining a focus on the link between drugs and violence.

At the end of 1987, a New York City police officer was shot and wounded. The *Daily News* on 14 December used a two-inch headline on its cover: "BLOODBATH." Headings of the related articles were: "Machine-gunner wounds cop; drug war kills 2 men," "In Bedford-Stuyvesant . . . Business as Usual—B'klyn Crack Den," ". . . A Drug War Bloodbath—Cop is Shot in Brooklyn—Was Probing Double Murder," and "Don't Worry, Mom." The year 1987 was over, and 1988, a congressional election year, was about to begin.

The year began with straightforward, general-interest reports. Then at the end of February 1988, a young police officer was shot point-blank while guarding the home of a witness in a drug case in Queens. At first the newspapers simply reported the event. Yet as the cold-blooded nature of the attack, the young age of the officer, and the perpetrators' involvement in the drug trade became widely known, the reports began to focus more generally on the violence committed by users and dealers of crack and other drugs.

During March the *New York Times*—the New York paper least likely to sensationalize the news—ran the following articles: "Machine Guns and Unpredictability Are the Hallmarks of Crack's Violence" (8 March) and "Brutal Drug Gangs Wage War of Terror in Upper Manhattan" (15 March). In April the *Times* ran a series of three articles on the drug war, ending with an article entitled "In the War on Illegal Drugs, Main Battle Is on the Home Front" (12 April). The series focused on drug trafficking and interdiction efforts as well as on law enforcement and corruption.

During this period the New York City Police Department reported that the murder rate in Queens had increased by 25 percent over the previous year. The *Times* reported this on 20 April and the next day published an article with the headline "Drug Violence Undermining Queens Hopes." The page B1 article began with these words:

> Queens officials and residents said yesterday that a police report showing that the borough's murder rate, fueled by crack, has increased 25% for the second year in a row confirmed their worst fears: that drug violence is threatening the very stability of what has long been considered New York's most middle-class borough.[21]

The threat to the middle class was the subject of the article, and it was noted that the "hardest-hit section is predominantly black middle-class southeastern Queens."

During the middle of the year it was quiet, but toward the end of the year, during election campaigns, things picked up again. In September the police announced that murder and manslaughter rates were up, and this was dutifully reported by the media. That month a story about a drug dealer who was set ablaze by three men on a Manhattan street corner was widely reported.

In December the New York City news media summed up the drug story of the year: in 1988 the city had experienced a record number of violent crimes and a notable percentage of these were considered by law enforcement officials to have been drug-related. A 30 December *Daily News* article entitled "Crack Whips Killing Toll" covered the police announcement on the year's record-setting murder rate. On 27 December 1988 the *Times* ran a short article on page B3 entitled "Police Term Homicide Data Too Raw and Not Definitive." However, the uncertain nature of the figures on which the big story was based was given little attention.

Early in 1989 the random drug violence theme first appeared. In its

Sunday edition on 22 January 1989, the *New York Times* included an article entitled "Drug Wars Don't Pause to Spare the Innocent." Citing "experts," the article dealt with the "killing of innocent bystanders, particularly in the crossfires of this nation's drug wars," suggesting that such killings had "suddenly become a phenomenon that greatly troubles experts on crime." Drug-related violence was spreading and suddenly even "innocent" people were at risk.

There was some evidence that innocent bystanders had been shot in the crossfire of drug battles. In a 22 January article, the *New York Times* estimated that in New York City there had been eight such cases in 1988. In a companion piece they reported that a twelve-year-old girl had been killed when she "was talking with a group of friends less than a block from her home when she inadvertently walked into a drug-related dispute on a sidewalk in Brooklyn."

For the first few months of the year, the random violence theme continued to be promoted by the media. On 23 January the *Daily News* published an article about the spread of crime into previously "safe" neighborhoods. Headlined "IT'S CALLED SPILLOVER, Silk-stocking areas share run on crime," the article quoted a "community leader" from Brooklyn who said, "There are no safe neighborhoods anymore." The article gave statistics showing the level of violent crime in each of the police precincts in the city. On 2 February the *New York Post* gave an example under the dramatic heading "HUMAN SHIELD—Snatched tot wounded in Brooklyn gun battle." The story was about a three-year-old boy who was "critically injured yesterday when a teen-ager snatched him from his mother's grasp and used him as a human shield in a gun battle."

There were also reports that drug-related violence had spread beyond the boundaries of New York City, threatening the smaller cities of upstate New York. The Rochester *Democrat and Chronicle* reported on 15 January 1989 that the per capita murder rate in that city was as high as that in most large urban centers. The headline read, "Rochester faces image of violence—12 drug-related killings last year were the highest ever in the city."

During this period the national media continued to view drug-related violence as being focused on inner-city neighborhoods. On 16 January 1989 *Newsweek* published a story called "A Tide of Drug Killing." The article emphasized the reactionary themes that drugs were behind a record-breaking level of violent crime and that crack was "uniquely evil." Yet it also clearly suggested that the drug-related violence was concentrated in poor and minority communities and went so far as to include the subheading "The crack plague spurs more inner-city murder." On 10 April 1989 *U.S. News & World Report* published a similar article. The main heading was "DEAD ZONES," and the subheading read, "Whole *sections* of urban America are being written off as anarchic badlands, places where cops fear to go and acknowledge: 'This is Beirut, U.S.A.' " (emphasis added).

An incident in April 1989 accelerated the objectification of the random drug violence theme. A young, middle-class white woman was jogging through Central Park in Manhattan when a large group of younger black males attacked her and brutally raped and beat her. After reporting the story, the news media followed up with articles suggesting that innocent people were increasingly likely to become victims of violence. For example, on 25 April the *New York Times* ran an article called "Gang Attack: Unusual for Its Viciousness," which stated:

> The random, apparently motiveless rampage in Central Park last week that the suspects call wilding was an extraordinarily ferocious version of group delinquency that usually takes less vicious forms, according to law-enforcement officials and psychologists.[22]

The people of the city were angry about the Central Park attack, and the news media fueled this anger. Though the question of a racial motive was raised—the victim was white and the suspects black—it was doubted. However, when an African American woman was found brutally murdered in Fort Tryon Park a few weeks later, on 6 May, only the *New York Amsterdam News*, the newspaper that gives "the new black view," argued that the two cases should be treated in a similar fashion. The article suggested that while African American women are frequently the victims of violence, their victimization is never given the same attention as that of white women.

While the Central Park case was not necessarily drug-related, it was violent, and it did draw attention to the vulnerability of white, middle-class people. Throughout the remainder of 1989, the news media continued to develop this theme, bringing in mention of crack whenever possible. On 28 May the *New York Times* published a full-length, double-column editorial called simply "Crack." Subtitled "A Disaster of Historic Dimension, Still Growing," the article claimed that "crack poses a much greater threat than other drugs. It reaches out to destroy the quality of life, and life itself, at all levels of American society." The theme of the editorial, itself a call for government action, was that crack is uniquely destructive and that as crack "spreads to middle America," the "fabric of society" itself is at risk.

On 1 October 1989 an article called "Crack's Destructive Sprint Across America" appeared in the *New York Times Magazine*. Its author argued that "now, in smaller communities, too, crack is striking with swift fury. From rural woodlands to shady suburbs, prairie townships to Southern hamlets, no community seems immune."[23] Also in its Sunday edition, the *Times* began a two-part series with a front-page article entitled "The Spreading Web of Crack," which stated: "Crack, which has been devastating entire inner-city neighborhoods, has begun to claim significant numbers of middle- and upper-class addicts, experts have found."

The year ended, again, with reports about the record number of homicides in the city. On 31 December the *New York Times* reported, "More Americans Are Killing Each Other." On 17 December the *Daily News* took a different angle by headlining: "Thugs Rule Subway." The *News* went on to provide a "log" of the crimes that took place on the subways, a common means of transportation for many New Yorkers.

The year 1989 began with an article in *New York* magazine that clearly explained the random violence theme. In "Fighting Back Against CRACK," the author wrote:

> For two years after the crack plague struck New York, in 1985, people who lived in solid neighborhoods around the city thought they could remain insulated from the havoc wreaked by the drug—at first crack was largely confined to the poorest neighborhoods, and many people thought it would be just another dreadful thing they read about in the tabloids or watched on the news.
>
> It hasn't turned out that way. Although there are a few parts of town where people still think of the crack epidemic as something distant and alien—the area around Gracie Mansion [the Mayor's residence] would seem to be one—most neighborhoods in the city by now have been forced to deal with either crack or its foul byproducts: if not crack houses and street dealers or users, then crackhead crimes such as purse snatchings, car break-ins, burglaries, knife-point robberies, muggings, and murders.[24]

By 1990 the theme of random violence had been objectified, and the news media continually argued for that position and reported stories that supposedly demonstrated its validity. An unusually high number of such incidents during the summer fueled that argument, and the random violence theme was brought to a new level of sensationalism. During one month in the summer of 1990, nine children in New York City were hit by stray bullets. Five of them died. The mayor compared New York to the television image of Dodge City. The news media were suggesting that now innocent bystanders were the targets of drug-related violence.

On 5 August the *Daily News*, which calls itself "New York's Picture Newspaper," gave the cover of its Sunday edition to the following headline in two-inch letters: "ENOUGH!" Just below the headline were white-bordered pictures of two of the latest "innocent" victims of the violence. Articles about each followed. One victim was a 33-year-old man who was shot to death "in a botched robbery" while he was making a call from a public telephone on a street corner of New York's Greenwich Village. The other, a nine-month-old boy, was killed standing in his walker when bullets meant for his uncle came through the door of their home. One of the many articles that followed had the headline "Innocent is Slain by the Damned." On 12 August the *New York Times* Sunday edition included an article with the title "Bystander Deaths Reshape City Lives."

Even *USA Today*, with its national focus, on 31 July featured an article about the shootings of bystanders in New York City. The article was called "New NYC Fear: Stray Bullets."

The innocent bystander motif of the random drug violence theme gained important symbolic support when a tourist to New York City was killed on a subway platform while trying to help his mother. On Labor Day a young man visiting New York from Utah was killed when, according to the *New York Post* on 4 September, he "tried to protect his mother from the bloodthirsty bunch stalking the 7th Avenue IND station at 53rd Street." Newspaper headlines highlighted the theme that, as had always been feared, even tourists to New York were now potential victims of the city's widespread and random violence. For example, the *Post* article was entitled "TOURIST SLAIN PROTECTING MOM."

The national news media also gave attention to the random nature of drug-related violence in New York. On 17 September, for example,

Time magazine had the headline on its cover "The Rotting of the Big Apple." Inside was an article called "The Decline of New York," followed immediately by the subheading "A surge of brutal killings has shaken the Big Apple to its core." The author wrote:

> A growing sense of vulnerability has been deepened by the belief that deadly violence, once mostly confined to crime-ridden ghetto neighborhoods that the police once wrote off as free-fire zones, is now lashing out randomly at anyone, even in areas once considered relatively safe.[25]

On 31 December 1990, the *New York Times* once again reported a record number of killings in New York City. On the first page of its Metropolitan section was an article called "Record Year for Killings Jolts Officials in New York." The author wrote:

> Crime in New York in 1990 was defined primarily in two ways, both of which tended to heighten anxiety. One was the large number of shootings of bystanders, whose victims were often children—crimes that frightened by their casualness and unpredictability. The other was crime that seemed to follow a pattern—like the Zodiac shootings and the livery-cab killings.[26]

The first "way" referred to innocent bystanders as victims. The second referred to the innocent victims of a person who had frightened the entire city for a time by shooting at people for no apparently logical reason, and also to attacks on innocent taxi cab drivers. In effect the newspaper was suggesting that crime in the city in 1990 was defined by the innocence of its victims and the randomness of their selection for victimization.

Reporting on drugs between 1986 and 1990, the news media in New York took its cue from the conservative political context of the state and nation. Then newsmakers developed their own theme, one that had the sensational quality that could attract people to buy the news. That theme said that drug-related violence in the city was widespread and random. A picture of reality was drawn in which all people were purported to be equally and indiscriminately subject to drug-related violent victimization.

Official Statistics and Research Findings

Drug scares are independent phenomena, not necessarily related to actual trends or patterns in drug use or trafficking.[27] In New York in the late 1980s, the alarm over random drug-connected violence was not related to what was known about street crime and violence through official statistics or to research findings.

A sample of people is considered random when that sample "has the property not only of giving each individual an equal chance of being selected but also of giving each combination of individuals an equal chance of selection."[28] Even news reporters knew in the late 1980s in New York that the observed increase in officially recorded drug-related violence was not truly random.[29]

Official statistics, to the extent that they are themselves an accurate reflection of actual conditions, show that not all people in New York City faced in the late 1980s the same risk of violent victimization—drug-related or otherwise. The conclusion that officially defined violent crime increased in New York City during this period is compelling.[30] The argument that such violence was randomly distributed, however, is not.[31]

Besides official crime statistics, the findings of a study on homicide by the national Centers for Disease Control support these conclusions. Using official mortality data, the study examined homicide as a cause of death in the United States between 1978 and 1987. The authors of the report found:

> From 1978 through 1987, annual homicide rates for young black males were four to five times higher than for young black females, five to eight times higher than for young white males, and 16–22 times higher than for young white females. Since 1984, the disparity between homicide rates for young black males and other racial/sex groups increased substantially.[32]

In addition they reported, "Despite common perception that the victims of homicide are usually killed by unknown assailants during robberies or drug-related crimes, more than half of all homicide victims are killed by persons known to them."[33]

Police statistics from New York City directly address the question of innocent bystanders. Despite the alarm, the number and proportion of victims of violence who are actually innocent bystanders remain very small. On 5 August 1990 the *New York Times* informed readers that the police had reported 1,051 homicides in New York City during the first six months of the year. The New York Police Department (NYPD) officially identified fifteen of those cases as having involved victims who were innocent bystanders. Thus, according to official statistics, during the first half of 1990 in New York City, 1.4 percent of all homicide victims were innocent bystanders.

Recent studies of homicide provide additional support for the conclusion that only a low percentage of homicide cases involves innocent bystanders. One study of 414 homicides in New York City in 1988 found that only 1.2 percent involved innocent bystanders as victims.[34] Another study of random shootings of bystanders in four U.S. cities between the years 1977 and 1988 concluded that "bystander shootings are a rare event."[35]

There is much research that demonstrates the link between observed violence and drugs, particularly crack.[36] Given the characteristics of crack itself and the nature of the crack market, however, this research suggests that the violence is a product of drug market instability and is aimed primarily at people who participate in, or whose lives touch upon, that market.

The research on drugs and violence suggests that most of the drug-related violence is confined to people who, by choice or circumstance, live in or near drug communities and neighborhoods.[37] Further, very few people are likely to be innocent bystander victims of the violence. Yet the media were able to suggest otherwise, since even a few cases of innocent people being victimized by violence held great symbolic value. As Sherman and his associates wrote:

> Bystander deaths violate the routine assumptions necessary for conducting daily life. . . . An increase in such killings, even a small proportion of all homicide, suggests a threat of spillover of street violence from the underclass to the middle and upper classes.[38]

In other words, poor and minority people should expect to be victims of violence and violent crime. Middle- and upper-class people, on the other hand, should not be expected to tolerate any increase in the risk of violent victimization.

It is safe to say that official statistics do show an increase in the amount of street violence over the past few years in New York City. Yet that violence has not become random. It continues to be directed at the same people it has always victimized: minorities, women, and most likely the poor and the young as well. This point is not meant to minimize or debase the great personal tragedy that any and every victim of violence is likely to suffer. It does suggest, though, that in New York City, if not elsewhere, all people are not equally likely to become the victims of street violence, drug-related or otherwise.

What's the Harm?

Reinarman and Levine pose an interesting question: "Given the damage that drugs can do, what's the harm in a little hysteria?"[39] They propose two answers. "First," they write, "drug scares blame individual immorality and personal behavior for endemic social and structural problems, and they divert attention and resources from those larger problems."[40] Such has been the case in New York. The fear of random drug violence, which invites policies that are tough on drug offenders,[41] bolstered and supported a major expansion of law enforcement, highlighted by a prodigious prison expansion program. Such policies place the onus on individual drug users and dealers, who have been viewed primarily as potential perpetrators of violent crime in need of control by the criminal justice system.

The federal strategy toward drugs and drug-related problems has been largely reactionary, with about 70 percent of all dollars proposed for spending on law enforcement and supply reduction programs.[42] In New York State, where much more consideration has been given to treatment and prevention,[43] official statistics show extremely large increases in the number of felony drug arrests, indictments, convictions, and sentences to prison from 1983 to 1988.[44] From 1983 to 1990 the New York State prison population grew from approximately 30,000 to about 55,000 inmates, with drug offenders accounting "for 45 percent of the total system growth since 1980 and 75 percent of the growth since 1986."[45]

As noted earlier, in his message to the state legislature in 1989, Governor Cuomo told legislators that the three most serious problems faced by the state were "drugs, drugs and drugs."[46] But what of homelessness and AIDS; illiteracy and unemployment; racism, ageism, and sexism? And what about the abuse of our children and the destruction of our environment? During a period when people believed that the greatest risk to their well-being came from random violence perpetrated by drug users and traffickers—a notion constructed by the media—attention and resources were diverted from the more intractable social and structural problems.

The second response to the question of harm, according to Reinarman and Levine, is that "drug scares do not work very well to reduce drug problems and that they may well promote the behavior they claim to be preventing."[47] The failure of the "war on drugs" strategy is well documented[48] alongside evidence indicating that policies and programs that address the larger and more basic social and structural problems would be more effective.[49]

Social scientists, political analysts, and even news reporters have acknowledged that drug abuse, drug trade, and drug-related violence have not been reduced to acceptable levels, even in those areas where enforcement and interdiction efforts have been strongest.[50] In fact, these efforts have resulted in several unintended and undesirable consequences.

As noted earlier, the war on drugs has overwhelmed federal, state, and local criminal justice systems,[51] including the one in New York City.[52] In addition, the war has contributed to the erosion of civil liberties, as in the case of the congressional amendment to the Posse Comitatus Act,[53] and through its assault on the Bill of Rights.[54]

In some ways the reactionary policies of the enforcement emphasis have exacerbated the very problems they were designed to solve. In his study of marijuana trafficking, Kleiman argued that marijuana enforcement "acts as a protective tariff" and thereby encourages "domestic commercial production, [which] tends to be quite violence-intensive."[55] Similarly, findings from a New York City study of homicides suggest:

> Given that most drug-related violence is related to conflicts over market share, violence is likely to increase as [inexperienced, young crack] dealers [with no links to any stabilizing organizational structure] compete for control of territories left unserved and unprotected as a result of successful enforcement activity.[56]

In his study of prostitution and drugs, Goldstein wrote, "When no social harm exists, there can be no justification for repressive legislation."[57] This insight remains true even in relative terms. The extent of repression in public policy should not exceed the harm caused by the problem that the policy addresses. By promoting the myth that citizens are all equally at risk of violence, especially at the hands of drug users and traffickers, the news media are at least partly responsible for encouraging the ill-founded and illogical expansion of law enforcement and the contraction of civil liberties in contemporary American society.

Conclusion

The reactionary agenda toward drug users and traffickers resulted from a constellation of forces. Liberal government officials in New York reacted to a perceived drug crisis by calling for a variety of programs. The news media, pursuing a sensational story that would sell the news and not contradict the policies of officials on whom they depended for information, mobilized the white middle class with an emphasis on the theme of random drug violence. Faced with an alarmed voting public that was calling for law and order, government officials promoted a drug scare that would permit spending on law-enforcement programs during a time of fiscal crisis and overcrowded prisons.

The drug scare around crack allowed the development of a conservative agenda even in a liberal political environment. In cases like this, social scientists should play a more active role.[58] For example, they can use their skills and positions to provide information, through government and through the media, to clarify the debate. In this case, for example, social scientists could have shown empirically that the fear of random drug violence, especially among white middle-class people, was unrealistic.

Epilogue

Due largely to the drug scare generated by government officials and the media, the prison inmate population doubled in New York State during the 1980s. Late in 1990 an article in the *Times Union* of Albany asked whether it is "proper" to continue to build prisons to satisfy "intense public demands to get tough on crime, particularly drug offenders." An "expert" and reform advocate from Washington, D.C., is quoted as having said, "The bills are coming due and they are quite large. At some point, it will force an examination of how much incarceration we can afford."

Just days before publication of the article, Governor Cuomo had announced that the state was faced with a major budget crisis, one that would cost the Department of Correctional Services alone an estimated $27 million during the current fiscal year. On the eve of the twentieth anniversary of the prison uprising at Attica in upstate New York, the sudden interest of the newspaper in the social and financial costs of incarceration was not surprising. It is only interesting.

Notes

The author wishes to thank Gregg Barak, Harry G. Levine, Nathan Riley, and anonymous reviewers from *Social Justice* for their comments on an earlier version of this chapter, and Elizabeth Briant Lee and Alfred McClung Lee for their encouragement. However, points of view and opinions expressed herein do not necessarily represent those of others, nor do they necessarily reflect or represent official policies or positions of the State of New York or any of its agencies, and no official endorsement should be inferred. An earlier version of this chapter was published in *Social Justice* in 1991, and portions are reprinted here by permission.

1. Peter L. Berger and Thomas Luckman, *The Social Construction of Reality* (Garden City, NY: Doubleday, 1966); Alfred Schutz, *Collected Papers I: The Problem of Reality*, ed. Maurice Natanson (The Hague: Martinus Nijhoff, 1962).

2. Robert S. Lichter, Stanley Rothman, and Linda S. Lichter, *The Media Elite* (Bethesda, MD: Adler and Adler, 1986); Tom Koch, *The News as Myth: Fact and Context in Journalism* (New York: Greenwood Press, 1990).

3. Alfred McClung Lee and Elizabeth Briant Lee, *The Fine Art of Propaganda: A Study of Father Coughlin's Speeches* (New York: Harcourt, Brace and Company, 1939); Alfred McClung Lee, *Sociology for Whom?* (New York: Oxford University Press, 1978); Alfred McClung Lee, *Sociology for People: Toward a Caring Profession* (Syracuse, NY: Syracuse University Press, 1988); Herbert J. Gans, *Deciding What's News: A Study of CBS Evening News, NBC Nightly News, Newsweek, and Time* (New York: Pantheon, 1979); Dan Schiller, *Objectivity and the News: The Public and the Rise of Commercial Journalism* (Philadelphia: University of Pennsylvania Press, 1981); John Chancellor and Walter R. Mears, *The News Business* (New York: Harper and Row, 1983); Martin Walker, *Powers of the Press: Twelve of the World's Influential Newspapers* (New York: The Pilgrim Press, 1983); Lichter, Rothman, and Lichter, *Media Elite*; David Broder, *Behind the Front Page: A Candid Look at How the News is Made* (New York: Simon and Schuster, 1987); Koch, *News as Myth*.

4. Compare Gregg Barak, "Newsmaking Criminology: Reflections on the Media, Intellectuals, and Crime," *Justice Quarterly* 5 (1988): 573.

5. Lichter, Rothman, and Lichter, *Media Elite*, 294.

6. See, for example, Lee, *Sociology for Whom?*; Lee, *Sociology for People*; Barak, "Newsmaking"; Koch, *News as Myth*.

7. Alfred McClung Lee, *The Daily Newspaper in America: The Evolution of a Social Instrument* (New York: Octagon Books, 1973); Lee, *Sociology for People*; Martin Mayer, *Making News* (Garden City, NY: Doubleday, 1987); Koch, *News as Myth*.

8. Lee and Lee, *Fine Art*; Lee, *Sociology for Whom?*; Barak, "Newsmaking"; Craig Reinarman and Harry G. Levine, "Crack in Context: Politics and the Media in the Making of a Drug Scare," *Contemporary Drug Problems* 16 (1989): 535–78; Koch, *News as Myth*.

9. Reinarman and Levine, "Crack."

10. Reinarman and Levine, 554–55.

11. Reinarman and Levine, 562.

12. Reinarman and Levine, 563.

13. Reinarman and Levine, 564.

14. See Governor's Office of Employee Relations, "Crackdown on Crack," *GOER News* 2 (1986): 16; Governor's Office of Employee Relations, "Crack— The Deadliest Cocaine of All," *GOER News* 2 (1986): 11–12.

15. Mario M. Cuomo, "Message to the Legislature" (Albany, 1987), 39.

16. Mario M. Cuomo, "Message to the Legislature" (Albany, 1989).

17. "State of New York Anti-Drug Abuse Strategy Report" (Albany: Statewide Anti-Drug Abuse Council, 1989).

18. From 1986 to 1990, I clipped and saved articles on drugs, drug policy, drugs and health, drug treatment and prevention, crime and drugs, and violence and drugs from the *New York Times*, the Albany *Times Union*, and *Newsweek* regularly, and from the *New York Post*, the New York *Daily News*, and other magazines and newspapers when relevant articles or events were brought to my attention. During the same period, a bureau at the New York State Division of Criminal Justice Services regularly clipped and circulated to staff articles relevant to crime and criminal justice practices and policies (including those about drugs, drug policy, and so on) from the major New York newspapers. Both of these sources were used for this analysis. Articles from the *New York Times* were oversampled, since that is the only major, mainstream New York City newspaper that is not a tabloid, and therefore least likely to sensationalize the news.

19. "Opium Dens for the Crack Era," *New York Times*, 18 May 1986, 38.

20. Reinarman and Levine, "Crack," 536.

21. "Drug Violence Undermining Queens Hopes," *New York Times*, 21 April 1988, B1.

22. "Gang Attack: Unusual for Its Viciousness," *New York Times*, 25 April 1989, B1.

23. Michael Massing, "Crack's Destructive Sprint Across America," *New York Times Magazine*, 1 October 1989, 38–41, 52–58.

24. Eric Pooley, "Fighting Back Against CRACK," *New York*, 23 January 1989, 32.

25. Joelle Attinger, "The Decline of New York," *Time*, 17 September 1989, 38.

26. "Record Year for Killings Jolts Officials in New York," *New York Times*, 31 December 1990, B1.

27. Reinarman and Levine, "Crack," 537.

28. Hubert M. Blalock, Jr., *Social Statistics* (New York: McGraw-Hill, 1960), 109.

29. Jonathan Greenberg, "All About Crime," *New York*, 3 September 1990, 20–32.

30. Uniform Crime Reports (UCR) statistics show that, overall, the level of violent crime in New York City did increase during the late 1980s. Up from 143,413 reported violent offenses in the city in 1986, there were 169,616 reported for 1989. In terms of the rate per 100,000 population, the increase was from 1,997.5 in 1986 to 2,301.6 in 1989. Comparing the first quarter of 1990 to the first quarter of 1989, the number of violent offenses reported declined from 37,443 to 29,833. See "Uniform Crime Reporting—Index Offenses Reported—Final Counts for 1989," *Office of Justice Systems Analysis Bulletin* (Albany: Division of Criminal Justice Services, 1990); and "Crime and Justice Trends in New York State: 1985–89," *Office of Justice Systems Analysis Bulletin* (Albany: Division of Criminal Justice Services, 1990).

31. National Planning Association population estimates and Supplementary Homicide Reports data for New York City for the period 1987 to 1989 show: (1) between 33 percent and 34 percent of the people in the city were non-white, but 55 percent of the victims of homicide were black; and (2) about 53 percent of the people living in the city were female, yet women accounted for less than 15 percent of all homicide victims.

32. "Homicide among Young Black Males—United States, 1978–1987," *Morbidity and Mortality Weekly Report* 39 (Atlanta: Centers for Disease Control, 7 December 1990), 870.

33. Centers for Disease Control, "Homicide," 871–72.

34. Henry H. Brownstein et al., "The Relationship of Drugs, Drug Trafficking, and Drug Traffickers to Homicide," *Journal of Crime and Justice* 15 (1992): 25–44.

35. Lawrence W. Sherman et al., "Stray Bullets and 'Mushrooms': Random Shootings of Bystanders in Four Cities, 1977–1988," *Journal of Quantitative Criminology* 5 (1989): 297–316.

36. Office of the Attorney General, *Drug Trafficking—A Report to the President*

of the United States (Washington, D.C.: U.S. Department of Justice, 1989); Paul J. Goldstein et al., "Crack and Homicide in New York City, 1988: A Conceptually Based Event Analysis," *Contemporary Drug Problems* 16 (1989): 651–87; Tom Mieczkowski, "Crack Distribution in Detroit," *Contemporary Drug Problems* 17 (1990): 9–29; Steven Belenko, "The Impact of Drug Offenders on the Criminal Justice System," in *Drugs, Crime, and the Criminal Justice System*, ed. Ralph A. Weisheit (Cincinnati: Anderson Press, 1990), 27–78; Paul J. Goldstein, Henry H. Brownstein, and Patrick J. Ryan, "Drug-Related Homicide in New York: 1984 and 1988," *Crime and Delinquency* 38 (1992): 459–76.

37. Henry H. Brownstein, "The Social Construction of Public Policy: A Case for Participation by Researchers," *Sociological Practice Review* 2 (1991): 132–40; Brownstein et al., 40.

38. Sherman et al., 299–300.

39. Reinarman and Levine, 567.

40. Reinarman and Levine, 567.

41. Compare James G. Fox, "The New Right and Social Justice: Implications for the Prisoners' Movement," *Crime and Social Justice* 20 (1983): 63–75.

42. Office of National Drug Control Policy, "National Drug Control Strategy" (Washington, D.C.: Executive Office of the President, 1989); Office of National Drug Control Policy, "National Drug Control Strategy" (Washington, D.C.: Executive Office of the President, 1990); Office of National Drug Control Policy, "National Drug Control Strategy" (Washington, D.C.: Executive Office of the President, 1992).

43. Statewide Anti-Drug Abuse Council, "Strategy Report."

44. Between 1983 and 1987, the number of felony drug arrests in New York State increased by 118 percent, indictments by 207 percent, convictions by 210 percent, and sentences to prison for drug convictions by 220 percent. From 1987 to 1988, felony drug arrests increased by an additional 23 percent, indictments by 12 percent, and sentences to prison for drug convictions by 22 percent (accounting for 37 percent of all sentences to prison in 1988). For New York City during the period from 1983 to 1987, the number of felony drug arrests increased by 122 percent, indictments by 305 percent, and sentences to prison for drug convictions by 237 percent. See Richard Ross and Marjorie Cohen, "New York Trends in Felony Drug Offense Processing" (Albany: Division of Criminal Justice Services, 1988); and "Crime and Justice Annual Report" (Albany: Division of Criminal Justice Services, 1988), 197.

45. Statewide Anti-Drug Abuse Council, "Strategy Report," 7.

46. Cuomo, "Message."

47. Reinarman and Levine, 568.

48. Ethan A. Nadelmann, "U.S. Drug Policy: A Bad Export," *Foreign Policy* 70 (1988): 83–108; Ethan A. Nadelmann, "Drug Prohibition in the United

States: Costs, Consequences, and Alternatives," *Science* 245 (1989): 939–47; James Ostrowski, "Thinking About Drug Legalization," *Policy Analysis, Cato Institute* 121 (1989); Henry H. Brownstein, "Demilitarization of the War on Drugs: Toward an Alternative Drug Strategy," in *The Great Issues of Drug Policy*, ed. Arnold S. Trebach and Kevin B. Zeese (Washington, D.C.: Drug Policy Foundation, 1990), 114–22.

49. Edwin Schur, *Narcotic Addiction in Britain and America: The Impact of Public Policy* (Bloomington: Indiana University Press, 1962); Joint Committee on New York Drug Law Evaluation, "The Nation's Toughest Drug Law: Evaluating the New York Experience, Final Report" (New York: The Association of the Bar of New York, 1977); Arnold S. Trebach, *The Heroin Solution* (New Haven: Yale University Press, 1982); Lynne A. Curtis, "The National Drug Strategy and Inner City Policy" (Testimony before the Select Committee on Narcotics Abuse and Control, U.S. House of Representatives, 15 November 1989); Milton S. Eisenhower Foundation, "Youth Investment and Community Resurrection—Street Lessons on Drugs and Crime for the Nineties, Final Report" (Milton S. Eisenhower Foundation, 1990).

50. Schur, *Narcotic Addiction*; Joint Committee on New York Drug Law Evaluation, "Nation's Toughest"; Malthea Falco, *Winning the Drug War: A National Strategy* (New York: Priority Press, 1989); Ralph A. Weisheit, "Civil War on Drugs," in *Drugs, Crime, and the Criminal Justice System*, 1–10; Mark Miller, "A Failed 'Test Case': Washington's Drug War," *Newsweek*, 29 January 1990, 28–29.

51. James Austin and Aaron D. McVey, "The 1989 NCCD Prison Population Forecast: The Impact of the War on Drugs," *NCCD Focus* (1989); Nadelmann, "Drug Prohibition."

52. Ross and Cohen, "New York Trends"; Belenko, "The Impact of Drug Offenders."

53. Steven Wisotsky, *Breaking the Impasse in the War on Drugs* (New York: Greenwood Press, 1986).

54. Paul Finkelman, "In War Civil Liberties Is the Second Casualty: The War on Drugs and the Bill of Rights" (Paper presented at the Annual Meeting of the American Society of Criminology, Baltimore, MD, 1990).

55. Mark A. R. Kleiman, *Marijuana: Costs of Abuse, Costs of Control* (New York: Greenwood Press, 1989), 73, 119.

56. Brownstein, "Demilitarization," 117.

57. Paul J. Goldstein, *Prostitution and Drugs* (Lexington, MA: Lexington Books, 1979).

58. Compare Barak, "Newsmaking"; Brownstein, "The Social Construction."

4 ‹ ‹ ‹
The New Mythic Monster

SU C. EPSTEIN

Introduction

Beginning in the late 1950s, researchers began to examine a phenomenon that was then termed "multicide," the killing of more than one person by a single assailant.[1] Although these crimes can be documented prior to the fifteenth century, the interest in such phenomena and the terminology for these types of behaviors were new.[2] As investigations increased, it was determined that not all multiple-victim–single-offender homicides were alike. "Evidence began to emerge on yet another form of murder that simply did not match with the concept of a mad killer running amok," and new terminology and typologies were developed.[3]

By the 1980s a variety of new terms were introduced to distinguish among different forms of multiple-victim–single-offender homicide situations, such as spree killing, mass murder, and serial killing.[4] While it appears that each researcher creates his or her own definition of the type of multicide under investigation, in the specific case of serial murder, there is a uniform definitional baseline. Criminologists and law enforcement representatives agree that the foundation of all definitions and typologies of serial murder entails killing in installments or intervals where the murders share common factors such as motive or method. Generally, supplements to the basic definition involve hypotheses of perpetrator characteristics and the assumption that serial killings are linked with sex crimes.[5]

Around the same time that researchers were taking interest in multiple-victim–single-offender homicides, and specifically, serial killing, the public also became concerned about these types of crime. After World War II, clearance rates for homicides dropped from 90 percent to 70 percent, while incidents of homicide continued to rise.[6] Acutely aware of an increasing number of homicides and fewer solutions, the media played a major role in publicizing sensational stories about multiple-victim killings. Media presentations suggested that serial killing could be responsible for numerous missing children and unsolved homicides; thus, the implication was that serial killers posed a tremendous threat to American society. Although the actual frequency of such crimes is unknown and greatly debated, by the mid-1980s the justice department was confirming media reports by suggesting that serial killing had reached "epidemic proportions."[7]

With the media focusing on multiple-victim homicides, serial killers attracted a great deal of attention. Public concern increased as it became apparent that serial killers were not the average hoodlums, but instead intelligent, thinking criminals who appeared to enjoy the act of killing. It frightened the public and angered law enforcement officials that such criminals kill for pleasure only and with increasing skill, thus reducing the odds of their apprehension. Public fears increased further as the media encouraged the belief that a serial killer could strike anyone, almost anywhere, and at any time. However, along with this fear came a deep curiosity as to what kind of person could engage in such extreme violation of social norms and evade capture for long periods of time.

Media and popular culture capitalized on public fear and curiosity, and a new icon appeared in popular culture: the serial killer. These criminals came to be referenced in songs and jokes, artistically illustrated on trading cards, featured in fanzines, discussed on weekly television shows, and promoted by art galleries that show and sell paintings created by convicted murderers. Seltzer even suggests that serial killer fiction has become so popular that it has replaced the Western in genre fiction.[8]

Film certainly did not avoid this craze. In 1989, much to his surprise, John McNaughton's film *Henry: Portrait of a Serial Killer* was deemed an "art film." During the 1990s American feature films featuring serial killers have enjoyed great box office success. *Silence of the Lambs* made over $100 million in box office sales, and for the first five weeks of its run held first place on the charts, while its killer character, Hannibal Lector, made it to the cover of *Newsweek* and became a household name. The attraction of serial killers also enabled the resuscitation of the slasher genre. Jason Voorhees returned, yet again, to be featured in *Friday, the 13th, Part 9*. The makers of this film, while not claiming to be creating high art, saw this installment to be a more serious and adult film than its predecessors, specifically stating, "Our competition will be *Hamlet*, or any other mainstream movies out there. . . ."[9] The notorious Freddy has now been resurrected in Wes Craven's new film, *Nightmare*.

In this discussion serial killer films are defined as those having a plot in which a single offender kills multiple victims over a period of time, and with some kind of identifiable pattern. Excluded are crimes of passion, occasions when the offender is acting in conjunction with other parties, and situations in which the killings take place in the context of another criminal activity, such as a bank robbery.

Although pattern and time period are significant criteria for inclusion in the category of serial killing, they intentionally are defined loosely in this study. In the criminological sense, serial killers engage in patterned behavior by having a common motive, method, and/or victim-type. While method and victim-type may be easily identified in film, a killer's motivation can be difficult to determine. To account for this, the pattern of common motive is expanded in this case to include a common pattern within the relationship between the killer and his or her victims.[10] Period of time is also defined in terms of any interval between hours and years. Although in the criminological sense it is unlikely that a murderer killing over a period of hours would be considered a serial killer, this time period is included in order to take into consideration cinematic convention.[11]

The following discussion is based on a study of 172 feature-length American films released between 1930 and 1992.[12] While all film genres are represented, most of these films fall into the categories of crime-action, psychological-thriller, and horror, with only a small portion of films belonging to the recently created slasher genre. Represented among these films are 155 distinct killers.[13]

Fictional Killers and Real Killers

There are some interesting parallels between the cinematic representation of serial killers and what is known about actual criminals. As is true of known serial killers, film characters are represented as older than most criminals, their ages typically ranging from twenty-six to sixty. Almost all serial killer characters are white, with a mere 1 percent represented as black, and no characters represented as Asian or Native American. This also parallels what is known about actual killers. Finally, serial killer characters, like actual murderers, are predominantly males who tend to victimize those they dislike or find offensive.

For many serial killer characters, as in actual cases, their pattern can be identified by victim-type, modus operandi, or a combination of the two. For example, in *The Love Butcher* (1982), the killer only murders women, whom he finds repulsive, with gardening tools. For other characters the pattern is found within the relationship between the killer and his victims. For example, the killer in *The Mutilator* (1985) murders his son's friends because he dislikes his son and anyone or anything associated with him.

While it may appear initially that serial killer characters are fairly realistically represented, closer inspection proves this to be inaccurate. While it is true that known serial killers are predominantly middle-aged white males, other significant characteristics that are notably absent.

Conspicuously absent, for example, is reference to male homosexuality, although homosexual acts and hate crimes have been connected to several known serial killers. Homosexual relations played a significant role in the prominent cases of John Wayne Gacy and Jeffrey Dahmer. In contrast to the vast number of actual cases that involve homosexual men and homosexual victims, only two films represent homosexual males. In both *Hide and Go Shriek* (1988) and *Too Scared to Scream* (1985) a homosexual male killer murders heterosexual people (both men and women) who he believes are standing in the way of his failed (homosexual) relationship.

Also notably inaccurate is the representation of female serial killers. Actual murders by women who meet the definitional requirements of serial killing frequently involve the killing of children, the elderly, or the sick. This type of serial murder is not depicted in film. Rather, female serial killer characters are typically presented as avenging a gang rape, as reacting to a wrong that they feel has been committed against a significant male character, or as motivated by an evil, supernatural force.

The consistent criminological linkage of serial killing and sex crimes is another facet of actual cases that films do not adequately or accurately explore. As a result they present a misleading picture. Frequently in actual cases of serial killing, a sexual crime takes place along with the murder. Often the sexual act, in conjunction with the killing, defines the murderer's sexuality. In engaging in the sex crime, the murderer becomes empowered by dominating victims who are socially less powerful than himself.[14] This pattern has led Caputi and also Cameron and Frazer to conclude that serial murder not only centers on the issue of power and domination but manifests misogynistic cultural attitudes.[15]

Sexual politics is clearly a dimension of serial killer film. Killer characters are empowered by their actions and frequently express misogynistic beliefs. However, in the serial killer film, sexuality and morality often become linked with cultural myths of romantic love and family. In many films the serial killer character is represented not as engaging in sex crimes, but as acting out of a sense of moral fortitude that becomes a means of legitimating violence.

In many serial killer films, the link between sex and violence, although continually present, becomes obscure and unrealistic. In film, characters murder to obtain the perfect family, to protect their loved ones, and for the sake of an abstract conception of love. Often these killer characters are trying to dominate their partner or control situational factors that prevent the mythic ideal of love from being realized. They are killing so that they may have fairy tale relationships with others. In *The Stepfather* series (1987–1991), for example, the serial killer murders in an attempt to possess the mythic family created by 1950s television programming. His goal is to exist in a trouble-free world where he is the idolized father with the dutiful and dependent wife and child.

Killer characters also murder when they believe that their victims are behaving immorally. Serial killer characters often murder young couples who are sexually active before marriage. Such characters also kill incidental victims. Many victims in serial killer films are people who happen to be in the wrong place at the wrong time or police officers who are near to apprehending the killer character. None of these situations are typical of actual serial killings. As a result serial killer films represent an inaccurate picture of the victim. While in actual cases, serial killers' victims are predominantly women, children, or young men, in film, serial killer characters' victims are adults and equally distributed between the sexes.

These cinematic representations, while not accurately portraying actual cases, are plausible characterizations. A serial killer could be a heterosexual man who kills sexually active couples because he feels they are committing a moral offense against society; however, there are currently no real-life cases that meet this description. More likely, the situations found in typical serial killer films are conventions that allow for the gratuitous display of nudity and sexual situations and are mainly attempts to draw box office success.

Serial killer characters are represented with similar demographic characteristics as actual killers. Their motivations are understandable, if not accurate, and their attitudes and actions reflect many dominant, cultural beliefs. Those unfamiliar with actual cases of serial killings would not be aware of the inaccuracies in the representation; thus, audiences typically are left with the superficial impression that they have seen realistic characterizations.

The Serial Killer as a Mythic Monster

The serial killer frequently is depicted as a fantastic character. Killer characters are often associated with occult forces that provide them with special powers. Some are represented as demonic or as evil personified; others are linked to classic mythic monsters like the vampire; and almost all are attributed some degree of superhuman ability.

Fantastical representation begins with a linkage between serial killer characters and the personification of evil. In numerous cases, such as *Torment* (1986) or *The Horror Show* (1989), even when a psychological diagnosis is given as an explanation of the character's behavior, the serial killer is described by others as "evil." In extreme presentations, such as *Def by Temptation* (1990) and *Night Angel* (1990), the character is presented as a demon from hell who has come to Earth. In others, such as *Witchboard* (1987) or *Killer Party* (1986), the killings are caused by evil forces that possess individuals.

In some cases the representation of the serial killer as a demonic, evil force is clear, but in others the presentation is much more subtle. For example, in the film *Body Parts* (1991), the limbs of a convicted murderer are removed and then attached to accident victims. The torso and head of the murderer are kept in stasis and later reanimated, at which point the murderer decides that he wants his old body parts back. Meanwhile, the recipients of the murderer's limbs undergo personality shifts in which they begin to have the killer's thoughts and begin to copy his behaviors. Recognizing his personality changes, one limb recipient wonders, "What is evil and where does it live? In the soul? Maybe it lives in the heart? Maybe it lives in the flesh?" While such a biological explanation is rather far-fetched, the film presents this view as a scientifically valid explanation. As in other films, it is suggested here that evil is a biological property. It is the fact that the accident victim has "a killer's blood in [his] blood" that makes him behave uncharacteristically.

The notion that the serial killer is evil is not limited to film. In his book *Serial Murderers and Their Victims*, lauded as "the best available book on the market" about serial killers, Hickey states, "Multiple homicide offenders, especially serial murderers, are incomprehensible to society. . . . Evil then becomes the appropriate label for those who apparently enjoy controlling and destroying human life."[16] He goes on to discuss the notion of evil and serial killers and notes, "Thus serial killers not only *do* evil, but they also possess various developmental characteristics that may contribute to evil."[17] Other researchers have likewise said that serial killers "are often evil but not crazy," or have referred to them as "devils."[18]

The conceptual connection between serial killers and evil has also fostered a link between the serial killer and mythic monsters. Noted experts on serial killing have even suggested that the fiends and monsters of legends are rooted in serial killers.[19] Numerous popular accounts of serial killing specifically refer to these criminals as *monsters*.[20] Other experts talk about "vampire killers" or criminals suffering from "the Dracula syndrome."[21]

The mythic monster as serial killer and serial killer as mythic monster are common representations in film. Sometimes by merely referencing other characters, film makers associate the serial killer and the mythic monster. For example, the killer is described as "a psychic vampire" in *One Dark Night* (1983), and the killer in *Fade to Black* (1980) dresses as Dracula. In *Stripped to Kill 2* (1989), upon the discovery that the victims' throats are not only slit with a razor but have traces of saliva on the cut, the officer jokes that he can see the headlines, "Vampire killer, cuts then sucks."

In other cases, such as *Dracula's Widow* (1988), murders are described within the film as being the work of a serial killer, when in fact, the killings turn out to be committed by a vampire. Conversely, in the film *Vampire at Midnight* (1988), the killer is believed to be a vampire, when, in fact, he is a more conventional serial killer.

The vampire is not the only mythic monster to be linked with serial killing in these films. The mythology of Lilith and the incubi is referenced in *Night Angel* (1990); a werewolf is responsible for the serial murders in the film *Berserker* (1988); and scientific creations, akin to Frankenstein's monster, are the culprits in movies such as *Silent Rage* (1982) and *Body Parts* (1991).

Given the widespread tendency to view actual serial killers as evil monsters, it is not surprising that the cinematic representation of serial killer characters would follow the same course. Likewise, if serial killer characters are depicted as evil, supernatural forces, it is not surprising that they should also display unnatural abilities.

The Serial Killer Character as Superhuman

Almost all cinematic representations imply that serial killers are special, atypical, and, therefore, possess unique capabilities. Only 20 percent of the serial killer characters are identified as supernatural by the use of such terms as *vampires, werewolves, demons, possessed*, or *aliens*. Yet, more than 60 percent of the serial killers in American films display obvious superhuman abilities.

Films represent serial killers as possessing extraordinary strength and physical abilities as well as an amazing capacity to recover from fatal circumstances. In *Burndown* (1990), for example, the serial killer character is said to have been exposed to massive amounts of radiation. Radiation poisoning is described as what actually kills the women he attacks, yet the radiation does not affect the killer in the same manner. In *Silent Night, Deadly Night 3* (1989), the killer character, awakening from a year in a coma and recovering from "reconstructive brain surgery," is able to rise from his hospital bed and kill the hospital staff before stiffly walking away. Films such as *Destroyer* (1988), *The Horror Show* (1989), and *Shocker* (1989) all depict "mass murderers" who survive the electric chair, at least temporarily, in human form.

While very few serial killer characters are actually presented as immortal, excessive force is typically required to stop the killer. Despite being severely beaten, sprayed in the face with mace, kicked in the groin, and shot and stabbed repeatedly and in combination, the serial killers in *Iced* (1988), *Lisa* (1990), *Open House* (1987), *The Hitcher* (1986), and *Eyes of a Stranger* (1980), among others, act as though nothing has happened and continue to attack their victims furiously. Other killer characters, after breaking handcuffs or being run over by cars and shot repeatedly, still are able to continue their attacks. *Hide and Go Shriek* (1988) shows the killer falling down an elevator shaft. Officials arrive, the crime scene is cleaned up, and the killer's covered body is loaded into the ambulance for transport to the coroner's office. Though several people have handled the body, in the final scene of the film, the audience sees the killer driving the ambulance away after having killed the attendant.

Perhaps the most interesting aspect of the cinematic representation of the serial killer as superhuman is that, in most cases, the evil entity is contextually presented and accepted as a regular mortal. The quintessential example of this is the horror classic *Halloween* (1978). In this film, although the killer, Michael Myers, is described by the psychiatrist as "evil" and "not human," he appears to follow a normal human development pattern, aging from a six-year-old boy to a twenty-year-old man. He also displays emotional ties to his family, which are considered ideologically characteristic of humans. These emotional ties are continually brought up and played upon within the story. Still, his murderous actions are simultaneously blamed on his evil nature and his involvement with "druid rituals." The first film of the series, in particular, clearly presents Michael as a human being, while simultaneously attributing superhuman abilities to him. In this film, Michael, having escaped from a mental institution, returns to his hometown, commits several murders, and finally attacks his sister. In the process of this attack he is stabbed with a knitting needle, poked in the eye with a hanger, beaten, and finally shot several times, causing him to fall backward out a second-story window. Moments later, when the other characters peer out the window, and the camera pans to the ground, he is gone. We later learn that, shot and bleeding, he has run through the woods and into a river that carried him downstream and away from the pursuing police.

Conclusion

Serial killers have become our culture's new mythic monsters in part because of the ways they are represented in popular cinema. Films create a paradoxical image of such criminals. On the one hand, they are realistically presented as mortal, human beings, and therefore constitute believable characters. Most killer characters not only appear to be "normal" but mirror the demographics of such killers drawn from actual case studies. In this way, the serial killer character is akin to actual killers, and the association between real killers and fictional characters is made. On the other hand, these seemingly mortal characters typically are capable of surviving the most brutal attacks and display astounding abilities. The character of Hannibal Lector in *Silence of the Lambs* (1991) commits gruesome acts while being able to consciously lower his heart rate sufficiently to appear on the verge of death. His senses are so keen that he can smell a bandage through a glass-encased cell. And yet, Lector is presented as an exceptionally intelligent, but biologically normal, mortal.

At the same time, expert and media presentations have encouraged viewing real-world serial killers as mythic monsters. Referring to such criminals as "monsters" and "evil" encourages people to think of the serial killer as unnatural, unreal, and inhuman. Referencing the unique "skill" of the serial killer and focusing on the fact that these criminals engage in their crimes undetected for long periods of time also encourage the public to view the killer as superhuman and unique.

Films and filmic presentations thus create an overall, collective impression of the serial killer. The realistic aspects of such characters and the familiar contexts in which they are presented enable killer characters to be accepted and associated with real killers. But simultaneously, films represent the serial killer as a supernatural force. In this way, both the characters and their real-world counterparts are presented within supernatural explanations, and are thus distanced from the rest of society. The serial killer becomes no longer human, but monstrous.

The public typically views the acts of the serial killer as so hideous as to be almost beyond comprehension. Hollywood's association of the serial killer with the supernatural provides both a rationale and a basis for assumptions about actual serial killers since, in viewing the serial killer as a supernatural force, the public is better able to come to terms with the killer's actions. The public can indulge its curiosity more readily if the serial killer is distanced; the serial killer's atrocities are harder to accept if we consider them to be committed by people like ourselves, our children, or our neighbors. The serial killer is more acceptable as a supernatural force who is outside of humanity and therefore divorced from us. Through film's reference to the supernatural, serial killers are dehumanized.

The association of serial killers with the supernatural also provides them with mythic status. The serial killer becomes nothing more than a characterization shaped by the fictional presentation, as opposed to an actual individual, a process illustrated by the mythology of Jack the Ripper.[22] By linking the serial killer with traditional monsters such as vampires or werewolves, the killer is incorporated into a conventional cinematic formula. The serial killer is characterized as immortal, like the vampire, living for eternity to prey on respectable living creatures. Situated within the established mythic monster formula, the characterization exists in a historical and cultural context that need not be questioned, and once again the fact that actual serial killers do exist can become obscured.

As a result the serial killer becomes not only legendary but iconic. Fan clubs and collectibles for noted fictional characters and actual killers exist side by side, without clear distinctions between what is real and what has been created. Both are idolized and emulated.[23]

In a nation concerned with crime in general and homicide in particular, it is not surprising that the serial killer should become prevalent in the media, both as an object of concern and an object of entertainment. It has been argued that people tend to mythologize that which they fear so that their anxieties may be dealt with in an informal, non-threatening manner.[24] Villela and Markin argue that movies serve in this way as modern myths.[25] To this end the serial killer character becomes a mythic monster that, once created by Hollywood, allows the public to come to terms with its fears of actual serial killings.

Media presentations affect, and intertwine with, public policy and public response.[26] In cases of homicide, for example, media coverage of a crime frequently elicits copy cat crimes. Similarly, the presentation of serial killer films has inspired actual killers to mimic the crimes they have witnessed on the screen.[27] In turn, the filmic representation of serial killers as mythic monsters may influence police response and public reaction toward this type of crime. Supernatural characters with superhuman strength are extremely threatening, and exceptional force is justified in apprehending them. Dehumanizing serial killer characters by connecting them to the supernatural legitimates the extraordinary measures that are seen as necessary to stopping them. But is it appropriate to apply the notions of superhuman abilities, or the belief in the necessity of excessive force, to actual killers?

While people typically are aware of the lines between the fictional and the real, distinctions between the fictional mythic monster and the actual serial killer have become blurred. Police have been known to release serial killers because they did not fit the mythic persona created by the media.[28] For example, in the case of the Yorkshire Ripper, the police released the guilty party from custody, basing their assessment on media-created profiles of Jack the Ripper and assuming the Yorkshire Ripper would have similar characteristics. Other examples of how such lines become blurred, and in turn have impact on policy decisions, can be found outside the realm of serial killing. For example, although he did not refer directly to the supernatural, reporter Roger Parloff described Rodney King as displaying "superhuman strength." He went on to claim that this legitimated the excessive force used against King by the L.A. police.[29]

Every century has had its mythic monsters, each representing the social concerns and fears of the time. In contemporary society we fear random and seemingly senseless violence, and it seems appropriate, therefore, that our mythic monster would take the form of the serial killer. However, unlike the monsters of the past, there is no debate as to the serial killer's actual existence. Serial killers do exist and, despite conventional media representations of such murderers, they exist not as a supernatural force akin to the vampire but as mortal beings.

Notes

1. Grierson Dickson, *Murder by Numbers* (London: Robert Hale, 1958).

2. Donald Lunde, *Murder and Madness* (San Francisco: San Francisco Book Company, 1976); Michael Newton, *Hunting Humans: The Encyclopedia of Serial Killers, Volume 2* (New York: Avon Books, 1990).

3. Ronald Holmes and James De Burger, *Serial Murder* (Newbury Park, CA: Sage Publications, 1988), 17.

4. Lunde, *Murder and Madness*; Holmes and De Burger, *Serial Murder*; Jack Levin and James Alan Fox, *Mass Murder: America's Growing Menace* (New York: Plenum Press, 1985).

5. Lunde, *Murder and Madness*; Holmes and De Burger, *Serial Murder*; Levin and Fox, *Mass Murder*; Steven Egger, *Serial Murder: An Elusive Phenomenon* (New York: Praeger, 1990); Eric Hickey, *Serial Murderers and Their Victims* (Pacific Grove: Brooks/Cole, 1991); Joel Norris, *Serial Killers: The Growing Menace* (New York: Doubleday, 1988).

6. Newton, *Hunting Humans*, 1.

7. Holmes and De Burger, *Serial Murder*; Levin and Fox, *Mass Murder*; Newton, *Hunting Humans*.

8. Mark Seltzer, "Serial Killers," *Differences* 5 (1993): 92–129.

9. Mark Shapiro, "Voorhees' Last Stand," *Fangoria* (August 1993): 125.

10. For example, included is the killer who on three separate occasions kills three unrelated individuals in three distinct ways, but the killer has killed all three individuals because they have stood in the way of the killer's achieving his or her goals or objectives. Another example would be the case when the killer's victims' shared characteristic is their relationship to the killer. Killings that are motivated by vengeance or a sense of moral injustice would be included within this conception as well.

11. According to Michael Hauge, *Writing Screenplays That Sell* (New York: McGraw-Hill, 1988), the plot of most feature films takes place within twenty-four to forty-eight hours. Given this time period limitation, events that occur over weeks or months in "real time" would be accelerated in film. It should be noted that most films did indicate that killings were taking place over extended periods of time, even if the movie did not show this time frame. There were only a few cases included where the killings occurred within hours of each other.

12. A comprehensive list of films was chosen by review of descriptions taken from Jay Robert Nash and Stanley Ralph Ross, eds., *The Motion Picture Guide, Volumes 1–12* and *Annual Editions* (Chicago: Cinebooks, 1985–1992). Films available on video cassette that met the definitional criteria of containing a serial killer character were reviewed. If they actually contained serial killer characters, they were included in the sample.

13. The discrepancy between the number of killers and the number of films results from the fact that some films contain multiple killers while others are a series of films that represent only one killer. In cases such as *Halloween*, although four separate films were included in the sample, the killer character, Michael Myers, is counted only once.

14. Most often serial killers are males. Their victims typically come from groups who have little or no social power, such as women, children, or homosexuals.

15. Deborah Cameron and Elizabeth Frazer, *A Lust to Kill* (Oxford: Basil Blackwell, 1987); Jane Caputi, *The Age of Sex Crime* (Bowling Green, OH: Popular Press, 1987).

16. Hickey, *Serial Murderers and Their Victims*, 29.

17. Hickey, *Serial Murderers and Their Victims*, 31, emphasis in the original.

18. Levin and Fox, *Mass Murder*, 210; Ronald Markman and Dominick Bosco, *Alone with the Devil* (New York: Bantam Books, 1989).

19. Joe Swickard, "Computer Programs Help Flesh Out Likely Mass-Killer Types," *Hartford Courant*, 27 October 1988, F1, F3.

20. Robert Ressler and Tom Shachtman, *Whoever Fights Monsters* (New York: St. Martin's Press, 1992); Howard Stevens and Mary Stevens, "Chained Beauties for the Prowling Sex Monster!" in *Serial Murderers*, ed. Art Crockett (New York: Windsor, 1990), 397–411; Hickey, *Serial Murderers and Their Victims*.

21. Crockett, *Serial Murderers*; Newton, *Hunting Humans*; Richard Monaco and Bill Burt, *The Dracula Syndrome* (New York: Avon Books, 1993); Ressler and Shachtman, *Whoever Fights Monsters*.

22. Caputi, *The Age of Sex Crime*; Jane Caputi, "The New Founding Fathers: The Lore and Lure of the Serial Killer in Contemporary Culture," *Journal of American Culture* 13 (1990): 1–12.

23. Devon Jackson, "Serial Killers and the People Who Love Them," *Village Voice*, 22 March 1994, 26–32; Caputi, "The New Founding Fathers." And in this light, see, of course, Oliver Stone's recent film/media event, *Natural Born Killers*.

24. James Twitchell, *Preposterous Violence* (Oxford: Oxford University Press, 1989).

25. Minnerly Lucia Villela and Richard Markin, "A Star Wars as Myth: A Fourth Hope?" *Frontiers* 5 (1987): 17–24.

26. Jack Shaheen et al., "Media Coverage of the Middle East: Perception and Foreign Policy," *Annals of the American Academy of Political and Social Science* 482 (1985): 160–73.

27. See, for example, the case of Mark Branch, who in 1988 dressed as Jason (from the *Friday the 13th* series) and stabbed a young woman in Greenfield, Massachusetts.

28. Caputi, *The Age of Sex Crime*; Cameron and Frazer, *A Lust to Kill*; Joan Smith, *Misogynies: Reflections on Myths and Malice* (New York: Fawcett Columbine, 1989).

29. Jerome Skolnick and James J. Fyfe, *Above the Law: Police and the Excessive Use of Force* (New York: Free Press, 1993), xii.

5...

A Cultural Approach to Crime and Punishment, Bluegrass Style

KENNETH D. TUNNELL

Introduction: A Brief History of Bluegrass Music

The roots of Southern American music can be found in the music of the English, Irish, and lowland Scots who migrated to North America in the eighteenth century. As some settled in Appalachia, and particularly in the Blue Ridge Mountains and Cumberland Gap, they brought with them, among other cultural attributes, songs that had been a part of their oral histories and traditions for centuries.[1] While some of these early mountain songs have been found outside the Appalachian region, that area, with its mountains and highlands, "acted as a giant cultural deep freeze, preserving these old songs and singing methods better than in other parts of the country."[2] In fact, the Appalachian region and its Euro-American residents remained isolated until after the Civil War, and as recently as 1916, in rural Tennessee and Kentucky, English ballads were still being sung much as they were when first brought there.[3] The long period of isolation combined with the eclectic cultural assimilation gave rise to a unique blend of musical styles that today is known as bluegrass music.[4]

As important as European cultures and their musical traditions were in shaping mountain or bluegrass music, other forces played a part. Since the South historically has been biracial, the predominant cultural influences on Southern music have been both Anglo-American and African American.[5] In the U.S., rural Southern blacks and whites, although segregated by law, shared a similar cultural milieu and exchanged cultural characteristics. Their ways of life, similar in that both races were rural, poor, often isolated, and dependent on agriculture, were reflections of their cultures and their social classes. As bluegrass music emerged from the union of these cultures, it was given shape by the dominant themes, values, and traditions specific to them.[6] Although bluegrass is Anglo, it also is blues—blues borrowed from African American culture and applied to the often mournful and lonesome folk ballads of Anglo-Americans' history.[7] Even the recognized "father of bluegrass" himself, Bill Monroe, recognizes the significance of African American music, saying, "Bluegrass music is a field holler, just like blues."

The commonly shared ways of life and social class among Appalachian mountain dwellers are important for understanding not only the early formative stages of bluegrass music but also its growing popularity. Just as European whites migrated to Appalachia during the eighteenth century, their descendants—poor, Southern whites—began their migration from the Appalachian region to the urban north during World War II and the years immediately following. And like their ancestors, these former Appalachians brought with them their cultural traits, including their music. As bluegrass music was removed from its insular setting and exposed for the first time to a wide variety of urban dwellers, it soon was embraced by many non-Southerners, largely because of its inherent Anglo and African American folk heritage and values expressed in song.[8] Such values are represented in bluegrass songs that address various issues, lifestyles, and actual historical events detailed from the perspective of rural mountain dwellers. These values have emerged as the dominant themes in bluegrass lyrics—themes that address not only the importance of family, home, and loved ones, but those that speak to the dark side of life, to violent crime and punishment in the community.

As the industrial working class evolved into a multicultural work force during the 1940s and 1950s, bluegrass music was on its way toward becoming a nationally recognized musical form. And it was during this period that bluegrass experienced its first real "take-off," as newly formed groups began performing on various radio shows and as studios began, in earnest, recording and marketing various bluegrass bands. Today bluegrass music has emerged from its Appalachian isolation; but, although not as regionally based as it once was, it still is primarily a class-based genre, appealing to both the Southern and Northern industrial working class.[9]

The Bluegrass Sound

While bluegrass music is growing in sales and concert attractions, it is not a major component of the music industry. Its fans and followers are small in number, and its profits pale in comparison with those of mainstream country and pop music. Thus, some readers may be unfamiliar with bluegrass music, its sound, and its essential elements. Bluegrass has been defined as

> polyphonic vocal and instrumental music played on certain unamplified instruments based on music brought from the British Isles to Appalachian regions and refined by additions of negro and urban music. Vocal lead parts are rendered in the high-pitched style of traditional British balladry, with chorus harmonies added by a high tenor sung a third or fifth above the lead, and lower baritone and/or bass lines.[10]

Bluegrass is the sound that comes together with particular acoustic stringed instruments (namely, the fiddle, banjo, guitar, bass, mandolin, and occasionally dobro) and with a particular timing, pitch, and vocal arrangement. Before 1940 string-band music, later to be called bluegrass, was rough-hewn; but Bill Monroe added elements of both jazz and blues to the country or hillbilly string sound.[11] Although Monroe first appeared on the Grand Ole Opry in 1939, the essential elements of what later came to be defined as bluegrass did not come together until 1940 in Monroe's band as "sacred and secular, black and white, urban and rural, combined to form an altogether new strain of American music."[12]

An essential element of bluegrass music, the singing, has come to be called "the high lonesome sound" because the lead and especially the tenor parts are pitched rather high, giving the song, along with its typically sad lyrics, a haunting, mournful, and lonesome sound. Like the songs themselves, this high lonesome sound may be the product of a centuries-ago singing style rooted in the oldest form of Christian worship—the psalm song. The psalm song, now known as the long-meter hymn and found predominantly in African American churches, may be a forerunner to the high lonesome sound of bluegrass music.[13] Again we see evidence of African American cultural influences on the sound of this musical genre. Although bluegrass singers may be unaware of, and thus unable to articulate, the significance of this heritage to bluegrass music, Monroe, an instrumental architect of the high lonesome sound, credits black blues music for giving shape to the high lonesome singing style. Monroe himself has said, "I would sing kindly the way I felt. I've always liked the touch of the blues, you know, and I put some of that into my singing. I like to sing the way it touches me."[14]

The union of black and white music is not unique to the bluegrass sound, for jazz shares characteristics of each musical form. But bluegrass, with its eclectic blend of blues, black-face minstrelsy, and Celtic musical forms, was transformed into something greater than the sum of its parts as it made its sojourn into Appalachia, was preserved there, and then, like some anomaly from the past, was spread throughout the country and into various parts of the world. Both the musical forms that gave bluegrass its shape and sound and the dominant themes found in the music, shaped by songs from the old world and songs from the new, transformed bluegrass into a uniquely appealing musical form.

Attention is now turned to the dominant themes found in bluegrass lyrics, with particular attention to the theme of violence.

Themes in Bluegrass Music

Today the words *bluegrass music* conjure up certain images in the minds of even mildly interested or informed listeners. Songs that inspire such images as mountain cabins (e.g., "Cabin Home on the Hill"), close-knit families ("Calling My Children Home"), loving mothers ("If I Could Hear My Mother Pray Again"), a God to fear ("God Who Never Fails"), highways ("Wreck on the Highway"), graveyards ("Snow Covered Mound"), wayfarers ("Wayfaring Stranger"), maidens ("Georgia Rose"), rogues ("Roving Gambler"), and longing for a home that is no longer there ("Mother No Longer Awaits Me at Home") exemplify dominant themes in bluegrass music. Bluegrass songs are ripe with visions of an "idyllic world to which the singer either longs to return or expresses his intention to return."[15] The singer typically represents one in exile who "can't go home again," and one who experiences the "contrast of memory and experience" (e.g., "The Old Home Place").[16]

Still other dominant themes in bluegrass include unrequited love (e.g., "Sweet Thing" and "Old Love Letters"), the deceit of urban women ("Girl in the Blue Velvet Band"), being orphaned in the city, ("I Was Left on the Street"), one's own impending death ("The River of Death"), the death of a loved one ("No Mother or Dad"), the love between parent and child ("Little Girl and the Dreadful Snake"), and the belief in an eternal life where loved ones shall never part ("Heaven" and "How Beautiful Heaven Must Be").[17]

Many of these songs aggrandize home, spiritual life, family values, and home-spun tradition (e.g., "Where No Cabins Fall" and "I'm on My Way Back to the Old Home"), while some bemoan their disintegration ("If I Had My Life to Live Over," "The Old Home Town," and "Georgia Mules and Country Boys"). Such themes-in-song were openly accepted and loved by rural mountain whites and later (immediately following World War II) by those Appalachian whites who migrated north in search of employment and a better way of life than they could expect by remaining in Appalachia.[18]

Given such dominant themes, bluegrass performers and aficionados contentedly claim that bluegrass music is clean family music representing wholesome themes—unlike those found in more widely accepted mainstream country music (themes such as infidelity, drinking, gambling, and divorce). Bluegrass performers take pride in offering clean, family entertainment, not only in their recorded music but also in their live performances. Some performers, for example, proudly claim that they play for the entire family and refuse to play where alcohol is served. Likewise, nearly all bluegrass festivals prohibit the audience from possessing and consuming alcoholic beverages.[19] Although a strong argument could be made that bluegrass music *is* to a large extent "wholesome," little is said about those themes that are neither wholesome nor family-oriented, and less is said about the oft-found violence in bluegrass music.

An Analysis of Bluegrass Murder Ballads

To understand violence found in bluegrass songs, I conducted a lyric analysis of bluegrass murder ballads. The base of bluegrass songs from which a sample could be drawn is voluminous. Yet the base of bluegrass murder songs is actually few in number, and as a result, sampling for this study was not necessary. Rather, I attempted to analyze the entire known universe of bluegrass murder ballads. Although few in number, these songs are essential elements to a bluegrass repertoire, not necessarily because murder songs are being written and recorded by bluegrass performers, but because they are still performed by both old-time and contemporary bluegrass bands at countless live bluegrass shows and festivals.

Because there is no universal list of murder ballads, I was left to my own devices to discover those songs representing units of analysis for this study. I used a variety of somewhat unconventional methods to compile a list of bluegrass murder ballads. First, I perused bluegrass song books, thematic books on bluegrass, and discographies that listed murder ballads.[20] Second, I questioned two long-time bluegrass fans and music collectors about such songs and also contacted two disc jockeys who host weekly bluegrass radio programs. From these four well-informed individuals, I learned of murder ballads that I could not have otherwise known. Third, I visited three record stores that specialize in marketing country and bluegrass recordings. From these visits I not only perused bluegrass recordings but informally learned of murder ballads by conversing with the shopkeepers. Fourth, I relied on my own personal knowledge, experiences, expertise, and bluegrass record collection. From these various sources of information, I discovered fifteen songs that give accounts of murder. The murders-in-song were then analyzed, revealing a disturbing latent content among the dominant themes.

Three distinct patterns emerged from this analysis. First, in almost every case, the murder occurs between acquaintances and nearly always involves a man killing a woman. Second, the woman's death is nearly always a violent one, with her body cruelly disposed of. Third, the murders depicted in song are characterized by either a lack of explanation for the violent acts or an explanation based on the man's jealousy and desire to possess the woman. And, as will be discussed subsequently, these lyrical patterns can in turn be contextualized within broader social, historical, and cultural explanations. These themes of violence in bluegrass music, and their larger context, are explicated in the remainder of this chapter.

Crime of Murder—Punishment of Death

The most popular British-derived murder ballad, "Pretty Polly" (c. 1750), originally known as "The Gosport Tragedy" and a mainstay among bluegrass songs, allegedly is based on a true story of a premeditated murder. In the song Polly discovers she is pregnant, and the child's father, her lover, kills her next to a grave that he had earlier prepared for her interment. Although there are several versions of the song, the most popular American version, oddly enough, focuses only on the murder and omits any mention of a courtship, seduction, and pregnancy:[21]

> Oh Polly, pretty Polly, come go along with me
> Polly, pretty Polly, come go along with me
> Before we get married some pleasures to see.
>
> He rode her over hills and valleys so deep
> He rode her over hills and valleys so deep
> Pretty Polly mistrusted and then began to weep.
>
> Oh Willie, oh Willie, I'm afraid of your ways
> Willie, oh Willie, I'm afraid of your ways
> The way you've been acting, you'll lead me astray.
>
> Oh Polly, pretty Polly, your guess is about right
> Polly, pretty Polly, your guess is about right
> I dug on your grave the best part of last night.
>
> She knelt down before him, pleading for her life
> She knelt down before him, pleading for her life
> Please let me be a single girl if I can't be your wife.
>
> He stabbed her in the heart and her heart's blood did flow
> He stabbed her in the heart and her heart's blood did flow
> And into the grave pretty Polly did go.
>
> He went to the jailhouse and what did he say
> He went to the jailhouse and what did he say
> I killed pretty Polly and tried to get away.
>
> Oh gentlemen and ladies, I bid you farewell
> Gentlemen and ladies, I bid you farewell
> For killing pretty Polly my soul will go to hell.

From the song, we learn that this murder obviously occurred between acquaintances, with the man killing the woman. The punishment for such an act of premeditated murder is death. But the punishment is farther-reaching in its consequences than simply a formal punishment of death; for in this case, Willie anticipates a never-ending punishment as his soul spends eternity in hell. Just as he can do nothing to change Polly's demise, he can do nothing to change his own fate. The logic of this message is causal—Willie killed Polly, thus he will die and his soul forever suffer. This represents a simple yet punitive ideology about misdeeds—one based on "an eye for an eye"—which mandates that Willie's life too should perish.

While the background facts of the case reveal the historical ins and outs, they are impossible to learn simply from the song. This component of violence in bluegrass songs is troubling, for while murder ballads in bluegrass music more than likely are based on true stories, often little is learned about the characters and their relationships from the songs themselves. The violence toward women in bluegrass songs has been recognized by others who make the claim that the most common motif in murder ballads is one where the woman becomes pregnant, is stabbed by her lover, and is promptly thrown into a river.[22] While it is true from these songs of murder that the most common motif is one where the woman's lover kills her and throws her into a river, it is *not* clear that pregnancy or immorality has anything to do with the murders in most of these songs.

"Down in the Willow Garden" (also known as "Rose Connally"), a murder ballad that may have descended from Ireland, again illustrates how the woman is killed by her lover. Three possible explanations emerge for this murder: the act may have been a desperate attempt to avoid marriage; the murderer may have anticipated monetary rewards as a result of her death; or the murderer may have felt compelled, based on his own father's prodding, to do the killing. The crime and ensuing punishment are described in the first person by the slayer.

Down in the willow garden
My love and I did meet,
And there we sat a-courting
My love dropped off to sleep.

I had a bottle of burgundy wine
My young love did not know,

And there I poisoned that dear little girl
Down by the banks below.

I stabbed her with a dagger
Which was a bloody knife,
I threw her in the river
Which was a dreadful sight.

My father had always told me
That money would set me free
If I would murder that sweet little miss
Whose name was Rose Connally.

He's sitting now by his cabin door
A-wiping his tear-dimmed eyes.
He's mourning for his own dear son
Who walks to the scaffold high.

My race is run beneath the sun,
The devil is waiting for me.
For I did murder that dear little miss
Whose name was Rose Connally.

From these lyrics we learn, as in "Pretty Polly," that the woman is killed by her lover. Her lover's punishment is death, as he and the scaffold confront one another. The most severe formal punishment that the state can impose is accompanied by informal sanctions—both his own guilt and recognition that his father is deeply troubled by his crime and impending death. He is overcome by the realization that he has ended a life and caused his father immense pain and suffering. While the slayer anticipates the most severe formal punishment, he also realizes clearly what grave consequences befall his family as a result of his own actions.

Again this depiction of violent murder in bluegrass songs reveals little about the characters and their connections and even less of what might explain why one punishment is imposed over another. Although capital punishment is described in bluegrass songs, just as often, the killer is punished by being confined to prison for a number of years.

Crime of Murder—Punishment of Imprisonment

No doubt, the majority of murder ballads are characterized by some form of man killing woman. One such song that does incorporate the depiction of a man murdering his pregnant lover is "Omie Wise," based on a true story and named for the victim, Omie, who is pregnant with the killer's child. He deceives her into believing that he will marry and care for her, when his real intention is to murder her in order to harbor the secret of their illegitimate child:

Oh listen to my story I'll tell you no lies
How John Louis did murder poor little Omie Wise.
He told her to meet him at Adam's Spring
He promised her money and other fine things.
So fool like she met him at Adam's Spring
No money he brought her nor other fine things.

"Go with me little Omie and away we will go
We'll go and get married and no one will know."
She climbed up behind him and away they did go
But away to the river where deep waters flow
"John Louis John Louis will you tell me your mind
Do you intend to marry me or leave me behind?"
"Little Omie little Omie I'll tell you my mind
My mind is to drown you and leave you behind."

"Have mercy on my baby and spare me my life
I'll go home as a beggar and never be your wife."
He kissed her and hugged her and turned her around
Then pushed her in deep waters where he knew she would drown.
He got on his pony and away he did ride
As the screams of Little Omie went down by his side.

Two boys went a fishing one fine summer day
And saw little Omie's body go floating away.
They threw their net around her and drew her to the bank
Her clothes all wet and muddy they laid her on a plank.
Then sent for John Louis to come to that place
And brought her out before him so that he might see her face.
He made no confession but they carried him to jail
No friends nor relations would go on his bail.

Although the punishment for this particular act is unclear (an anomaly in bluegrass crime ballads), we do learn from the song that John Louis is taken to jail. Furthermore, this crime clearly shocked and outraged the community. His family and friends were perhaps outraged and ashamed to the extent that they refused to bail him out of jail. In other bluegrass songs we sometimes learn that the jailed criminal has no friends or relations in a particular town. But in this song, Louis has both; they simply refuse to come to his aid. Today in rural Appalachia (where Omie Wise was murdered), murderers are often left in jail awaiting trial because their family and friends refuse to help them when all evidence points to their guilt. Families are disappointed and ashamed of such violent actions and of the "bad name" with which they are socially labeled because of a single family member's misdeeds.[23] This song, unlike others, is narrated in the third person, as a story of oral tradition where this awful deed, no doubt, has been recounted time and time again.

Still other songs are mysteries that offer no explanation for the murder. For example, "Little Sadie" begins with the woman's murder but then turns to the killer's flight, capture, trial, and punishment and well illustrates the absence of any explanation for Sadie's death. Unlike those songs mentioned earlier, here the penalty is not death, but a prison sentence of forty-one years and forty-one days. It also is interesting, and somewhat unusual for this genre, that in this song, the killer, who narrates the story line, confesses to his crime:

I went out last night for to make a little round
I met Little Sadie and shot her down
Went back home, got into bed
44 pistol under my head.

Woke up the next morning at half-past nine
The hacks and the buggies all standing in line
Gents and gamblers gathered round
To carry Little Sadie to the burying ground.

Well I began to think of what a deed I'd done
Grabbed my hat and away I run
I made a good run but a little too slow
They overtook me in Jericho.

I was standing on the corner reading the bill
When up stepped the sheriff from Thomasville
Said, "Young man ain't your name Brown
Remember the night you shot Sadie down?"

I said, "Yes sir but my name is Lee
I shot little Sadie in the first degree
First degree and second degree
If you got any papers won't you read 'em to me."

Well they took me downtown and dressed me in black
And put me on the train and started me back
All the way back to that Thomasville jail
And I had no money for to go my bail.

The judge and the jury took the stand
The judge held the papers in his right hand
41 days and 41 nights
41 years to wear the ball and stripes.

This song is typical of murder ballads in bluegrass music, except that the punishment is not "an eye for an eye," but time in prison for taking the life of Sadie. No explanation is offered for either Sadie's murder or the imposition of this punishment rather than death.

Another song with similar victim-victimizer relationships is "Poor Ellen Smith," a ballad allegedly composed by the murderer, Peter De-Graff, who was convicted of killing Ellen Smith in Winston-Salem, North Carolina, in August 1893.[24] While no explanation is offered for the murder, this particular song is unusual, for there is a sexual component to the crime that does not appear in other songs. Apparently, Ellen was sexually assaulted. The killer, who narrates the story in song, is apprehended by a posse, convicted by a jury, and serves twenty years in prison. While his punishment is less than that of Little Sadie's killer, it has other dimensions than simply time in prison. We learn that his punishment is also an informal one, for he suffers immense guilt for his act.

Poor Ellen Smith, how she was found
Shot through the heart, lying cold on the ground.
Her clothes were all scattered and thrown on the ground
And blood marks the spot where poor Ellen was found.

They picked up their rifles and hunted me down
And found me a-loafing around in the town.
They picked up her body and carried it away
And now she is sleeping in some lonesome old grave.

I got a letter yesterday and I read it today
The flowers on her grave have all faded away.
Some day I'll go home and say when I go
On poor Ellen's grave pretty flowers I'll sow.

I've been in this prison for twenty long years
Each night I see Ellen through my bitter tears.
The warden just told me that soon I'll be free
To go to her grave near that old willow tree.

My days in this prison are ending at last
I'll never be free from the sins of my past.
Poor Ellen Smith, how she was found
Shot through the heart, lying cold on the ground.

Perhaps one of the most graphically violent bluegrass songs of man killing woman was brought to this country by English settlers. In England it appeared as "The Wittam Miller" and "The Berkshire Tragedy," and in America as "The Oxford Girl," "The Bristol Girl," "The Wexford Girl," "The Lexington Girl," and most recently as "The Knoxville Girl." The man's desire to possess "his" woman appears to be the explanatory dimension of this crime. It appears that Willie did not completely possess the Knoxville girl's attention, for she, according to the murderer, had "roving eyes." The killer, who sings the song, is apprehended and sentenced to life in prison. He, like the murderer of Ellen Smith, reports suffering enormous guilt because of killing the woman he loved:

I met a little girl in Knoxville,
A town we all know well,
And every Sunday evening
Out in her home I'd dwell,
We went to take an evening walk
About a mile from town,
I picked a stick up off the ground
And knocked that fair girl down.

She fell down on her bended knees,
For mercy she did cry,
"Oh Willie, dear, don't kill me here,
I'm unprepared to die."
She never spoke one other word,
I only beat her more,

Until the ground around me
With her blood did flow.

I took her by her golden curls,
I dragged her round and round,
Throwing her in the river
That flows through Knoxville town,
Go down, go down, you Knoxville girl
With the dark and roving eyes,
Go down, go down, you Knoxville girl,
You can never be my bride.

I went back to Knoxville,
Got there about midnight,
My mother she was worried,
And woke up in a fright.
Saying, "Son, oh Son, what have you done
To bloody your clothes so?"
I told my anxious mother
I was bleeding at my nose.

I called for me a candle
To light my way to bed
I called for me a handkerchief
To bind my aching head.
I rolled and tumbled the whole night through
As trouble was for me
Like flames of hell around my bed
And in my eyes could see.

They carried me down to Knoxville,
They put me in a cell
My friends all tried to get me out
But none could go my bail.
I'm here to waste my life away
Down in this dirty old jail
Because I murdered that Knoxville girl,
The girl I loved so well.

In the following song, "99 Years and One Dark Day," the killer tells his tale of killing "his woman" and now spends his time laboring in prison. In this song, no reason is given for his slaying of his woman, and no reason for his receiving this particular punishment over another.

> I've been in this prison 20 years or more
> Shot my woman with a 44,
> I'll be right here till my dying day
> I got 99 years and one dark day.
>
> Well the free days pass and the beds are hard
> I spend all day breaking rocks in the yard,
> Well there ain't no change it's gonna stay that way
> I got 99 years and one dark day.
>
> Ain't no singer can sing this song
> To convince this warden that I ain't wrong,
> It's my fate it's gonna stay that way
> I got 99 years and one dark day.
>
> Didn't learn to read I never learned to write
> My whole life has been one big fight,
> I never heard about the righteous way
> I got 99 years and one dark day.
>
> I committed a crime many years ago
> Shot my woman with a 44,
> I'll be right here till my dying day
> I got 99 years and one dark day.

The murder of a woman by a man in some bluegrass songs is intertwined with love and marriage plans. Although the motive is still unclear, marriage does seem to have something to do with the murder in some of these songs. "Banks of the Ohio," one of the most popular folk-bluegrass songs, illustrates this theme in murder ballads:

> I asked my love to take a walk
> Just a walk a little way,
> As we walked along we talked
> All about our wedding day.
>
> And only say that you'll be mine
> And our home will happy be
> Down beside where the waters flow
> On the banks of the Ohio.

I held a knife close to her breast
As into my arms she pressed,
She cried, "Oh, Willie dear, don't murder me.
I'm not prepared for eternity."

I took her by her lily white hand
Led her down where the waters stand,
There I pushed her in to drown
And watched her as she floated down.

I started home, 'tween twelve and one
Thinking of the deed I'd done
I killed the girl I love you see
Because she would not marry me

The very next day, bout half past four
Sheriff Smith knocked on my door
He said, "Young man, come now and go
Down to the banks of the Ohio."

The man's jealousy and his desire to possess "his" woman explain
still other murders found in bluegrass music. For example, "Little Glass
of Wine," a once very popular bluegrass song, tells the story of how a
jealous lover poisons his Molly. Marriage is a part of this song and part
of the explanation for the crime. It appears that Willie wanted to get
married, Molly did not, and Willie resolved that if he could not have
her, nobody would. The following is a portion of the song:

Come little girl let's go get married
My love is so great how can you slight me,
I'll work for you both late and early
And at our wedding my little wife you'll be.

Oh, Willie dear, let's both consider
We're both too young to be married now,
When we're married, we're bound together
Let's stay single just one more year.

He went to the bar where she was dancing
A jealous thought came to his mind,
I'll kill that girl, my own true lover
'Fore I let another man beat my time.

He went to the bar and he called her to him
She said, "Willie dear, what you want with me?"
"Come and drink wine with the one that loves you
More than anyone else you know," said he.

While they were at the bar a-drinking
That same old thought came to his mind,
He killed that girl, his own true lover
He gave her poison in a glass of wine.

As earlier researchers have observed, punishment for capital crimes varies considerably among a few explanatory variables (with the exception of race, which is not relevant here).[25] As in reality, the punishments in song also vary, as some murderers receive sentences of death and others sentences of life or a few years less. Although it is difficult to account for the use of prison as punishment in lieu of death, interestingly, the prison sentences are rather lengthy, ranging from twenty to ninety-nine years. This may indicate that judicial responses to these crimes, perhaps some of the most senselessly violent of their era, disallowed plea bargaining a murder charge to a less serious charge. But beyond this, what broader social and cultural patterns account for the presence of these violent crimes in bluegrass music?

Violent Crime in Bluegrass Music: A Cultural Explanation

Although songs that describe property crimes (e.g., "I Just Got Tired of Being Poor"), outlaws as heroes ("Pretty Boy Floyd" and "Jesse James"), women killing men ("Barbara Allen"), the confining life of prison ("Sad Prisoner's Lament," "Old Richmond Prison," and "Doing My Time"), murder as revenge ("Hills of Roane County"), crimes of disorderly conduct ("Six Months Ain't Long"), and even victimless crimes ("In the Jailhouse Now") emerge in bluegrass lyrics, the violent crime of man killing woman dominates crime stories found among bluegrass songs.

Though firmly entrenched in the culture of the old world, the genre of these songs has evolved into a truly American phenomenon. As art imitates life, we are left to wonder what factors might explain the emergence and persistence of such violent songs—songs that relate stories of specific violent acts and that often reflect violence in the broader society. These songs, their emergence and historical persistence, can be situated within at least four larger explanations: (1) as a result of oral tradition and communication, (2) as representative of the functions that crime has served and continues to serve in American society, (3) as a reflection of a subculture of violence, and (4) as an indication of historically held punishment ideologies for capital murder.

First, these songs of murder and punishment often represent historical facts, or some version of history, that individuals put to music. The violent acts depicted in these songs were no doubt shocking to the rural mountainous community and represented actions that could not go untold. To both communicate and preserve these stories, they were put into song form, passed on to others in the community, and passed down through the years, becoming a part of oral tradition and what we now call bluegrass music. These songs of violent crime and punishment became a part of the history of the region immediately affected by such violent acts and reflected, for the most part, actual historical incidents preserved in song form. Early in the history of these songs, the telling and singing of acts of violence were modes of communicating what was of interest to nearly everyone—shockingly violent crime. Later, with mass communication and the recording and marketing of these songs, they continued to be popular, as these stories of violence fell on new ears. Today these songs certainly are not recorded by bluegrass bands as often as they once were, but they remain fundamentally important to many a bluegrass band's repertoire and can be heard at nearly every live bluegrass show. Thus, within the rhythms of oral history and tradition, we today hear stories of violent crimes and subsequent punishments that have survived 100 years or more.

Second, these songs can be explained, in part, by the function that crime served at the time of the songs' inception and by the function that crime continues to serve. Americans' interest in crime may be functional, serving to reinforce conduct norms.[26] Social theorists have commented that Americans (among other societies) need crime to wonder about, to be shocked about, to reinforce socially approved norms and values, and to gaze in awe and disdain at the criminal who does what most cannot and would not do.[27] Americans historically have made folk heroes of criminals; today, in the midst of a growing crime-control industry, crime stories fill the daily newspapers, the nightly news, top-selling magazines, political rhetoric, and everyday conversation, as Americans consume crime, crime stories, and crime-related commodities.[28] Violent crimes such as those described here certainly are not desired by the community. However, as they occur, the subtle differences between normal and abnormal behavior become more clearly delineated within the shocked community. The parameters of official behavior, marked sharply by the shockingly violent behavior occurring beyond moral boundaries, are symbolically strengthened as the community shares its mutually held values and standards for normative behavior. These songs of violent crime and punishment act to further bolster conduct norms and consensual forms of punishment.

The third potential explanation, and perhaps the most telling, is subcultural. Although the South and Appalachia have received the attention of social scientists, the subculture of violence has only recently been alluded to. These songs certainly fit within what we know about that culture and its historical levels of violence. From the various attempts at understanding this phenomenon, both the attributes of a subculture and individuals' integration into it have emerged as potentially useful components of an explanation. Earlier researchers, focusing on subcultural explanations for aggregate murder rates, found that

> the highest rates of homicide occur, among a relatively homogeneous subcultural group. . . . Similar prevalent rates can be found in some rural areas. The value system of this group, we are contending, constitutes a subculture of violence. [T]he greater the degree of integration of the individual into this subculture, the higher the probability that his behavior will be violent in a variety of situations.[29]

These statements suggest that such a proclivity toward violence in rural areas may be explained by the cultural acceptance and reproduction of such behavior. Thus, for the fairly homogeneous and well-isolated rural area of Appalachia, such an explanation for a subculture with a wide acceptance of violence seems likely.

Violent behavior is explained not only by cultural differences but by social class. Research shows that lower-class young boys are more likely to be socialized into relying on direct expressions of aggression than middle-class young boys. This finding is related to, among other things, the types of punishment meted out by parents of different social classes and the various roles and responsibilities of fathers among different social classes. As compared to middle-class mothers, lower-class mothers report that their children are more likely to be struck, and the fathers in lower-class households often play a less-important role in the family than fathers in middle-class households.[30] As youngsters become integrated into a culture where violence is considered a viable option, violence as a way of resolving life's matters becomes socially reproduced.

These dimensions of both culture and social class are analytically useful when applied to Appalachia. The South, and especially Appalachia, not only has its own unique subcultural values but historically has been a very depressed area where poverty and disease have run rampant, while educational, occupational, and financial opportunities have been limited. The distribution of social classes in Appalachia, where many of these songs originated and are still revered, is clearly skewed toward the lower class.

The South, some historians posit, has been addicted to violence at nearly every level in society since long before the Civil War.[31] Violence in the name of one's honor has been considered acceptable behavior in Southern culture. From such a culture, Appalachians, especially men, who have relied on a "frontier" mentality have developed an ideology of independence.[32] The tendency for violence became a part of the Southerner's frontier existence and development. The Southern character, and especially the Appalachian, was (and is) entrenched with individualism and back-country pride. Throughout history, and even today, the Southerner "would knock hell out of whoever dared to cross him."[33] As a result Appalachian men have independently handled their own affairs, taken the law into their own hands, refrained from meddling in other people's business, and disciplined their children and their women however they saw fit, with full knowledge that their neighbors did not dare interfere. After all, in the cultural history of Appalachia, such behavior has been considered normal rather than deviant. It may well be that as eighteenth-century culture, stories, and songs were preserved in the southern Appalachian area, so were primitive attitudes about discipline, gender, and violence.

As part of conquering their environment with both frontier independence and machismo, Appalachian men have developed an attitude of dominance over women and have expected women to be subservient. In Appalachia clearly delineated and articulated gender differences have been imposed on youngsters early in life. Clear gender roles (e.g., the man as ruler of the household) have been reinforced and socially reproduced in the isolated area of Appalachia, where such ideologies were preserved as they went undisturbed by more enlightened outside forces.[34]

This frontier mentality and dominance over women are exemplified among themes found in Southern literature and bluegrass music—music that is almost entirely dominated by men.[35] Such themes have the latent effect, at least, of terrorizing women, further subjugating them, making them more dependent on males, threatening them by suggesting that murder is a viable alternative within interpersonal relationships, and propagating the independence of the Appalachian male. Art, after all, intertwines with life, and bluegrass music reproduces, among other things, the dark and violent side of Appalachian mountain life.

Beyond these social explanations, the crimes and punishments described in song reflect something of the historical period in which they were conceived. They certainly reflect the singing styles and traditions of centuries ago. But just as important, they inform us of the then-held ideologies on punishment for capital crimes—ideologies that, just as today, vary on the fundamental issues of capital punishment as retribution, capital punishment and imprisonment as deterrence, and incapacitation policies.

Retribution, as ideology, places the state in the role of executioner, to do what the victim's immediate family wants to do and wants to have done—to take the life of the one who takes. Although retribution in the form of state-sanctioned capital punishment offers a social response rather than a familial one, the response is the same—social vengeance, which is evident in many of these bluegrass murder ballads.

Deterrence ideologies are also present in these songs. When the murderer narrates the story of his crime and punishment, whether it be his own impending death or years in confinement, he does so to warn others of the terrible consequences for such behavior. The murderer's telling the story of his deed and his doom is a powerful medium, for through a dark tale we learn of the emotions of both the victim and the victimizer. We learn of the act itself and, just as important, of the killer's capture and punishment. His telling of the story serves as a warning as much as a story—a warning to avoid similar misfortunes. His punishment and words of insight are designed to affect society. In other words, the social hope is that his punishment deters at least some future violence. A punishment of death has other powerful implications for the community. Death is a symbolic punishment and the murderer a symbolic common enemy. His death punishment reaffirms conduct norms that were violated and also, ideally, sends a warning to others.

Support for incapacitation as punishment is evident in some of these songs where retribution in life is not levied, but rather a lengthy prison sentence is designed to isolate the murderer from the community. This policy undoubtedly represents a more progressive response to capital murder than a penalty of death. This shift in punishment types, reflected in song, may indicate fluctuating support for capital punishment. As public support for death as punishment waned and as lengthy prison sentences rather than death were meted out, murder ballads reflected those broader social changes.

These murder ballads reveal the historical culture of their inception. They tell stories of violent, senseless crimes that no doubt shocked communities, angered residents, and all but destroyed victims' families. They indicate some of the details of the murders, some of the reasons for the violence, and often some sense of the killer's capture or escape. But as with any good story, they also often end with a moral—a moral that serves as closure for the song and as important instruction about acceptable behavior and the consequences of deviance and crime.

Notes

This chapter is a revision of two of the author's previous publications and is reprinted here by permission: "Blood Marks the Spot Where Poor Ellen Was Found: Violent Crime in Bluegrass Music," *Popular Music and Society* 15 (1991): 95–115; "99 Years is Almost for Life: Punishment for Violent Crime in Bluegrass Music," *Journal of Popular Culture* 26 (1992): 165–81.

1. Bob Artis, *Bluegrass* (New York: Hawthorn Books, 1975); Steven D. Price, *Old as the Hills: The Story of Bluegrass Music* (New York: Viking Press, 1975). The Blue Ridge Mountains, the eastern range of the Appalachian Mountains, extend from southern Pennsylvania to northern Georgia; they constituted a formidable barrier during western migration. The Cumberland Gap is a natural passage through the Cumberland Mountains near where Virginia, Kentucky, and Tennessee meet; this passage served as Daniel Boone's Wilderness Road. Today, as then, subsistence farming is readily found throughout that area.

2. Charles Wolfe, *Kentucky Country: Folk and Country Music of Kentucky* (Lexington: University Press of Kentucky, 1982), 5.

3. Charles Wolfe, *Tennessee Strings* (Knoxville: University of Tennessee Press, 1977). The Appalachian region commonly includes the hilly and mountainous areas of ten states: Kentucky, Tennessee, Georgia, Alabama, North Carolina, South Carolina, Virginia, West Virginia, Ohio, and Maryland.

4. Fred Hill, *Grass Roots: Illustrated History of Bluegrass and Mountain Music* (Rutland, VT: Academy Books, 1980); Bill C. Malone, *Southern Music, American Music* (Lexington: University Press of Kentucky, 1979). Although I use the term *bluegrass,* bluegrass music itself did not evolve as a distinct genre until about 1950. Before then mountain string or hillbilly music had been simply *country music.* There was no separate bluegrass music category until Bill Monroe and his Bluegrass Boys brought the elements and dynamics together into a new sound that we today, in respecting Monroe and his home state of Kentucky, call bluegrass music. For simplicity, I use the term *bluegrass* throughout this chapter.

5. Bill C. Malone, "Music," in *Encyclopedia of Southern Culture,* ed. Charles R. Wilson and William Ferris (Chapel Hill: University of North Carolina Press, 1989), 985–92.

6. Not only did the people of this region experience a cultural integration of music, stories, and themes, they also shared and exchanged musical instruments. The banjo, an essential element of bluegrass music today, is African in origin. And the guitar, an instrument that was introduced relatively late to the Appalachian region and is essential to bluegrass music, was first played with skillful finesse by African Americans.

7. Although black music (ragtime, blues, country blues, minstrelsy, spirituals, and jazz) in this country has enjoyed wide exposure since the mid-nineteenth century, white folk music was "discovered" relatively late in the history of traditional American music. In fact, hillbilly music was not discovered until 1916 and was first recorded in the 1920s. The two most famous discoverers of folk music—John A. Lomax and Cecil Sharp—made very significant contributions toward both popularizing and preserving Appalachian folk music (Malone, "Music"). While Lomax collected and profited from what he mistakenly believed were racially homogeneous white cowboy songs, Sharp, with his assistant Maud Karpeles, traveled through the states of Kentucky, Virginia, Tennessee, North Carolina, and West Virginia during the years 1916–1918. They often stayed with local mountain people and encouraged them to play and sing their songs. As they did, Sharp wrote musical notes for what he heard as Karpeles wrote the lyrics in shorthand. They collected hundreds of songs and found that many, as a result of generations of oral tradition, had numerous versions and were widely known within their narrow region of observation. They collected

the bulk of their material in the region between Tennessee and North Carolina, for, according to Sharp and Karpeles, it "was in this region that the most primitive conditions prevailed." As a result of their research and discovery, they published a book of 274 songs with 968 tunes. Later, Francis Child did likewise by publishing a multitude of English and Scottish ballads along with an analytical commentary of them. See Cecil Sharp and Maud Karpeles, *English Folk Songs from the Southern Appalachians* (London: Oxford University Press, 1932), xv; Francis J. Child, *The English and Scottish Popular Ballads, Volume 5* (New York: Dover, 1965).

Still later, during the 1920s, the Okeh Recording Company sent Ralph Peer to locate mountain musicians to record. As Peer made his way into fairly isolated areas, he advertised in local newspapers for musicians. As pickers and singers came out of the mountains and hollows, Peer recorded them. The record company sold their records primarily to mountain dwellers, and country music experienced its first golden era during the years 1925–1935; see Artis, *Bluegrass.*

8. Neil V. Rosenberg, "Bluegrass," in *Encyclopedia of Southern Culture*, 993–94; Neil V. Rosenberg, *Bluegrass: A History* (Urbana: University of Illinois Press, 1985).

9. Robert Cantwell, *Bluegrass Breakdown: The Making of the Old Southern Sound* (Urbana: University of Illinois Press, 1984).

10. Price, 2.

11. Actually, the label *country music* was not applied to the hillbilly string band musical form until sometime after 1940. Rather, the more common labels were *mountain music, old-time music,* and *hillbilly music.* See Charles Wolfe, "Bluegrass Touches: An Interview with Bill Monroe," *Old Time Music* 16 (1975): 6–12. Most Southern musicians at that time had no use for the label *hillbilly* because of the many negative implications. This dislike is easy to understand, given commonly accepted definitions of the term by non-Appalachian residents. For example, the *New York Journal* in 1900 defined a "hill-billie" as "a free and untrammelled white citizen of Appalachia who lives in the hills, has no means to speak of, dresses as he can, talks as he pleases, drinks whiskey when he gets it, and fires off his revolver as the fancy takes him"; see Archie Green, "Hillbilly Music: Source and Symbol," *Journal of American Folklore* 78 (1968): 204.

Bill Monroe was asked, during an interview, about the use of the word *hillbilly.* He responded, "I have never liked the name, the word 'hillbilly'. It seemed like maybe another state out west would call you hillbilly if they thought that you'd never been to school or anything. I've never liked that and I've never used it in my music" (Wolfe, "Bluegrass Touches," 6). Like Monroe, most country music performers and country people have found *hillbilly* offensive.

12. Cantwell, xi. Monroe, during his early performances on the Grand Ole Opry, had Dave "Stringbean" Akeman playing banjo with him. Akeman played clawhammer or frailing style rather than the three-finger style. It was this element, the three-finger style, popularized by Earl Scruggs, that ultimately redefined the music that Monroe played as bluegrass.

13. Cantwell, *Bluegrass Breakdown*.

14. Charles Wolfe, "Bluegrass Touches," 7.

15. Cantwell, 226.

16. Cantwell, 228; Thomas Wolfe, *You Can't Go Home Again* (New York: Harper, 1940).

17. Ivan M. Tribe, "The Hillbilly versus the City: Urban Images in Country Music," *JEMF Quarterly* 10 (1974): 41–51.

18. This lack of hope was epitomized in a scene from *Coal Miner's Daughter*, a film about the life of country music star Loretta Lynn. The scene is a classic, where Doo, the man Loretta later married, bemoans the fact that since his return from military service, he has found little work available in the mountains of home. A local moonshiner offers some bleak words of advice by saying, "Hell, Doo, up here there's only three things a man can do—coal mine, moonshine, or move on down the line." This scene vividly captures the limited alternatives available for improving one's lifestyle and material conditions in Appalachia.

19. Bluegrass festivals are outdoor events typically held over a three-day weekend where at least a dozen acts perform. Festivals have dramatically increased in number in the past ten to fifteen years, giving bluegrass performers a steady circuit during the spring, summer, and fall, and giving the fans ample opportunity to hear bluegrass music. Fans usually camp at the site for the duration of the festival and the entertainers come and go in their touring buses. If not for bluegrass festivals, bluegrass performers, more than likely, would go hungrier than they already do.

20. Wayne Erbesen, *Backpocket Bluegrass Songbook* (New York: Pembroke Music, 1981); Rosenberg, *Bluegrass: A History*; Happy Traum, *Bluegrass Guitar* (New York: Oak Publications, 1974); Peter Wernick, *Bluegrass Songbook* (New York: Oak Publications, 1976).

21. Wolfe, *Kentucky Country*.

22. Erbesen, *Backpocket Bluegrass Songbook*.

23. Terry C. Cox and Kenneth D. Tunnell, "Competency to Stand Trial or the Trivial Pursuit of Justice," in *Homicide: The Victim-Offender Connection*, ed. Anna Wilson (Cincinnati: Anderson, 1993), 415–40.

24. Erbesen, *Backpocket Bluegrass Songbook*.

25. Ruth D. Peterson and William C. Bailey, "Murder and Capital Punishment in the United States: The Question of Deterrence," in *Criminal Law in*

Action, ed. William J. Chambliss (New York: Wiley, 1984), 435–48; Marvin E. Wolfgang and Marc Riedel, "Race, Judicial Discretion, and the Death Penalty," in *Criminal Law in Action*, 449–61.

26. Emile Durkheim, *The Division of Labor in Society* (New York: The Free Press, 1984).

27. Karl Menninger, *The Crime of Punishment* (New York: Viking, 1966).

28. Nils Christie, *Crime Control as Industry* (London: Routledge, 1993); Kenneth D. Tunnell, "Film at Eleven: Recent Developments in the Commodification of Crime," *Sociological Spectrum* 12 (1992): 293–313.

29. Marvin E. Wolfgang and Franco Ferracuti, *The Subculture of Violence: Towards an Integrated Theory in Criminology* (Beverly Hills: Sage, 1982).

30. Wolfgang and Ferracuti, *The Subculture of Violence*.

31. Raymond D. Gastil, "Violence, Crime, and Punishment," in *Encyclopedia of Southern Culture*, 1473–76.

32. Although other nations have their own histories of the frontier (e.g., Canada and Australia), they do not have histories or current levels of violence like those found in America, and especially in the rural South.

33. Wilbur Joseph Cash, *The Mind of the South* (New York: Random House, 1941), 44.

34. Cantwell, *Bluegrass Breakdown*.

35. Richard Hofstadter, "Reflections on Violence in the U.S.," in *American Violence*, ed. Richard Hofstadter and Michael Wallace (New York: Vintage, 1970), 3–43. Also, the works of Jesse Stuart, Tennessee Williams, and James Agee well illustrate this mentality among Southern and Appalachian males.

6 . . .

Electric Eye in the Sky: Some Reflections on the New Surveillance and Popular Culture

GARY T. MARX

Electric eye in the sky
Feel my stare—always there
There's nothin' you can do about it
Develop and expose
I feed upon your every thought and so my power grows.

—"Electric Eye," Judas Priest

Stare. It is the way to educate your eye and more. Stare, pry, listen, eavesdrop. Die knowing something. You are not here long.

—Walker Evans

The country doesn't give much of a shit about bugging. . . . Most people around the country think it's probably routine; everybody's trying to bug everybody else; it's politics.

—President R. Nixon on Watergate

Most analyses of information technology use printed words and numbers. As important as historical, social, philosophical, legal, and policy analyses are, they are not sufficient for a broad understanding. We also need cultural analysis. This chapter considers elements of surveillance as they are treated in popular media. Attention to visual images and music can tell us about cultural themes and values. The images we hold of surveillance methods are incomplete and partially independent of the technology, per se. Images are social fabrications (though not necessarily social deceptions). Images speak to (and may be intended to create or manipulate) needs, aspirations, and fears. They communicate meaning.

Surveillance technology is not simply applied, it is also *experienced* by users, subjects, and audiences. Cultural analysis can tell us something about the experience of being watched, or of being a watcher.

One may well ask whether the serious social questions raised by surveillance technologies (such as computer dossiers, video and audio monitoring, drug testing, satellites, or electronic location monitoring and undercover methods) are not trivialized by considering mass media depictions. But here Erving Goffman's admonition to look for big meanings in little things, as well as Shakespeare's "by indirections find directions out," apply. There are strong intellectual and political grounds for studying popular culture and information technology.

To understand the threats (as well as the opportunities) posed by these devices, we must look at their cultural backdrop and ask how culture supports or undermines our most cherished values. For example, as a result of surveillance devices for monitoring and surveillance toys, children are now raised to believe that being watched and watching others through sense-enhancing technologies is the normal order of things. As adults how will they respond to requests for information that in the past might have been seen as inappropriate? Conversely, will they be more likely to use privacy-invading technologies than their parents? Will this mean changes in interaction and in the meaning of intimacy and trust?

If liberty is indeed at risk from these tools, we need to know how the public perceives them and what sense it makes of media depictions. Where are the soft spots? What are the contours of public resistance or support for technologies that cross boundaries that in the past had been impenetrable and even sacrosanct? What themes and representations do the supporters and opponents of the new technologies offer or fail to offer? What is referred to only by innuendo or euphemism?

The various actors involved with the culture of surveillance are engaged (whether they realize it or not) in a struggle to shape popular images. Should social scientists choose to merge their science and politics, the right picture and/or sounds can be worth much more than words, or our words alone, in bringing about or blocking the spread of invasive technologies. Apart from any advocacy issues, as social scientists we can better understand the technologies by looking at the meanings and symbolism that surround them. The images are socially patterned, not random.

Popular culture of course reflects developments in technology. For example, contrast Paul Simon singing in 1967, "Coo coo ca shoo, Mrs. Robinson, we'd like to know a little about you for our [presumably manual] files," or about the spy in a gabardine suit whose "bow tie is really a camera," in the song "America," to his "lasers in the jungle" and "staccato signals of constant information" in the 1980s song "Boy in the Bubble."

But this works the other way as well. Art, science fiction, comic books, and films have anticipated and even inspired surveillance devices and applications to new areas. Take for example the 1927 film *Modern Times*, in which Charlie Chaplin's private reverie of smoking a cigarette in the bathroom at work is shattered by the sudden appearance of his boss on a wall-sized video screen, gruffly saying, "Hey, quit stalling and get back to work." The boss has a two-way video camera. H. G. Wells, Dick Tracy, James Bond, and Star Trek are some other familiar examples. In another example, a Spider Man comic inspired a New Mexico judge to implement the first judicial use of electronic location monitoring equipment.

I approach the popular media with many questions (only some of which are dealt with here): How have culture creators depicted the new technologies? What images, symbols, and themes appear most often? A more difficult question is to note what symbols and themes are not used. Familiarity with materials from other times and cultures and from critical media can help discover this. What kinds of symbols are used for new, unseen, and unfamiliar aspects of emerging technologies, such as DNA sequencing? What assumptions do the creators appear to be making about the technologies? Is there an art of glorification as well as denigration? What shared understandings are these believed to communicate? How is the desire for security balanced with the desire to be free from intrusions? How do social factors affect the behavior and redefinition of the surveillant and the surveilled? What conclusions can be drawn about how characteristics such as gender or race of the artist (or of the intended audience) affect the work? Is there understandable variation across media and types of surveillance devices (e.g., visual vs. auditory, physically invasive versus noninvasive techniques, self vs. other surveillance)? How do depictions of surveillance technology intended to help one person watch another differ from depictions of technologies intended to protect the individual from the surveillance of others? What separates the more moving and enduring creations from the less? How have themes evolved as the power and potential of the techniques have become clearer in the last two decades? How much consistency is there across media? How do treatments relate to the written ideas of social scientists and critics? How are these treatments affecting popular conceptions and understandings?

A particular challenge lies in linking the cultural images of surveillance to social, political, economic, and technical factors. Rather than a reductionist model stressing the causal primacy of any one of these factors, they are interactive. Culture both shapes and is shaped by the available technology.

Another important issue involves the connection between what individuals perceive and experience and what the creators and/or owners of the cultural form intend them to experience. There are two parts to this—do such depictions accurately reflect personal experiences with surveillance, and how are they perceived by the audience? These are not necessarily independent. Through their educational role, the media help prepare individuals for what they should experience as watchers or the watched.

Artistic statements, unlike scientific statements, do not have to be verbally defended. But the social scientist can ask about their social antecedents and impacts. Do they move the individual? Do they convey the experience of being watched or a watcher? Do they create indignation or a desire for the product? Do they make the invisible visible?

In this chapter I will consider depictions of surveillance technology in popular music, jokes and cartoons, illustrations, advertisements (whether for products or ideas), and art. Like the material it is based upon, this chapter seeks to communicate immediately and viscerally. In offering examples my initial goal is for the reader/viewer/listener to consume and experience the materials. The message is to be found directly in what the song writer, cartoonist, illustrator, advertiser, or artist suggests to the audience. The materials can descriptively stand by themselves. But I seek to go beyond being a collector, even at the risk of treading in alien interpretive waters, by asking how these depictions can be organized and what they may tell us about society and surveillance.

Habermas has stated "my question is my method." My approach is driven by a desire to understand surveillance in a broad fashion, but I also seek to systematize. In the first instance I have simply observed. The material presented is an illustrative sampling from a larger collection of materials gathered over the last decade. Clearly surveillance is *not* a theme in most popular songs, jokes, or art. Not having taken a representative sample, I can't say how minimal it is. However, I am confident that the materials presented here represent the popular materials that *do* deal with surveillance.

There is, of course, a leap from impressions to meaning. Subjectivity must be a part of any broad understanding of human affairs. Yet it can mislead if we claim that our subjective experience is necessarily representative. While what is offered here is primarily my personal experience and interpretation of the materials, I hope it is suggestive of questions for more systematic and quantitative research.

Popular Music

Surveillance themes are pervasive in popular culture, although we often do not think of them as that. Consider for example the familiar song "Santa Claus is Coming to Town." The words to this religious panoptic song are well known—Santa "knows when you are sleeping, he knows when you're awake, he knows if you've been good or bad, so be good for goodness sake." The message here is be good not because it is right but because you will be externally rewarded, and you won't get away with bad behavior. Someone is watching—consistent with computer dossiers, "he's making a list, checking it twice."

I was surprised at how many surveillance songs could be identified, once one starts listening for this. One well-known genre represents the positive, protective side of surveillance as something an individual seeks. Many religious songs involve the theme of an appeal to, or statement about, an all-powerful and knowing God looking over humankind. Another version involves the yearning for a lover and/or protector by someone who feels weak or vulnerable. The song "Someone to Watch Over Me" is an example. It contains the lines "Looking everywhere. . . . Tell me, where is the shepherd for this lost lamb? . . . Won't you tell him please to put on some speed, follow my lead. Oh how I need someone to watch over me." Such songs (at least until recently) were much more likely to be sung (and perhaps written) by females than by males. They are the passive expression of a hope or a plea, rather than an active seeking out of the individual. In contrast males have been more likely to write and sing about their prowess as active watchers and discoverers.

Our concern here will be more with the process of actually being a watcher, or with the experience of being watched, rather than with pleas for protective surveillance; and we will be concerned with changes in the music as more powerful surveillance technologies have appeared. Popular songs in this genre tend to involve either a love-inspired male surveillant or a chronicle (often of protest or satire) of what a surveillant does to others. Some suggest the erotic fantasy of secret watching.

The love songs can be categorized with respect to whether they involve (1) an equation of watching and knowing with love, (2) a search for a true love, (3) the surveillant's power to discover deception, or (4) voyeurism. These songs all refer to extrasensory powers of cognition possessed by the male singer as he watches a female. As sophisticated surveillance technology came into wider use in the 1970s, there was a shift from magical, intuitive powers to sense-enhancing technologies. In most cases the power of the surveillance is greatly overstated. The ability to know more than could be known with the senses is equated with the ability to know everything.

The film *Rear Window* appeared at the height of a Cold War–generated climate of suspiciousness and the availability of new imaging technologies such as zoom lens. It contains the classic line by Thelma Ritter, "We have become a nation of peeping toms." Its syrupy theme song sung by Bing Crosby, "To See You Is to Love You," is a traditonal ballad of adulation, attesting to the powers of the love object. Here the mere sight of the woman is sufficient to make the singer love her. This song has none of the hard-edged obsessive watching and/or covert surveillance of later decades in which the woman must be watched because she cannot be trusted. The singer is infatuated: "To see you is to love you, and you're never out of sight." Her charm means that the male singer sees her "anyplace I look" and "I see you all the time." Real watching and fantasy merge. Hitchcock juxtaposes the professional surveillance of Cary Grant as a photographer suspiciously watching a neighbor's window with the male gaze in which he watches his girl-friend, Grace Kelly, and a scantily clad female entertainer in another window.

The Clovers' 1954 song "I've Got My Eyes on You" contains the es-sential elements of the possessive, all-powerful male gaze typical of many such songs, including Sting's "Every Breath You Take," which appeared almost thirty years later. The Clovers' song has a strategic goal: "I'm gonna make you mine." The singer can "see everything you do." He watches "you all day long. I watch you all night, too. Know everywhere you go." The song can also be seen as offering a public marker. In singing "I've got my eyes on you," the singer announces his intentions and choice. To say "I have my eye on that" need not literally mean it is being intensively watched, but rather "I choose that." This song conveys the idea of the woman as an active stimulant of his atten-tion: "the way you wiggle when you walk, it'd make a hounddog talk." In most other songs the object of attention is passive or unknown, not realizing that she is "performing" or she has behaved badly, thus call-ing forth the intense male surveillance. The Doors sing about "a spy in the house of love" who "can see you and what you do" and who knows your dreams and fears, and "everywhere you go, everyone you know."

In their 1957 song "Searchin' " the Coasters express a common bal-lad theme—the search for true love. Unlike later songs, this is not a threat, nor is it bragging. Its actions are not motivated by the suspi-ciousness of a woman who can't be trusted or by the desire to gratify a secret obsession. Instead the song represents a statement of determina-tion, optimism, and yearning in proclaiming that the singer will "find her"—the ideal woman.[1]

This song links directly to the search of the detective: "I'm like that Northwest Mountie—you know I'll bring her in someday. . . . yeah, Sherlock Holmes, Sam Spade, they got nothing on me. Sergeant Friday, Charlie Chan, and Boston Blackie." Unlike the song in the Hitchcock film, here there is an explicit and easy link between the male gaze and the professional surveillant.

The surveillance in "On Every Street," by the Dire Straits, has as its theme an effort to locate a particular individual. The song refers to the tracks increasingly left by inhabitants of an electronically marked world: "There's gotta be a record of you someplace, you gotta be on somebody's books" and "somewhere your fingerprints remain concrete." This involves a sadder, less hopeful search than for the Coasters; perhaps the yearning is deepened because the singer knows exactly what he has lost and is looking for.

Suspicion-Driven Surveillance

In 1956 in "Slippin' and Slidin'," Little Richard has been "peepin' and hidin' " to discover the jive of his baby, and as a result he "won't be your fool no more." Bobby Vee says that "the night has a thousand eyes" and that these eyes will see "if you aren't true to me." If he gets "put down for another" or told lies, he warns, "I'll know, believe me, I'll know." The Who more directly imply the possession of extra-sensory powers in singing "there's magic in my eyes." The singer knows he has been deceived because "I can see for miles and miles and miles and miles and miles." Hall and Oates sing about the inability to escape my "Private Eyes," which, while "looking for lies," are "watching you. They see your every move."

In a more contemporary song, the Alan Parsons Project makes direct use of technology to discover lies and to tell the deceiving lover to "find another fool" because "I am the eye in the sky looking at you; I can read your mind."

Perhaps surprisingly for a group called the Information Society, the emphasis in their song "What's on Your Mind" is not on sophisticated communications technology but on traditional means, perhaps involving intuition, and a gentle plea to inform the singer. The song contains the lines "There are some things you can't hide" and "I can see behind your eyes," yet the song asks "If you hide away from me, how can our love grow?"

The classic song to discuss here is "Every Breath You Take," by Sting, who reports that it is about "the obsessiveness of ex-lovers, their maniacal possessiveness"—a song he had written after a divorce. It is about surveillance, ownership, and jealousy.[2] Sting was surprised that many people thought of it as "a very sweet love song." Many listeners heard the affirmative, protective, and positive aspects of surveillance, as when parents look out for children or caretakers watch those who are ill. While Sting reports that he reads critic Arthur Koestler, his song is personal, not political. The female is warned that her fake smiles and broken bonds and vows will be known by the singer. In a wonderful example of life imitating and using art, the song was popular with police doing surveillance (thus, detectives in Boston, and likely elsewhere, played the song while they tailed organized crime figures).

While the song does not mention technological supports for this omnipresent and omnipotent surveillance, it is easy to connect it with contemporary tools. One can hear the song to suggest the following:

> every breath you take [breath analyzer]
> every move you make [motion detector]
> every bond you break [polygraph]
> every single day [continuous monitoring]
> every step you take [electronic monitoring]
> every word you say [bugs, wiretaps, microphones]
> every night you stay [light amplifier]
> every vow you break [voice stress analysis]
> every smile you fake [brain wave analysis]
> every claim you stake [computer matching]
> I'll be watching you [video]

In most of the songs already discussed here, we see surveillance as a means of protection and discovery, and even prevention, often in a context of doubt. Yet in other songs we see the pleasure of watching as an end in itself. For example, consider Queensryche's unsettling (from a standpoint of the object of surveillance) song, "Gonna Get Close to You." Here the singer is "outside your balcony; I have a room with a view and I'm watching you." He knows "when you're alone, I know when you turn out the light." In "Voyeur," by Lizzy Borden, we hear a similar theme: "I'm watching you, you're in my sights. I know you so well, I know your every move." In this song there is an element of compulsiveness ("I can't stop watching you"), and the singer is distraught "because you don't even know me."

Chronicles of Surveillance

In the chronicles the voice is that not of the surveillant but of an individual subject to surveillance, or of a third party telling us about it, frequently in the form of a satirical warning. The songs are concerned with threats to liberty, the chilling effects of being spied upon, and the loss of privacy. A central theme is "they are watching us." Here the voice is not that of the swaggering, boastful, omnipotent watcher who makes veiled threats about his power, but the voice of the subject, victim, or concerned chronicler warning us about surveillance.

One form of chronicle deals with the negative impact on the watcher. The 1966 theme song "Secret Agent Man" for a long-running TV series warns of threats to life ("odds are you won't live to see tomorrow") and depersonalization ("they're givin' you a number, and takin' away your name"). For the Dire Straits "Private Investigations" results in being "scarred for life —no compensation." At the end of the day you are left with whiskey and lies and a "pain behind the eyes."[3]

The Robbins in "Framed" offer a first-person account of victimization by an informer. The lead singer is put in a police line-up and he realizes he was a victim of "someone's evil plan. When a stool pigeon walked in and said, 'That's the man.' "

Bob Dylan's "Subterranean Homesick Blues" expresses many themes. One is the threat of covert surveillance involving a "man in a trench coat" with "badge out," microphones planted in the bed, and telephone taps. As a result youth are satirically warned to look out, "Don't matter what you did. Walk on your tiptoes. Don't try 'No Doz.' " The song suggests that youth are being watched, regardless of whether they have actually done anything wrong or not. To avoid surveillance "don't wear sandals" and "get dressed, get blessed, try to be a success."

In "Talkin' John Birch Paranoid Blues" Dylan parodies the search for communist conspiracies. What is initially omnipresent here is not surveillance but communists. But to overcome the problem requires a search that satirizes in its breadth. Communists are looked for "under my bed," "in the sink and underneath the chair," "up my chimney hole," even "deep down inside my toilet bowl," "in my TV set," at "the library," and among "all the people that I knowed."

Sy Kahn, in "Who's Watching the Man," poses a classic issue for social control theory in asking, "who is watching the man who's watching the man who's watching me?" He doesn't understand why he is a target since he pays taxes and doesn't vote or criticize. He reports a truck with a telephone company sign next to his house, which has no phone, and new wires on his roof. Unrealistic paranoia toward the end of the song makes its satirical intent clear. He wonders about three men in his barn "trying to read my electric meter through a telescope" and about someone living in his TV set.

In Orwell's *1984* a video device linked mass surveillance with mass communication.[4] Individuals had almost no control over being seen, nor over what they saw. Hence, they were doubly controlled. Allusions to either (or both) mass surveillance and mass communication can also be found in a number of songs.

XTC's 1979 song "Real by Reel" protests the secret "invading our privacy" as "we play for the ministry." The most mundane acts and private recesses are now subject to documentation: "Now I lay me down to sleep knowing that your lenses peep; now I eat my daily bread and into the tape spool I'll be fed." "They" can film you everywhere—in bed, in the bath, when you cry or laugh. The camera can distort "so you won't know what's 'real by reel.' " It can even record "everything you feel."

The TV viewer as a manipulated voyeur is a theme in several songs. Siouxsie and the Banshees in "Monitor" express discomfort in seeing a victim who "looked strangely at the screen." Something too personal has been communicated to a mass audience in the comfort of their living rooms. They suggest a double meaning in singing about a "monitor outside for the people inside." This could refer to outside leaders watching citizens, or to a TV monitor for citizens who are outside the system of power to watch and be conditioned by. The monitor offers both a "prevention of crime [and] a passing of time."

Vigil Cliché, in "The Voyeur," deal with predictable themes such as "private lives up for auction," information overload, and living vicariously through the mass media ("I like to watch disasters in replay and rerun in slow mo; I like to watch on the spot interviews kicking in front doors"). As in the Peter Sellers film *Being There*, in which the lead actor's persona is formed by reflecting back what he sees on television, the singer lacks a firm identity.

The song also directly suggests a rarely acknowledged aspect of being captured on video—narcissism and exhibitionism. TV permits the singer to identify with media stars and to fantasize that he too is a celebrity. More generally, negative reactions to video invasions of personal space are very much tempered by the allure of seeing one's self on the video and feeling important as a result. In this song we hear, "[I like] to watch as my face is reflected in blank TV screens; when the programmes are over I like to pretend that that's me up there making headlines, camera closeups; . . . I don't care if it's only a moment, as long as it's peaktime, just as long as all of my friends and my family see me, the world will know my name."

"Spy in the Cab," by Bauhaus, is a song protesting the meters that record the driving behavior of truckers. The electronic extension of the employer's vision is resented by the drivers. "Hidden in the dashboard the unseen mechanized eye" with "a set function to pry" brings a "coldy observing" twenty-four-hour "unblinking watch."

In their 1979 "Fingerprint File," the Rolling Stones complain about "feeling followed, feeling tagged." The fingerprint file "gets me down." In a rare direct attack: "There's some little jerk in the FBI a keepin' paper on me ten feet high." Concern is expressed over "listening to me on your satellite," informers who will sell out and testify, and "electric eyes." As in the Bob Dylan song, listeners are urged to be suspicious, lay low, and watch out. The song ends in a whisper: "These days it's all secrecy, no privacy."

Rockwell begins "Somebody's Watching Me" with a synthesized voice asking, "Who's watching me?" Like Sy Kahn, he makes the point that he is just an average man who works "from nine to five" and all he wants "is to be left alone in my average home." The listener is led to ask, "Why would anyone want to monitor him?" The implied answer is that the surveillance is out of control. Even ordinary people, whom there is no reason to suspect, become targets, not simply those who "deserve" to be surveilled. We can't be sure if this is an out-of-control system or a logic of random application to create deterrence via uncertainty.

Rockwell always feels "like somebody's watching me and I have no privacy." Unlike the singers of religious songs, he does not get a feeling of safety from this surveillance. He wonders, "Who's watching me?" It might be neighbors, the mailman, or the IRS. Yet these realistic questions give way to satirical unreality. He wonders if the persons on TV can see him, and he is afraid to wash his hair " 'cause I might open my eyes and find someone standing there." The latter could also be interpreted as satirizing those who complain about the loss of privacy. It takes something serious to a ridiculous extreme.

Judas Priest's 1982 "Electric Eye" offers us the bragging voice of an electronic surveillant "up here in space," which has truly awesome powers: it watches all the time; its "lasers trace everything you do"; it probes "all your secret moves"; it is always in focus; its subjects "don't even know I'm there"; it is accurate, offering "pictures that can prove." It correctly equates knowledge with power: "I feed upon your every thought and so my power grows." People think they have private lives but they should "think nothing of the kind." Unlike some of the songs that encourage resistance, this one advises, "There is no true escape" and "there's nothing you can do about it."

Paul Simon's "Boy in the Bubble" suggests ambivalence. He catches the power and frenetic rhythms of telecommunications with "lasers in the jungle" and "staccato signals of constant information." With heart transplants and the boy in the bubble, these are "days of miracle and wonder." Yet this appears to be sarcastic, as it comes with remote bombs in baby carriages.

Mojo Nixon applies Nancy Reagan's "Just Say No" to his defiant 1987 "I Ain't Gonna Piss in No Jar." He can be fired from his job, but something more important can't be robbed: "my freedom and my liberty." He urges everybody to go to Washington. If "they want our piss we ought to give it to 'em. Yeah, surround the White House with a urinary moat."

"California Uber Alles," sung by Disposable Heroes of Hiphoprisy, tells of a long series of perceived negative policies by the governor of California and warns, "Close your eyes it can't happen here; Big brother in a squad car's comin' near." "Now it's 1992, knock knock at your front door—hey, guess who? It's the suede denim secret police. They've come to your house for your longhaired niece."

While social control is a major theme in rap songs, in general (as with graffiti wall art), they don't deal with the more subtle forms of surveillance. The emphasis is on direct coercion, harassment, and arrest at the hands of uniformed patrol officers. One exception is a Public Enemy song on the FBI infiltration of the Black Panther Party.

Cartoons, Comics, and Jokes

A colleague of Samuel Johnson wrote to him in 1778, "I have tried too in my time to be a philosopher; but, I don't know how, cheerfulness was always breaking in."[5] The same sentiment applies to the analysis of some of these materials. I have tried in my time to be a serious, analytic, systematic sociologist and a righteous social reformer, but in working with these materials, cheerfulness was always breaking in.

I have identified four types of surveillance humor: (1) accommodation, (2) machine/human frame breaks, (3) dystopias, and (4) reversals. A given example may fit more than one category, and other categories could be added. I will illustrate these with cartoons and comic strips.[6]

The accommodation or cultural-assimilation theme involves routinizing and folding into everyday activities new (and sometimes shocking) devices. The technology is domesticated and made familiar through its association with commonplace activities. It may serve as a functional alternative to traditional means.

Some illustrations of this are the following:

♦ Two businessmen are in an office concluding a deal, and the one behind a desk offers his hand while saying, "A handshake is good enough for me, Jack. The whole meeting's on videotape anyway." The camera is not seen.

♦ Just before going to bed, a small boy in pajamas says, "I'm clean, Mommy." In successive frames the mother checks his hands, face, and ears and then says, "Urinalysis." In the final frame, the child hands her a bottle with a urine sample.

♦ Two men are riding exercise bikes at a gym and one says, "I think we're getting serious—she's springing for a credit check *and* a surveillance on me."

♦ A man visiting a bank's loan department is told, "That's right, sir, no collateral is necessary. However, we will have to chain this little electronic device around your neck."

♦ Two couples are standing talking at a cocktail party, and one of the women says, "Franklin can't discuss that—he's under constant electronic surveillance."

♦ A man approaches a suburban house with a white picket fence and encounters a sign reading, "Beware of the technology."

♦ In an office meeting at the IRS audit division, a supervisor, accompanied by an employee, tells the director, "Good news! McDonald [the employee] broke into a taxpayer's home computer."

♦ A sign in front of a building with a long line of cars waiting to enter identifies it as "Joe's Drive-Thru Testing Center," offering a variety of testing including emissions, drugs, blood pressure, polygraph, stress, loyalty, and cholesterol.

A second type of surveillance humor involves an element central to much humor—the breaking of frames. In this case, machines, humans, or animals act like each other and cross the boundaries of what is conventionally expected of the type in question. Many of these are part of a broader genre of person/machine jokes in which the frames that keep these distinct are crossed, and the juxtaposition of things we "know" don't go together is humorous. Examples of this include:

♦ A man receiving money from an ATM machine hears the machine say, "Now, remember that this has to last all weekend, so don't spend it foolishly. And don't forget the phone bill." The caption beneath reads, "Why the Automated Talking Teller Never Caught On."

♦ In a national park, a ranger wearing a bear costume (minus the head) is standing in front of a sign reading, "Do Not Feed the Bears," and writing a citation to two tourists who had previously offered the fake bear food.

♦ A sign on the floor of a hotel room reads, "This Way, Marion Barry." A woman sits seductively on the bed, waiting to activate a large mouse trap, and a voice from a closet with hidden video equipment says, "Now remember, no entrapment."

♦ A man puts his feet up on his desk, and a sign appears on his computer reading, "Take your feet off the desk."

♦ The computer screen of a data entry worker reads, "Faster! Faster! You're working 12 percent slower than the person next to you. . . ." Next to her is a smoking robot also entering data into a terminal.

♦ A boss cracking a whip inside a galley ship with data entry personnel lined up in columns is yelling "Keystroke! . . . keystroke! . . . keystroke!"

Finally, four "Far Side" cartoons:

♦ At night a cow is sitting around a campfire and telling some cowboys, "A few cattle are going to stray off in the morning, and tomorrow night a stampede is planned around midnight. Look, I gotta get back. . . . Remember, when we reach Santa Fe, I ain't slaughtered."

♦ A man walking past a dog's house is met by the dog pointing a device at him that reads "Fear-o-sensor."

◆ The caption beneath a couple that has passed out in their backyard, wearing electronic collars, reads, "Hours later, when they finally came to, Hal and Ruby groggily returned to their yard work—unknowingly wearing the radio collars and ear tags of alien biologists."

◆ From the inside of a house occupied by whales, a picture window opens onto humans with cameras and is captioned with one whale saying to the other, "Uh-oh, Norm. Across the street—whale-watchers."

The third type of surveillance humor is the "1984 dystopia," in which the image-maker intends to shock us through satire. This says that surveillance and surveillance technology is all-powerful, it's everywhere, it's inhuman, it's crazy, and this is what it could/will logically lead to. This also suggests the question, "Where will it end?" Examples include:

◆ A classic Doonesbury cartoon shows a black congressional aide delivering a proposal to his employer in Palm Beach, Florida. At the entry to the town he is stopped by police and asked for his pass card. He responds, "My pass card? You guys are kidding, right?" (This cartoon was in response to a proposed law requiring nonresidents to carry such identification.)

◆ A drawing of Manhattan is captioned, "Under new zero-tolerance rules, the entire island of Manhattan has been confiscated by federal agents after a marijuana seed was found on West 23rd St. (see detail). Entire island will be sold at auction soon. Includes Brooklyn Bridge."

◆ A second-grade classroom in the midst of great student pandemonium shows FBI agents entering and the teacher responding, "Thank heaven you're here." It is captioned, "Following their orders to investigate domestic terroristic organizations, the FBI checks on Miss Toog's second grade."

◆ Three men are in the restroom looking in (unbeknownst to them) a one-way mirror. One says, " . . . company lie detector tests, company urine tests, I swear, where's it all gonna end?" What they don't see is the man on the other side of the mirror taking notes on their conversation.

◆ Two men are talking, and the first says, "Your wife just gave you that beautiful gold watch a week ago—now she's divorcing you?" The second, holding up his wrist, says, "It has a surveillance camera in it."

◆ The cartoon "Sylvia" shows a SuperCop exhorting a couple in bed: "The national average is 2.5 times a week." The man says, "She's here again," and the woman, "Tell her we're doing the best we can."

A final form of surveillance humor involves reversals. Here an action may backfire, and machines go out of control or end up being used in unanticipated ways. Charlie Chaplin's *Modern Times* remains the classic example of this, where he is literally drawn into the assembly line. The hubris of humans in thinking they are in control is revealed, as is the latent threat of tampering with the unknown. Actors become stuck on their own petards. Unintended consequences and surprise accompany innovations. Mistakes occur. The reliability and validity of the machine's results are questioned. The last laugh or revenge may even be had by the subject of the surveillance. The usual power relations enhanced by the technology may be reversed, or the device is so out of control that everything gets destroyed. Some illustrations include:

◆ In a "Bloom County" cartoon, police with drawn weapons break into a man's house, having been called by the man's young son, who told them the father was using drugs. The son, in obvious response to educational efforts at school, says, "I just couldn't stand by and watch you flush your life down the toilet, Dad!!" The police officer next asks the son what drugs were involved. The boy replies, "Tobacco, caffeine, Schlitz . . . you name it."

◆ A couple sitting on a sofa is about to kiss when suddenly a loud siren goes off. The man then explains, "Damn! I forgot to disconnect my personal alarm system."

◆ A couple is lying in bed, and the man says, "Not tonight, Hon. It'll just wreak havoc with the motion sensors again."

◆ A couple at home is watching a politician on TV giving a campaign speech. A voice-stress analyzer is attached to their TV set. The husband states, "According to the voice-stress analyzer, he is not going to lower taxes."

◆ A barricade in the middle of a blocked-off street has written upon it, "POLICE LINE. NO VIDEO CAMERAS BEYOND THIS POINT."

Illustrations

Newspaper and magazine articles; editorial page political cartoons; and professional, business, and social movement communications concerned with surveillance and technology are often illustrated by drawings.

Given the continuous flow of social interaction and words in everyday life, the communication of meaning through a single frozen frame is an accomplishment. As Erving Goffman notes, this is accomplished by a variety of conventionalized cues.[7] The best-known visual symbol of surveillance is the eye, followed by the ear. It is also more difficult to visually depict the contents of smelling, touching, and feeling, and even the activity of the latter two. The eye is a commonplace symbol—for example, in the reminders sent out by medical offices.

The emblem of the Pinkerton National Detective Agency—a simple eye with the slogan "We Never Sleep"—is a good illustration. This suggests the agency's dedication to duty and the threat in its omnipresence. A public service poster from the M.I.T. police shows a large, computer-drawn eye with visible dots and this message: "Counting your eyes, there are about 18,000 eyes on our campus. There are only 52 in the M.I.T. Campus Police Department. If you see something suspicious, give us a call." An article on databases uses the familiar cue of an eye looking through a keyhole. WAC, a social movement concerned with stopping violence against women, has as its symbol an eye surrounded by the phrase "WAC IS WATCHING WOMEN TAKE ACTION." These have a direct, literal quality. We immediately understand the implications of a watchful eye.

Yet literal visual representations of surveillance are not common. The medium of drawing offers creative possibilities beyond traditional photography or testimony in court, which are more bound by reality. Common to many illustrations is the breaking of frames in which things that are not usually together, or could never be together in the real world, are joined. As in humor, breaking frames is attention-getting and often is seen as "interesting." Many of the illustrations involve grafting two discrete elements together with a transfer of meaning (whether reciprocal or one-way) between objects. As with much linguistic communication, something new comes to be understood by reference to something already known. The familiar serves to inform or offer a new way to think about the unfamiliar.

As with the surveillance jokes, a common frame break involves merging the human and the nonhuman. Eyes, ears, and technologies for enhancing seeing or hearing (magnifiying glasses, binoculars, tele-scopes, microphones) are joined to elements that they are not (and generally could not be) joined to in reality. We see human-like technology and humans as machines.

Examples of this include:

- a drawing accompanying a story about caller ID in which the telephone earpiece contains an eye behind a peephole
- an eye coming out of a computer, monitoring a worker
- a boss with X-ray vision, peering at a worker
- putting an eye in the center of a computer disk
- converting the wings of the U.S. eagle into elongated ears in response to Watergate
- putting a microphone in the raised arm and binoculars to the eyes of the Statue of Liberty
- a Superman-like figure coming out of the top of a telephone
- a computer printout coming from a man's chest while he holds his shopping bag and TV set, illustrating marketing research that joins television ad watching with shopping
- an illustration for a story entitled "From G-Man to Cursor-Man" shows a large mainframe computer wearing a jacket and a hat
- a phone following a man around as an illustration of personal mobile phones
- the individual standing under the lens of a giant microscope or under a magnifying glass, intended to illustrate DNA testing
- A bar code half covering a face (the symbol of a Dutch social movement concerned with data protection)

While the vast majority of the articles these illustrations accompany have at least an implied warning and some ambivalence about the technology, images of individuals as direct victims are not common. One example is the individual holding up a hand to block the spotlight shining down on him. In other examples we see persons cowering inside their homes with an unfriendly surveillance eye shining down. In one case the roof is lifted off the house to permit the outside in.

Helping us understand something new by reference to something old can be seen in the DNA identification card. This shows a double helix and some numbers that would be meaningless to most people. Yet when it is added onto a familiar "identification card," its meaning is very clear.

The idea of one's "data shadow" or "data image" is illustrated by showing a person with a shadow or a head made up of the kind of personal data in the computer. This shows the person as visible and suggests new meanings of the self or personhood.

The use of a visual metaphor can be seen in the case of the politician skewered on the antenna of his cordless phone. He was overheard talking to his mistress, and when this information became public it damaged his political career. Here we see a literal rendering of damage.

The illustration of a verbal cliché is shown by the drawing of a wall with eyes and ears ("the walls have ears") and a federal agent holding up a spider's web with a gun in the center. The latter illustrated a news story about a gun purchase sting that bordered on entrapment. A web was spun for the suspect and bait was offered.[8]

Exaggeration is also used in humorous illustrations of this type. For example, a story about parents using beepers to locate their teenagers shows a youth wearing four different-colored beepers on a belt.

A final aspect involves the extent to which the illustration is moving and memorable. Does it make the individual take notice and want to comment on it to others? Is it something that stays with the observer (much as most people who have seen Edvard Munch's "The Scream" or the last scenes in *Casablanca* are likely to remember them)? There is, of course, variation, but this is likely patterned and related to the characteristics of the individual and the material. What are some of the characteristics of memorable images? To more fully answer this requires a phenomenological analysis of the materials in which one studies how individuals make sense of the material. But to judge from my own responses, mixing the sacred and the profane and building upon the historical memory of the viewer makes such a response more likely.

The images of the U.S. eagle and the Statue of Liberty joined to the dirty tools of eavesdropping are memorable. The wrist with the bar code (from a book of German political cartoons) is moving, when viewers bring to it their memory of concentration camp victims with numbers on their wrists.

Advertisements

In contrast to the illustrations, the ads generally show less creativity and frame breaking. They are more straightforward. They describe a product or service and make greater use of words along with the images. This greater realism reflects their partisanship in the promotion of a tangible product, rather than abstract ideas and actions to illustrate in a more balanced, or at least broader, fashion. In showing only a representational photograph of the product, they let it speak for itself, although assumptions are made about how the audience will fill in the blanks.

This direct approach is illustrated by an ad that shows a variety of devices and simply asks, "Where can you go to see and hear what your eyes and ears can't?" No explanations or justifications are offered. The ad implies it is obvious why you would want to do this, and there is no lurking moral ambiguity. Even more minimalist are the handwritten signs I saw on the University of Washington campus: "Seattle Surveillance Specialists—the cheapest rates in town."

However, when the ads are undertaken to promote the political interests of a business or to promote a film (e.g., the file cabinet coming out of the telephone with a reference to the IRS, or an ad for the film *Kafka* showing a man peering out of a file cabinet), we see greater imagination and frame breaking.

Western culture, and in some ways particularly the United States, is ambivalent about surveillance as a reflection of its more general attitudes toward power. We seek to be protected by surveillance and welcome the watchful eye of the protector. Yet we also fear the invasive or evil eye that breaks the boundaries between self and others and between the group and society.

Not surprisingly, the ads emphasize the positive and ignore the negative aspects of surveillance. They deal with volatile material and are as interesting for what they say as for what they fail to say. Legitimations may be provided, and the nasty potential and normative violations made possible by surveillance are denied. A televison ad for a directional microphone asks, "Are you a curious person?" An ad for a device to hear from the other side of a wall euphemistically invites the viewer to "diagnose sounds through a solid surface from any source." An ad for an eavesdropping device that looks like a radio "focuses ambient sounds onto a sensitive microphone." A children's ad for "Super Ears" pushes its uses for listening to the sounds of nature. A Washington State appeal for motorists to report those driving illegally in special carpool lanes says, "Thanks for being a HERO," and invites them to call 764–HERO. A purveyor of surveillance technologies reports that his goods "empower the consumer."

Relatively few of the ads show the direct and honest appeal of one inviting you to "eavesdrop for under $80!" And such a bargain!—"You'd expect to pay double for a mini-recorder . . . especially one that's voice-activated." Similarly, an ad for "electronic ears disguised as a radio" shows a happy image of birthday domesticity and the caption, "People assume you're listening to a radio. In fact, you're hearing every word of their conversation. . . . Literally gives you superhearing." It is also "fun for amateur spying."

An ad for a surveillance book shows a wolf's eyes peering out and asks, "Are You a Hunter or the Hunted?" The obvious implication is it is better to be a hunter and to strike first. Consistent with the idea that the best defense is a good offense, some ads glide over the potential for aggressively gathering information on others and redefine the technology as a defensive measure to protect oneself from snooping. There is line-blurring with respect to the often morally suspect offensive uses and more easily justified defensive uses of the technology.[9]

The name of a national chain that sells spying devices—"Counter Spy Shop"—suggests justification via the need for protection. One of its products, "the briefcase that sees everything," can be used to "capture theft, conspiracy or break-ins on tape!" Unstated is that it can just as easily be used as part of a theft or conspiracy, and whatever its ostensible goal, its secret use in some states may constitute a felony.

Similarly, an ad for the widely publicized "secret connection briefcase" simply asks, "Bugged?" This implies a need to be protected. The first item listed is a "micro-miniature hidden bug detection system [which] lets you know if someone is secretly recording your conversation." It also includes an "incredible 6-hour recorder—so small it fits in a cigarette pack." While not said, the latter is intended for you to secretly tape others, assuming they don't also have a detector.

Some of the largest security companies profit from this amoral mix by selling both surveillance and antisurveillance devices. Outside of specialized publications, there are fewer ads for devices to protect oneself from the snooping of others. The public market for snooping seems much larger than that for protective devices.

Deception and lying may be defined as "pretending." Thus, an ad for a call-forwarding device reports that you can be at home and pretend to be at the office, and "best of all, the person calling never knows."

Rather than words such as *secret, hidden, covert, snoop,* or *spy,* we see *discreet viewing,* the possibility of *less conspicuous use,* the ability to *unobtrusively snap a photo* or to gather information *unobserved.*[10]

A telephone conversation recorder "automatically records your conversations for replay so that you can concentrate on your call and later retrieve information without the bother of time-consuming note taking." Unstated are the advantages that a secret recording can offer "without the bother of having to ask permission."

Attention may be focused away from what the product is used for, or the conditions of its use, to its other attributes such as design or materials. This offers other reasons for the purchase. For example, "The M3 is housed in a nice Parker knock off pen, so you not only get the best recording possible, the pen housing shows a bit of class as well." A camera hiding in a lighter has an "impressive enamel-like finish and gold trim."

An osmosis-like transfer of legitimacy may be suggested by reference to valued symbols. The aura of science with its suggestion of modernity, power, efficiency, and certainty is often drawn upon with terms such as "sophisticated technology," "high tech," "the scientific measure of truth," "ultra miniaturized," "solid state electronics," "integrated circuitry," "voice stress computer," and "electronically analyzes."

Hiding a video camera or an alarm in a warm cuddly object such as a teddy bear not only is intended to deceive but may make the transition to secret spying or alarms easier. A picture of a child hugging a big doll accompanies an ad for a baby monitor that permits you "to listen to what the children are up to."

The transference may involve esteemed sponsors or carriers whose use sanctifies, or vouches for, use by the ordinary person. The technology may be "built to military specifications," "originally designed for the DEA," "the same sophisticated technology used by professionals," or "used by U.S. Government agencies." An ad for "electronic ears disguised as a radio" invites the user to "hear like a super hero."

The advertisements seek to show how the product is needed by, or serves the interests of, the consumer. In extreme cases this is even extended to the subject of the surveillance. For example, an ad regarding "new technology in the office," from United Technology, informs us that it's all about "fun."

The ads may attempt to create or manipulate fear. They may draw on a sense of responsibility or obligation. Some of the ads for protective devices for children imply that if you really love your child, you have a duty to purchase the product.

The effort to generate anxiety and then to offer a means of coping with it via the product or service is most clear in defensive means. An ad for an intrusion detector shows a shadowy burglar breaking in with the caption "Chances are that your home and both your vehicles don't have security alarms. Your daughter or son, away at college, are probably relatively defenseless as well." But not to worry, the simple "Security Monitor" will solve all problems. An ad for "Child Guardian" shows a smiling child wearing his electronic sensor on a belt but warns that "the number of child abductions each year grows increasingly alarming." But with "Child Guardian," "your active youngster is under a 'watchful eye' every moment." An ad for "Guardian Angel" includes an idyllic picture of a child playing and warns, "It can happen anywhere: one moment your child is playing at your side. The next, he or she is gone." An ad for a drug-testing system reports that "teenage drug abuse is our #1 problem" and shows a worried mom saying, "Something was wrong with my son, but he'd insist things were O.K." Ordering the drug-testing kit helped her "find the problem and helped put my family back together." An ad for a "memo muncher" asks, What is the cost of a memo seen by "a wrong person"? Is "your competition looking through your garbage at night?" Even absent that, you can't be certain—"people are naturally inquisitive and you can never be quite sure that some private document doesn't end up in the wrong hands"—unless, of course, you spend $300 on their product. An ad in a computer magazine advises, "GET DEFENSIVE! YOU CAN'T SEE THEM, BUT YOU KNOW THEY'RE THERE. Hackers pose an invisible but serious threat to your information system."

The legal or ethical uses may be mentioned, but with the understanding that other uses are possible. The choice then is the user's and not in the product as such. Thus, a "Voice Stress Computer" "can sit on a desk or inside a drawer." The "PB1 Mini Parabolic Mic System" "should find application in situations from big-game hunting to legal recording." An automatic telephone conversation recorder is "small enough to fit discreetly underneath or next to your telephone."

While the technology is new, the marketing of surveillance in work settings is not. A series of ads for "accounting and writing machines" from *Business Week* magazine of 1929, which by today's standards seems crude and even eerie in their directness, makes visible verbal clichés such as "An eye for every angle of your business."

Computer programs called PEEK and SPY are more contemporary versions that let the employer do just that. To increase security, monitor production, and aid in training, the operator may peek at a "target" user's computer, but with the user's permission, and he or she "may disallow watching at any time." The SPY program permits monitoring computer use without the user's knowledge or permission. In trying to literally convey the surveillance, an ad intended to be humorous shows a manager's neck stuck into a computer screen, a wire running to a work station, and then a head coming out of the screen watching.

The relative absence of actors/actresses makes these materials more difficult to analyze than the gender commercials studied by Erving Goffman. Yet there is a clear gender component when humans are depicted. In most cases when a user is shown, it is a man. Consistent with muting what actually goes on, and to avoid stimulating a sympathetic counterreaction, rarely is the object of the surveillance shown. When it is, it is likely to be a subordinate such as a child, worker, or prisoner. Women are more likely to serve as objects than men.

This illustrates what Foucault calls the male gaze and may reflect erotic curiosity and men's generally greater interest in technology. An implicit link between sex and violence may be seen in ads that show an attractive female within the viewscope of a camera, which could equally be a rifle scope. For example, an ad for a book on surveillance shows an attractive woman in the scope, and an ad for a "Nite-Scope" device frames a scantily clad woman within the scope. It is captioned, "The dark holds no secrets with the night penetrator." This is "ideal for discreet viewing or map-reading, nocturnal wild life and astronomic observation, or maritime navigation." If that is so, one wonders why the ad shows a woman as the subject of surveillance. I found only two ads that involve women as users, and I found no examples of the female gaze, where a man is the object of technology applied by a woman.[11]

The ads reflect normative patterns in which it is more common for men to look at women than the reverse. Whether or not the male impetus to look is stronger, it is less socially inhibited.[12] Increased feminist consciousness and awareness of sexual harassment may further enhance the male market for covert surveillance devices, as the normative boundaries become more restricted. But it may also mean greater equality in the gaze. We might expect more ads showing females as users with males as objects of surveillance.[13]

Visual Art

Contemporary artists, in reflecting the material culture and cultural themes of their time, have turned to surveillance media and the topic of surveillance—using the technology to reveal unseen elements and to help us experience surveillance.

While the inert eye, from Dali and Magritte to the engraver of the U.S. dollar bill, has always been a theme, video and related technologies offer new possibilities—particularly for performance art, which directly involves the audience and which merges, or at least breaks down the conventional differences between, subject and object. Video art, because of its real-time quality and mixing of image and sound, is an ideal medium for the artist concerned with surveillance themes. It offers temporal continuity and breadth and hence is more comprehensive than a still photo.

Illustrative of the breakdown between art and reality is the work of artist Julia Scher.[14] She obtains loans and donations of equipment to reveal the conflict between the need for protection and the possibility of being victimized by the particular apparatus. Her art exemplifies what it seeks to communicate. Unlike fiction, it does not imitate reality. Rather as with cinema verité, it tries to capture something that is there. It reflects and creates reality. In a group exhibit in Los Angeles entitled "Surveillance," she placed the gallery itself under surveillance. Viewers became part of the spectacle. The viewers' body heat tripped invisibly projected infrared beams at the entrance to the building. This caused flashing lights and an alarm embedded in a representation of a human torso on the wall to go off.

In another exhibit she created a mock interrogation room in which subjects enter their name into a computer and then see their image on the screen and a list of crimes they are [wrongly] accused of committing. Surveillance cameras were set up in various rooms, permitting subjects to see themselves and others as they pass through the rooms.

Reality and art fuse, as do target and agent. The surveillance cameras are not an invented form that mimics reality. This situation differs from "real" surveillance only because of its context and goals. The technology is recontextualized to critique and even expose it. Here, the technology's goal is to educate or entertain rather than to surveil. The viewer experiences video surveillance as both the object who is watched and as the subject who is watching.

This self-monitoring is a form of bio-feedback and illustrates one theme of contemporary surveillance societies. The voyeur and the exhibitionist may be merged. For those who are there, it is participatory art. It can be a mocking form and involve play-acting, as the participant chooses it and is aware of it, but it is not simply pretend. Further mixing elements is the fact that when Scher is not doing art, she runs a company called "Safe and Secure," which installs surveillance systems.

Artist Richard Lowenberg uses contemporary military and industrial surveillance technology to reveal protected or unseen things—such as an Air Force satellite communications receiver or invisible heat patterns from dancers. Absent technical supports, these are unseen because of distance, darkness, or barriers such as walls and skin.

Lowenberg's unobtrusive night work uses darkness-illuminating technologies. There is no telltale flashbulb to give it away. While his photographic art is hidden in darkness, the technology he uses pierces a barrier that for most of human history has protected information. The image intensifier (or nightscope) amplifies star light 20,000 times, and "flirs" (forward looking infrared systems) need no light at all. The flir uses infrared sensors to provide a high resolution thermal video display. It makes visible what (if we were aware of it at all) we would experience only as temperature variations, even though the infrared spectrum is omnipresent. The flir offers a shifting window into an ever-present thermodynamic world unaffected by light or darkness. This technology permits seeing in the dark and seeing things that for normal communications purposes are not really (or at least practically) there.

For Lowenberg thermal patterns serve as a kind of invisible ink. Temperature prints are produced using a heat-reflective screen. We see variations in temperature rather than light—the darker the color, the warmer the area. In one example using the flir imager he videotaped a dance performance that occurred in complete darkness. Dancers dipped their hands in water and fingerpainted on a blank wall. As the temperature of the water gradually changed, amazing patterns were seen on the wall, even though neither the audience nor dancers could see this, absent the conversion of heat variations to light and dark hues.

In another example of using technologies to surface the unseen (but not purposively hidden), Nina Sobel offers a visual representation of ever-present but rarely seen brain waves. Her "Encephalographic Video Drawings" records brainwaves on video. In a unique example of self-monitoring, individuals confront their own previously unseen "mediated images." What is reflected is "real," although the medium for showing it is not the phenomenon as such.

Given a free market and the double-edged, multiple-use potential of any technology, the usual workings of surveillance from the more to the less powerful can also be highlighted and reversed. Paul Ryan and Michael Shamberg use video technology to watch the watchers—to catch them in the act, so to speak. In a 1969 video called "Supermarket," they document a video surveillance system in a Safeway store—recording a large sign that says, "Smile. You Are on Photo-Scan TV." The store manager tells them to stop and that it is illegal to shoot images in the store—to which they respond, "You're taking pictures of us, so why can't we take pictures of you?" This, of course, raises the first question of social analysis: "Says who?"

Another example of using the technology to survey the surveyors can be seen in the film *Red Squad*, based on a New York collective following and interviewing police red squad members. This becomes reciprocal as they become the subject of the red squad's gaze as well. Artist Lewis Stein takes pictures of surveillance equipment. And Rick Preliner in an audio-scanning installation called "Listening Post" permitted the gallery-goer to eavesdrop on airwaves used by federal agents and local police in the Los Angeles area.

Another form of artistic expression does not focus directly on surveillors as subjects but intercepts their data on others. This represents an egalitarian sharing of the data or, in Susan Sontag's words, the "democratization of the evidence." Here the artist, like the control agent, invades the private space of the subject, but with a different purpose—to demythologize, authenticate, or question. We are shown what authorities see and hear about others.

Maria Kramer's video installation goes straight to the source. "Jean Seberg/the/FBI/the/Media" uses FBI documents to report on the U.S. countersurveillance activities directed at the actress. By enlarging and then displaying the documents, Kramer exposes both photographically and politically the surveillance activities that may have shortened the life of the actress.

Michael Klier's "Der Reece" ("The Giant") uses images from video surveillance cameras in a variety of urban settings to create a composite work. Louis Hock's "Mexican Tapes: A Chronicle of Life Outside the Law" is a video narrative using night-vision technology applied to three illegal Mexican immigrant families.

In "Abscam" ("Framed") Chip Lord mixes real surveillance data with fictional material. He plays a whispering newsman who returns to the scene and thus adds "fake" material. But given the fact that Abscam itself was, to a large degree, an artifact of the agent's intervention (creating a fake setting with some very attractive, unrealistic inducements), such work raises deeper questions about just what "real" means. The ability to digitally retouch or create photo images (e.g., as with the National Geographic's altering the size of a pyramid to fit its cover) raises related questions.

Gary Lloyd's "Radio Painting" is a canvas with a low power FM radio transmitter embedded in it so that anyone speaking within the presence of his work has his or her voice transmitted within a five-block range. Here the artist exercises some control over the "critic" by enforcing publicity, and he broadens the number of critics. The artist is in a position to know the remarks made in front of the painting.

Artists also use more conventional tools to invade privacy and make public what is usually not recorded. Photographers traditionally have done this. Walker Evans used a concealed Leica camera for his famous series of New York subway photos.

French photographer and conceptual artist Sohie Calle has done things such as (1) randomly picking a man from a crowd and following him to Venice, photographing him and keeping notes of his activities; (2) taking a job as a hotel maid and photographing the possessions and interiors of the same room over a three-week period as different persons stayed there; (3) inviting strangers to her own apartment and photographing them while they slept; (4) having her mother hire a private detective to follow and photograph her on a particular day. The detective did not know the artist knew and had arranged it. She then recorded her feelings and imaginings as she went about the day— knowing she was being recorded and watched, but not when, where, or by whom. She juxtaposes the surveillance photos with her own conjectures and artificially manufactured emotions. This powerfully conveys her experiences of suspiciousness and paranoia, as the detective might be anyone she sees.

In a variation of a Garfinkle or Goffman experiment, she reports finding an address book and photocopying it before returing it to its owner. She then called everyone in it and asked if she could interview them about its owner, without ever encountering him.

Some Implications

To begin with, these materials literally or symbolically speak for themselves. Like a good meal, the value comes from the experience. Films such as *Rear Window*, the *Conversation*, or *Kafka* and songs such as "I Ain't Gonna Piss in No Jar," and the robotic arm with its hint of a skeleton cradling or crushing the flowers give us a jolt and a type of understanding that is otherwise unobtainable. This involves not only *verstehen*, or imagining, what another person experiences, but a nonreflective shock. These certainly can (and must) be considered on their own terms. There is wisdom in E. B. White's observation that "humor can be dissected as a frog can, but it dies in the process."

I would certainly not want to profane the sacred by connecting urine in a cup with the president's wife, nor would I have abstract, emotionless analysis detract from the artistic experience. The broad, exploratory approach taken in this chapter does not lend itself to a rigorous model of scientific hypothesis testing. Rather than deductively straining these materials through varieties of available theory, I will proceed inductively and indicate the theoretical implications that I find in the material.

Social scientists generally draw too rigid a line between their data and the offerings of the artist. Artistic creations can significantly inform us about surveillance and society. They can be approached from a standpoint of the sociology of knowledge, and we can ask about the messages conveyed, how this has changed, and how it correlates with the characteristics of the creator and the context. Here the art is treated as a dependent variable. But the materials can also inform us about broader societal issues, and we can speculate on their social impact.

I will consider seven implications involving (1) education, (2) conflict, (3) power, (4) conflicting and uncertain values, (5) contextual meaning, (6) the need for research on the social impact of such material, and (7) comparisons between art and science as ways of knowing.

1. *These materials can help us see and understand (whether emotionally or cognitively) new developments in surveillance.* They offer an alternative language through visual metaphors. The meaning of authoritarianism, repression, domination, intolerance, and spying is likely to be different when experienced vicariously through seeing and hearing, rather than through reading and quantifying. The traditional role of the artist in making the unseen visible has a particularly appropriate meaning here. Such media can educate in a distinctive and perhaps more profound sense than the exclusively verbal. They can help us see and experience in different ways, especially things that are new. For example, electronic data and microscopic DNA sequences become more imaginable when they are transformed through artistic representations.

These new ways of seeing may involve:

a) The idea of an alternative way of constructing the self, such as through the data image or shadow.[15] The meaning of personhood is changing. An image depicting a human form that is nothing more than credit card transactions and identifying numbers gives one the sense that there is another "you" out there, largely beyond your knowledge and control, that others have access to and even own.

b) The ease with which data can be distorted and manipulated—for example, the distortion of a face or physical presence (the film *Rising Sun* gives a good example), or the mixture of real and nonexistent elements. By actually seeing a "real" photograph or image of something that has never existed (a horse's head on the body of a person, or altered proportions of a pyramid) we can more easily come to appreciate the increased possibilities for deception and to question the validity of visual images. In this sense "seeing is believing"—at least believing not to believe. This has major implications for courtroom evidence and for new presentations. It can communicate the fragmented and movable quality of the "realities" we perceive. This may lead to a healthy skepticism or an immobilizing paranoia.

c) The changing line between the human and nonhuman—robots, cyborgs, and implants—is more easily grasped when we actually see these through the artist's imaginary creations.

d) Helping us grasp the scale, totality, comprehensiveness, and simultaneity of the new forms of surveillance across multiple dimensions. We can literally more easily see the big picture. The cartoon showing the drive-in testing service is a good example of this, as are video pastiches made from far-flung surveillance cameras.

Artistic materials can educate and politicize by telling us what is happening and by offering warnings. They bring the news to broader audiences (e.g., the cartoon about the Florida city requiring passcards or computers displaying signs about not working as fast as the person next to you). Here the materials are like any other mass media account, yet because of a broader reach and a potentially more powerful and poignant means of conveying the message, they may be better understood.

2. A struggle is going on over what surveillance technology means and how it ought to be viewed. While we must be skeptical of simplistic determinisms, image and interest are often linked. To oversimplify, this involves conflicts over symbols and words, with vendors and dominants on one side (e.g., security companies, managers, various guardians), and subordinates, civil libertarians, skeptics, and resisting social movements on the other. Each side has allies in culture production. For the former, it tends to be advertising and its glorification of surveillance. For the latter, it tends to be cartoonists, popular songwriters, and artists who demystify, expose, and delegitimate. Reduced to essentials, the art tends to view technology as the enemy or problem and the ads as the savior or solution. They are mirror opposites. It is an interesting exercise to fill in the other half of the story. Such work is as revealing for what it says as for what it does not say.

Art and politics are often treated as if they were more independent than is the case. Scottish poet Ernest Fletcher said, "Let me write poems, I care not who writes the laws." Yet Plato wanted poets to be controlled by the state—and with good reason, from an Establishment perspective.

3. *A related point is that these materials remind us that surveillance is often about power.* Many of the visual and textual messages make it clear that there is a controller and the controlled (managers and workers, men and women, parents and children, guards and prisoners, merchants and consumers, and so on). The notion of the all-powerful and knowing entity—whether involving God, superheroes, government, bosses, or parents—is so embedded in our culture as to be commonplace, and note is rarely taken of it. It is against this backdrop that many of these materials are offered. As subordinates in some or many of the roles we play, we are in a position to understand this and can readily identify with the subject's experience.

4. *The materials also suggest that our relatively democratic and egalitarian society is uncomfortable with the naked facts and brute force of power.* Hence, many of the messages are subtle, use euphemisms (bugging devices as "diagnostic tools"), deal only with the positive aspects (nightscopes as great for watching nocturnal animals), and seek to transfer warm feelings from one object (a teddy bear) to unpleasant items (such as a hidden camera).

Such treatment indicates the value conflicts and resulting profound ambivalence of our culture toward surveillance. Such work may convey the omnipresent, omnipotent, omniscient character of surveillance and in so doing portray an all-knowing God. We are both fascinated (especially in North America) and repelled by it. It honors our fantasies of omnipotence and desire for control and reinforces our fears of the inhuman and the inhumanly mechanistic. This ambivalence can be seen more generally in the contrasting views of the evil eye and the eye of God. The technology can protect and violate. An important issue for study is whether this ambivalence has lessened in recent decades as concerns about security, productivity, and health have increased.

The ambivalence one can read into this material also reflects *value uncertainty* beyond value conflicts, in which meaning is unclear and still being negotiated as new products and uses continually appear. Conflicting laws, policies, and public opinion data also suggest this.

In this sense culture is not a perfectly integrated system, but an ever-changing crazy quilt made of bits and pieces that are barely held together by weak threads that often pull in opposing directions. Whether in physics or morality, this results in tension.

5. *We see that the meaning is not in the object but in the context and in*

how it is interpreted. Thus, for example, electronic location monitoring technology to confine those under judicial supervision may be presented and viewed differently than when the same technology is used to protect abused spouses, children, and those with Alzheimer's disease.

6. *This material calls attention to areas for social research*. It is important to study the social functions and consequences of this material. How do audiences fill in the blanks? Like paint-by-number kits, these materials are often unfinished, and they rely on our *bringing* the connecting lines and colors to them. We need a better ecology of perceptions and values that will tell us what people see, or hear, when given a vague surveillance stimulus. The creators and owners of culture think they know (especially advertisers). But what images and assumptions do they hold, and are they correct? To what extent do they lead or follow? Do they reflect or create?

On balance what is the net effect of popular media in creating an environment that welcomes, tolerates, or opposes the new surveillance? Does it educate for citizenship in a democratic society and create a healthy skepticism and even indignation? Does it demoralize and depress and create an immobilizing paranoia and the beliefs that the technology is more powerful than it really is, and that we are in the iron grasp of an unstoppable technological determinism? Does this material subtly prepare us, prime the pump, create a receptive (if not necessarily overly welcoming) public, softening us up, much as long-range artillery does, before an assault? As social fictions and reality are blurred, what happens? What is the impact of songs such as "Secret Agent Man" and the television programs associated with it? What was the impact of "Candid Camera" in making a joke out of video invasions and deception; or of today's home-video shows, which treat surveillance as entertainment or merely as competitions to win prizes? Does constant media exposure normalize, routinize, domesticate, and trivialize surveillance?

7. *Finally, this material reminds us of the parallel between science and art, as both may seek to go beneath surface realities and question conventions.* For example, Richard Lowenberg's unmasking of the electromagnetic environment shares the goal of some researchers in mapping and making visible the invisible world. The sociologist does this when analyzing latent functions and unintended consequences, demystifying social practices, and identifying the obfuscatory role that ideology and words

can play. It would be useful to compare the work of artists and scientists here with respect to subjects, presentation, and audience response, as well as to understand reciprocal influences among these two somewhat different, if overlapping, ways of knowing.

Notes

This chapter draws from Gary T. Marx, *Windows into the Soul: Surveillance and Society in an Age of High Technology*, ASA-Duke University Jensen Lectures, forthcoming. I am grateful to Ann-Marie Wood, Jen Owen, Deborah Irmas, Mathieu Deflem, and Eve Darian-Smith for help.

1. It is, of course, possible that the search is for a particular individual who does not want to be found, yet given our notions of choice, that would then put the singer in a negative light in pursuing someone who had rejected him. By the 1990s anti-stalking laws criminalized this.

2. *Rolling Stone*, 1 March 1984.

3. Of course, the adventure, bravery, self-sacrifice, and patriotism the song suggests can also be viewed positively.

4. James B. Rule, "1984—The Ingredients of Totalitarianism," in *1984 Revisited: Totalitarianism in Our Century*, ed. Irving Howe (New York: Harper and Row, 1983), 166–79.

5. Murray Davis, *What's So Funny?* (Chicago: University of Chicago Press, 1993).

6. Unfortunately, permissions restrictions conflict with a major purpose of this chapter, which is to communicate about surveillance beyond script. The author (c/o Dept. of Sociology, University of Colorado, Boulder, Colorado, 80309) would be pleased to send images to anyone requesting them.

7. Erving Goffman, *Gender Advertisements* (Cambridge, MA: Harvard University Press, 1979).

8. Comprehending these requires effort, since most people respond to images directly and, initially at least, literally, rather than looking for linguistic and other referents and symbols. I had the ears and eyes in the walls image for several years before I "saw" the artist's intent. Where there are levels of meaning, as with this illustration, differences in individual styles of perception and knowledge condition how much is seen.

9. With respect to offensive and defensive uses, we need to differentiate a defensive device such as a bug detector, which only has one use, from a more neutral tool such as a bug that can be used defensively (e.g., in response to a perceived threat) or offensively.

10. The ad for the M3 is an exception to the neutered language of most ads.

This device is "small enough to be secreted in a coat sleeve" and is designed for "surreptitious" recording. However, this ad appears to be directed toward security professionals.

11. One illustration did involve this, but the observed man is himself calling a hot line to report a tip.

12. This may be turned around and exploited. Consider the marketing of "Anne Droid," an attractive department store surveillance mannequin with a camera in her eye and a microphone in her nose. This has something of a "last laugh" quality to it, as the leering male may himself be observed. The culture of surveillance may also be transferred back to ads for more conventional products such as lingerie.

13. There are, however, advice manuals specifically directed toward women, such as Joseph T. Culligan, *When in Doubt Check Him Out* (Miami: Hallmark Press, 1993), and Gigi Moers, *How and Why Lovers Cheat and What You Can Do About It* (New York: Shapolsky Press, 1992).

14. The work reported here is from LACE, *Surveillance* (Los Angeles: LACE, 1984). A copy of the catalogue containing many of the works discussed in this section may be obtained from LACE.

15. Kenneth C. Laudon, *Dossier Society* (New York: Columbia University Press, 1986).

7 ◆ ◆ ◆
Media, Crime, and Justice:
A Case for Constitutive Criminology

GREGG BARAK

Introduction

In *Rape and Criminal Justice*, Gary LaFree thoroughly examined the social construction of sexual assault from the perspective of those who must respond formally to the claim that a rape had occurred.[1] Among his findings are some very useful analogies for the study of crime news construction. For example, "legal agents, no less than other human beings, must actively construct their own perceptual world. This world is always at least one step away from the world 'as it really is.' "[2] He continues that "the distance between perception and reality is likely to be especially great in the case of the criminal-selection process, because legal agents most often respond to events that they did not actually observe."[3] What Lafree argues about legal agents and processes is no less true for media agents, sources, and processes of news construction.

The sociology of "social construction" in relation to issues of deviance and control has been represented historically by three prominent theoretical traditions: "symbolic interactionism,"[4] "labeling,"[5] and "postmodernism."[6] Presently, in the study of crime and justice there is an emerging theoretical model—constitutive criminology—that combines insights from the two older traditions and from a more recently developed synthesis of postmodernism and cultural Marxism. I believe that constitutive criminology, as articulated by Henry and Milovanovic, yields an ideal theoretical venue from which to study media, crime, and justice. They represent the world of constitutive criminology as that which is

> concerned with identifying the ways in which the interrelationships be-
> tween human agents and their social world constitute crime, victims, and
> control as realities. It is oriented to how we may deconstruct these reali-
> ties, and to how we may reconstruct less harmful alternatives. Simultane-
> ously, it is concerned with how emergent socially constructed realities
> themselves constitute human agents with the implication that, if crime is
> to be replaced, this necessarily must involve a deconstruction and recon-
> struction of the human subject.[7]

Moreover, the constitutive version of criminology that incorporates both postmodernism and Marxism involves grasping both discourse and practice in order to retain the coexistence and mutual determina-tion of practices and discourses, structure and agency.[8] Unlike many critical Marxists who recognize only the negative side of postmodern-ism, grounded in its basic nihilistic and relativistic tendencies, Henry and Milovanovic also recognize the positive change-oriented side, grounded in the possibilities of critical opposition, transpraxis, and re-constitutive effects. Constitutive criminology, in other words, works toward the development of a "replacement discourse." As Henry and Milovanovic explain, replacement discourse captures "the fluid nature of criminal violations and the legal processing of such infractions. . . . [It also envelops] not just the declarations of policy but the ways its practitioners and policy makers distinguish their reality from the total-ity" of offenders, victims, criminal justice agencies, and the wider polit-ical economies. Finally, it requires "a 'bringing back in' of the under-emphasized, informal, unofficial, and marginalized practices (the un-spoken) that are part of the totality of power that passes for crime control."[9]

Applied to the general study of mass communications or to the spe-cific study of crime and justice news, constitutive criminology like "newsmaking criminology"[10] argues that mass media realities of crime and justice, and societal reactions to various crimes, criminals, and vic-tims, reinforce selective models for addressing crime and crime control. A primary objective of both of these criminologies is to expose the un-derpinning cultural and political-economic nature of the crime problem, and to draw the necessary connections between this nature and the way in which crime is defined as a particular type of individual or social problem. At the same time, constitutive and newsmaking criminologists seek to "overthrow" the mainstream discourses, views, points of perception, and policies associated with crime and justice, replacing them with alternative conceptions and practices, such as those that are part of an emerging "criminology of peacemaking." Peacemaking criminology refers, in part, to those proposals and programs that foster mediation, conflict resolution, reconciliation, and community. It is a criminology that "seeks to alleviate suffering and thereby reduce crime . . . that is based necessarily on human transformation in the achievement of peace and justice . . . [and that] takes place as we change our social, economic, and political structure."[11] All three of these critical criminologies converge around the shared agreement for the development of a replacement discourse.

The need to change the mass-mediated understanding of crime and justice is strongly supported by the available research on media, crime, and criminal justice. Recognizing the tremendous influence that the mass media have on the development of beliefs and attitudes, and on the subsequent development of policies of criminal justice, Surette underscores that "these policies determine what behaviors we criminalize, what crimes we tolerate, how we treat criminals, and how we fight crime."[12] As the mass media create a social reality of crime and justice for their audiences, they also shape their audiences' perceptions about crime, control, and the larger world. In fact, the research of Gerbner et al. demonstrates an association between television viewing and what they call a "mean world view."[13] This view is characterized by "mistrust, cynicism, alienation, and perceptions of higher than average levels of threat and crime in society."[14] The work of Barrile has likewise revealed an association between television viewing and a "retributive justice perspective" that supports authorities and favors punitive policies such as harsher punishments and the death penalty.[15] Marks provides further evidence of the effects of television exposure on the increased fear of crime and perceived vulnerability, and on the adoption of self-protective anticrime behaviors.[16] All of this "translates into attitudes regarding who can employ violence against whom, who are appropriate victims of crime, and who are likely to be criminals."[17]

Constitutive Criminology and Moral Evaluations

Constitutive criminology takes the view or assumes that crime and justice are both *in* and *of* society. It provides a framework for "reconnecting crime and its control with the society for which it is conceptually and institutionally constructed by human agents."[18]

Constitutive criminology can help to integrate the perception and construction of crime and justice. In the study of humankind, the concept of perception has a long and complex history. In this century perception has generally been more identified with psychology than sociology. In the case of psychology, however, perceptions have come to denote primarily the neurophysiological rather than the cerebral-cognitive processes, with the former's emphasis on sensory perception, thresholds of perception, and the illusions of perception that view the recipient or beholder as a "passive subject" or "object of" rather than as an "active agent" in the production of.

On the other hand, the perceptual concern of sociology has been with the content of the views and attitudes that people hold, including the very way they frame social actions, interactions, objective situations, and themselves. While constitutive criminology reflects and is integrative of psychological perceptions, especially those of a cerebral-cognitive nature, it springs mostly from the sociology and social psychology of such turn-of-the-twentieth-century thinkers as Max Weber, W. I. Thomas, and George Herbert Mead. It is also informed by the German phenomenologists, the American pragmatists, the sociologists of knowledge, the students of nationalism and ethnocentricism, the disciples of Alfred Schutz, the ethnomethodologists, the interactionists, the labeling school, and the microsociologists influenced by Erving Goffman.

The argument implicitly, if not explicitly, developed here maintains that with respect to crime and justice, constitutive criminology—with its distinctly Marxist and postmodernist synthesis—contributes a fuller understanding of the newsmaking process than earlier social constructionist approaches. The fundamental differences between constitutive criminology and the other sociological constructionist traditions (as they have been applied to criminology) are that the former moves beyond the relativism of the latter, whose emphasis has been away from "what is" and toward "what relevant actors/actresses think is." By contrast, constitutive criminology's emphasis is on integrating the relationship between what is and what people think is. A related difference has to do with the traditional constructionists' reification of the status quo and the critical constructionists' search for a reflexive reconceptualization of crime and justice. Instead of passively accepting the prevailing perceptions, distortions, and constructions of reality by elites and masses alike as the traditionalists do, the critics are actively attempting to develop a replacement discourse rather than an oppositional one, a peacemaking discourse, for example, rather than a conflicting or competing one.

Succeeding Giddens,[19] constitutive criminologists view "social structure and its constituent control institutions as the emerging outcome of human interaction that both constrains and enables criminal action and recognizes that those structures are simultaneously shaped by crime and crime control talk that is part of their reproduction."[20] Thus, constitutive criminology is not an exercise in polemics, and human agencies are not to be separated from the structures that they make. What sets constitutive criminology apart from, for example, labeling, with its emphasis on role engulfment and deviancy amplification, or from symbolic interactionism, with its emphasis on individual interpretation and negotiation with others over the meaning of specific criminal and justice events, is an appreciation of the ways in which audiences are constructed, constituted, and undermined by human agents in the context of a historically specific political economy. Constitutive criminology also underscores the missing importance of the dialectic of control on the way audiences are made during their attempt to control labels for others.

The point, then, is that constitutive criminology recognizes the power of people to undermine the structures that confront them and asserts that people both use and are used in the propagation of knowledge and truth about what they and others do in this world. Hence, the attention given to crime and justice in relation to moral evaluations by constitutive (or newsmaking) criminologists is not an exercise for exercise' sake, but rather an attempt to understand the construction of crime and justice for the purposes of reconstruction.

In the United States, the relationship between moral evaluations and the construction and reconstruction of media images (or characterizations) of crime and crime control is constituted within the core of the social, political, and psychological makeup of American society. Mass news representations in the "information age" have become the most significant communication by which the average person comes to know the world outside his or her immediate experience. As for the cultural visions of crime projected by the mass media, or the selections and presentations by the news media on criminal justice, these representations are viewed as the principal vehicle by which the average person comes to know or make sense out of crime and justice in America.

Crime stories produced by the news media in this country reveal as much about the American experience and U.S. values as they do about control and the administration of justice. Moving back and forth between society's primary information system—the mass media—and its primary system for legitimizing values and enforcing norms—the criminal justice system—are morality plays or struggles between bad guys and good guys. While "the tendency to make moral evaluations is of course not limited to thinking about crime," it does seem that crime is a "focal point for the human need to hold positive and negative attitudes toward social objects."[21]

Throughout society there are both individuals and groups of people with a wide range of perceptions about crime and justice. These perceptions are influenced by the different ways in which the interplay between criminals, apprehenders, and victims are socially and ethically perceived by ordinary citizens, criminal justice policy makers, those responsible for carrying out legal norms, criminologists, and the press. The mass communication of these perceptions constructs a cultural awareness of crime, of victim/offender encounters, and of the administration of justice.

The cultural formation of moral evaluations does not randomly occur. They are not the unadulterated byproducts of logic and facts. Moreover, cultural evaluations are not the offspring of some kind of all-powerful elite of the Left or Right. Nor are the moral or social panics associated with urgent societal problems the exclusive territory of moral or social entrepreneurs. Whether the subject is civil disturbances like the L.A. riots that erupted in response to the Rodney King beating verdict in the spring of 1992, everyday activities like rape and domestic violence that are commonly committed by both strangers and intimates, or homeless victims of the AIDS epidemic who are dying on the streets, what emerges in the construction of social and criminal crises is the tendency for the political parameters of discussion to become rather fixed by a limited public discourse. Pro or con, supportive or oppositional, these discourses typically reinforce a status quo where the underlying structural and institutional relations are taken as a given. As Watney demonstrates in *Policing Desire: Pornography, AIDS, and the Media*,[22] there is an important need for analysts of media to deconstruct culturally taken-for-granted factuality. In his study Watney did precisely that by showing how the British government and media based their approach to the AIDS crisis on an agenda of sexual uniformity and conformity, fueled by a not-so-subtle homophobia, that had little, if any, impact on the problem but was of ideological service in the struggle to reproduce a repressive sexuality.

Contemporary cultural fascination or preoccupation with certain kinds of anomic violent crime—for example, like that involving serial killers—is reflected in the "true crime" sections of popular bookstores and is not disconnected from the minds and imaginations of news media audiences that are nurtured on a constant diet of an unsafe world where subhuman criminals apparently run rampant. As these types of statistically rare and gruesome crimes are merged in the public (mass) mind with the crimes of fiction, a distorted view of crime (and justice) is perpetuated. At the same time, these mixed perceptions of real and make-believe criminals produced by the mass media not only "provide modern audiences with an outlet for their needs to participate vicariously in the struggle between good and evil forces," but with "accounts of real struggles between the established moral order and threats to subvert it" that satisfy those same needs.[23] Numerous films, docudramas, and prime-time television shows such as *America's Most Wanted*, *Top Cops*, *American Detective*, and *Unsolved Mysteries* testify to this mass-media construction of law, order, and justice.

Deconstructing Media, Crime, and Justice

The interaction of journalists, sources, and audiences that coexist within a diverse and eclectic cultural and social system coproduces mass mediated images of crime and justice. As employed here, the model of media, process, and the perception of crime assumes that the social construction of crime news, or how we regard victims, offenders, and agents of crime control, emerges out of a historically evolving mass discourse on crime and justice. More specifically, for the purposes of developing a replacement discourse, crime and justice news deconstruction and reconstruction necessitate a scrutiny of the interaction between the production of crime news stories and the wider social order. It further entails an appreciation that crime news, like other news, emerges from struggles that are ultimately resolved, at least momentarily, by the prevailing if not necessarily dominant relations of power. Like news in general, crime news is chiefly a reflection of "the exercise of power over the interpretation of reality."[24] Like students of news media generally, students of constitutive criminology are concerned with the degree of distortion and bias in the news, or with the distance between the social reality of crime and the newsmaking reality of crime. Unlike other analysts of the news media who are merely interested in seeing that the news media tell it like it is, constitutive criminologists are also interested in telling it like it could or should be.

In an attempt both to articulate the processes of news coproduction and to clarify how these are more fully grasped through the lens of constitutive criminology, I will now turn my attention to three dynamic and interrelated themes of mass communication as they constitute crime and justice: (1) media reflection, cultural diversity, and crime news; (2) mass media, public order, and symbolic deviance; and (3) social control, news media, and political change.

Media Reflection, Cultural Diversity, and Crime News

In *Media Performance*, McQuail argues that "the degree of correspondence between the diversity of the society and the diversity of media content is the key to assessing . . . whether or not the media give a biased or a true reflection of society."[25] It has been shown that despite the expanding media pluralism (many channels) in this and other societies, message pluralism (diversity of content) has not grown accordingly.[26] This is generally the case for media coverage of political, racial, ethnic, class, or sexual diversity. Instead of reflecting the increasingly greater diversity, the media have continued to provide homogenized, mainstream, and uniform versions of reality that tend to avoid fundamental controversy. What accounts for this consistency in the lack of diversity of news media is a reliance on shared journalistic routines, on the same news sources, and on the interaction between fundamental news values and society's core values. Put another way, since the news media compete for the same audiences, and since they reflect the narrow topical and selection criteria of significance and relevance to the concerns of their audiences and their media organizations alike, it is not surprising that what constitutes "news" does not necessarily conform with reality.

Distortions abound with the portrayals of issues related to race, ethnicity, gender, and class in the news media. Blacks, Hispanics, and other minorities such as Asians and Middle-Easterners are generally underrepresented in the positive news. However, when it comes to negative news, which is often thought to be more newsworthy than "good news," blacks and other ethnic minorities are more likely to be identified in negative contexts (e.g., crime), even when they are cast as victims.[27] The same kinds of patterns exist with the depictions of women in the news. For example, the economic role of women is usually underestimated. The media typically report on women of lower status, in subordinate positions to men, or in some statistically uncommon negative role like mistress or prostitute, while other roles, which are no less common in real life, are neglected.[28] When it comes to class, occupation, and social status, the same kinds of news reporting prevail. Here "media portrayals accentuate higher skilled, better paid and higher status occupations, both in terms of frequency and often in direction of valuation. Routine or normal working class jobs are rarely seen, except for service roles."[29]

As for portrayals of crime, distortions also exist.[30] The news media consistently underplay petty, nonviolent and white-collar offenses while they overplay interpersonal, violent, and sexual crimes. Invariably, media portrayals of criminals tend to be one-dimensional reflections of the crimes commonly committed by the poor and the powerless and not those crimes commonly committed by the rich and powerful.[31] By contrast, with respect to news media images of the criminal justice system in general and of crime fighters in particular, distortions persist that are contradictory in nature. For example, while the docudramas and news tabloid shows repeatedly represent the police as gallant warriors fighting the forces of evil on the one side and mainstream news constructions on the other side, they often personify the agents of crime control as negatively ineffective and incompetent. Nevertheless, the outcome or "the cumulative effect of these portraits is support for more police, more prisons, and more money for the criminal justice system."[32]

Mass Media, Public Order, and Symbolic Deviance

When it comes to reporting crime news there is journalistic tension between those objective norms that call for images that reflect actual crime in amount and type, and those organizational norms that recognize that crime stories are a commodity whose audience or market value "may be higher than its value according to other criteria: relevance, accuracy, concern about effect, real significance."[33] In newsmaking practice, however, crime reporting is shaped more by the way the system of law enforcement and crime control works than by either official or unofficial crime statistics or by audience demand.[34] The lessons learned from news stories about successful and unsuccessful "crime fighting" tend to reinforce and thus support the dominant power relations in society, as individuals rather than social relations are inevitably portrayed as the problem. Such lessons are also consistent with more general media stories that cultivate a mainstream set of outlooks, assumptions, and beliefs about behavior[35] that confront symptoms divorced from their institutional and constitutive elements.

The model of the media as a process that contributes to social conformity and consensus is thought to work through the symbolic rewarding and punishing of good and bad deeds. Symbolic rewarding is accomplished primarily by identifying heroes, villains, and neutral characters and associating them with specific traits, beliefs, or kinds of behavior. Symbolic punishment is achieved through labeling or stigmatizing certain activities or traits as antisocial, deviant, or undesirable. Sometimes this rewarding and punishing is done explicitly; sometimes it is accomplished by way of unspoken assumptions or by the framing of news accounts. The essentially ideological construction of symbolic deviance occurs against the backdrop of a taken-for-granted normality of existing social arrangements. The outcome of this symbolic policing process is the resolution of short-term conflicts and the restoration of public orders for the primary benefit of the status quo.

This is not to suggest that the media are fixed and stagnant; on the contrary, by their very nature, media are active and subject to changing norms and values. The mass media also have a dialectical relationship with their object matter. For example, although there is still great concern over the racism and sexism found in fictional and nonfictional media accounts of criminals and victims, there has been a shift in media presentation away from a strongly normative control of marginals and toward one of increasing ambivalence, tolerance, and even solidarity with minorities and other "deviant" groups such as single parents, homosexuals, the mentally ill, and the homeless.[36] Sometimes the media follow social trends and the dictates of their audiences; sometimes they are out front of their audiences, creating social trends.

Examples of mass media following the trends in economic and social development include two of the most successful prime-time television situation comedies of the early 1990s, *Roseanne* and *Murphy Brown*. Both shows reflect different responses to the breakdown of the traditional nuclear family under the stress of advanced capitalism, and both fulfill the respective needs of their changing demographic audiences. In very distinct yet related ways, these shows also reflect the way gender relations are changing in American society. In the first sitcom, a white working-class nuclear family barely "makes ends meet" through the relatively shared economic obligations and responsibilities of mother and father. In the second sitcom, as Rapping[37] has discussed, the unmarried and independent Murphy Brown represents the triumph of decades of work by feminists, inside and outside the media industry, to change the way gender issues—at least as they pertain to white, middle-class women—are understood and portrayed.

Social Control, News Media, and Political Change

Both functional and critical theories of communication associate the working of mass media with social order. Functional theories attribute to mass media the purpose of securing stability and continuity by establishing a broad consensus of values. Critical theories argue similarly that powerful class elites use the mass media to impose dominant views while marginalizing/delegitimating views of opposition.

The dialectical view employed here recognizes the interactive and contradictory processes inherent in the functional and critical relations of mass communications. It also assumes that people as individuals and groups are actively struggling throughout society, with very uneven degrees of success and failure, to create through the mass media their own social order out of the materials made available to them from the political economy. As McQuail correctly points out, "Whatever the choice of theory, no evaluation can be made without first determining *whose* order might be sustained or disrupted by mass media: that of society, of ruling elites or [of] what individuals choose to construct for themselves."[38]

Clearly the mass and news media are both intricately connected to the maintenance of public order. Nevertheless, in the process of social control, the news media in particular can be viewed as exhibiting value or normative contradictions that may facilitate both order and change. For example, during the Vietnam War, as Lefever, Gitlin, and Paletz and Entman[39] have shown, and contrary to popular and critical belief, the press did not undermine the patriotic cause but actually shifted its coverage over a ten-year period in reflection of the changing political momentum. What transpired was that the news media helped to frame opposition to the war as respectable only after the war had lost its legitimacy not only with the anti-war activists and demonstrators but with a section of the established elite as well.

By comparison, during the Gulf War of 1991, the news media experienced much angst about its manipulation by the government. In fact, the press took a great deal of heat from media critics as it was characterized as a lapdog for the Pentagon.[40] Faced with the kind of censorship that the press received, its role became one of primarily cheerleading and propagandizing for the U.S. forces of good against the evils of Saddam Hussein. And, while critics decried the media's unexplicated attachment to the "national interest" and to the values of "patriotism," news media pundits of all political persuasions were shedding buckets of tears in print and on the air about the repressive censors at the Pentagon. The point is simply that the press's constricted views reveal multiple and even contradictory roles, including that of an alleged "lapdog" on behalf of the powers that be, "watchdog" on behalf of the citizens that be, and "neuterdog" on behalf of the value-neutral journalists that be. Therefore, the news media should be correctly understood as multi- rather than one-dimensional.

Similarly, when it pertains to civil disturbance, domestic unrest, and localized violence, media performance has varied according to the nature of the case and local conditions. Generally, however, there seem to be at least two widely shared perspectives, both inside and outside the media: "First, that media *ought* to report such happenings fully and fairly, because of the public 'need to know'; secondly, that their reporting should not itself contribute to illegal behaviour."[41] Of course, these roles sometimes come into conflict with each other.

On close observation, it appears that the news media have reacted both to the conventional norms of media performance and to what is viewed as "in the public interest." On the one hand, when legitimacy has been claimed for civil disturbance and when the aim has been to redress some known and considerable grievance, or where a deep political division has been present, the news media have tended to distance themselves from authorities. Those cases, for example, have included anti-war protests, major strikes, and political and civil rights demonstrations. On the other hand, when those more illegitimate forms of civil disturbance (i.e., responses to alleged police misbehavior or unfair jury verdicts) have occurred and involved violent rioting or crimes against property, the news media have been more likely, within and without the boundaries of "truth" and "balance," to side with the existing forces of law and order.[42]

Finally, despite its sometimes adversarial role, the news media typically follow rather than lead the masses or elites in social or political change. Moreover, the mass media generally subscribe to the cultural norms of solidarity and social identity. In the words of McQuail, "there is a latent power to advance collective ends and humanitarian goals, but it is very sporadically and selectively exercised."[43] In part this is a result of the fact that the news media are not primary social actors. In part this also is due to two of the fundamentals of newsmaking: "one is the primacy of media organizational goals, another the fact that media are generally instruments, not instigators, of other social forces."[44]

The relationship between news media and social solidarity refers to the capacity of the mass media, in general, to promote "pro-social" or "positive" values, to symbolically sympathize or empathize with individuals or groups in trouble or need, as well as to the "public recognition of shared risks, sorrows and hardships, which reminds people of their common humanity."[45] The pro-social values are also part of the domain of social control, bringing us full circle to the question of policing versus changing the symbolic environment. The news media in particular are capable of making their audiences feel intimate with the wider community, society, or "global village" as it were, thereby aiding audiences in their ability to share in or experience the collective life of humankind.

Both the categories of media formats and the social problems in which the collective expression of empathy appear are varied and numerous. Media formats include news background, documentary and docudrama, realistic fiction such as TV soap operas, editorial comments, letters to newspapers, appeals for support, fund-raising efforts and media campaigns on behalf of groups, advertising in the media, and attention to talk shows. With respect to social problems, the list is practically endless, but it also includes a "social desirability" factor that is reflected in the distribution of empathic attention by the media.[46] Some of the more identifiable problems that receive sympathetic attention are all kinds of illness and disability, homelessness and poverty, old age, racial and sexual discrimination, and victimization through child abuse and neglect. Some of the less identifiable problems that can still receive sympathetic attention include drug addiction, juvenile delinquency, conditions of criminalization, and dehumanizing prison conditions.

Between the "more" or "less" identifiable problems lies the arena in which newsmaking criminologists can draw fundamental relations that constitute all social problems. By seizing and redefining the empathy or affective factor within the processes of newsmaking, criminologists can not only assist the press in their quest to provide the most accurate information about crime and justice, about criminals and victims, and about what works and does not work in the struggle to reduce crime and punishment, but they can also inform and alter public attitudes and understanding of law and order. Concomitantly, newsmaking or constitutive criminologists can deconstruct and reconstruct the perceptions of crime and justice, and provide the necessary public service of assisting to demystify both the structural causes of crime and the cultural obstacles to social and economic justice.

Reconstructing Crime News: The Worst, the Bad, and the Good

Both the news media and the public find themselves trapped, seemingly forever, in morality plays of "good" versus "evil." Accordingly, the deconstruction and reconstruction of crime news involve the development of a "replacement discourse" that understands that both the production of crime news and its performance evaluation, in terms of how well it explains and demystifies reality, require that newsmaking criminologists and others transcend dualistic analyses of mass media or crime news. As an illustration, I will now provide a limited overview of the shifting trends in crime news production as a means of revealing how a constitutive criminology can be used in evaluating the quality and transformative potential of various scenarios in crime and justice construction.

Worst News

While the medium may still be the message, *the* medium is still television. With respect to crime and justice, the news media's medium is the "reality" and tabloid news series. Coming into their own during Bush's tenure as president, the number of shows in this genre "have multiplied and garnered audiences at a terrifying rate."[47] By 1992 there were ten of these shows, mostly low-budget syndication deals, occupying the prime-time (family) viewing hours from 7 P.M. to 9 P.M. Among the best known are probably *Hard Copy* and *America's Most Wanted*: "Both feature a confusing mix of 'live footage' and dramatic re-creations of 'actual events.' And they both present a world view that . . . flirts dangerously with certain aspects of fascist ideology."[48] Concerning the social construction of crime, this is probably the worst news, especially if one believes in communications theory, which argues that attitudes and beliefs develop gradually in response to significant trends in media representation. Making these shows particularly dangerous is the absence of commentary by informed criminologists and other students of justice and social control.

Making these shows socially dangerous is the fact that serious commentary by media analysts or by political and cultural elites is conspicuously absent. It is somehow taken for fact by media pundits and commentators that these programs "address themselves to an audience assumed, implicitly, to be incredibly illiterate, gullible, and 'outside the loop' of serious social discourse."[49] In short, these television tabloids, obsessed with serial murderers, sexual abusers, scandals without political relevance, weird religious rites, and the occult, present themselves as "outside" the cultural and political mainstream. In reality, however, the high ratings of these shows reveal that they are integral to the cultural and ideological production of social control and crime.

For example, these shows mix in news stories about important members of the cultural and political world caught in scandal and intrigue, men and women who also may serve as positive role models and leaders of democratic institutions, together with news stories about degenerates and "nut cases." This interesting mixture of "high lives" and "low lives" for the mass consumption of "mid lives" helps to fuel political cynicism and apathy, if not outright despair.

Of course, while such portrayals of urban America may capture an important dimension of criminality, they fail miserably to communicate any sense of the constitutive elements of crime, and they mistakenly imply that the resolution of criminality and related social problems remains within the reach of law enforcement.

By contrast, the relatively unfocused, unprecedented, and short-lived attention paid by the news media to violence by local police forces in the context of their routine operations, brought about by the repeated replay of the Rodney King beating by the Los Angeles police, is related to the fact that then-Attorney General Dick Thornburgh and his staff, a year after the beating, still had no clear answer to the query of whether there are any local, regional, or national patterns of police misconduct or brutality. Not only does the federal government not know the answer to this question for Los Angeles, it does not know the answer for any police organizations across the nation. In particular, the Bureau of Justice Statistics within the Justice Department, which collects all kinds of data on crime and law enforcement, does not collect statistics on police violence in American society. Conspicuously absent from the annual publication of the Bureau's 700-plus-page *Sourcebook on Criminal Justice Statistics* are any data on the number of civilians shot by the police, times police use deadly force, citizen complaints against the police, officers disciplined by departments and the nature of their offenses, or police processed for local crimes. Quietly and privately, however, some of these data have been collected. For example, the FBI maintains records of the number of complaints filed yearly against its agents. There is also the National Center for Health Statistics' poorly kept data on the number of persons killed by the police use of deadly force.[50] In short, since the government does not widely disseminate records of police misbehavior for public consumption, its agencies and the reporting media cannot tell us either how common or uncommon police brutality and violence are or in what cities they are most prevalent. Consequently, neither criminologists nor the public can study or compare how the police are doing in different localities across the country, establishing, if you will, a "quality of police" index for rating cities.

Without this kind of rudimentary knowledge of police behavior, no one has any answers; and so the news media ask no questions, rarely even addressing anecdotal evidence that they stumble upon. And, in the absence of a newsmaking reality, nothing can be done about a (significant or insignificant) social problem but to forget about it until the next time urban America erupts in response to real or imagined police oppression. As Chevigny has written, because "we have no systematic knowledge on the national level—either of the prevalence of police violence or what can be done about it—we simply don't recognize it as a persistent problem. The systematic ignorance of the federal government works very well to keep police violence off the national agenda."[51]

Meanwhile, it appears that camcorders and videotapes of police misbehavior in the hands of citizen sources will periodically circulate images locally and nationally through the electronic news media, reminding society of this police problem. Of course, these relatively rare crime news stories by amateur reporters are no match for the everyday reporting of the news media generally and for the prime time television fare of "reality" and tabloid news journalism particularly. With respect to the dearth of police violence stories, there are no government sources or newsmaking criminologists with the data to make sense of or to provide perspective for these media representations. Without context for explaining complex behavior, both the mass and news media tend to revert to their simplistic "good" versus "bad" cop scenarios, rather than to analyses that examine the social, institutional, organizational, and environmental interactions of police-citizen, police-criminal, and police-victim encounters. The end results are that much about police work remains unknown, or at least, hidden from mass consumption. And, therefore, much about police behavior that might change remains in place.

Bad News

When it comes to the social reconstruction of crime, there is an obvious need for newsmaking/constitutive criminologists to confront, challenge, and expose the "worst" crime news. Equally important is the need to confront "bad" crime news that figures so prominently in reproducing the very language, discourse, and thinking about crime and justice that needs replacement. What distinguishes the worst crime news from the bad crime news is that the former is more subtle and unconscious, the latter much more overt and recognizable by both experts and lay people.

Benedict's ethnomethodological, historical, and critical analysis of how the press covers sex crimes is here very instructive. Benedict argues that the coverage of sex crime has been steadily declining since the early 1980s:

> All in all, rape as a societal problem has lost interest for the public and the press, and the press is reverting to its pre-1970 focus on sex crimes as individual, bizarre, or sensational case histories—witness the furor over the celebrity rape case against William Kennedy Smith. Along with the loss of interest has come a loss of understanding.[52]

Benedict's book is based on a detailed examination of four very specific and prominent sex-crime cases: the 1979 Greta and John Rideout marital rape case in Oregon; the 1983 pool table gang rape of a woman in a New Bedford, Massachusetts, bar; the 1986 sex-related killing of Jennifer Levin by Robert Chambers in New York; and the 1989 gang rape and beating of a Central Park jogger in New York. In chronological order these four cases raised questions about marriage, ethnicity, class, and race. All of them should have raised questions of gender, but for the most part, the media coverage was silent on the subject. This news media omission reveals much about power/gender relations, about cultural attitudes, and about how public opinion and the press regard sex, women, and violent crime.

According to Benedict and others, the news media portrayals of these sex crimes generally reflected journalism's predominantly male and white constituency, especially in relationship to crime coverage; the still prevalent stereotypes associated with both rape and sex; the absence of any recognition or reference to misogyny in American society; and the tendency of the press to prefer individual to societal or cultural explanations of crime. They also revealed that these reporters and editors seemed more able to admit to their racism than their sexism. In short, these news people were more able to recognize the sick socialization of blacks in urban ghettos than the sick socialization everyone receives at schools, fraternities, and in society at large. Benedict further argues that the extent to which the press would not research and explain gang rape or cover the rape of the jogger as a gender-based crime exposed both the racism of coverage and the backlash against feminism in the United States during the 1980s.

Besides, even those news stories that bothered to examine "the mind of the rapist" were grounded in a familiar combination of individual pathology and such myths as "rape is sex" or "rape is motivated by lust." More fundamentally, the press's lack of understanding of the crime of rape was revealed by its inability to describe even the gruesome, bloody rape of the jogger, who became comatose and was near death, in nonsexual terms. Rather than talking in terms of the boys *grabbing* or even *touching* the jogger's breasts and legs, news accounts used such terms as *fondling* and sexually *exploring*. Instead of substituting such terms as *having sex with* for the rape, implying consent on the part of the victim, why not use the term *penetrate*, or why not the more realistic terms used by defendant Kharey Wise in his description of his "running" buddies' acts that night, which appeared in the *City Sun*: "Steve and Kevin both f——ed her. Ramon was holding her too and he was grabbing her tits and Antron was laughing and playing with her leg." The latter phraseology refers to the acts of rapacious behavior; the former phraseology refers to the acts of making love. It seems that the news media "still don't get it"—that is, the difference between rape and sex.

The common "spin" that kept these sex crime news stories alive was the press's ability to once again revert to its formulaic presentation of the "good" and "bad" morality play. Found in this familiar drama are the images of two Western puritanical classics portrayed "in the story of Eve as temptress and corruptor (the 'vamp'), and in the later Victorian ideal of woman as pure and uninterested in sex (the 'virgin')."[53] Combined with these antiquated and unrealistic thematic representations of women as either whores or Madonnas are the postmodern habits of media journalism. Whatever the gauge, women fare badly at the hands of the mass media. Taken in its totality, the representations of sex, crime, and rape, both in myth and in news media construction, serve to reinforce negative images of women and of social justice.

Sex crime victims tend to be squeezed into one of two images: either a wanton female who provoked the assailant with her sexuality; or pure and innocent, a true victim attacked by monsters. As Benedict explains:

> Both of these narratives are destructive to the victims of rape and to public understanding of the subject. The vamp version is destructive because it blames the victim of the crime instead of the perpetrator. The virgin version is destructive because it perpetuates the idea that women can only be Madonnas or whores, paints women dishonestly, and relies on portraying the suspects as inhuman monsters.[54]

Finally, in terms of replacement discourse, Benedict reminds us that the stigmatization of women by the coverage of sex crime victims in general and of victims of rape in particular will only be eliminated when these victims are taken seriously without having to hide behind the narratives of innocence and virginity, and when the mainstream news media assert in their representations "the role of women and the way men are trained to see them as objects of prey," as demonstrated in the jogger case.[55]

Good News

If there is any "good news" to report, it has to do with the fact that the news business has at least acknowledged its racist past and is sensitive to questions of race and racism in its contemporary practice. In relation to the Central Park rape, Lichter, Lichter, and Amundson offer another interpretation of the overall media coverage of crime in New York City. While they corroborate many of the findings of Benedict, especially as related to gender, the two analyses reach mixed conclusions with regard to the issues of race, class, and crime. With respect to gender, Lichter et al. agree with Benedict that lost in these news reports was the fact that this attack by a group of "wilding" teenagers was essentially a crime against women. But Lichter and her associates' analysis of local crime news reporting on the gang beating and rape makes the argument that both print and broadcast news media have improved their historically biased and racially stereotyped images of criminals and victims.

Set against the background of such racially charged "crimes" as Howard Beach, Tawana Brawley, and Bernhard Goetz, their content analysis determined that news media framed the Central Park rape case, first and foremost, by what the police called it, a "crime of opportunity." The attack also was portrayed as one of randomness, apparently lacking any purpose or meaning beyond the immediate gratification of its perpetrators. Amid the charges of racism and sensationalism that were raised and debated by media reports of the Central Park rape, Lichter et al. analyzed the topics, themes, and language of local media coverage beyween 20 April and 4 May 1989. In all they studied 406 news items from the evening newscasts of six New York television stations and from the city's four daily newspapers and one black weekly.

Consistent with most studies on the mass media, their content analysis revealed that news is not uniformly reported. It is not a mirror on reality but rather a prism "whose refracted images are formed not only by events but by the choices and perspectives of journalists and news organizations."[56] In other words, although the news prism is essentially the same, journalists and news organizations did differ, as the Lichter et al. study revealed, with respect to issues of race. By comparison, the variation or difference in mainstream news coverage of crime and justice was of less significance or consequence. As these researchers concluded about the reporting of the rape, it was "split between a populist tabloid approach (emotional language, focus on public outrage, and calls for "law and order" measures) and concerns about social responsibility (the frequent denial that race was relevant to crime)."[57] At the same time, however, as Lichter et al. point out, "the media missed an opportunity to confront racial undertones that well up in cases of interracial violence, even when no overt racial motive is present."[58]

Conclusion

In summary, the news media do not cover systematically all forms and expressions of crime and victimization. They emphasize some crimes and ignore others. They sympathize with some victims while blaming others. At the same time, with respect to the crime and justice covered by the news media, the performances vary in both quality and quantity. Some of that coverage has been characterized above as "worst," some as "bad," and some as "good." These distinctions refer not only to the distance between "objective" realities of crime and justice and their portrayals in the mass media but to the distortions between the crimes covered and the degree to which they are explained relative to the criminological knowledge base. These distinctions also refer to the varying potentials for each to facilitate what Henry and Milovanovic refer to as "transpraxis," or the ability of critical opponents of the status quo to be aware of the reconstitutive effects in their very attempts to neutralize or challenge "the reproductions of relations of production."[59]

Notes

An earlier version of this chapter was published in the journal *Humanity and Society* (1993), and is reprinted here by permission.

1. Gary D. LaFree, *Rape and Criminal Justice: The Social Construction of Sexual Assault* (Belmont, CA: Wadsworth, 1989).

2. LaFree, 236.

3. LaFree, 236.

4. Herbert Blumer, "The Crowd, the Public and the Mass," in *New Outline of the Principles of Sociology*, ed. Alfred M. Lee (New York: Barnes and Noble, 1939), 185.

5. Howard S. Becker, *Outsiders: Studies in the Sociology of Deviance* (New York: The Free Press, 1963).

6. Dragan Milovanovic, *Postmodern Law and Disorder: Psychoanalytic Semiotics, Chaos and Juridic Exegeses* (Liverpool: Deborah Charles Publications, 1992).

7. Stuart Henry and Dragan Milovanovic, "The Constitution of Constitutive Criminology: A Postmodern Approach to Criminological Theory," in *The Futures of Criminology*, ed. David Nelken (London: Sage, 1994), 110.

8. Alan Hunt, "The Big Fear: Law Confronts Postmodernism," *McGill Law Journal* 35 (1990): 507–40.

9. Henry and Milovanovic, "The Constitution of Constitutive Criminology," 130.

10. Gregg Barak, ed., *Media, Process, and the Social Construction of Crime: Studies in Newsmaking Criminology* (New York: Garland, 1994); Gregg Barak, "Newsmaking Criminology: Reflections on the Media, Intellectuals, and Crime," *Justice Quarterly* 5 (1988): 565–87.

11. Harold Pepinsky and Richard Quinney, eds., *Criminology as Peacemaking* (Bloomington: Indiana University Press, 1991), ix.

12. Ray Surette, ed., *The Media and Criminal Justice Policy: Recent Research and Social Effects* (Springfield, IL: Charles C. Thomas, 1990), 3.

13. George Gerbner et al., "Cultural Indicators: Violence Profile No. 9," *Journal of Communication* 28 (1978): 176–207; George Gerbner et al., "The Demonstration of Power: Violence Profile No. 10," *Journal of Communication* 29 (1979):

177–96; George Gerbner et al., "The Mainstreaming of America: Violence Profile No. 11," *Journal of Communication* 30 (1980): 10–29.

14. Surette, *The Media and Criminal Justice Policy*, 8.

15. L. Barrile, "Television and Attitudes about Crime" (Ph.D. diss., Boston College, 1980).

16. A. Marks, "Television Exposure, Fear of Crime and Concern about Serious Illness" (Ph.D. diss., Northwestern University, 1987).

17. Surette, *The Media and Criminal Justice Policy*, 8.

18. Stuart Henry and Dragan Milovanovic, "Constitutive Criminology: The Maturation of Critical Theory," *Criminology* 29 (1991): 307.

19. Anthony Giddens, *The Constitution of Society* (Oxford: Polity Press, 1984).

20. Henry and Milovanovic, "Constitutive Criminology," 295.

21. Daniel S. Claster, *Bad Guys and Good Guys: Moral Polarization and Crime* (Westport, CN: Greenwood Press, 1992), ix.

22. Simon Watney, *Policing Desire: Pornography, AIDS and the Media* (Minneapolis: University of Minnesota Press, 1987).

23. Claster, 3.

24. Herbert J. Gans, *Deciding What's News: A Study of CBS Evening News, NBC Nightly News, Newsweek and Time* (New York: Vintage Books, 1980).

25. Denis McQuail, *Media Performance: Mass Communication and the Public Interest* (London: Sage Publications, 1992), 162–63.

26. W. T. Gormley, "An Evaluation of the FCC's Cross Ownership Policy," *Policy Analysis* 6 (1980): 61–83; George Gerbner et al., "Charting the Mainstream: Television's Contributions to Political Orientation," *Journal of Communication* 32 (1982): 100–127.

27. Paul G. Hartman and Charles Husband, *Racism and Mass Media* (London: Davis Poynter, 1974); Teun Adrianus van Dijk, *Racism and the Press* (London: Routledge, 1991).

28. S. H. Miller, "The Content of News Photos: Women and Men's Roles," *Journalism Quarterly* 52 (1975): 70–75; Roy E. Blackwood, "The Content of News Photos: Roles Portrayed by Men and Women," *Journalism Quarterly* 60 (1983): 710–14.

29. McQuail, 166.

30. F. James Davis, "Crime News in Colorado Newspapers," *American Journal of Sociology* 57 (1952): 325–30; Mark Fishman, "Crime Waves as Ideology," *Social Problems* 25 (1978): 530–43; Doris Appel Graber, *Crime News and the Public* (New York: Praeger, 1980); Fred Fedler and Deane Jordan, "How Emphasis on People Affects Coverage of Crime," *Journalism Quarterly* 59 (1982): 474–78.

31. Vicky Munro-Bjorklund, "Popular Cultural Images of Criminals and Convicts Since Attica," *Social Justice* 18 (1991): 48–70.

32. Ray Surette, *Media, Crime and Criminal Justice: Images and Realities* (Pacific Grove, CA: Brooks/Cole, 1992), 249.

33. McQuail, 253.

34. Steve Chibnall, *Law-and-Order News* (London: Tavistock, 1977); Mark Fishman, *Manufacturing the News* (Austin: University of Texas Press, 1980); Surette, *Media, Crime and Criminal Justice.*

35. Gerbner et al., "Charting the Mainstream"; Nancy Signorielli and Michael Morgan, eds., *Cultivation Analysis* (Newbury Park, CA: Sage, 1990).

36. G. I. Berry, "Multicultural Role Portrayals on Television as a Social Psychological Issue," in *Television as a Social Issue,* ed. Stuart Oskamp (Newbury Park, CA: Sage, 1988), 88–102; Richard Campbell and Jimmie L. Reeves, "Covering the Homeless: The Joyce Brown Story," *Critical Studies in Mass Communications* 6 (1989): 21–42; Gregg Barak, *Gimme Shelter: A Social History of Homelessness in Contemporary America* (New York: Praeger, 1991).

37. Elayne Rapping, "Tabloid TV and Social Reality," *The Progressive* (August 1992): 35–37.

38. McQuail, 237.

39. Ernest W. Lefever, *Television and National Defense: An Analysis of News* (Washington, D.C.: Brookings Institution, 1976); Todd Gitlin, *The Whole World Is Watching* (Berkeley: University of California Press, 1980); David Paletz and Robert Entman, *Media, Power, Politics* (New York: The Free Press, 1981).

40. John R. MacArthur, *Second Front: Censorship and Propaganda in the Gulf War* (New York: Hill and Wang, 1992).

41. McQuail, 244.

42. McQuail, *Media Performance.*

43. McQuail, 273.

44. McQuail, 273.

45. McQuail, 263.

46. McQuail, *Media Performance.*

47. Rapping, 35.

48. Rapping, 35.

49. Rapping, 35.

50. Roy Roberg and Jack Kuykendall, *Police and Society* (Belmont, CA: Wadsworth, 1993).

51. Paul Chevigny, "Other Rodney Kings?: Let's Make It a Federal Case," *The Nation* 257 (23 March 1992): 371.

52. Helen Benedict, *Virgin or Vamp: How the Press Covers Sex Crimes* (New York: Oxford University Press, 1992), 251.

53. Benedict, 18.

54. Benedit, 24.

55. Benedict, 266.

56. Linda S. Lichter, Robert S. Lichter, and Daniel Amundson, "The New

York News Media and the Central Park Rape" (New York: Center for Media and Public Affairs, 1989), 15.

    57. Lichter, Lichter, and Amundson, "The New York News Media," 2.

    58. Lichter, Lichter, and Amundson, "The New York News Media," 2.

    59. Henry and Milovanovic, "Constitutive Criminology," 295.

PART THREE...
SUBCULTURE, STYLE, AND CRIME

8 ◆ ◆ ◆

Style Matters:
Criminal Identity and Social Control

JEFF FERRELL

A variety of social groups and events occupy the common ground between cultural and criminal activities—that is, between those activities organized around imagery, symbolism, and shared meaning, and those categorized by legal and political authorities as criminal. Bikers and skinheads, Bloods and Crips, 2 Live Crew and Robert Mapplethorpe all construct symbolic networks and cultural identities while they themselves are constructed by others as criminal. And in all of these cases, this interplay of cultural and criminal practices is in turn entangled with the practice of power, as played out in inequalities of social class, ethnicity, gender, and sexuality. Given this, the intersection of cultural and criminal activities constitutes an appropriate—indeed, essential— focus within the larger purview of criminology. If we are to understand emerging forms of legal and political authority, the inequalities embedded within contemporary legal and political arrangements, and the responses of people and groups to these inequalities, we must pay attention to the confluence of cultural and criminal processes in everyday life.

This chapter critically examines that most delicate but resilient of connecting tissues between cultural and criminal practices: style. As will be seen, *style* is considered here not as a vague abstraction denoting form or fashion, but as a concrete element of personal and group identity, grounded in the everyday practices of social life. *Style* is in this sense embedded in haircuts, posture, clothing, automobiles, music, and the many other avenues through which people present themselves publicly. But it is also located *between* people, and *among* groups; it constitutes an essential element in collective behavior, an element whose meaning is constructed through the nuances of social interaction. When this interaction emerges within a criminalized subculture, or between its members and legal authorities, personal and collective style emerges as an essential link between cultural meaning and criminal identity.

Style Past and Present

If we reconsider past research in criminology and related fields with an eye toward these sorts of issues, we can begin to see the importance of style in defining criminal and cultural activities. In research conducted some forty years ago, Finestone found that young black drug users were characterized not simply by their drug use but by precise forms of music and "proper dress," which they utilized, along with "charm, ingratiating speech . . . and unrestrained generosity," in an effort to make their "day-to-day life a gracious work of art."[1] During the 1960s Werthman and Piliavin reported that "the most important factor affecting the decision of juvenile officers is the attitude displayed by the offender," including the "style and speed with which the offender confessed." They added that "certain kinds of clothing, hair, and walking styles seem intrinsically to trigger suspicion" of black youth by police officers.[2]

By the 1970s a variety of studies began to substantiate these sorts of conclusions. Chambliss's classic report on the Saints and the Roughnecks demonstrated that the Roughnecks' "demeanor"—that is, the "hostility and disdain," or alternately the transparent "veneer of respect," that they presented to adult authorities, the "posture affected by the boys of the Roughneck ilk"—served as a "cue" that confirmed for the adults their criminality.[3] Allen and Greenberger also proposed (and tested) around this time an "aesthetic theory of vandalism," which highlighted the "sheer enjoyment" associated with the "aesthetic experiences" and symbolically defiant meanings of youthful vandalism. Here not only the style of the criminal but the stylishness of the criminal event itself began to define the meaning of criminality.[4]

During the 1970s and 1980s, those involved in British cultural studies and the British "new criminology" also began to investigate style as a crucial component in cultural and criminal activities. Clarke's classic essay, "Style," was reflected throughout the larger collection of which it was a part, and in in-depth case studies by Cohen, Willis, Hebdige, Cosgrove, and others.[5] In his study of working-class youth, for example, Willis found that the kids' deviation from and opposition to school authority

> is expressed mainly as a style. . . . Opposition to staff . . . is continuously expressed amongst "the lads" in the whole ambience of their behaviour, but it is also made concrete in what we may think of as certain stylistic/symbolic discourses centring on . . . clothes, cigarettes, and alcohol.[6]

Hebdige's study of punks and related youth subcultures echoed this notion of style as inherently intertwined with deviant identities and alternative subcultures; and Cosgrove's report on the criminalization of black and Latino zoot suiters in the 1940s pointedly labeled this conflict "style warfare."[7]

Contemporary research in criminology and related fields continues to expose the role of style in defining cultural practices, criminality, and social control. Like Cosgrove, Moore has elegantly described the process by which "youths wearing the zoot-suit costume anywhere in [Los Angeles] were chased and beaten, regardless of their behavior," and she traced larger linkages between style and crime as well.[8] Katz has developed an analysis of particular criminal exchanges and identities, and in so doing has located the various, negotiated meanings of personal style and aesthetics within both criminal events and subcultures, and larger patterns of age, social class, and ethnicity.[9] Anderson has carefully documented the sort of "street wisdom" involved in learning "the meaning of certain styles of hats, sweaters, jackets, shoes, and other emblems," as well as the emergent process by which black youths "camouflage themselves" through changes in clothing and presentation of self so as to minimize police harassment.[10] And in a recent analysis of black popular culture(s), Hall—in an updating of the British cultural studies perspective he helped establish two decades ago—likewise points out that "within the black repertoire, *style*—which mainstream cultural critics often believe to be the mere husk, the wrap-

ping, the sugar coating on the pill—has become *itself* the subject of
what's going on." He proceeds to discuss stylistic strategies and manifestations reminiscent of Finestone's and of Werthman and Piliavin's
accounts:

> . . . linguistic innovations in rhetorical stylization of the body, forms of
> occupying an alien social space, heightened expressions, hairstyles, ways
> of walking, standing, and talking, and a means of constituting and sus-
> taining camaraderie and community.[11]

Significantly, bell hooks and other writers have of late also discussed
the black experience in the United States in terms of politically charged
stylistic strategies and have linked these stylistic orientations to patterns of ethnic discrimination in housing, jobs, media—and the criminal justice system.[12] Likewise, much of the recent ethnographic
research on minority youth crime and youth gang involvement links
this sort of criminality to involvement in the alternative style and symbolism of youth subcultures and, drawing directly and indirectly on
Willis's classic analysis, demonstrates how these subcultural/stylistic
orientations help lock kids into cycles of criminalization and failure.[13]
Speaking for the public record, sociologist Malcolm Klein further links
increases in minority gang activity to the "diffusion of gang culture . . .
from caps to shoes to baggy pants to posture," and he warns the public
that "youths' emulating" of these styles "often ends up in gang activity."[14]
Other recent studies of Anglo and ethnically mixed youth subcultures engaged in criminal(ized) activities also find that style plays a key
role in both criminal identity and action and in official responses.
Hamm, for example, documents the role of subcultural style in the development of skinhead ideology and violence and exposes the homologous process by which ideology, violence, and style intertwine.[15] I argue
elsewhere that contemporary hip-hop graffiti writing exists *essentially* as
a "crime of style," for both its practitioners and the legal and political
authorities who work to stop it. Graffiti "writers" organize their painting around personal and collective style, gain status and visibility from
both stylistic conventions and innovations, and in so doing develop a
stylish resistance to corporate culture and political power. Legal and
political authorities, caught within an "aesthetics of authority," in turn

launch elaborate campaigns to criminalize graffiti writing and to erase graffiti from the surfaces of the city.[16]

Contemporary controversies continue to confirm the power of style. In cities around the country, minority kids risk getting shot, or pulled over by the police, for wearing—perhaps accidentally, perhaps with deadly purpose—a red shirt or bandanna in a blue neighborhood. Others report police harassment based on the style of their cars or on the style and volume of music that emanates from their big-bass car stereos.[17] School authorities, amusement park owners, and shopping mall security forces ban sports team clothing, backward baseball caps, particular brands of boots and shoes, Dickie's work clothes, and other personal styles they view as gang-related; and an Arizona school principal reprimands a student for wearing a Batman/Penguin shirt, alleging that the shirt "was a sign of devil worship."[18] A juvenile detention facility dresses all prisoners in "identical yellow jumpsuits" in an attempt to "break down gang ties based on colors and clothing styles."[19] Parents worry about buying the professional sports team jackets their kids want. Forty-five Denver kids were robbed of their jackets in one seventy-five-day period during the winter of 1992–93, for example, and the pace continues—to the point that local police now run jacket-theft sting operations, sports store owners and athletic-wear manufacturers consider putting "no gang" patches on the jackets, and a sixteen-year-old is "shot to death because someone wanted his Broncos jacket."[20]

In many cases the subtleties of style shape the ambiguous boundaries between cultural traditions and crime. In southern California, school and legal authorities wonder whether the self-styled "posses" to which more and more kids belong constitute gangs, or gang alternatives; as one school administrator says, "It's all very confusing. The kids might know what they're talking about but most adults don't."[21] In Denver a concerned citizen writes to the sports editor of the local paper about the new baseball team's jerseys:

> Unfortunately, black is the favorite color of gangs, and others who are in the business of intimidating "the other guys." Because most of us want the Colorado Rockies to be a family-oriented sport, and it goes without saying that children will emulate sports figures, let's not have our kids running around in black.[22]

Also in Denver, friends of a young man shot to death take pains to point out that, despite his involvement in hard-core rap music and his personal style, he was "definitely not a gang-banger. To look at him with his braids and his droopy jeans and stuff, you'd think he's just another gang kid, but that's just the way kids look today."[23] In New Hampshire, the owner of Drive-By Fashions riddles clothing with bullet holes "to his customers' specifications"; when criticized for "profiting from gang violence," he responds, without apparent irony, "It's just a fashion statement. If you try to read anything into it, you're just dead wrong."[24] In Denver, Los Angeles, and throughout the West, young Latinos and Latinas wear t-shirts designed by local artists to reflect their ethnic heritage. The artists note, again with no apparent irony intended, that their most popular t-shirts feature 1940s zoot suiters, and that they hope the t-shirts will not be identified with gangs![25] And in Los Angeles, the *Los Angeles Times* runs a half-page photo of a thirteen-year-old graffiti tagger above a story entitled "War of the Walls." Leaning against a tagged wall, his face covered by a black baseball cap and black bandanna, his body engulfed in ultra-baggy shirt and pants, he does indeed seem to share with the zoot suiters of a half-century ago a remarkable extremism of style.[26]

Clearly, then, both past scholarship and contemporary controversies confirm that kids, criminals, and authorities engaged with the criminal process are at the same time engaged in matters of style. They further reveal that kids, criminals, and authorities take style seriously; for all of them, style matters. But what are we, as criminologists, to make of this? In what ways should style, therefore, matter to us?

Style, Interaction, Authority, and Amplification

Style

To begin with we must pay attention to style because style defines the social categories within which people live, and the communities of which they are a part. For kids (and adults), style serves as a ready and visible medium for negotiating status, for constructing both security and threat, and for engaging in criminality. When kids participate in mainstream, noncriminal activities and cultures, they operate within an elaborate system of commercial appeal and consumption; with great care and grave consequences, they negotiate status, identity, and community through styles and makers of clothing, shirttails tucked and untucked, over- or under-sized garments, precisely cut hair, subtleties of eyeliner and blush, and a host of other devices. Why should we expect that alternative or criminal youth cultures should operate differently?

Can we really imagine, for example, that youthful gang members are defined by their violence, their association with drugs, or their criminal records, and then just happen to adopt intricately symbolic clothing styles, flash gang colors and hand signals, take on stylish street names, and write highly stylized graffiti? Could it be that young (and old) bikers are defined simply by owning and riding motorcycles and then just happen to sort and signify themselves and their bikes through an elaborate system of motorcycle models and accessories, tattoos, hats, gloves, boots, key and wallet chains, and "colors"? Can it be that the particular styles of those noted previously—drug users, Roughnecks, British working-class kids, punks, zoot suiters, skinheads, graffiti writers—somehow stand apart from the lived experience of their criminal identities? A careful look at these and other cases tells us that style cannot be dismissed as epiphenomenal; in the same way that style gives substance to noncriminal group life and identity, it shapes the substantive experience of those engaged in criminal(ized) subcultures and communities.[27]

Moreover, style defines the lived experience of ethnicity, social class, and other essential social (and sociological) categories. When Stuart Hall asserts that "within the black repertoire, *style* . . . has become *itself* the subject of what's going on," when bell hooks proclaims that "my 'style' ain't no fashion," we begin to see that ethnicity is largely constructed and presented in everyday life through collective stylistic strategies.[28] When we consider the many differences between Armani suits and soiled coveralls, between older American automobiles and newer imports, between proper words chosen and improper gestures made, we begin to see also the styles through which social class is expressed and evaluated in everyday life. In this sense ethnicity and social class reside less with skin color or dollars than they do with participation in various collective styles; they emerge from socially symbolic stances that locate individuals and groups in the larger society. In the moments of lived experience, style becomes the medium through which social categories take on meaning.[29]

To participate in a community—large or small, ethnic or ideological, criminal or noncriminal—is therefore to participate in style as collective action. When members of a community each choose particular haircuts, clothes, or postures, they knowingly and unknowingly engage in collective behavior—collective behavior lodged in the particular styles adopted. Collective style serves, in Durkheim's terms, as the social glue that holds subcultures and communities together; in terms of differential association, stylistic codes and conventions constitute a significant portion of the "techniques" and "motives" learned within a criminal community. A multitude of historical and cultural forces intersect in a baseball cap turned backward, a pair of Doc Marten boots or Chuck Taylor hightops, a team sports jacket; and to acquire these items is to acquire not just the items but at least a faint taste of these forces as well, and the meanings and consequences they carry for the individual and the community.

To wear particular clothes, drive certain cars, or listen to distinctive types of music is in this sense to make oneself *stylistically visible*, to those both inside and outside the subculture or community. Whether intentionally or not, it is to declare one's membership. My research among Texas bikers, for example, revealed that the wearing of "colors" references issues of group loyalty and territoriality. A biker not wearing colors can therefore enter a tough biker bar with a sort of immunity that a biker sporting colors cannot, because he is, in stylistic terms, invisible. Similarly, the adoption of certain gang or hip-hop styles can lead to conflict or harassment on the streets, not necessarily because the individual sporting such styles is perceived as a direct threat, but because such styles present that person as a visible player in the larger game of street style and toughness. It is little wonder, then, that a mother whose son was robbed of a sports team jacket "had no idea of [the] trouble she was buying" in buying her son the jacket.[30]

This perspective leads us to reconsider, for example, the meaning of membership in youth gangs, and similarly, apparent predilections toward violence among gang members and other kids. If, as is often alleged, youth gangs exist in part out of a desire by their members to "belong," gangs may fulfill this desire largely by providing a sense of *aesthetic* belonging, of membership in an *aesthetic or stylistic community*. As a gang member, one carries the stylistic markers of membership at school and on the street, and thus lives out in hairstyle, dress, and comportment membership in the gang, even when physically apart from it. And this stylistic portability begins to explain the allure of gang-affiliated styles for other kids as well; with the right sorts of clothes or haircuts, they can participate, second-hand, in a meaningful stylistic community.

Similarly, kids' fascination with guns and violence may be built as much on the sensual aesthetics of weaponry and violence as on some raw desire to assault others. Certainly, the mass media have not only glorified weaponry and violence but eroticized and aestheticized them; that is, they have converted violence into a style of identification and action, and weaponry into a glamorous appendage essential to the identities of action heroes, tough guys, and cops. In this cultural context, gang members and other kids play with their guns, fondle and polish them, pass them around at parties, and utilize them as fantasy-world props.[31] In other words, they employ them as faddish symbols of status, as stylistic devices for constructing their evolving identities. As a recent mass media report on "gangsta rap" noted,

> For the gangsta rappers . . . guns are symbols of toughness and arrogance, the necessary elements of ghetto survival. For the wannabes cultivating a street-wise image, the implied menace of a pistol jammed into the waistband of baggy jeans is more a show of style.[32]

Violence itself—beatings, blood, and scar tissue—likewise becomes meaningful in this context as a stylized show of status and identity, as a ritualized mark of membership and belonging. Thus, Hamm's conclusions regarding skinheads may well characterize other youth gangs as well: "Violence is their signature trademark because *violence is part of subcultural style*."[33]

Here, of course, we see a remarkable intersection of individual identity, group interaction, market forces, and meaning—that is, a sort of stylized political economy of everyday life. For each person style becomes the medium for "presentation of self" and for defining that presented self as lodged within the larger stylistic orientations of the group, subculture, or community. These orientations, though, do not emerge from within the group alone but under the weight of heavy advertising campaigns, manipulative marketing strategies, and media saturation. Gang members, graffiti writers, and others invent their own styles less than they literally and figuratively buy into various sectors of mass, commodified fashion markets, and then homologously rework and reinvent the stylistic fragments that they pry loose for their own purposes.[34]

Reconfigured in this way, these styles do, in fact, come to represent internal group identity, but in so doing point once again beyond the group itself. At the level of capitalist commodification, these styles are often reincorporated into the mass markets from which they come, in an unfolding dialectic of subcultural innovation and market appropriation. Of more interest here, group styles become in everyday life *epistemic* and *symbolic* markers through which those *outside* the group also "read" group membership and subcultural identity, and thus come to "know" who is a gang member or a graffiti writer. That is, these styles acquire further layers of meaning in the intricacies of social interaction.

Interaction

When gang members or other kids wear gang-related styles, these styles confirm their membership in an aesthetic community not only because the kids recognize their meaning, but because others react to them as markers of gang identity. In this sense the styles draw the response that their wearers intend. But subcultural styles and their shadows also draw reactions not intended. Recently, for example, a young man told me of having his hair burred in the sort of buzz-cut style that is currently popular among a variety of youth subcultures. Though his intentions had only vaguely to do with experimentation and stylishness, the results were directly violent. He was soon thereafter assaulted by two young black men who accused him of being a racist, neo-Nazi skinhead. And though his hair is now longer, he refuses to return to the inner-city neighborhood where the assault took place. A student of mine, who identifies herself as "Hispanic, though I don't look it," also explained to me that she and her boyfriend had let their close-cropped hairstyles grow out because these styles regularly caused misunderstandings with others in regard to their ethnicity and politics. In Chicago a deaf-mute teenager who signed "I love you" was shot by gang members who mistook the sign for a rival gang's sign.[35] And the Denver mother who bought her son a team sports jacket likewise only intended to buy her son "the gift he'd wanted," and after the jacket was stolen, even talked with a store clerk who assured her that a second jacket wouldn't "get her son in trouble." After this second jacket was stolen at knifepoint, though, she sent her son out of town to live with relatives.[36]

In this context a Denver newspaper therefore publishes a guide to "deciphering the signals sent by teens' clothes." The guide includes a warning that "an innocent young baseball fan . . . may learn too late not to wear his team cap in some neighborhoods where it can symbolize gang membership"; the article also quotes a hospital psychologist: "It can be dangerous. . . . Here at the hospital we see kids who have been injured, beaten up, abused in awful ways because they were in the wrong place at the wrong time, wearing the wrong kinds of things."[37] Similarly, the director of a local gang-alternative program emphasizes that kids who wear sagging pants and other popular styles of clothing

> "are setting themselves up as targets." The best way to avoid being shot or mislabeled by police, he said, is to give gangs, gang fashion, and the gang lifestyle a wide berth: "Many of these kids think this is a game, but it's a very serious game. A lot of them don't know the rules to the game. And if you don't know the rules to the game, you're going to get beat."[38]

And a Denver police officer tells kids, "Put on a Chicago Bulls jacket and a pair of pricey sneakers and you might as well paint a bull's eye on your back," and warns them "of the hazards of stylin'."[39]

Such cases confirm that style operates not only as a manifestation of individual and group identity but as a critical component in social interaction. Put differently, style constitutes much of the "symbolic" in the symbolic interactions of everyday life.[40] When others react to you based on the style you present, and you then react to their reactions, an interactive dynamic has emerged that reinforces and reconstructs the meaning of that style for you and others. As just seen, this dynamic may carry the individual beyond his or her own intentions and create consequences beyond those that could have been anticipated. For kids who choose to wear a buzz-cut or a team sports jacket, reactions to these choices alter their understandings of themselves, others, and the styles involved. Thus, as before, style comes closer to being a causal factor than a casual epiphenomenon; it shapes the nature of social interaction and the meanings that evolve from it.

Style in this sense exists not as a stationary entity but as a negotiated social process. The meaning of style resides not only in clothes and on the body but *between* people, in the interplay of identities, in the reading and counterreading of stylistic cues. This stylistic process goes on within criminal and noncriminal subcultures—thus creating various stylistic communities—and between subcultural members and those whom they encounter in their daily lives. And of all these stylistic encounters, certainly the most critical in shaping daily experience and determining crime and criminality are those with legal and political authorities.

Authority and Amplification

This notion of style as an essential component in symbolic interaction returns us to some of the research already seen. Werthman and Piliavin, it will be recalled, reported that for juvenile officers, "certain kinds of clothing, hair, and walking styles" caused suspicion of black kids and others, and that "the attitude displayed by the offender" often decided the case.[41] Willis likewise noted that the conflict between working-class kids and school authorities "is expressed mainly as a style"; Chambliss found the "demeanor" of the lower-class Roughnecks to be a deciding factor in their harsh treatment by school and legal authorities; and both Cosgrove and Moore reported on the "style warfare" between black and Latino/Latina zoot suiters and the police.[42] As already seen, contemporary controversies regarding police and judicial responses to gang involvement, graffiti writing, and other subcultural activities also sketch connections between social power, legal status, and style.

These past and present cases point to a single conclusion: legal authorities read and respond to the styles of lower-class and ethnic minority kids (and adults), to their collective presentations of self and constructions of identity, and in so doing push them into downward cycles of criminalization. As before, ethnicity here becomes a factor in criminalization not as an abstraction having to do with color of skin but as a set of stylistic orientations that both construct one's ethnic identity and draw the sort of attention from authorities that will further define and limit it.[43] Similarly, poverty connects with criminalization not from a simple lack of money or power but by way of stylistic cues that "invite" police attention and harassment. And thus, discriminatory policing or differential enforcement in turn become meaningful, not simply as statistical residues of arrest rates, but as interactive dynamics through which authorities pay more attention to one group than another and read (and misread) the stylistic patterns that construct group identity. To put it bluntly, trouble with the police or other authorities comes less from being "black" or "poor" or "young" as such than it does from particular automobiles, clothes, haircuts, and postures that signify these statuses to those in authority.

Style in this sense exists as the *medium* through which disadvantaged groups and legal authorities interact, the *locus* of inequality and power—the place where power relations are played out and resisted—and therefore, the *catalyst* that precipitates the sorts of inequitable interactions that further label and amplify group activities as criminal. The power of subcultural styles is such that they become important cultural currency, not only for those "outsiders" who develop and adopt them but for legal and political authorities as well.

Miller's essay in this book (Chapter 10), for example, exposes the many ways in which gang symbolism and style exist as the medium of meaning for both gang members and the probation officers who attempt to control them. Probation officers read gang styles as emblematic of defiance and gang immersion, enforce court orders prohibiting gang clothing, confiscate gang paraphernalia, and display their confiscated collections on office walls. As Rodriguez shows, Immigration and Naturalization Service officials likewise detain and deport Latino/Latina kids "simply because they were caught dressed like 'gang-bangers' and without proper identification." And in the countries to which the kids are deported, style continues to matter; as Rodriguez reports, "recently, a Salvadoran police officer burned and then cut off the 'homeboy' braid of a deported Los Angeles youth."[44] Plaza similarly documents "the look"—"polyester pants, loud makeup, or cowboy boots with slanted heels"—that constitutes for U.S. border patrol agents an informal "illegal alien" profile in El Paso, Texas. She also documents extensive legal and extra-legal harassment of Mexican Americans based on this sort of stylistic profile, and her own experiences in being tailed by border patrol agents while "dressed . . . as a low-income Mexican woman."[45] The "drug courier profiles" integral to the contemporary "war on drugs" in the United States of course manifest this same dynamic, with their ethnic and social-class characterizations linked to make and model of car, tinted windows, clothing, and other stylistic factors.[46] In each of these cases, legal authorities interpret particular configurations of ethnic and social-class style as indicators of criminality, and in so doing push those who exhibit them into criminal(ized) identities.[47]

The stylistic orientations of disadvantaged groups thus symbolize prior social inequality and group identity, and at the same time propel group members toward further victimization and criminalization. For members of these groups, style carries the history and future of group affiliation, and criminalization; it incorporates past encounters with the legal system and precipitates new ones. In the lived experience of identity and inequality, personal and group style exists as a badge of resistance and honor and, at the same moment, a stigmata.[48] It sets in motion, and keeps in motion, spirals of criminalization and inequality.

To examine subcultural styles and legal response in this way is not, of course, to blame the victim, to imply that those who adopt these styles somehow cause their own failure. Rather, it is to reveal the interactional dynamic by which subcultural styles, when played out in a context of vast inequality and powerful legal authority, become interpersonal markers through which inequality is amplified, and those caught up in inequality are criminalized. More broadly, a focus on style begins to expose the lived dynamics of inequality and injustice, the ongoing social process by which discriminatory legal practices and emerging criminal identities are constructed and continued in the situations of daily life.

Criminology, Social Interaction, and Style

In sketching the meaning of style for legal authorities and those they seek to control, the previous discussions also highlight the meaning of style for criminology. As these discussions show, core concerns of criminology—criminal and subcultural identity, the links between criminality and social inequality, the nature of legal control—are manifest in the stylistic orientations of subcultures and communities. Shared styles define the social and cultural boundaries of criminal and noncriminal communities alike and give texture and meaning to the experience of membership in these communities. Broad categories of social class and ethnicity also find expression in stylistic orientations, which further construct identity and difference along fault lines of social inequality. And these stylistic orientations, constructed as they are from mediated images and advertised commodities, in turn reveal the many ways in which people and groups convert the economic inequalities of mass, capitalist culture into the popular culture of everyday life.[49]

Perhaps most importantly, stylistic orientations are of concern to criminology because they are the medium through which inequitable legal practices take shape. If style constitutes the connecting tissue between cultural practices and criminal identities, it also forms the connecting tissue between disadvantaged groups and agents of legal control. As we have seen, legal authorities read and react to subcultural styles as the stains of prior criminality and the predictors of future crime. In so doing, of course, they set up self-fulfilling prophecies in which these styles become catalysts for further legal entanglement. In a context of inequitable legal control, then, subcultural styles exist for legal authorities as both the cause and effect of criminality, and for marginalized groups as both symbols of resistance and invitations to control. Such styles engage legal authorities and subcultural members in spiraling cycles of interpretive interaction, which shape and expand existing inequalities.

An understanding of style thus develops both critical and interactionist criminologies and begins to integrate them as well. It sharpens the political edge of symbolic interactionist and labeling theories of crime, revealing how symbolic exchanges around criminality reproduce social inequalities. In the same way, it grounds the essential insights of critical criminology—as to the social class and ethnic dimensions of crime, differential enforcement, and legal injustice—in an awareness of the daily processes of social interaction. Certainly broad critiques of inequality and injustice are important. But as the many subtleties of style remind us, we must ask, in situation after situation, precisely how and why such inequalities are constructed. As Hebdige argues, "Rather than presenting class as an abstract set of external determinations," we must reveal class "working out in practice as a material force, dressed up, as it were, in experience and exhibited in style."[50] This attentiveness to the lived experience of inequality and injustice moves criminology past the old antinomies of structure and agency, society and small group. It also points, time and again, back to style. For kids, criminals, and legal authorities caught up in a process of symbolic meaning and official reaction, and for criminologists who work to unravel the lived politics of this process, style matters.[51]

Notes

1. Harold Finestone, "Cats, Kicks, and Color," in *The Other Side: Perspectives on Deviance*, ed. Howard S. Becker (New York: The Free Press, 1964), 284–85.

2. Carl Werthman and Irving Piliavin, "Gang Members and Police," in *The Sociology of Juvenile Delinquency*, ed. Ronald Berger (Chicago: Nelson-Hall, 1991), 359, 362.

3. William Chambliss, "The Saints and the Roughnecks," in *Down to Earth Sociology*, 6th ed., ed. James Henslin (New York: The Free Press, 1991), 273, 274. See alternately David Klingler, "Demeanor or Crime? Why 'Hostile' Citizens Are More Likely to Be Arrested," *Criminology* 32 (1994): 475–93; and also Richard Lundman, "Demeanor or Crime? The Midwest City Police-Citizen Encounters Study," *Criminology* 32 (1994): 631–56.

4. Vernon Allen and David Greenberger, "An Aesthetic Theory of Vandalism," *Crime and Delinquency* 24 (1978): 310. See similarly Nick Lowe's song, "(I Love the Sound of) Breaking Glass," in Nick Lowe, *Basher: The Best of Nick Lowe* (1984).

5. John Clarke, "Style," in *Resistance Through Rituals*, ed. Stuart Hall and Tony Jefferson (London: Hutchinson, 1976), 175–91; Stanley Cohen, *Folk Devils and Moral Panics* (London: MacGibbon and Kee, 1972); Paul Willis, *Learning to Labor* (New York: Columbia University Press, 1977); Dick Hebdige, *Subculture: The Meaning of Style* (London: Methuen, 1979); Stuart Cosgrove, "The Zoot-Suit and Style Warfare," *Radical America* 18 (1984): 38–51.

6. Willis, 12, 17.

7. Hebdige, *Subculture*; Cosgrove, "Zoot-Suit"; see Tricia Henry, *Break All Rules! Punk Rock and the Making of a Style* (Ann Arbor: UMI Research Press, 1989).

8. Joan W. Moore, "Isolation and Stigmatization in the Development of an Underclass: The Case of Chicano Gangs in East Los Angeles," *Social Problems* 33 (1985): 6. See also Ralph Turner and Samuel Surace, "Zoot-Suiters and Mexicans: Symbols in Crowd Behavior," *American Journal of Sociology* 62 (1956): 14–20.

9. Jack Katz, *Seductions of Crime: Moral and Sensual Attractions in Doing Evil* (New York: Basic Books, 1988); see Jeff Ferrell, "Making Sense of Crime: A Review Essay on Jack Katz's *Seductions of Crime*," *Social Justice* 19 (1992): 110–23.

10. Elijah Anderson, *Streetwise: Race, Class, and Change in an Urban Community* (Chicago: University of Chicago Press, 1990), 231, 197.

11. Stuart Hall, "What Is This 'Black' in Black Popular Culture?" *Social Justice* 20 (1993): 109, emphasis in original; Finestone, "Cats"; Werthman and Piliavin, "Gang Members."

12. See, for example, bell hooks, "My 'Style' Ain't No Fashion," *Z Magazine* 5 (May 1992): 27–29; bell hooks, *Black Looks: Race and Representation* (Boston: South End Press, 1992); Richard Majors and Janet Mancini Billson, *Cool Pose: The Dilemmas of Black Manhood in America* (New York: Lexington, 1992); Holly Sklar, "Young and Guilty by Stereotype," *Z Magazine* 6 (July/August 1993): 52–61. See also Robin D. G. Kelley, "Know the Ledge," *The Nation* 258 (14 March 1994): 350–55.

13. See, for example, Mercer Sullivan, *"Getting Paid": Youth Crime and Work in the Inner City* (Ithaca: Cornell, 1989); Joan W. Moore, *Going Down to the Barrio: Homeboys and Homegirls in Change* (Philadelphia: Temple, 1991); Moore, "Isolation"; Felix Padilla, *The Gang as an American Enterprise* (New Brunswick, NJ: Rutgers, 1992); John Hagan, "Structural and Cultural Disinvestment and the New Ethnographies of Poverty and Crime," *Contemporary Sociology* 22 (1993): 327–32; Willis, *Learning*.

14. In Thaddeus Herrick, "Sociologist Says Gang Culture Saturating Society, Los Angeles Not to Blame for Denver's Ills," *Rocky Mountain News*, 24 October 1993, 10A.

15. Mark S. Hamm, *American Skinheads: The Criminology and Control of Hate Crime* (Westport, CT: Praeger, 1993).

16. Jeff Ferrell, *Crimes of Style: Urban Graffiti and the Politics of Criminality* (New York: Garland, 1993).

17. See, for example, Brian Weber, "Cruisers Lose on West 38th," *Rocky Mountain News*, 23 April 1992, 7A; Bill Scanlon, " 'Harassing' of Youths Gets Hearing," *Rocky Mountain News*, 23 August 1993, 16A; and Tony Arguello, "Doing the Right Thing Sparks Controversy," *El Semanario* (*The Denver Post*), 14 April 1994, 1, 19, who reports that Latino/Latina youth in Denver "feel they have no rights, as to how they dress, how they wear their hair, or how their vehicles look. And all this determines if they will be stopped [by the police]." Recent interviews that I have conducted with former Latino/Latina gang and graffiti crew members in Denver confirm this sense of style as instrumental in defining not only subcultural identity but the nature and number of contacts with police.

18. "Arizona Teen Chewed Out in School for Wearing 'The Penguin' T-shirt," *Rocky Mountain News*, 12 November 1992, 41. See Karen Bailey, "Schools Target Gang Colors," *Rocky Mountain News*, 10 October 1990, 8, 11; John Ensslin, "3 Arrested as Elitch's Fights Gangs," *Rocky Mountain News*, 27 May 1991, 6; Robert Tomsho, "Dowdy Work Duds Make Fashion Statement," *Rocky Mountain News* (*Wall Street Journal*), 15 May 1993, 46A; "Mall Outlaws Backward Caps," *Rocky Mountain News*, 8 January 1994, 39A. Schools around the country have also banned kids from wearing saggy pants, noserings, and other personal paraphernalia; also banned is the wearing of Doc Marten boots, with or without the customized laces that allegedly signify subcultural affiliation.

19. Marlys Duran, "Teens Behind Bars," *Rocky Mountain News*, 6 March 1994, 22A, 32A.

20. John Ensslin, "Coat Bandits Terrorize Denver-Area Youths," *Rocky Mountain News*, 14 February 1993, 8; John Ensslin, "Mom Had No Idea of Trouble She Was Buying," *Rocky Mountain News*, 14 February 1993, 8; "Youths Steal Team Jackets," *Rocky Mountain News*, 10 November 1993, 27A; "Thieves Get 2 Sport Jackets," *Rocky Mountain News*, 17 November 1993, 23A; "Teen Arrested in Jacket Theft," *Rocky Mountain News*, 24 November 1993, 23A; "Boy Robbed of Jacket," *Rocky Mountain News*, 30 November 1993, 15A; "Cops Bait Jacket Thieves," *Rocky Mountain News*, 1 December 1993, 31A; Lynn Bartels, "Teen Nabbed in Sports Jacket Sting," *Rocky Mountain News*, 9 December 1993, 4A; J. R. Moehringer, "Killers Wanted Boy's Jacket," *Rocky Mountain News*, 3 December 1993, 5A; Charlie Brennan, "Sportsfan Stores Pushing 'No Gangs, No Drugs' Patches," *Rocky Mountain News*, 4 December 1993, 4A; Charlie Brennan, "Company May Put Anti-Crime Patch on Jackets," *Rocky Mountain News*, 10 December 1993, 20A; "Boys Robbed of Jacket, Cap," *Rocky Mountain News*, 11 April 1994, 15A; "Boy Gets Jersey Back," *Rocky Mountain News*, 8 June 1994, 29A; Ann Carnahan, "Teen Names Pal as Kid Who Killed for Jacket," *Rocky Mountain News*, 9 September 1994, 4A, 6A; "Sports Jacket Theft Reported," *Rocky Mountain News*, 25 October 1994, 22A; Lynn Bartels, "It Was a Night of Bad Tricks," *Rocky Mountain News*, 2 November 1994, 5A, 6A.

21. John Glionna, "Pals in the Posse," *Los Angeles Times*, 28 February 1993, B1, B3.

22. LeRoy Leapoldt, "Please, No Black Jerseys," *Rocky Mountain News*, 22 March 1992, 56. The local press subsequently reported that "three boys waiting for a bus were beaten by gang members . . . for wearing black"; see "Teen Trio Beaten by Gang," *Rocky Mountain News*, 31 October 1994, 12A.

23. In Charlie Brennan, "Death Played Muse for Carl Banks," *Rocky Mountain News*, 7 November 1993, 15A.

24. "He'll Put Bullet Holes in Your Clothes," *Rocky Mountain News*, 19 July 1994, 96A.

25. See Hector Gutierrez, "T-shirts Make a Cultural Statement," *Rocky Mountain News*, 3 May 1993, 26A; Hector Gutierrez, "Young and Proud Hispanics Wear Their Hearts on Their T's," *Rocky Mountain News (Las Noticias)*, 5 September 1993, 4N. See similarly Laquita Bowen Smith, "Kente Cloth Is a Symbol of African Heritage, Pride," *Rocky Mountain News (Scripps Howard)*, 9 June 1994, 90, on the emerging cultural meanings of kente cloth.

26. Michael Quintanilla, "War of the Walls," *Los Angeles Times*, 14 July 1993, E1. See similarly Ellison's description of zoot suiters, quoted in Cosgrove, 39. Remarkably, the Dickie's clothing, which some school officials have banned because of its alleged gang connotations, today thrives simultaneously in two

cultures—as blue-collar work attire and subcultural youth fashion; see Tomsho, "Dowdy."

27. See Jeff Ferrell, "The Brotherhood of Timber Workers and the Culture of Conflict," *Journal of Folklore Research* 28 (1991): 163–77; Ferrell, *Crimes*; and "Special Issue on Latin America," *Border/Lines* 27 (1993), for descriptions of the stylistic dimensions of youth cultures in Latin America. And as Iain Chambers, *Popular Culture: The Metropolitan Experience* (London: Methuen, 1986), 11, says, "Caught up in the communication membrane of the metropolis, with your head in front of a cinema, TV, video or computer screen, between the headphones, by the radio, among the record releases and magazines, the realization of your 'self' slips into the construction of an image, a style, a series of theatrical gestures."

28. Hall, "What Is This 'Black,' " 109, emphasis in original; hooks, "My 'Style,' " 27.

29. See similarly Michele Lamont and Marcel Fournier, *Cultivating Differences: Symbolic Boundaries and the Making of Inequality* (Chicago: University of Chicago Press, 1992); Fred Davis, *Fashion, Culture, and Identity* (Chicago: University of Chicago Press, 1992).

30. Ensslin, "Mom," 8.

31. See, for example, Romel Hernandez and Dean Krakel, "Teens, Guns and Violence in the Suburbs," *Rocky Mountain News*, 23 May 1993, 5A–6A, 8A–12A; also 24 May 1993, 8A–11A, on kids' rituals surrounding guns; and Grant Mc-Cracken, *Culture and Consumption* (Bloomington: Indiana, 1988), on similar new-commodity rituals among noncriminal groups. See similarly Ned Polsky, *Hustlers, Beats, and Others* (Garden City, NY: Anchor, 1969), 130–31, on attitudes toward guns among professional "heavy men." These rituals also return us to the aesthetics of crime, as discussed in Allen and Greenberger, "Aesthetic Theory"; Ferrell, *Crimes*; and elsewhere.

32. Michael Saunders, " 'Gangsta' Rap: Rising with a Bullet," *Rocky Mountain News (The Boston Globe)*, 27 October 1993, 24D.

33. Hamm, *Skinheads*, 62, emphasis in original. The practice of "beating in" new gang members and "beating out" ex-members clearly embodies the often ritualized, stylized, and symbolic nature of subcultural violence. See also Adrian Nicole LeBlanc, "While Manny's Locked Up," *New York Times Magazine*, 14 August 1994, 30–31, who reports on the scars that one youth gang member "wears like badges," and on how, for another, "the feeling of cutting . . . helps her escape."

34. See Hebdige, *Subculture*; Hamm, *Skinheads*; Alan Tomlinson, ed., *Consumption, Identity, and Style: Marketing, Meanings, and the Packaging of Pleasure* (London: Routledge, 1990).

35. Reported in Ray Hutchison, "Blazon Nouveau: Gang Graffiti in the Bar-

rios of Los Angeles and Chicago," in *Gangs: The Origins and Impact of Contemporary Youth Gangs in the United States,* ed. Scott Cummings and Daniel Monti (Albany: State University of New York Press, 1993), 171.

36. Ensslin, "Mom," 8.

37. Karen Abbott, "Dress Code," *Rocky Mountain News,* 2 November 1993, 8D, 10D.

38. Charlie Brennan, "Give Gang Culture a Wide Berth, Open Door Director Advises," *Rocky Mountain News,* 14 December 1993, 28A.

39. Steve Waldman, "'Stylin': Gangs and Good Kids: It's Getting Harder and Harder to Tell Them Apart," *Up the Creek,* 23–29 April 1993, 8–9.

40. See, for example, Norman K. Denzin, *Symbolic Interaction and Cultural Studies: The Politics of Interpretation* (Cambridge, MA: Blackwell, 1992); Howard S. Becker and Michal McCall, eds., *Symbolic Interaction and Cultural Studies* (Chicago: University of Chicago Press, 1990).

41. Werthman and Piliavin, 362, 359.

42. Willis, 12; Chambliss, "Saints"; Cosgrove, "Zoot-Suit"; Moore, "Isolation."

43. As Hall, "What Is This 'Black,' " 111, notes, "The essentializing moment is weak because it naturalizes and dehistoricizes difference, mistaking what is historical and cultural for what is natural, biological, and genetic. . . . There is no escape from the politics of representation."

44. Luis J. Rodriguez, "Los Angeles' Gang Culture Arrives in El Salvador, Courtesy of the INS," *Los Angeles Times,* 8 May 1994, M2.

45. Tina Plaza, " 'Let's See Some Papers': In El Paso, Looking Latin Is a Crime," *The Progressive* 57 (1993): 18, 23.

46. See Andrew Schneider and Mary Pat Flaherty, " 'Profile' Stops Called the New Racism," *Rocky Mountain News (The Pittsburgh Press),* 12 August 1991, 4, 20, 22; Christina Johns, *State Power, Ideology, and the War on Drugs: Nothing Succeeds Like Failure* (New York: Praeger, 1992); Sue Lindsay, "Ruling Tromps on Racism in Drug Arrests," *Rocky Mountain News,* 11 November 1993, 48A.

47. Or as Jack Kerouac notes in *On the Road* (New York: New American Library, 1955), 112, "There was a mean cop in there who took an immediate dislike to Dean; he could smell jail all over him."

48. See, for example, Cosgrove, "Zoot-Suit"; Moore, "Isolation"; Marcos Sanchez-Tranquilino and John Tagg, "The Pachuco's Flayed Hide: Mobility, Identity, and Buenas Garras," in *Cultural Studies,* ed. Lawrence Grossberg, Cary Nelson, and Paula Treichler (New York: Routledge, 1992), 556–70; and Dick Hebdige, *Hiding in the Light* (London: Routledge, 1988), 35, who notes that subcultural styles constitute both "a declaration of independence, of otherness, of alien intent, a refusal of anonymity, of subordinate status," and at the same time "a confirmation of the fact of powerlessness, a celebration of impotence."

49. See John Fiske, "An Interview with John Fiske," *Border/Lines* 20/21 (1991), 4–7; John Fiske, "Cultural Studies and the Culture of Everyday Life," in *Cultural Studies*, 154–65.

50. Hebdige, *Subculture*, 78.

51. On possible interplays of critical and interactionist criminologies, see, for example, Katz, *Seductions*; Ferrell, "Making Sense"; Ferrell, *Crimes*; Dario Melossi, "Overcoming the Crisis in Critical Criminology: Toward a Grounded Labeling Theory," *Criminology* 23 (1985): 193–208; Ruth Triplett, "The Conflict Perspective, Symbolic Interactionism, and the Status Characteristic Hypothesis," *Justice Quarterly* 10 (1993): 541–58. Feminist criminologists have also integrated critical and interactionist, macrosocial and microsocial approaches in their groundbreaking work; see, for example, Susan Caulfield and Nancy Wonders, "Personal AND Political: Violence Against Women and the Role of the State," in *Political Crime in Contemporary America: A Critical Approach*, ed. Kenneth Tunnel (New York: Garland, 1993), 79–100. This movement past the dualisms of microsociology and macrosociology, agency and structure, is, of course, evolving in fields beyond criminology as well; see, for example, George Ritzer, *Frontiers of Social Theory: The New Syntheses* (New York: Columbia University Press, 1990).

9 ◂ ◂ ◂

Hammer of the Gods Revisited: Neo-Nazi Skinheads, Domestic Terrorism, and the Rise of the New Protest Music

MARK S. HAMM

He's a skinhead and a Fascist,
He's bald-headed and a racist,
Moral and heart, he has not;
Hate and violence mark his face.
He loves war and he loves violence;
And if you're his enemy;
I'll kill you.

—*Destructive Force (Störkraft), "Mercenaries," Berlin, 1992*

"John, you look like a fucking tramp!"
"Yes, Dad! I've got style."

—*Conversation between Johnny Rotten and his father, London, c. 1977*

Scholars have long debated the effects of contemporary music on audience values and behavior. Historically, this debate has centered on that genre of popular music known as the "protest song."

Modern Protest Music

Modern protest music took root in mass American culture between the Great Depression and World War II. Following the legends of Woody

Guthrie, Leadbelly, Pete Seeger, and John Lee Hooker, the poet Bob Dylan emerged during the mid-1960s to redefine the genre. In so doing, he created an artistically unrivaled affirmation of the values being expressed by the prevailing international youth subculture of those days—the hippies.[1]

These values (generally defined as the quest for unconditional love and peace in a world becoming progressively more flawed) were expressed in such hippie catch phrases of the day as Dylan's own "Dig Yourself," Timothy Leary's "Tune In, Turn On, and Drop Out," and perhaps best-known of all, "Make Love, Not War." Hippie values, recorded in such Dylan anthems as "Like a Rolling Stone," "Mr. Tambourine Man," and "The Times They Are A-Changin'," were supported and sustained by an easily identifiable and richly textured subcultural style (including eroticism; spirituality; playfulness; a oneness with nature; long hair; excessive drug use—especially marijuana, hashish, and LSD; "love beads"; peace symbols; well-worn bluejeans; buckskin boots; and so on) that congealed into what French cultural anthropologist Claude Lévi-Strauss defined as *homology*, or the tightness of fit between countercultural values, style, and musical expression of values and style.[2]

Recent research shows that listeners pay little attention to the lyrics of popular music. Yet this was not the case during the late '60s. Then listeners of protest music understood song lyrics quite well. After all, these protest songs, according to all manner of music criticism (for example, in 1971 Dylan was awarded an honorary doctorate degree from Columbia University for his contributions to contemporary American music) contained lyrics that were rendered with a rare artistic eloquence—an eloquence that ultimately resonated in the hearts and minds of young people far beyond the hippie scene.

In his Pulitzer prize-winning book on U.S. involvement in Vietnam, *A Bright Shining Lie*, Neil Sheehan recalls that the best-known song among combat soldiers in Vietnam—especially in the horrific days following the Tet Offensive of December 1968—was Pete Seeger's "Where Have All the Flowers Gone?"[3] For those who have never heard it, and for those who will never forget it, the last verse of the protest song—important for the discussion to follow in this chapter—is:

Where have all the young men gone?
   Long time passing.

Where have all the young men gone?
　　Long time ago.
Where have all the young men gone?
Gone to soldiers every one.
When will they ever learn?
When will they ever learn?*

Because of their emotional affinity with this verse—along with their affinity for other popular protest songs of the era, such as the Animals' "We Gotta Get Out of This Place," Edwin Starr's "War," Creedance Clearwater Revival's "Fortunate Son," and Dylan's masterpiece, "Blowin' in the Wind"—soldiers at war on foreign soil, for the first time in U.S. military history, began to festoon themselves with the trappings of a youth subculture. Inspired by the little-known U.S. Pacification Program (a branch of the Pentagon established by the Johnson administration to curtail the massive killing and torture of Vietnamese civilians by American troops), there emerged, in fact, a homologous anti-war countersociety among the young combat soldiers of Vietnam.

On their helmets these young American infantrymen—predominantly black and white kids from working-class backgrounds—wore drawings of flowers, inscriptions of protest song lyrics, and peace symbols. They frequently wore love beads around their necks, and around their wrists bracelets made from the scraps of downed evacuation helicopters. Division patches appeared on field jackets alongside hippie and biker regalia. Bivouac hootches from Long Binh to Da Nang were converted to "hippie pads" complete with Day Glo posters shimmering in the soft luminescence of black lights. Here, amid the killing fields of war, many of these young soldiers—with Dylan, Jimi Hendrix, Creedence, and Smokey Robinson blasting in the background—became regular users of the extremely intoxicating marijuana grown in Vietnam and Cambodia. Some dabbled with the cheap but brutally addictive heroin produced in the Golden Triangle. And still others experimented with a host of new mind-altering psychedelics smuggled into Nam via "care packages" from the outside world.[4]

As a result of this incorporation of hippie values, style, and music into military affairs (as a result of homology), sympathy for the Vietnam soldier began to inform the world of popular culture. And during the acid-filled days of the late '60s, the American hippie movement gave birth to a highly popular subgenre of cosmic protest music. The historic anti-war performances at Woodstock by Country Joe and the Fish ("Fixin' to Die Rag"), Richie Havens ("Handsome Johnny"), Joan Baez ("Truck Drivin' Man"—written by Gram Parsons, the original "Cosmic Cowboy"), the Jefferson Airplane ("Volunteers"), and Jimi Hendrix ("The Star Spangled Banner") gave poignant testimony not only to rock's sympathy with the hundreds of thousands of U.S. soldiers killed and wounded in the Vietnam War, but also with the millions of Vietnamese lives being lost to the massive U.S. military machine that was then rolling across Southeast Asia in a terrible thunder of death and annihilation.[5]

Meanwhile, closer to home, Dylan's music was defining the character of a more militant youth movement dedicated to ending a host of perceived social injustices. In 1966 the original Black Panther Party of Oakland, California, adopted Dylan's "Ballad of a Thin Man" as their guiding anthem in the struggle to overthrow the institutional oppression of all African Americans.[6] Two years later the notorious Weatherman Underground organized itself around the lyrics of Dylan's "Subterranean Homesick Blues" ("ya' don't need a weatherman to know which way the wind blows").[7] Like Country Joe MacDonald and Paul Butterfield at Woodstock (who dressed in combat jackets), and Joan Baez, Arlo Guthrie, Richie Havens, and Carlos Santana (who wore bracelets from the scraps of downed helicopters), both the Panthers and the Weathermen adopted a strident paramilitary look—including combat boots, guerrilla jackets, black berets, and machine guns made fashionable by Fidel Castro and Che Guevara in the legendary battle of the Sierra Maestra. To be sure, these were more than a bunch of hippies. During this period the Weathermen bombed two courthouses, a police statue, and a urinal at the U.S. Capitol Building; and the Panthers fought bloody gun battles with police in Oakland, Detroit, Chicago, and Los Angeles, and engaged in deadly knife fights with prison guards behind the walls of San Quentin, Soledad, and Attica.[8]

By decade's end it seemed the nation was headed for anarchy. The madness of assassinations, race riots, and Vietnam had taken a serious toll on the moral constitution of American society. Then in 1970, in the year following Woodstock and the massive anti-war demonstration held in front of the White House on 11 November 1969, President Richard M. Nixon began in earnest a plan to reduce U.S. military involvement in Vietnam.[9]

Two months after the ensuing Attica riot, the bloodiest prison rebellion in American history, Dylan released one of his most passionate recordings about the ravages of social injustice—the memorial ballad of prisoner "George Jackson." Six months later unprecedented reforms began to take place within the New York and California prison systems, reforms that would influence the course of American corrections for the next decade.[10]

Protest music had come of age. The protest song had given rise to a somewhat nebulous but truly authentic political movement, which in turn had created a subgenre of cosmic protest music and a homologous youth subculture dedicated to its values. By the early '70s, this progressive sociopolitical consciousness had somehow inspired a fundamental shift in U.S. foreign and domestic policy. And then Dylan and the hippies turned inward, toward affairs of the heart and soul. By 1972 the golden age of protest music was over.

But was it?

The Current Debate

The current debate among scholars engaged in the study of music and behavior is concerned with whether topical music of the post-Vietnam era carries a message viable enough to ensure any resulting sociopolitical action on the part of its listeners. At base, there are two sides to this debate: contemporary music either *does* or *does not* provide the messages necessary to elicit sociopolitical action.

The overwhelming body of research published in the United States supports the latter proposition. As early as 1971, the ever-prolific R. Serge Denisoff pointed out that listeners of topical songs often "would not or could not" interpret their meaning.[11] Similar conclusions were drawn throughout the 1970s. In his influential book *Minstrels of the Dawn*, Jerome Rodnitzky argued that protest music had been overtaken by a "terminal illness. . . . Somewhere along the way folk-protest was swallowed up by the general musical category called rock. . . . Rock musicians moved around, but not toward anything. . . . [Rock] lacked any tangible reason for being, beyond commercial success."[12]

The 1980s saw a continued affirmation of the proposition that the protest song had all but disappeared with the demise of the anti-war movement. Kizer, for one, argued that "protest music currently tends to be less sharply defined than in the past. . . . [There is] a dramatic lack [of] specialized lyrics created for social movements."[13] Similarly, Tucker noted that popular music had become a "betrayal of rock's past as a tool for the expression of social consciousness."[14] Tillman suggested that rock was "inherently apolitical . . . too sensual and aesthetic and lacks the purposive-rational orientation that is required to realistically engage in political action."[15] And the Plasketes sardonically asserted that "protest songs and Yamaha guitars [have been] traded in for upward mobility and air-conditioned cars."[16] "Rock is not now, nor will it be," wrote London, "an assault on traditions as was the case in the past."[17]

Thus, the prevailing consensus among U.S. commentators is that topical messages expressed in post-'60s rock have little if any effect on the listener. "The weight of the existing empirical evidence," concludes Orman, "suggests that rock music has no mystical power that can make people change their basic political values or orientations. Rock music cannot be said to be a primary political socializing agent."[18]

Research published in Great Britain over the past two decades, though, reveals a very different picture. This research has been concerned almost exclusively with topical messages presented in the lyrics of punk music. Specifically, it has been interested in the effects of such Sex Pistols protest sirens as "God Save the Queen," "Holiday in the Sun," and "Anarchy in the U.K."[19] But unlike their U.S. counterparts, British scholars have considered the effects of music not on the general population but on listeners within the context of subculture. Moreover, this body of literature shows that the punk subculture has been dominated by working-class youths who have, in fact, come to embrace a countercultural ideology as a result of their exposure to the subculture's music. Simply put, punk music—with its intense social content—effectively raises the political consciousness of listeners who hang around the punk scene.

According to this school of thought, punk music—and its attendant subcultural style—operates as "a spectacular means of expressing lived relations in which distinct objects, symbols, and rituals (stylistic elements) congeal into a system of meaning."[20] Stylistic elements of punk, a function of this "system of meaning," include specific haircuts, costumes, jewelry, and theatrical violence—that is, violence expressed abstractly, including acts of self-mutilation.[21] Thus, punk style (technicolor mohawks, safety pins pierced through the nose or ears, studded dog collars and razor blades worn around the neck, ripped and soiled t-shirts, pogo or slam dancing, and, importantly, Nazi tattoos and Third Reich regalia) became an integral part of punk music's popularity, providing listeners with what Paul Gilroy describes in *There Ain't No Black in the Union Jack* as "an ability to be political without being boring."[22] Far from having no effect on the sociopolitical consciousness of its audience, then, punk music created a "theater of rage" which offered the wondrous "means through which ordinary consumers [could] not only appropriate new technologies [and] new media skills to themselves," writes Dick Hebdige in his celebrated book, *Subculture*, but could also "learn a new principle of assemblage."[23] Although they disdained the stylistic creations of the hippie era, Neil Nehring concludes in his authoritative work on youth subcultures in post-war England, *Flowers in the Dustbin*, that punks "did remember the belief in the late sixties that youth culture could change the world."[24]

The U.S. and British Research

The U.S. and British research is distinguished not only by conclusions on the effects of contemporary topical messages on audience values and behavior, but by research methodologies as well. In the United States, the predominant method employed over the past three decades has been lyric analysis (often combined with historical review). This method is based not on individual listeners' perceptions of song lyrics but on literary interpretations made by music critics themselves. The approach is based on the assumption that the mass effects of protest music can be best understood "as a personal response to music, of exploring one's feelings that music evoked."[25] Moreover, lyric analysis is considered "the richest and most useful kind of criticism because it respects the work as it was actually perceived, by people in general."[26]

Yet rarely have U.S. scholars employed social science research methods in their analyses of protest music and its effects on audience values, and never has a study examined its effects on audience behavior. In fact, there appears to be an antiscientific bias in the U.S. literature. Rodnitzky, for example, argues that "the influence of protest music cannot be measured statistically."[27] In those rare cases where social scientific methods have been used to measure audience value orientations, researchers have typically relied on populations of convenience (i.e., college students).[28] Never has a U.S. study examined the effects of protest music using the apparatus of a youth subculture as the primary unit of analysis. There is, then, actually very little "existing empirical evidence" on the sociopolitical influence of modern protest music.

By contrast British scholars have relied on a wide range of methods in their research on the punks. British studies typically include combinations of ethnomethodology, participant observation, historical review, literary criticism, and lyric analysis. But like their U.S. counterparts, the British researchers offer little quantitative evidence on musical tastes, values, and subcultural style; hence, once again little is known about the empirical intersection of protest music and sociopolitical behavior.

Finally, U.S. and British researchers are distinguished by their portrayal of the protest singer. Whereas British scholars clearly demonstrate a fascination with the London punk artists of 1977, they generally have not expressed a solidarity of interest with these performers. Indeed, the performances of Sex Pistol Johnny Rotten are generally described as "snarling lyrics as though they tasted of his own piles, dancing like a rotten corpse . . . glassy eyes burning . . . amphetamine-parched lips turned back in savage contempt as he went for the jugular."[29] The U.S. literature, however, is replete with sentiments of solidarity with the protest singer. Rodnitzky, for one, has argued that "what protest music needs [today] is another young Bob Dylan—not an entertainer with good voice inflections and a perfected musical style, but an artist with specific social visions."[30]

The remainder of this chapter is dedicated to the study of such a musician. But unlike previous U.S. researchers, I have no intention of laboring under a romanticized illusion about the contemporary protest singer. The times, after all, they have a-changed.

White Power Heavy Metal

White power heavy metal, by any definition of the genre, qualifies as protest music. It is a musical idiom, to use the definition coined by Denisoff, that is "inherently linked to some supportive organizational form such as a social movement."[31] The social movement, in this case, is a modern form of Nazism.

The creation of white power heavy metal resulted primarily from the musical talents of an Englishman named Ian Stuart Donaldson (a.k.a. Ian Stuart) and his band Skrewdriver. Successful protest singers, like Bob Dylan and Johnny Rotten, become social icons because they offer an unrivaled artistic expression of the values and style of a prevailing international youth subculture; that is how they change the world. And homologous youth subcultures are in turn invariably shaped by the historical context in which they emerge. Skrewdriver became the world's premiere skinhead band during the early 1980s as a result of three important historical trajectories.

First, by the time Margaret Thatcher became prime minister of England in 1979, unemployment had already reached unprecedented post-war proportions in the working-class neighborhoods of London, Manchester, Birmingham, and a dozen other British cities. Four years earlier, the social problems associated with this massive unemployment had been compounded by a series of prolonged industrial strikes, housing shortages, hospital closures, and three-day work weeks.[32] It was out of this space that seventeen-year-old Johnny Rotten—an emaciated, unemployed, hemorrhoid-afflicted speed freak with spiky hair and green teeth—donned an "I Hate Pink Floyd" t-shirt and set upon the boutiques, pubs, and art schools of London's West End with "no concept of a melody, tune, or anything." Punk was born, born from the seams of a world where young people "had no money, no jobs, no nothing." "So the Pistols projected that anger," says Johnny Rotten in his memoir, "that rock-bottom working-class hate."[33]

Second, in 1981 the British government began moving toward a conservative approach to immigration. Mrs. Thatcher inaugurated her tenure as prime minister by declaring that she "understood the feelings of those who fear that the British culture may be swamped by an alien one."[34] In essence, this rhetoric of nationalism led a number of analysts to conclude that Thatcherism had facilitated the incorporation of a common-sense form of racist logic into mainstream political thinking.

Third, in concert with her most influential global ally, U.S. President Ronald Reagan, Thatcher introduced a series of public policies to facilitate the pursuit of self-interest in British society. Neil Nehring has eloquently described this phenomenon:

Thatcherism and Reaganism . . . robbed the word *public* of any positive resonances. . . . The two leaders damned long-established efforts at social remediation as inherently repressive. Thatcher went so far as to declare that Jesus Christ's self-sacrifice for others was a matter of idiosyncratic personal preference. When the people of the United States and England allowed common sense about the state to be defined in this way early on, by Reaganism and Thatcherism, those demagogic, populist appeals could then be accompanied by the imposition of authority and order—the actual expansion of state power—against the supposed drags on the economy. . . . The ruling economic interests broke more expansive labor and curtailed spending on social relief, while fueling the immensely profitable military industry.[35]

These crucial historical developments—the punk movement with its legacies of *hate*, *rage*, and *Nazi fetishism* among working-class youth; the rhetoric of *nationalism* with its legacy of racism; and self-interest with its attendant rise of *militarism*—created the basis for what sociologist Stuart Hall has referred to as Britain's "new authoritarianism."[36] Ian Stuart reworked this trend into a highly attractive form of protest music designed to appeal to a growing number of English teenagers who, by 1981, had been shoved into a near-lumpen status by the troubled British economy. Yet early white power heavy metal was altogether void of English parochialisms; instead, it was designed as world music. In effect, Stuart appropriated the new authoritarianism for his own political purposes and then transformed it into a seductive form of lowbrow entertainment designed to capture the attention of millions of alienated white kids from London to Berlin, from Stockholm to Los Angeles. History reveals that he was monumentally successful in this endeavor.

Stuart accomplished this artistic feat by mixing two hugely compatible forms of contemporary British music. He began by drawing from a subgenre of punk that by the early eighties had adopted the devolved, back-to-the-basics sound of British "Oi!" music. ("Oi!" is an old gypsy term used by cockney workers years ago meaning, "Hey!" ["Oi! You."].) The punked-up version of this retrogressive form of entertainment was created by a group of now-defunct British bands of middling renown: Accident, Cocksparrer, Oi Polloi, Last Resort, Criminal Class, Cockney Rejects, the Gonads, and 4-Skins. To polarize themselves against the left-wing, "new romantics" of the era—such as the Clash, Elvis Costello, the Police, the Pretenders, Bob Marley and the Wailers, and the Boomtown Rats—the Oi! punks began trading on the traditions of British pub singalongs and male surge-chanting about the "glory of the British state."[37] Oi! became much more than a "music to steal hubcaps by," as one observer has described it.[38] Instead, Oi! created an angry and aggressive "us-versus-them" orientation for its listeners. Consider, for example, this act of bricolage committed in 1980 against Pete Seeger's famous anti-war song by the Oi! band Slaughterhouse and the Dogs, entitled "Where Have All the Boot Boys Gone?"

> Wearing boots and short haircuts,
>   We will kick you in the guts.
> I don't know just what I've done,
>   I just know I'm having fun.
> Where's the bloody boys gone?
>   Gone, gone, gone, gone.

Stuart then integrated this drunken, nationalistic, and exceedingly violent form of Oi! music with the din-of-battle threnodies of heavy metal in the tradition of Led Zeppelin.[39] Anyone who has listened carefully to Led Zeppelin knows that the occult messages rendered in their songs were based on the proposition that human affairs were much better in the past, a million years ago when the forces of nature ruled the everyday activity of men and women who roamed the Earth as heathens, barbarians, and shamans. This message can be read in the text of such Zeppelin classics as "Dazed and Confused," "The Crunge," and "The Battle of Evermore." It can be clearly read in the band's famous spiritual evocation of teenage redemption, "Stairway to Heaven"—perhaps the most popular rock song of all time. Yet among delinquent youth of London during the developmental stages of the British skinhead movement, British research shows that "the most popular song" of the era was Led Zeppelin's crypto-historic saga of death and annihilation, entitled "The Immigration Song."[40] In his extraordinary historical treatise on Led Zeppelin, *Hammer of the Gods*, Stephen Davis concluded that the band demonstrated

> a fascination with Celtic Britain and the tides of English history, especially the four-hundred-year period from the eighth to eleventh centuries when the English fought for their island with generations of Viking invaders from Denmark and Sweden. "The Immigration Song," with its images of

barbarous Norse seamen and pillaged abbeys, was the first of Led Zeppelin's many hammers-of-the-gods threnodies.[41]

Fantasy

Fantasy, then, is at the moral root of Skrewdriver's music. When combined with the banality and violence of Oi!, Stuart's brand of heavy metal produced a sort of mystical, occult-oriented, "bully boy" appeal for a "clean white Britain" in which the Viking—that barbarous Celtic warrior of Led Zeppelin mythology—once again emerges to rule the British Isles. Essentially, "Skrewdriver turned the clock back hundreds of years and glorified the age where life was a day to day battle for survival, disease was rife, war ever present, and the mass of people lived as virtual slaves."[42]

In 1982, White Noise Records of London (owned and operated by the British National Front, a neo-fascist organization with offices in London, Paris, Berlin, and Rome) released Skrewdriver's seminal album of white power heavy metal, entitled *Hail the New Dawn*. The album cover displayed a group of Vikings standing on a conquered European beach in front of a glorious sunrise. Rendered in a raw, edgy, blues-based intonation reminiscent of Howlin' Wolf via Mick Jagger—or what a young British Bob Seager might have sounded like had he played too long in the ruins of the Führersbunker during the final days of the war—*Hail* contained Stuart's anthems of human survival for white youth of the 1980s. These songs were designed to project the prevailing nationalism, racism, hate, and rage of British working-class society onto the rest of the world. They included "White Power," "Race and Nation," "Rudolf Hess (Prisoner of Peace)," and a vicious, two-chord heavy metal number called "When the Boat Comes In":

Nigger, nigger get on that boat.
Nigger, nigger row.
Nigger, nigger get out of here.
Nigger, nigger go, go, go.

Never had a protest singer stated a more clearly defined social vision. And never had a vision been expressed with such vitriolic hatred; a hatred reserved for "the drags" on the prevailing economic systems of Britain and the U.S. White power heavy metal *was not* an artistic rebellion against Thatcherism and Reaganism. It was, instead, a hyperactive endorsement of these regimes. Spurred by the political action of the fascists at the National Front, in 1983 Skrewdriver emerged as the world's leading "white power" heavy metal band. This occurred by dint of the fact that a number of hard-core London punks were still flirting with the violent and reactionary symbols of Nazism—the swastika, the SS badge, the Iron Cross, and so on. Suddenly, Ian Stuart was in the right place at the right time. Breathing intendment into the otherwise "meaningless" punk symbols of Nazism, Stuart and his associates created a homologous paramilitary youth subculture dedicated to rapacious acts of violence against persons because of their race, religion, or sexual preference—people who are members of the classic "outgroups" of society.

The Neo-Nazi Skinheads

The neo-Nazi skinheads of the 1980s and 1990s have been organized around the intersection of subcultural values, style, and musical expression of values and style. In order of importance, Skrewdriver presented to the world's white youth a value system that was anti-immigrant (anti-black), anti-communist, anti-Semitic, anti-gay, and anti-IRA. This system of values has been supported and sustained by a subcultural style that includes excessive beer drinking, shaved heads, hiked-up jeans, red suspenders, flight jackets, Doc Marten work boots with white shoelaces, and Viking and Nazi regalia. The skinhead style also includes such random acts of violence as "Paki bashing," "hippie bashing," "queer bashing," and "nigger bashing"—or what has become known within the skinhead subculture as "berserking" and "sidewalk cracking."

Hence, to date skinheads have amassed an unprecedented record of vandalism, racial assault, and murder. In Britain alone, the number of racial attacks provoked by skinheads has increased to an estimated 70,000 incidents per year, including seventy-four murders of Afro-Caribbean, Asian, and Pakistani men.[43] And with the collapse of communism and the destruction of the Berlin Wall, violent nationalism has spread like a deadly virus throughout Western Europe and has spilled into such former East-bloc nations as East Germany, Poland, and Russia. Exacerbated by massive movements of poor immigrants across borders into the West, German skinheads have used clubs, knives, beer bottles, brass knuckles, firebombs, Oriental throwing stars, explosives, and guns to grievously injure an estimated 80,000 foreigners from such third-world nations as Nigeria, Uganda, Mozambique, Pakistan, Turkey, and Vietnam. This iniquitous wave of terrorism has included at least forty homicides, mostly against old men, women, and children.[44]

Yet what is perhaps most striking about the international neo-Nazi skinhead movement is that its style of violence against social outgroups mirrors perfectly the larger social and political contentions of the times. During the Persian Gulf War, for example, British skinheads volunteered to serve in the military, and others were implicated in the bombing of more than twenty mosques in the greater London area.[45] Meanwhile, German skinheads have joined mercenary movements in Croatia, supporting the policy of "ethnic cleansing" against Muslims, and in Iraq, supporting Saddam Hussein's attempt to eradicate the nation's Kurdish population.[46]

With the growth of the skinhead movement has come, of course, an expansion of both the number and influence of ultramodern protest singers in the tradition of Ian Stuart. Accompanied by the international marketing of Nazi memorabilia (which has now become a $100-million-a-year commercial enterprise), record companies in Germany, France, and the United States have created a growing stable of racist bands (such as No Remorse; Brutal Attack; Vengeance; and RaHoWa, or Racial Holy War) and a thriving market for white power heavy metal music, fictionalizing violent nationalism with such skinhead anthems as "Turks," by the popular German band Dark Skins:

> Put them in jail
> Or put them in concentration camps
> Away from me in the desert.
> But send them away.
> Kill their children, molest their wives.
> Destroy their race,
> And they will fear you.
> Turks, Turks, Turks.[47]

The American Skinheads

The American skinheads took root in popular culture during the mid-1980s, as the mainstream culture of the U.S. became anchored in conservatism, Republicanism, patriotism, militarism, and traditional "family values" that were at the heart of both Reaganism and a growing religious revival waged by the Fundamentalist Christian Right. Since then, the tally of skinhead violence includes more than 100 murders of young African Americans and third-world immigrants; at least four homicides of gay men; nearly 400 assaults against African American males; more than 300 cross burnings; fourteen firebombings of African American churches; more than 200 assaults against gays and lesbians; some forty desecrations of Jewish cemeteries; and nine acts of violence perpetrated against worshipers at Jewish synagogues, including one attempted mass murder in Dallas, Texas.[48]

Evidence

Evidence regarding the interplay of skinhead culture and violence can be found in an estimation of the influence of white power heavy metal music—as an element of skinhead homology—in the geometry of domestic terrorism. Between 1989 and 1991, I conducted thirty-six structured interviews along these lines with skinhead gang leaders in various cities and prisons across the nation. (The methodology used in the study is explained in my book *American Skinheads*.)

The first element of skinhead homology, neo-Nazi values, was measured by responses to the "authoritarian aggression" scale designed by Theodor Adorno and associates in their historic attempt to dissect fascistic mentality within broad populations (the well-known "F Scale"). According to this measure, the skinheads were generally found to be racist, anti-semitic, and homophobic.

The second element, the style of racial violence (or domestic terrorism), was measured two ways. First, the skinheads were asked to report the number of fights they participated in during the past two years. This was followed by the question, "How many of these fights were against people of another race?" In total the thirty-six skinheads were involved in more than 120 acts of violence over the two-year period (the mean number of fights was three), and roughly 42 percent of these fights were against racial minorities (including two homicides and two attempted homicides). Second, the skinheads were asked to report on those intoxicants, if any, they had ingested prior to these racial attacks. In the overwhelming number of cases, the skinheads were drunk on beer.

The third element of homology, white power heavy metal music, was examined by responses to the following question: "Perhaps the most important aspect of youth culture is music. List your favorite bands (beginning with your most favorite)." A total of twenty-three skinheads reported that their favorite band was Skrewdriver, and most of them listened to Skrewdriver records on a daily basis.

The Results

The results are presented in Table 1. The table shows that neo-Nazi values are positively correlated with both a preference for the music of Skrewdriver and variances in terrorism. Likewise, the style of beer intoxication is strongly correlated with terrorism and preference for Skrewdriver. Finally, terrorism and a preference for Skrewdriver are also positively correlated.

Taken together, these findings indicate that there is a homogeneous musical preference and a coherent ideology among skinheads that facilitates the subcultural style of racial violence. The music is white power heavy metal, the ideology is neo-Nazism, and the subcultural style is alcohol-induced domestic terrorism. In other words, preference for new forms of protest music is statistically homologous with sociopolitical values and criminal behavior.

Criminological Perspectives on Collective Violence

Criminological perspectives on collective violence have traditionally been shaped by strain theory. According to this well-known explanation, structural dysfunctionalism in society leads to individual ends/

Table 1 **Skinhead Homology: Statistical Correlates (Pearson's *r* reported, *N* = 36)**

	Preference for Skrewdriver	Terrorism
Neo-Nazi Values	.57	.57
Beer Intoxication	.68	.77
Terrorism	.67	

Note: All coefficients are significant at the .05 level, with a critical effect size of .40.

means discrepancies among lower-class youth who then rebel against dominant ideologies by joining a youth subculture with its own deviant set of values and customs.[49] Recently, however, a small but influential group of postmodern criminologists has rejected this view on the grounds that it fails to link a person's background to the foreground of criminal action via an understanding of the experiential setting of crime and delinquency. By ignoring the linkage between background and foreground, strain theorists have left a "black box in the center of the criminal enterprise, or by default provide[d] a simplistic rational choice theory."[50] In either case, postmodernists argue that mainstream criminological theories do not contain the requisite intellectual capacity to explain the vitality, the emotions, and the sheer excitement of committing violence against another human being.

In an attempt to fill this "black box" with texture and meaning, postmodern criminologists have advanced several alternative theories.[51] Foremost among these has been the theory of moral transcendence advanced by Jack Katz. In his celebrated book, *Seductions of Crime*, Katz argues that London skinheads carved out their subcultural space by searching out provocation with racial minorities. Katz describes skinheads as "street elites" who drunkenly saunter into racially mixed neighborhoods looking for a fight. For these youth, Katz asserts that "violence is essential so that membership [in the skinheads] may have a seductively glorious . . . significance. . . . Being in this world of experience is not simply a matter of detailing posture and using violence to raise the specter of terror. It is also a contingent sensual involvement."[52]

In advancing this theory, however, Katz seems to have created yet another black box. That is, while Katz lucidly describes what it *feels like* to engage in collective violence, he tells us little about the thought, speech, rituals, and aesthetics that produce such action—that is, the everyday culture of collective violence as it is lived and experienced by its practitioners. Put another way, *Seductions of Crime* ignores what Jeff Ferrell has so aptly referred to in his critically acclaimed book, *Crimes of Style*, as the process of "doing things together."[53] As such, Katz's theory fails to view skinhead violence as a collective political act that challenges the rationalistic individualism of democratic societies. How does a small group of neo-Nazi skinheads come to the point where they are willing and able, for example, to construct and throw a molotov cocktail through the window of a Turkish home, killing a fifty-four-year-old woman and her three grandchildren—as they did in Mölln, Germany, in November 1992? How do they come to the point of hiking to the rooftop of a Jewish community center and placing two cyanide gas pellets in the air-conditioning system—as they did in Dallas, Texas, in July 1990? How do they come to single out a spastic woman confined to a wheelchair, douse her with Schnapps, and burn her to death—as they did on a Berlin street in broad daylight in February 1994? Or how do they come to the point of picking up a baseball bat and beating a poor immigrant to death on a city sidewalk—as they have done countless times in the U.S., Germany, and Great Britain since the fall of the Berlin Wall?[54] Katz suggests that such acts of terrorism provide skinheads with the means necessary to achieve a moral transcendence over conditions they perceive as being morally intolerable. But what, then, are the group dynamics that generate the transcendent experience? What ties these youths together and propels them toward their criminal edge-work?

I have argued that the substantive materials used to fill this black box of criminological theory on collective violence—shared values, popular music, and subcultural style—must first be organized. If they are not organized, the phenomenon cannot be understood. If it is not understood, it cannot be controlled. And if it is not controlled, in the case of the neo-Nazi skinheads of post-communist Europe and beyond, it has the potential to become what William Chambliss has recently referred to as "perhaps the major social problem of the next century."[55] In his book *Apocalypse Postponed*, renowned Italian linguist Umberto Eco has suggested that the culture of terrorism "only becomes explicit when confronted with a critical analysis of the way it functions."[56] In this vein, I have maintained that explanations of domestic terrorism must be organized around the principle of homology, which must in turn be studied for its statistical correlates. Without an understanding of these empirical associations, we can never fully contemplate what it means to experience the righteousness, rage, and the "contingent sensual involvement" associated with acts of evildoing. Through an understanding of their forbidden values, seductive style, and untamed musical expression of values and style, we are able to view the neo-Nazi skinheads as a self-sustaining terrorist youth subculture capable of reproducing itself in a variety of social milieus.

Consider, in closing, the case of a seventeen-year-old skinhead from Milwaukee who goes by the street name of the "Raging White Rhino"—one of the subjects in the present study. The Rhino is from a working-class background. A junior in high school, he is drug-free and usually gets along with his parents. He was introduced to white power heavy metal music when he was fifteen by a friend with a shaven head and a swastika tattoo, and he has listened to this music every day since. He has even fronted his own garage band—in his parents' home—by playing three-chord rhythm guitar, covering such Skrewdriver classics as "When the Boat Comes In" and "White Power." Along with his companions (nigger bashing, berserking, and sidewalk cracking are always group affairs), he has been involved in more than ten racial attacks; each time he was intoxicated on beer. These aspects of doing things together are more than simple accouterments attached to the criminal project; they are, instead, the very building blocks of moral transcendence.

I met the Rhino on a sweltering, late Saturday afternoon in August 1990, crossing a railroad spur in front of a working-class tavern in inner-city Milwaukee. He was dressed in a "No Remorse" t-shirt, hiked-up bluejeans, and Doc Marten boots. His face was covered with acne, his head was shaved up, and he had a Viking tattoo running down his left forearm. He was drunk and wore a set of brass knuckles. He was what Katz would call "a bad ass"—mean, angry, and with a giant piss stain on his pants. The Raging White Rhino was, especially in the industrial sadness of a Milwaukee sundown, a pathetic sight to behold and a living embodiment of Durkheim's worst nightmares about the anomic breakdown of social order:

Author: (sitting on the railroad tracks and sweating profusely because of the humidity):	So tell me, why did you become a skinhead?
Raging White Rhino (sitting on a railroad tie, drinking a Budweiser, and sweating even more than the author):	Cause niggers suck. Niggers and Jews. What the fuck do you care anyhow?

Author (an hour later, after sundown):	Have you ever done violence against somebody because of their race?
Rhino (after a few more beers):	Yeah. Shit, yeah! But they usually provoke it. Like they'll say some shit about white power. That's when we throw down. I beat one nigger in the head with a beer bottle. Fucked him up good! Just goin' berserk on that nigger's skull.

Postscript

Ian Stuart was killed in a car wreck in 1993. John Rotten (Lydon) now tours Europe and Latin America with his band PiL (Public image Limited). He has finally learned how to play three-chord rhythm guitar. In August 1994 more than a half-million rock fans returned to Woodstock for a twenty-fifth anniversary concert. Headlining the event was a sleek and sensuous fifty-three-year-old Bob Dylan.

Notes

1. See generally Emmett Grogan, *Ringolevio: A Life Played for Keeps* (Boston: Little, Brown, 1972); Bob Spitz, *Dylan: A Biography* (New York: McGraw-Hill, 1989).

2. Dick Hebdige, *Subculture: The Meaning of Style* (London: Methuen, 1979); Claude Lévi-Strauss, *The Elementary Structures of Kinship* (London: Eyre & Spottiswood, 1969).

3. Neil Sheehan, *A Bright Shining Lie: John Paul Vann and America in Vietnam* (New York: Viking, 1988), 23.

4. See generally Lewis B. Puller, Jr., *Fortunate Son: The Autobiography of Lewis B. Puller, Jr.* (New York: Bantam Books, 1991); Steven Wright, *Meditations in Green* (New York: Bantam Books, 1983).

5. See Joan Baez, *And a Voice to Sing With: A Memoir* (New York: Summit Books, 1987); David Crosby and Carl Gottlieb, *Long Time Gone: The Autobiography of David Crosby* (New York: Doubleday, 1988).

6. Eldridge Cleaver, *Soul on Ice* (New York: McGraw-Hill, 1967).

7. Peter Collier and David Horowitz, *Destructive Generation: Second Thoughts About the Sixties* (New York: Summit Books, 1989).

8. Collier and Horowitz, *Destructive Generation*.

9. Sheehan, *A Bright Shining Lie*.

10. John Irwin, *Prisons in Turmoil* (Boston: Little, Brown, 1980).

11. R. Serge Denisoff and Mark H. Levin, "The Popular Protest Song: The Case of 'Eve of Destruction,' " *Public Opinion Quarterly* 35 (1971): 120.

12. Jerome Rodnitzky, *Minstrels of the Dawn: The Folk-Protest Singer as Cultural Hero* (Chicago: Nelson-Hall, 1976), 138–39.

13. Elizabeth J. Kizer, "Protest Song Lyrics as Rhetoric," *Popular Music & Society* 9 (1983): 10.

14. Karl Tucker, "Rock into the Future," in *Rock of Ages: The Rolling Stone History of Rock and Roll*, ed. Ed Ward et al. (Englewood Cliffs, NJ: Rolling Stone/ Prentice-Hall, 1986), 614.

15. Cited in James R. McDonald, "Politics Revisited: Metatextual Implications of Rock and Roll Criticism," *Youth & Society* 19 (1988): 488.

16. George M. Plasketes and Julie Grace Plasketes, "From Woodstock Nation to Pepsi Generation: Reflections on Rock Culture and the State of Music, 1969–Present," *Popular Music & Society* 11 (1987): 33.

17. Cited in McDonald, 488.

18. Cited in McDonald, 489.

19. See generally Hebdige, *Subculture*; Mike Brake, *Comparative Youth Culture* (London: Routledge and Keagan Paul, 1985); Bruce Dancis, "Safety-Pins and Class Struggle: Punk Rock and the Left," *Socialist Review* 8 (1978): 58–83; Simon Frith, *The Sociology of Rock* (London: Constable, 1978).

20. Caroline Kingsman, "High Theory . . . No Culture: Decolonizing Canadian Subcultural Studies" (Unpublished manuscript, Carlton University, Ottawa, Ontario, n.d.), 2.

21. Hebdige, *Subculture*.

22. Paul Gilroy, *There Ain't No Black in the Union Jack: The Cultural Politics of Race and Nation* (Chicago: University of Chicago Press, 1991), 121–22.

23. Hebdige, *Subculture*, 64.

24. Neil Nehring, *Flowers in the Dustbin: Culture, Anarchy, and Postwar England* (Ann Arbor: University of Michigan Press, 1993), 272.

25. Chet Flippo, "The History of Rolling Stone: Part III," *Popular Music & Society* 3 (1974): 295.

26. Robert Christgau, *Any Old Way You Choose It* (Baltimore: Penguin, 1973), 25.

27. Jerome Rodnitzky, "The Decline of Contemporary Protest Music," *Popular Music & Society* 1 (1971): 49.

28. See Denisoff and Levin, "The Popular Protest Song." For rare exceptions, see Lorraine E. Prinsky and Jill Leslie Rosenbaum, " 'LEER-ICS' or Lyrics: Teenage Impressions of Rock 'n' Roll," *Youth & Society* 18 (1987): 384–97; H. Stith Bennett and Jeff Ferrell, "Music Videos and Epistemic Socialization," *Youth & Society* 18 (1987): 344–62; and Anthony Pearson, "The Grateful Dead

Phenomenon: An Ethnomethodological Approach," *Youth & Society* 18 (1987): 418–32.

29. Julie Burchill and Tony Parsons, *The Boy Looked at Johnny* (London: Pluto Press, 1978), 34.

30. Rodnitzky, *Minstrels of the Dawn*, 150.

31. R. Serge Denisoff, *Sing a Song of Social Significance* (Bowling Green, OH: Bowling Green University Press, 1972), 51. It is important to note that skinheads have been seen in the streets of London since the late 1960s. However, they were not aligned with any identifiable fascistic or neo-Nazi movement until the Thatcher era. The present discussion is concerned only with the skinheads of that era.

32. Brake, *Comparative Youth Culture*; Hebdige, *Subculture*.

33. John Lydon, *Rotten: No Irish, No Blacks, No Dogs* (New York: St. Martin's Press, 1994), 86–87.

34. Cited in Mark S. Hamm, *American Skinheads: The Criminology and Control of Hate Crime* (Westport, CT: Praeger, 1993), 30.

35. Nehring, *Flowers in the Dustbin*, 97–98.

36. Stuart Hall, *The Hard Road to Renewal: Thatcherism and the Crisis of the Left* (New York: Verso, 1988).

37. Hamm, *American Skinheads*, 34.

38. Jack B. Moore, *Skinheads Shaved for Battle: A Cultural History of American Skinheads* (Bowling Green: Bowling Green State Popular University Press, 1993), 47.

39. Hamm, *American Skinheads*.

40. R. E. Shain and K. Higgins, "Middle-Class Delinquents and Popular Music: A Pilot Study," *Popular Music & Society* 2 (1972): 23–42.

41. Stephen Davis, *Hammer of the Gods: The Led Zeppelin Saga* (New York: Ballantine Books, 1985), 117.

42. Hamm, *American Skinheads*, 34.

43. Hamm, *American Skinheads*.

44. Mark S. Hamm, "Conceptualizing Hate Crime in a Global Context," in *Hate Crime: International Perspectives on Causes and Control*, ed. Mark S. Hamm (Cincinnati: Academy of Criminal Justice Sciences/Anderson, 1994), 173–94.

45. Hamm, *American Skinheads*.

46. Michael Schmidt, *The New Reich: Violent Extremism in Unified Germany and Beyond* (New York: Pantheon Books, 1993).

47. See Eric Jensen, "International Nazi Cooperation: A Terrorist-Oriented Network," in *Racist Violence in Europe*, ed. Tore Bjorgo and Rob Witte (New York: St. Martin's Press, 1993), 80–95.

48. Hamm, "Conceptualizing Hate Crime in a Global Context."

49. See generally Robert Agnew, "Foundations for a General Strain Theory of Crime and Delinquency," *Criminology* 30 (1992): 47–86.

50. Pat O'Malley and Stephen Mugford, "Crime, Excitement and Modernity," in *Varieties of Criminology: Readings from a Dynamic Discipline*, ed. Gregg Barak (Westport, CT: Praeger, 1994), 190.

51. See Martin D. Schwartz and David O. Friedrichs, "Postmodern Thought and Criminological Discontent: New Metaphors for Understanding Violence," *Criminology* 32 (1994): 221–46.

52. Jack Katz, *Seductions of Crime: Moral and Sensual Attractions in Doing Evil* (New York: Basic Books, 1988), 128, 139.

53. See Mark S. Hamm, "Doing Criminology Like It Matters: A Review Essay on Jeff Ferrell's *Crimes of Style*," *Social Justice* 20 (1993): 203–10.

54. See Hamm, *American Skinheads*; Hamm, "Conceptualizing Hate Crime in a Global Context"; Schmidt, *The New Reich*; Alexis A. Aronowitz, "Germany's Xenophobic Violence: Criminal Justice and Social Responses," in *Hate Crime*, 37–70; and Wilhelm Heitmeyer, "Hostility and Violence Against Foreigners in Germany," in *Racist Violence in Europe*, 17–28.

55. William J. Chambliss, foreword to *American Skinheads*, xiii.

56. Umberto Eco, *Apocalypse Postponed* (Bloomington: Indiana University Press, 1994), 119.

10 ...

Struggles Over the Symbolic: Gang Style and the Meanings of Social Control

JODY A. MILLER

Charles White is a probation officer with the Los Angeles County inten-sive gang-supervision program.[1] As I walked into his office for the first time, the wall caught my eye. A large collection of black caps, probably twenty-five of them, hung one on top of the other. Some said "Raid-ers"; others were plain; others had various logos or letters on them. Interspersed among them were several dark wool hats. Below this dis-play of hats was hung a row of black nylon belts with small silver belt buckles. Some of the buckles were plain; others had initials punched or scratched into them. Next to these were rows of posters, each with a black-and-white mug shot of a young Latino or African American man. The photo was centered on the poster; under it was listed the individu-al's name, crime(s), and the length of his sentence. Each poster was covered with red vertical bars, and across the top in bold letters was emblazoned the slogan "GANGS = PRISON." As I studied this wall, I couldn't help but wonder . . . what does all of this mean?

While the gang "problem" has spread rapidly across the United States in the last decade, gangs have been a feature of Los Angeles for many years, and southern California has an especially dense population of gang members, with an estimated 100,000 to 150,000 gang members in Los Angeles County alone.[2] These gangs have created unique styles for their members, including dress, hair, tattoos, graffiti, and body language. As a result, style has become a vehicle through which social control agents interact with gang members. This chapter examines the ways institutional agents in charge of monitoring and controlling gangs come to understand and mediate this symbolism. Specifically, it examines how one branch of the juvenile justice system—the intensive gang supervision unit of the Los Angeles County Probation Department— interacts with gang members based on style.

Background

Guided by the work in the 1970s of British cultural theorists such as Stuart Hall and Dick Hebdige, a number of researchers have recently called for an integration of cultural studies with the study of crime and deviance.[3] As Ferrell points out, "Many social groups and events traditionally conceptualized as 'criminal' are in fact defined in their everyday operations by subcultural meaning and style."[4] Though research on street gangs has rarely focused specific theoretical attention on the significance of gang style, it has been noted in many ethnographic studies of gangs.[5] Moore, for example, examines the influence of the zoot suit among Chicano gangs in the 1940s, describing how "[y]ouths wearing the zoot-suit costume anywhere in the city were chased and beaten, regardless of their behavior."[6] For these young men, regardless of gang affiliation, clothing style became synonymous with the deviant gang label.

Comparatively little attention has been paid to contemporary gang style, though there are reasons to consider it significant. The contemporary situation is unique in terms of the sheer number of gang members and the widespread proliferation of gangs. In part, this is a result of deteriorating economic conditions in many cities across America.[7] In addition, Klein suggests that popular media attention to gangs and gang style has contributed to youthful identification with gang culture. This "cultural diffusion" has also contributed to the formation of youth gangs across the United States.[8]

The growth in gangs comes at the time of an intense increase in punitiveness within the juvenile and criminal justice systems and within public discourse. This punitive shift has been witnessed in a widening of social control, especially in communities of color.[9] The handling of gangs and gang members (or those perceived to be gang members) by the juvenile and criminal justice systems has shifted as well, with the social control of youths of color often accomplished through the application of the label "gang member."[10] These changes are both cause and result of the public's concern about gangs, which is so heightened in the current era that it constitutes a moral panic, one based on negative stereotypes of youths of color.[11] According to Moore, "Gangs sharpen and simplify middle-class . . . notions of what lower-class maleness is."[12]

In addition, Klein and Maxson point to the proliferation of sophisticated gang intelligence-gathering among law enforcement agencies, a result of the shift from rehabilitation to deterrence goals in recent decades.[13] This is evident in the expansive development of anti-gang legislation, which provides greater latitude in the intervention on gang members based on "expert" knowledge of the nature of gangs,[14] as well as the development of specialized police, probation, and prosecution units. What is particularly significant for the study of gang style are the explicit goals of these specialized gang intervention programs. According to Maxson and Klein:

> The gang arena is now dominated by efforts that stress deterrence and control through surveillance, incapacitation, and retribution. . . . [Probation] officers' explicit goals are to apply intensive surveillance to their gang probationers and to "violate" them—return them to incarceration for technical or legal violations—wherever feasible.[15]

Within the Los Angeles County Probation Department, specialized intelligence-gathering and gang monitoring are accomplished in part through the intensive gang supervision unit. In this probation unit, each officer is exclusively assigned probationers who are alleged to be active gang members. While regular probation supervision averages caseloads of approximately 150, gang supervision officers typically have caseloads ranging from forty to fifty-five, providing officers in the gang unit more time to spend on each case. In this investigation I will suggest that it is in part at the level of style that gang supervision officers interact with their probationers, intervene in their daily lives, and "violate" them for their continued gang affiliation. I will explore the means by which style is called upon by probation officers to interpret and monitor youths' behaviors.

Method

This research is based on in-depth interviews with six officers from one area division of the Los Angeles County Probation Department, including five deputy probation officers in the specialized gang unit and their supervising officer, who oversaw the activities of the gang unit officers in his division. All were male; two were African American, two Latino, and two white. Interview data were supplemented with informal discussions that occurred while I spent time at the probation department gathering data for a separate project, as well as with ethnographic notes gathered during several "ride-alongs" with two of the gang supervision officers as they went into the field and interacted with gang members on their caseloads.

The interviews were semi-structured and open-ended. They began with general questions as to how long the officers had worked in the gang unit and what made them interested in doing so, as well as information about the gang situation in the areas to which they were assigned. Next I asked how they could tell if someone was a gang member, and from this question probed issues of gang style and symbolism. Having gathered taxonomies of gang symbols, I asked the officers what they felt the meanings behind gang style were, what information it provided them, and how important they felt it was to interact with gang youths based on these symbols. All of the officers indicated the importance of addressing gang style, and from there we discussed their methods of doing so.

One problem the interviews revealed was the difficulty of ascertaining the source of probation officers' information about gang style—whether from direct experience with gang members on the streets, discussions with other probation officers, information located in reading materials such as gang manuals, media portrayals, or some combination of these. This was revealed to me most clearly with the repetition of a specific example. Gary Reed, an African American probation officer, told me about a new probationer on his caseload who was a member of the 75th Street gang and had "LXXV" tattooed on his forehead.[16] This new probationer and his tattoo seemed to take on mythic proportions among the probation officers I interviewed after Reed. For example, Dan Schwartz, a white probation officer in the gang unit, explained that he had "recently heard a kid had a seven-five across his entire face." Similarly, Robert Baiza, a Latino probation officer, told me that "75th Street is probably the boldest [gang], where they have 75th Street [tattooed] right above their eyebrow." In these instances, it is difficult to know how much of the officers' statements were extrapolated and amplified from the stories and photograph of Reed's one probationer. The exaggerated quality that this tattoo took on in their conversations does clearly indicate, though, the significance of gang style in their understanding of gangs.

The goals of this project are to ascertain the amount of knowledge probation officers have about gang style, and to explore the degree of importance they place on interacting with gang members around the use of style and symbols. The interviews, ride-alongs, and informal discussions all reveal that style is frequently a contested issue in the interactions of probation officers and their gang-affiliated clientele. Probation officers use a number of methods, both formal and informal, in their attempts to supervise and diminish gang members' participation in gang activities and to violate them for continued affiliation. These methods often rely on the mediation of gang style for their success. However, the officers I spoke with sometimes differed in their approaches and beliefs concerning gang symbols. These complexities of style, perception, and control are explored next.

Elements and Meanings of Gang Style

Symbols, clothing, and artifacts are adopted and used in a variety of ways—for the construction and presentation of self; the announcement of value, mood, attitude, and identity; and the promotion of group cohesion and solidary relationships.[17] In the case of youth groups such as gangs, the objects adopted and their intended meanings are often in opposition to dominant cultural ideals.[18] Specific cultural rituals or activities (such as dress, the use of graffiti, tattooing, and communication styles) can serve to "represent and heighten the importance of social solidarities and social divisions."[19]

The significance of these activities and symbols was not lost on the probation officers I interviewed. In the sections that follow, I will discuss the meanings the officers attributed to gang style: the ways in which they used their probationers' dress and appearance to measure their level of gang involvement, the messages of defiance and disrespect the officers read into gang members' symbolic displays, and the dangers they perceived as resulting from youths' adoption of gang-oriented style.

There is no doubt that the officers with whom I spoke saw gangs as masculine enterprises. Throughout the interviews, gang members were consistently described as male, and it was only when I asked about girls that the officers would discuss them. The majority expressed a lack of in-depth knowledge about female gang participation, and often discussed girls in stereotyped ways, sometimes as sexual objects, always as subordinate to the "real" gang problem. This belief that gangs are almost exclusively a male phenomenon shaped the meanings probation officers attached to gang style and to their concerns about controlling gangs. The threat posed by gangs, then, was, in part, their enactment, or perceived enactment, of uncontrolled, violent masculinity.[20]

Labeling Youths' Levels of Gang Involvement

Ferrell points out that members of criminal subcultures "develop elaborate conventions of language, appearance, and presentation of self, and in doing so participate, to greater or lesser degrees, in a sub-culture, a collective way of life."[21] Recognizing this, the officers I spoke with held the belief that a gang member's dress can reveal "the tightness he is with the group." As a result, they often looked to the styles of probationers and other youths they came across to determine their level of gang involvement. While most articulated a recognition that this scheme is not entirely foolproof, they nevertheless drew upon it regularly. Dan Schwartz explained:

> I've heard the expression if he looks like a duck and talks like a duck and walks like a duck, it's a duck. And I think that's true for a gang member also: if he looks like a gang member, and he acts like a gang member and he, he walks the walk of a gang member, you know, so to speak, then he's probably a gang member.

Because of the importance they placed on gang style as a tool for measuring involvement, the officers with whom I spoke were able to characterize a range of symbols adopted and employed by gangs, including clothing styles, graffiti, tattoos, and verbal and nonverbal communication styles. All of these were used as clues for examining a youth's gang participation. Gang clothing is comparable to "a uniform," according to Reed, and is composed of a variety of elements: shoes, socks, pants, shirts, belts, hats, and jackets.

However, the officers recognized that gang-style fashions have become increasingly popular among non-gang youth, causing the potential for misidentification, at least among the unknowledgeable. Schwartz explained:

> If you go to the high schools and the junior highs, I mean, baggies are in. Kings, Raiders clothes are in. Teachers are wearing Raiders clothes, administrators, um, it's in. That is the style. The gang style, the gang quote "style" is in.

Because of the problems gang-type fashions can cause for identifying gang youths, the officers often looked more specifically for aspects of the gang "uniform" that were particular to individual gangs, including the insignias found on their hats and belt buckles, graffiti, tattoos, colors, and subtle consistencies in the style of members of the same gang. Typically, the officers with whom I spoke could provide detailed descriptions of such things as the brand names preferred, the color and style of shoes favored, and the sports team logos adopted by members of various gangs on their caseload. These elements were deemed more foolproof measures of serious gang involvement; thus, the officers believed that their knowledge and ability to recognize gang members were more sophisticated than the general public's. Baiza explained:

> There's a lot of little identifying markers more than just the obvious Kings and Raiders hats and jackets. That's . . . everybody knows that. But there's a lot of other things, what color shoelace they wear, uh, whether they tie the shoes from the underneath or over the top, OK? Uh, what side they wear their earring on sometimes, you know. There's a lot of things that we look at other than the obvious. . . . Their combs can all be one color— you know, different stuff like that. The cars, the license plate covers might be all one color. People don't pick up on that.

The officers perceived tattoos and graffiti to be particularly foolproof measures of youths' commitment to their gang. For example, because graffiti functions for gangs in a variety of ways—to mark territories, to promote and affirm solidarity within the gang, to challenge rival gangs, and to create memorials for those gang members who have been killed—the officers expressed the belief that graffiti could provide vital information about which members were most active within the gangs on their caseload. Knowing a member's moniker and seeing it in graffiti around the neighborhood gave the probation officer clues as to the individual's activity level. Schwartz described the neighborhood surrounding a gang member on his caseload, which indicated to him that the youth was actively participating in his gang again: "You look on his street, and his, all the apartments are hit up with his name. Painted, I saw it up and down the street."

Other officers shared Schwartz's belief that examining the nature and extent of youths' adoption of particular gang style elements provided evidence as to the seriousness of their involvement. These details were viewed as providing officers with specific and definite information concerning the affiliation of the youths they encountered. For example, Jim Ewart, a white probation officer, explained that if youths have "a particular gang logo tattooed physically on their bodies," this provides convincing evidence, "because most people wouldn't put an impression that is so permanent onto their bodies unless they had an affiliation with the gang." The officers were most disturbed by tattoos that they considered blatant because of their locations. Schwartz explained, "It's one thing to hide it, and it's quite another to have it displayed in, very openly on your face and neck. . . . He's telling you, 'Hey, I'm a gang member. This is me.'" Youths whose tattoos were in visible locations were considered more committed to "the gang lifestyle."

Defiance and Outlaw Masculinity

For the probation officers with whom I spoke, elements of style within gang culture were perceived as significant specifically because of the defiant messages they allegedly send concerning the rejection of mainstream cultural ideals, and the redefinition of status as coming from immersion in "the gang lifestyle." Richard Martinez, a Latino probation officer, explained that a gang member, "by dressing the way he's dressing, is indicating to us that he's choosing to identify with the gang lifestyle and everything that goes along with it." This concern was illuminated by the officers' discussions of the meanings they attached to gang affiliation, which they saw reflected in the various elements of style that gang members adopt. These meanings were perceived as projections of a tough, "outlaw" masculinity. Reed explained:

> The hardcore gang member doesn't care about anything but his gang. His gang is, you know, he doesn't respect any other system. His morals are around the gang, you know; if the law says one thing, what does his gang say? That's what matters more.

This hardcore philosophy, the officers believed, was captured in the masculine styles adopted by gang youth and incorporated into an outlaw image. These styles include violent sports team logos, prison symbolism, and oversized clothing—the latter thought to provide them with both a means of carrying concealed weapons and of making themselves look larger and more threatening.

For example, the officers with whom I spoke argued that the adoption of sports clothing by gang members illustrates the defiant gangster image the gang members have adopted. Sometimes a specific sports team may be adopted because of the symbolic meanings that can be extracted from the team logo; other times they are chosen because of the name or letters in the name of the team. For example, Reed told me that many Crip gangs incorporate the Duke Blue Devils: "Blue. Devils. Blue meaning Crips. Devils are gangsters, they're devious, they're into that kind of stuff." Likewise, White, an African American officer, explained:

> Georgetown shirts mean "gangster." Raiders mean outlaw. Um, the Bulls, because of the violence of the bull, it means to, uh, you know, to run over people. You will find out that a lot of gangs have taken up the sports clothing and it's a really big industry now, and you'll notice that a lot of them wear the violent-type animals, like the Bulls and the Bulldogs. And you see, like the Raider, you see the patch with the eye, you know it's a pirate, outlaw, you know, outcast from society.

In addition to the incorporation of sports paraphernalia, gang members use a variety of other artifacts to create their symbolic "gangster" style. A widely known example is the preference of many Crip gang members for British Knights tennis shoes. Reed explained, "That means 'Blood-Killer.' You're gonna see Crips wearing those shoes. They love 'em.'' A similar but less publicized example is Burger King, where again, the BK stands for Blood-Killer. Baiza explained, ''All the Crips go and eat at Burger King. And they, and they, walk around with their hamburgers and cups, Burger King, back to their neighborhoods, and drive around with Burger King cups, which is saying, ''Blood-Killer.' ''

Several probation officers also focused on gang members' use of non-verbal communication to send the message that they are tough and dangerous. For example, Reed described ''the walk'' of a gang member as a stroll in which ''they're trying to act like they're warriors.'' And Ewart noted, ''He's trying to express himself in a certain way, maybe he feels he's tough, strong, bad, insane, and they'll try to incorporate those feelings into a physical walk or gait, or the way they stand sometimes.''

Hairstyles provide another example of the adoption by gang members of a defiant stance, drawn from the look found in penal institutions. Reed explained that ''a lot of Hispanic gang members will wear their hair almost, um, shaved really close, some almost bald. . . . They keep it like that to give them the look like as if they're in state prison—that hardcore look.'' Likewise, the probationer on Reed's caseload who had ''LXXV'' tattooed on his forehead was, according to Reed, ''just basically saying 'I'm 75th Street gang member. I'm hardcore. And I'm ready to battle.' '' He elaborated: ''That's telling others he's a threat, and, you know, deal with him accordingly.''

These messages of defiance and threat that the officers saw as the essence of gang style contribute to their belief that gang style in and of itself is, at least in certain contexts, menacing and dangerous. In fact, several of the officers expressed their belief that gang style in fact exists as a public safety issue.

The Dangers of Gang Style

Gang style was perceived by the officers as posing a threat, both to individual gang members and more generally to public safety. At the most basic level, it was seen as allowing those youths who adopt gang style to be threatening. For example, some officers argued that gang members wear oversized clothing so that they can, in Ewart's words, ''actually store a shotgun or rifle inside, and you cannot observe it.''

According to White, those youths who dress down[22] most overtly are often members who are trying to make a name for themselves and are therefore more likely to engage in criminal activity. There was also a belief, expressed by Baiza, that a youth's decision to adopt gang style could result in "his furtherance in the gang lifestyle, which could result in him hurting somebody else."

In addition to the perceived threat that gang members pose by dressing down, the officers expressed even greater concern for the negative attention they attract by publicly adopting gang style. Even if a youth is not engaged in any gang activities outside of dressing down, there allegedly remain social consequences that place him and others around him in danger. First and foremost, dressing in gang-style attire makes youths visible targets—for the police and also for rival gangs. White surmised, "You're gonna be singled out, not only by law enforcement, you're gonna be singled out by other gangs." Martinez explained:

> If the gang member is dressed in gang attire, and he's walking down the street, and another gang member from an opposing gang sees him, there's a better possibility that he's going to get shot or jumped or hurt dressed as a gang member than if he were not dressed as a gang member.

Likewise, White explained that often when gang members go into rival territories looking for vulnerable targets, they don't necessarily look for individuals they know by face, but instead target youths who look like gang members. "You ask the typical gang member a lot of times, 'Do you know who you shot?' 'No, they was dressed as a gang member.' That's what the kid'll tell you." Reed, again describing the youth on his caseload with "LXXV" tattooed across his forehead, said, "I look at it as a bull's eye, something to shoot at. Point blank, you know?" And Baiza surmised, "It's almost a death wish."

In addition, when youths dress down, they seem not only to make targets of themselves, but to bring risk to others around them. For that reason, some of the officers expressed the belief that gang style is a public safety issue. Martinez explained that intervention into gang style is:

> important for the safety of those he's associating with, who may or may not be gang members, who just happen to be standing on the street corner and then some gang members from an opposing gang drive by and see him and shoot at him but miss him and hit somebody else.

Finally, the officers discussed their concern that the adoption of gang style narrows the life options of the youths on their caseloads. One way it does so is by narrowing their mobility. Baiza described a youth on his caseload for whom he had trouble finding a school placement that didn't cross rival gang neighborhoods: "If you have to cross too many barriers, he can't go. 'Cause he can't ride the bus, 'cause they'll pick up different gang members on the way, and he'll never make it." And White noted that "there's some kids in Richmond Street that never leave the Richmond Street area. They can't." Martinez explained:

> The tattoos that might identify them with a particular gang makes it difficult for them to go anyplace outside of their own area. Um, whether it's to a doctor's office in another area or whether it's shopping with their parents in another area, whether it's just going to a park in another area, once they have marked themselves up as belonging to a particular gang, then they have to, they have to conceal that as best they can in order to be safe in another area.

Gang style also allegedly narrows their options when they attempt to move into the "straight" world. As Reed noted, "People will treat you like a criminal because of the way you are dressed." For example, gang style makes employment very difficult. According to Baiza, many restaurants will not hire youths with visible gang identification because it is too risky. He explained:

> Let's say a kid from Cuyahoga West gets a job at McDonald's selling food there. And on his hand he has CHW. And some guy from a rival gang comes in and sees him, you know. And then he goes back and tells everybody, then they come back and do a drive-by, there are gonna be innocent people hit. So employers have to be pretty watchful.

Gang styles, especially permanent marks such as tattooing, were seen as locking youths into lives with few options for the future.

The meanings probation officers attached to gang style provided for them powerful justifications for intervening on the youths' lives and for criminalizing otherwise noncriminal behavior. When youths' attire was used as a measuring rod for their level of gang involvement, when it was read as defiance of authority and disrespect toward the probation officer and the justice system, and when it was viewed as placing them and others in danger, the probation officers felt it was both their right and their duty to criminalize that style. In the section that follows, I will discuss their methods for doing so.

The Social Control of Gangs and Gang Style

Interacting with gang members based on their clothing and style is often an explicit expectation of gang supervision officers. Schwartz explained that "every kid has orders of the court, probation conditions that they have to abide by. And if they don't, it's the probation officer's duty to deal with it in some way, and to inform the court." The court orders are written to encourage the officers to monitor gang style. Condition 15A of the Los Angeles County Juvenile Conditions of Probation stipulates that the minor "not participate in any gang activity." This statement leaves wide latitude for interpretation.

In addition, Condition 40 simply states "other" and has several blank lines that the probation officer or judge can check and fill with additional stipulations. This is sometimes specifically used to dictate that the youth abandon gang style. For example, Baiza described one incident in which "the judge ordered me on Condition number 40 to check and see if [a probationer's] tattoo that he had put on his neck that the judge saw, when he had it done. 'Cause if it's new, if he in fact put it on since he's been put on probation, that's gang identification, the judge wants to know that." He explained that it is against the law for these youths to wear clothing "if it's identified as gang clothes and you're in the gang."

In addition to the implicit or explicit reference to issues of style in the conditions of probation, the officers felt it was important to consistently monitor and challenge youths' modes of dress or appearances because of the deeper meanings attached to gang style—defiance, disrespect, and dangerousness. As a result, much of the contact between gang supervision officers and the gang members on their caseloads occurred within the community, because the officers felt they could better monitor the youths' performance, as well as dress and appearance, through surprise visits at home and school.

When probation officers went out into the community to interact with gang members, their social control activities took a number of forms. For this analysis, I will discuss a range of methods employed by probation officers, which can be understood as a continuum of intervention strategies. These often involved a progression from informal to increasingly more formalistic intervention, culminating in formal probation violation.

Informal social control consisted of making youths aware that the officers knew they were dressing down, in addition to attempting to get the youths to abandon their gang style. These attempts to change gang style involved warning the youths to stop, attempting to negotiate with them or reach a compromise, and finally, at times confiscating gang-related articles when they were found in the probationers' possession. When these methods were deemed insufficient for dealing with a particular gang member, the officers would document evidence of the youth's involvement, with the specific goal of bringing the probationer back to court on formal charges of violating conditions of probation.

Making Gang Meanings Explicit

While riding with White, I witnessed an encounter that illustrates probation officers' efforts to let youths know, at the very least, that the officers were aware that they were dressing down. We went to the home of one of White's probationers; the youth had on a white Georgetown t-shirt and long, oversized shorts that were red, yellow, and green, and came below his knees. White walked into the home, along with me and the police officers with whom we were riding. As he was talking to the young man, he asked him what the Georgetown t-shirt symbolized. When the youth hedged, White told him he knew it stood for his gang, and he warned the young man to admit it. The goal of this encounter seemed to be to make it clear to the young man that he wasn't getting anything past White. White made no effort to intervene any further than simply mentioning that he recognized the shirt and getting the youth to admit that his recognition was a valid one.

Regardless of whether they deemed it necessary to intervene, the officers felt it was important to project the message to the youths that they knew what was going on, that the young men were not slipping forms of gang affiliation past them unnoticed. White explained:

> Every time I talk to a kid, and I see him dressed that way, for what it's worth, I tell him, "I know you're dressin' down, man. You still dressin' down." You know, I let them know that regardless of how minimal it is,

"you're still dressin' as a gangster." So that means that he does still have affiliation with the gang. Regardless of what he tells me. Show me. When you're telling me you're not a gangster, you don't dress with any of the Raiders clothing on. Or the Georgetown, or the sports clothing.

Similarly, Baiza explained that when they see youths in sports paraphernalia, the officers often ask questions like, "Well, who's the new center for the Kings then? If you like the Kings, who in the hell is the new center?" In doing so, they let the youths know that they were aware of the gang meanings attached to their attire.

Advising Gang Members to Abandon Gang Style

An explicit goal of the gang supervision officers was to get the youths on their caseloads to stop dressing like gang members. Many expressed the belief that this could be the first step in getting youths to move out of "the gang lifestyle" altogether. On a more practical level, they also felt it was necessary to address the youths' appearance because otherwise "they'd think it's OK." Often this informal intervention progressed from warning the youth to abandon aspects of his gang uniform to outright confiscation of items in his possession.

For example, during one ride-along with Reed, we visited a probationer whom he had visited a couple of weeks earlier. At that time, Reed had noticed the juvenile was wearing a gang-style belt buckle with gang initials scratched into it. Attempting to compromise with the young man, Reed had given him a warning and told him to either get rid of it or get rid of the etched insignia. When we visited the second time, the youth was still wearing the belt buckle and it still had the same gang-identifying scratches in it. Reed ordered the young man to take off the buckle and give it to him for disposal. He had no plans to write the youth up but merely took the belt buckle away from him.

Several of the officers, notably those who grew up in communities with gangs, were sensitive about not imposing rigid dress codes on the youths, and these officers often attempted to reach compromises with their probationers rather than trying to change their style of dress completely. For example, Reed noted that "instead of buying clothes ten sizes too big, if you can get 'em to buy clothes one size larger or two sizes larger it doesn't look as bad. At least that's a start." He recognized that peer acceptance remains an important motivating factor, explaining, "If they wear normal clothes, then the guys will call them a buster, you know, stuff like that. Ranker, you know, these little nicknames that are disrespectful." Baiza also explained his reasons for compromising with his probationers:

> If he's dressed sort of semi-gang, and not heavy, doesn't have the slits,[23] doesn't have any Kings stuff on . . . I can accept a guy, and I know he's dressing to be one of the gang, and I know he has to live in a gang group. I can handle that. But when he's openly displaying slits, or whatever I think is, or the way he ties his shoes, or his earring, the way he has his shirt buckled, uh, if he's openly defying, and trying to tell everybody else in the school that he's from Southside, or "I'm from Westside," and he doesn't care, then I'll hit him up. But if he dresses and doesn't have the little indications, sophistication, I'll let him slide. I mean, he's gotta live there; I don't have to live there.

Officers not raised in communities with gangs showed less sensitivity and awareness of the stylistic negotiations these youths must go through in their day-to-day lives. For example, Ewart said he tells kids, "You're to get rid of this clothing, and you're to get standard student-style dress clothing or citizen-style dress clothing." Baiza critiqued this type of approach: "As long as they're trying to maintain, you gotta understand where they're from; you can't expect them to wear Jordache and surfer shirts, you know, and some Reeboks." Baiza respected the youths by giving them some room to dress in the styles with which they were comfortable. As long as their clothing style was not overtly gang-oriented, he was willing to "give 'em a lot of play."

Formal Intervention

While some of the probation officer/probationer interactions remained at the informal level, at times probation officers confiscated items or made photographic evidence of them with the explicit goal of sending the juvenile back to court on a violation. Often, they turned toward more formal methods of intervention when their attempts at informal control were ignored or challenged by the youths, or when they suspected a youth was involved in more serious activities for which they were unable to get evidence. In these cases, documenting gang style and violating youths on these grounds provided a means of intervening on kids who were otherwise uncontrollable.

The officers used a number of methods for gathering information to formally intervene on their probationers. In addition to confiscating items, some chose to take photographs of probationers when they were dressed down or photographs of items they found, such as clothing, notebooks with gang-type writing in them, drawings, or newspaper clippings. In addition, photographs in the probationers' possession that were incriminating—for example, pictures of the youth "throwing signs"[24]—were sometimes used as evidence. Schwartz told me that he had "taken kids back to court on pictures I've found in their bedrooms." Often this documentation of gang attire occurred over time, as the probation officer built a case against his probationer.

At times the goal was to document enough evidence to take the gang member out of the community, at least temporarily. Other times, the goal was simply to use the threat of formal actions to increase the probation officers' leverage with the youths on their caseloads, particularly when the judges included orders not to dress in gang attire. As Reed noted: "When you get backup from a judge, that helps a lot; then when I talk to them then it matters 'cause then they feel that if I keep seeing 'em dress in gang attire, then when I inform the court then they're gonna be in trouble."

In addition, when youths were brought back to the court for new charges or some other violation, the officers' documentation of their clothing and style could be used, as White described, to "make a strong case. I use the attire as a strong case." He elaborated: "If a kid gets in trouble I'm going to definitely let the court know that he dresses in gang attire on a regular basis." Even when the youths are not specifically violated for dressing down, that behavior can be called upon to justify recommending harsher sanctions from the court for other offenses.

All of these efforts at intervening on gang youths at the level of style—both informally and formally—signify the relationship the probation officers perceived between the way youths dress and present themselves, and more serious aspects of gang involvement. As Martinez summarized:

> It's more than just being dressed down, it has to do with his lifestyle, which has led him to one of crime. And we're trying to show him that

this lifestyle has caused him problems, and that to help himself he's going to have to change his lifestyle, and part of that change has to do with his clothing and his outlook of himself.

Discussion

In this study, I have examined the process by which probation officers in the intensive gang supervision unit of the Los Angeles County Probation Department come to define gang style as problematic and attempt to intervene on it in the lives of their probationers. Gang style and symbols adopted by probationers—clothing, graffiti, tattoos, and gestures—are constructed as measures of a youth's commitment to the gang, as defiant rejections of mainstream culture, and as dangerous threats to public safety.

However, the fetishistic emphasis on gang symbolism is not unique to the probation officers I interviewed; it is part and parcel of the current law enforcement philosophy toward gangs, in which intelligence-gathering is emphasized, specialized units are developed, and officers within these units are trained to orient themselves toward the suppression of gangs, gang members, and gang style. In fact, numerous manuals are made available to probation officers and other law enforcement officials that provide detailed taxonomies of gang symbolism.[25]

Gang style is seen as a reflection of an outlaw lifestyle adopted by gangs and their members. The reading of youths' symbolism in these ways allows for the construction and maintenance of "the gang" as trouble, danger, and violent threat. Viewing gangs only via this narrow construct justifies formal intervention that is punitive, mean-spirited, and surprisingly individualistic in its solution (e.g., "GANGS = PRISON"), considering the group nature of gangs themselves and the social and economic contexts in which they emerge.[26] In addition, the very attention paid to gang style—its glorification as evil in the eyes of mainstream culture and the law—is likely a contributor to the diffusion of gang culture among youths across the United States.[27]

Gang policies are rarely based on strategies that are grounded in an assessment of the causes of gang affiliation. Instead they tend to be measures taken with little thought given to the sources of gangs within communities.[28] The current thrust in gang policy is toward gang suppression and deterrence at the expense of prevention, rehabilitation, and efforts to change the social and economic conditions that today make gangs viable options for more and more youth.[29] The preoccupation with gang style among gang supervision officers is a manifestation of this circumscribed approach.

Notes

1. All names have been changed, and personal characteristics have been altered as necessary to conceal individual identities.

2. Malcolm W. Klein, *The American Street Gang: Its Nature, Prevalence and Control* (New York: Oxford University Press, forthcoming).

3. See Stuart Hall and Tony Jefferson, eds., *Resistance Through Rituals: Youth Subcultures in Post-War Britain* (London: Hutchinson, 1976); and Dick Hebdige, *Subculture: The Meaning of Style* (London: Methuen, 1979), for works from the 1970s. For contemporary arguments, see Stanley Cohen and Jock Young, eds., *The Manufacture of News: Deviance, Social Problems and the Mass Media* (London: Constable, 1981); Jeff Ferrell, *Crimes of Style: Urban Graffiti and the Politics of Criminality* (New York: Garland, 1993); and Clinton R. Sanders, ed., *Marginal Conventions: Popular Culture, Mass Media and Social Deviance* (Bowling Green, OH: The Popular Press, 1990).

4. Jeff Ferrell, "Towards a Critical Criminology of Culture" (Paper presented at the Annual Meeting of the Academy of Criminal Justice Sciences, Kansas City, MO, March 1993), 1.

5. Leon Bing, *Do or Die* (New York: Harperperennial, 1991); Anne Campbell, *The Girls in the Gang* (New York: Basil Blackwell, 1984); Martin Sanchez Jankowski, *Islands in the Streets: Gangs and American Urban Society* (Berkeley: University of California Press, 1991); Jack Katz, *Seductions of Crime* (New York: Basic Books, 1988); Joan W. Moore, *Going Down to the Barrio: Homeboys and Homegirls in Change* (Philadelphia: Temple, 1991); Joan W. Moore, "Isolation and Stigmatization in the Development of an Underclass: The Case of Chicano Gangs in East Los Angeles," *Social Problems* 33 (1985): 1–12; James Diego Vigil, *Barrio Gangs: Street Life and Identity in Southern California* (Austin: University of Texas Press, 1988).

6. Moore, "Isolation," 226.

7. John M. Hagedorn, *People and Folks: Gangs, Crime and the Underclass in a Rustbelt City* (Chicago: Lake View Press, 1988); Pamela Irving Jackson, "Crime, Youth Gangs and Urban Transition: The Social Dislocations of Postindustrial Economic Development," *Justice Quarterly* 8 (1991): 379–96.

8. Klein, *American Street Gang.*

9. For a general discussion of these changes, see Barry Krisberg, Ira M.

Schwartz, Paul Litsky, and James Austin, "The Watershed of Juvenile Justice Reform," *Crime & Delinquency* 32 (1986): 5–38; and Stuart A. Scheingold, *The Politics of Law and Order: Street Crime and Public Policy* (New York: Longman, 1984). For juveniles, in addition to increased incarceration rates, the growth of diversion programs has served to widen the net of social control as well. See Christine Alder, "Gender Bias in Juvenile Diversion," *Crime & Delinquency* 30 (1984): 400–414, for a discussion of this trend. This punitive shift and its disproportionate impact on communities of color is reflected most acutely in recent incarceration rates. See Marc Mauer, "Men in American Prisons: Trends, Causes, and Issues," *Men's Studies Review* 9 (1993): 10–12, for a discussion. According to Mauer, the number of Americans incarcerated in prisons and jails more than doubled between 1980 and 1990, giving the United States the highest incarceration rate in the world. Mauer reports that those facing incarceration are disproportionately young men of color—nearly one-quarter of African American men between twenty and twenty-nine years of age are caught in the criminal justice system.

10. In fact, in Los Angeles County, 47 percent of all African American males between twenty-one and twenty-four years of age are listed in the police gang database, despite the fact that research consistently reveals that only a small proportion of youths in gang-involved communities are gang members. See Ira Reiner, *Gangs, Crime and Violence in Los Angeles: Findings and Proposals from the District Attorney's Office* (Los Angeles: District Attorney, County of Los Angeles, 1992). For research on the rates of gang participation in gang-involved cities, see Beth Bjerregaard and Carolyn Smith, "Patterns of Male and Female Gang Membership," Working Paper No. 13 (Albany: Rochester Youth Development Study, 1992); Klein, *American Street Gang*; and L. Thomas Winfree, Jr., et al., "The Definition and Measurement of 'Gang Status': Policy Implications for Juvenile Justice," *Juvenile and Family Court Journal* (1992): 29–37.

11. Meda Chesney-Lind, "Girls, Gangs and Violence: Anatomy of a Backlash," *Humanity & Society* 17 (1993): 321–44; Moore, *Going Down*.

12. Moore, *Going Down*, 137.

13. Malcolm W. Klein and Cheryl L. Maxson, "Street Gang Violence," in *Violent Crime, Violent Criminals*, ed. Neil Weiner and Marvin Wolfgang (Newbury Park, CA: Sage, 1988), 198–231.

14. For a discussion of anti-gang legislation, see Patrick Jackson, "In Search of Gangs and Social Policy: A Literature Review" (Unpublished manuscript, University of Missouri, 1988); Los Angeles City Attorney Gang Prosecution Section, *Civil Gang Abatement: A Community Based Policing Tool* (Los Angeles: Office of the Los Angeles City Attorney, 1992); and Alexander A. Molina, "California's Anti-Gang Street Terrorism Enforcement and Prevention Act: One Step Forward, Two Steps Back?" *Southwestern University Law Review* 22 (1993): 457–81.

15. Klein and Maxson, 227–28.

16. Examples of gang style or symbolism that are specific to particular gangs have been changed to maintain the anonymity of the officers interviewed.

17. Carl J. Couch, *Social Processes and Relationships* (Dix Hills, NY: General Hall, 1989); Mihaly Csikszentmihalyi and Eugene Rochberg-Halton, *The Meaning of Things* (New York: Cambridge University Press, 1981); Daniel Miller, *Material Culture and Mass Consumption* (Oxford: Basil Blackwell, 1987); Chandra Mukerji and Michael Schudson, "Introduction: Rethinking Popular Culture," in *Rethinking Popular Culture: Contemporary Perspectives in Cultural Studies,* ed. Chandra Mukerji and Michael Schudson (Berkeley: University of California Press, 1991), 1–61; Gregory P. Stone, "Appearance and the Self," in *Social Psychology Through Symbolic Interaction,* ed. Gregory P. Stone and Harvey A. Farberman (Waltham, MA: Xerox College Publishing, 1970), 394–414.

18. Hall and Jefferson, *Resistance Through Rituals*; Hebdige, *Subculture*.

19. Mukerji and Schudson, 21.

20. For a discussion of the relationship between masculinity and crime, see James W. Messerschmidt, *Masculinities and Crime: Critique and Reconceptualization of Theory* (Lanham, MD: Rowman and Littlefield Publishers, 1993).

21. Ferrell, "Towards," 3.

22. "Dressing down" is a phrase used to describe the act of wearing gang-style attire.

23. Many gangs make one- or two-inch cuts at the bottom of their pants. The location of the cuts can reveal geographic information about the gang, and are a way of claiming affiliation.

24. Gangs use hand signals as a way of claiming their gang affiliation or communicating other messages. This is referred to as "throwing signs."

25. For examples of this, see "Gang Manual" (Santa Rosa, CA: National Law Enforcement Institute, 1991); "Investigating Street Gangs for the Street Police Officer" (Burbank: Burbank Police Department, n.d.); Robert K. Jackson and Wesley D. McBride, *Understanding Street Gangs* (Costa Mesa, CA: Custom Publishing Company, 1985), 59–83; and Operation Safe Streets Street Gang Detail, "Los Angeles Style: A Street Gang Manual of the Los Angeles County Sheriff's Department" (Los Angeles: Sheriff's Department, County of Los Angeles, 1992).

26. Hagedorn, *People*; Jackson, "Crime"; Vigil, *Barrio Gangs*.

27. Klein, *American Street Gang*.

28. Irving A. Spergel and G. David Curry, "The National Youth Gang Survey: A Research and Development Process," in *The Gang Intervention Handbook,* ed. Arnold P. Goldstein and C. Ronald Huff (Champaign, IL: Research Press, 1993), 359–400.

29. John M. Hagedorn, "Gangs, Neighborhoods and Public Policy," *Social Problems* 38 (1991): 529–42; Malcolm W. Klein, "Attempting Gang Control by Suppression: The Misuse of Deterrence Principles," *Studies on Crime and Crime Prevention: Annual Review* (1993): 88–111.

11 . . .

Squaring the One Percent: Biker Style and the Selling of Cultural Resistance

STEPHEN LYNG AND MITCHELL L. BRACEY, JR.

Introduction

With the publication of *One Dimensional Man* in 1964, Herbert Marcuse produced a timely, critical statement on the political-economic system that would usher in the postmodern era within the United States.[1] One of the culminating products of a long tradition of critical thought initiated by Frankfurt School theorists in the 1930s, this work spoke presciently of the new political and economic culture taking shape in the early 1960s. Marcuse was able to discern within the emerging system the seemingly paradoxical institutional linkage between the forces of creative innovation within the "free-market" economy and the social control of all creative cultural forms that challenge the existing political-economic system. Marcuse's analysis of this relation pointed to a new type of totalitarianism inhering in the "free" society model of democratic capitalism.

In addition to providing important insights about the control of dissidence in capitalist society, this framework also exposes one important source of innovative products for the postmodern market economy. The same dissenting groups that create the need for social control responses by authorities often serve as sources of creative new-product designs and mass marketing strategies. The subcultural stylistic creations of these groups can be exploited by companies looking for new marketing ideas. What Marcuse surely could not have envisioned in 1964 is the explosive growth over the next three decades in the number of industries that succeeded in marketing product-lines inspired by various forms of subcultural resistance. Business success in the postmodern era has increasingly depended upon this strategy.

Our goal in this chapter is to describe a dramatic example of the interplay between corporate marketing strategy and subcultural resistance. The case we will describe illustrates the dynamic that Marcuse conceptualized so brilliantly in his 1964 study—the synchronicity between the imperative for an ever-expanding market economy and the social control mandate to respond effectively to the challenges posed by dissident forces.

We will illustrate this dynamic through a detailed account of a contemporary business success story. The story concerns the inspiring return to profitability of an American company that was close to collapse less than ten years ago. Harley-Davidson, Inc., the sole U.S. manufacturer of motorcycles remaining since the mid-1950s, posted record earnings in the last several years and now controls the largest share of the U.S. market for motorcycles in its heavyweight class (751 cc or larger engines). In what has been described as "one of the greatest comebacks in U.S. business history," Harley-Davidson rose to its current position of preeminence after a restructuring plan saved it from bankruptcy in 1985.[2]

At this writing, the waiting period for a new top-of-the-line Harley is from ten to twelve months, quite remarkable considering its $18,000 selling price, which is many thousands of dollars more than comparable models offered by Harley-Davidson's competitors. The company's recent success has been reflected in shifting media images of Harley ownership as well. While the popular culture in the post-war period produced a picture of the typical Harley enthusiast as a lower-class deviant with a proclivity for violent behavior, a counter image of the elite Harley owner developed during the 1980s. For example, stories circulating in the electronic and print media indicated recently that millionaire publisher Malcom Forbes valued his stable of Harley-Davidsons as much as his collection of Fabergé eggs. In a recent issue of *Texas Monthly*, a slick regional magazine marketed to an affluent readership, the cover photo reveals then-Governor of Texas Ann Richards sitting astride her pearl-white, custom Harley.[3] Numerous celebrities from the sports and entertainment industries, including NBC *Tonight Show* host Jay Leno, actor Arnold Schwarzenegger, and rock star Billy Joel, among others, have publicly expressed their passion for Harleys. In an ironic transformation of the ultimate symbol of sleaze, "America's motorcycle" has acquired a special mystique for some within the ranks of the rich, the powerful, and the famous.

Much has been written about Harley-Davidson's remarkable return to financial solvency, but none of the existing accounts tells the complete story. The missing chapter deals with the connections between Harley's effort to establish the largest possible market for its primary product and the subculture that embraced this product as its central icon. In relating this story, we will focus on several interrelated themes. One of our concerns is to explain how a population of individuals that the American Motorcycle Association once branded as the deviant "one percent" of sport motorcyclists could become a dissident force in American society. Another theme deals with the transformation of this dissident challenge into instances of criminal conspiracy, both real and imagined. In developing both of these themes, we draw on a cultural criminology perspective to explore the interrelated social processes that give rise to "the culture and subcultures of crime and the criminalization of culture."[4] And it is here that we can begin to account for the deep connections between subcultural resistance, the social control and criminalization of dissidence, and business success in the postmodern order.

The One-Percenter Subculture of Resistance

Two years after the publication of Marcuse's classic work, another soon-to-be classic of a very different sort was published by a young journalist named Hunter S. Thompson. Although Thompson would later develop a cult following among college students and members of the '60s drug culture, he was a relatively obscure freelance writer when he published his first book in 1966, entitled *Hell's Angels: A Strange and Terrible Saga*.[5] This book's status as the definitive account of the emerging biker subculture can be attributed to an accident of timing and to the unusual combination of journalistic skills and unique character traits of its author. Thompson developed an interest in motorcycle gangs at precisely the point that key events catapulted the previously unknown Hell's Angels motorcycle club to national prominence. But more importantly, Thompson's personal proclivity for some of the same marginal behaviors practiced by Hell's Angels gave him special access to this group as a participant observer. As Thompson explains in an interview statement:

> I just went out there and said: "Look, you guys don't know me, I don't know you, I heard some bad things about you, are they true?" I was wearing a fucking madras coat and wing tips, that kind of thing, but I think they sensed I was a little strange—if only because I was the first writer who'd ever come out to see them and talk to them on their own turf. . . . They were a bit off balance at first, but after about 50 or 60 beers, we found a common ground, as it were. . . . Crazies always recognize each other. I think Melville said it, in a slightly different context: "Genius all over the world stands hand in hand, and one shock of recognition runs the whole circle round." Of course, we're not talking about genius here, we're talking about crazies—but it's essentially the same thing. They *knew* me, they saw right through all my clothes and there was that instant karmic flash. They seemed to *sense* what they had on their hands.[6]

With one foot planted firmly in the world of journalism, and the other in the world of outlaw bikers, Thompson was able to describe, with a certain degree of sociological sophistication, the process by which the Hell's Angels came to be perceived as a threat to the moral and social order. His book also provided a rich and comprehensive ethnographic account of the biker subculture surrounding the Hell's Angels. Indeed, almost thirty years after its initial publication, it remains the most important ethnographic study of the motorcycle outlaw subculture currently available.[7]

Because of its seminal status among works dealing with motorcycle gangs, Thompson's book serves as a key empirical reference for the present analysis. This evidence is supplemented with additional data from other published ethnographic studies, as well as participant observational data collected by the authors.[8]

The Amplification of Lower-Class Lifestyle Patterns

To examine the distinctive pattern of resistance embodied in the biker subculture, we must first locate this group within the class structure of

American society. Although hard evidence on the class status of biker groups is unavailable, descriptive material from ethnographic studies suggests that early clubs like the Hell's Angels were made up largely of lower- and working-class individuals. Ethnographic accounts of the lifestyle patterns typical of many motorcycle outlaws reveal all of the elements of a class-based cultural system that sociologists have variously conceptualized in terms of the "hard living lifestyle," the "culture of poverty," and "lower or working class focal concerns."[9]

Alcohol and drug abuse and interpersonal or marital instability are, for example, two "ingredients of hard living" that very often distinguish the biker lifestyle. Thompson's descriptions of Hell's Angels "runs" and of their other social gatherings offer a graphic account of the rampant hedonism that pervades these events. In the typical gathering, the consumption of large amounts of alcohol serves as a backdrop for the copious use of a wide variety of illegal drugs:

> A righteous Angel loading up on a run will consume almost anything, and in any quantity, combination or sequence. I recall a two-day party . . . at which Terry began the first day with beer, had a stick of the grass at noon, then more beer, and another joint before dinner, then to red wine and a handful of bennies to keep awake . . . more grass in the middle of the evening, along with a red for some odd feeling, then all through the night more beer, wine, bennies and another red to get some rest . . . before taking off again for another twenty hours, on the same diet, but this time with a pint of bourbon and five hundred micrograms of LSD to ward off any possibility of boredom setting in.[10]

The indiscriminate use of alcohol and other drugs during biker social gatherings is typically accompanied by unrestrained sexual behavior as well, although some researchers describe normative principles that govern sexual relations in these contexts.[11] The present authors' participation in several "runs" yielded evidence that supports other descriptions of sexual activities during these events: large numbers of women responding to shouted requests by male bikers to "show your tits," men and women engaged in a full range of public sex acts, and club "mamas" administering to the sexual needs of several club members at once ("pulling a train").

The substance abuse and sexual license that characterize official biker events reflect a more general lifestyle pattern of more or less continuous drinking and drug use and unstable relations between men and women. As participants in the "saloon society" milieu, many club members' primary aspiration is to "live at the bar."[12] The female associates of bikers typically share this aspiration and are often drawn into the one-percenter subculture through prior participation in the saloon culture either as prostitutes, exotic dancers, or dedicated bar patrons. Once they become affiliated with a particular club, however, these women are exposed to a continuous cycle of exploitation and abuse by their male consorts.

In a study of gender roles within the biker subculture, James Quinn provides a detailed description of the various status positions open to females who become club associates. All of these positions involve functions focused on servicing the affective, sexual, and/or economic needs of male superordinates.[13] Women attached to particular club members ("ol' ladies") are expected to turn over all of their economic resources, acquired through legal or illegal (i.e., prostitution) means, to their "ol' men." Unattached women affiliated with a club chapter ("mamas") are considered club "property" available for the sexual gratification of any male member desiring this service. In addition, any woman tied to the club chapter, regardless of her status position, can be "loaned" by her ol' man for sexual services to other bikers either inside or outside of the club. This exploitative gender role structure predictably contributes to a pattern of unstable relationships between men and women:

> Many veteran biker women (in reaction to their use as a sexual commodity) come to see their male companions as somewhat interchangeable agents of status and protection. This is *not* to say that sincere and loving relationships are unheard of within the outlaw subculture. They are, however, more the exception than the general rule. The longevity of even the best of relationships in this milieu is hampered by the sporadic poverty (and occasional wealth), extreme mobility, and physical excesses that permeate it. While a few biker couples manage to maintain long-standing relationships, most break up after a few months or years since it is more expedient to find a new partner, or do without one, than it is to work out the problems of a troubled relationship.[14]

The evidence presented here on substance abuse and gender relations among bikers reveals the underlying process by which this subculture of resistance is carved out of the dominant culture. Rather than negating key elements or values of the dominant culture to produce a counterculture, or expropriating and redefining elements of the dominant culture, one-percenters create a unique cultural domain by exploring the most extreme edges of the class culture from which they emerge.[15] This tendency to exaggerate lower-class focal concerns applies not only to substance abuse and sexual relations but to all the other lifestyle patterns emphasized by past researchers. Hence, the biker subculture is defined by extreme expressions of toughness, the active cultivation of "trouble" and "excitement," violence, rootlessness, political alienation, individualism, and a present-time orientation.[16]

Ethnographic studies of the outlaw subculture offer both empirical and conceptual support for this analysis. For example, Watson finds the experience of "trouble" to be an overriding theme within the world of one-percenters.[17] The greatest ambition one can have in this group is to be a "righteous" club member, which is achieved through a wide range of outrageous and/or illegal pursuits. Indeed, the more outrageous one's appearance and behavior, the better, as Hunter Thompson documents:

> An outlaw whose normal, day-to-day appearance is enough to disrupt traffic will appear on a run with his beard dyed green or bright red, his eyes hidden behind orange goggles, and a brass ring in his nose. Others wear capes and Apache headbands, or oversize sunglasses and peaked Prussian helmets. Earrings, *Wehrmacht* headgear and German Iron Crosses are virtually part of the uniform—like the grease-caked Levis, the sleeveless vests and all those fine tattoos: "Mother," "Dolly," "Hitler," "Jack the Ripper," swastikas, daggers, skulls, "LSD," "Love," "Rape" and the inevitable Hell's Angels insignia.[18]

The high value bikers place on outrageous appearance is matched by their enthusiasm for anarchistic behavior. As Thompson puts it, "There are few Angels who won't go far out of their way to lay a bad jolt on the squares [i.e., non-bikers]."[19] For example, Montgomery's subjects often engaged in "homosexual horseplay" consisting of "clumsy grabbing, embracing, and rolling around on the bed . . . public displays of French kissing and flying tackle embraces," all initiated by men who take great pride in their status as heterosexual predators and gay-bashers.[20] The ongoing search for the most extreme expressions of lower-class lifestyle patterns pushes many bikers beyond merely outrageous behavior to illegal acts such as street fighting, reckless riding, highway vandalism, motorcycle theft and stripping, and running cons.[21] Consequently, many bikers find themselves in a never-ending orbit of antagonistic exchanges with social control agents of one sort or another. A life full of "troubles" may be common among lower-class individuals, but most seek to avoid them if possible. By contrast, bikers do not avoid lower-class troubles; they amplify them as a way of demonstrating their distinctiveness.

Other exaggerations of lower-class normative elements and focal concerns are ontologically connected to stylistic forms that help distinguish this group as a subculture. The value assigned to masculinity and male physical strength in lower-class culture is magnified in the subcultural context into the quintessential biker physique—a large-bodied individual made obese through excessive eating and drinking. As Montgomery notes, "Fellows considered by most people to be ugly and repulsive due to their excessive body hair, barrel chests, tree-trunk arms and beer bellies are ideal in Outlaw bikers' eyes."[22] Similarly, bikers elaborate the lower-class value placed on "toughness" by creating distinctive styles of motorcycle design and clothing. The preference for "hardtail" motorcycle frames, which lack any spring rear suspension, and the removal of all nonessential accessories (windshields, farings, turn signals, mirrors) reflect the contempt that bikers have for comfort and safety. Of similar stylistic derivation is the signature article of clothing associated with outlaw bikers—the infamous denim jacket with the sleeves removed. According to Watson, removing the sleeves from clothing that could potentially serve to protect a rider against "road rash" (skin abrasions caused by skidding across the pavement) also functions as a way to express contempt for safety.[23]

A related stylistic theme that occupies a central place in the subculture's symbolic system is the celebration of death. Almost all analysts of lower-class culture designate fatalism as one of the most enduring features of lower-class existence. But while many lower-class individuals grudgingly accept the hazards of their occupational or leisure-time activities, members of the one-percent fraternity project a pronounced fascination with death. In addition to configuring their motorcycles in the most dangerous way possible, bikers promote reckless riding as a means of demonstrating "righteousness." Indeed, high status is often conferred on individuals whose recklessness has resulted in serious crashes—individuals who have succeeded in "wiping out with class."[24] Watson's entrée into the biker group he studied was a direct consequence of prestige he achieved by crashing his motorcycle:

> Although I had ridden motorcycles for years, I became aware of the local biker group while building my first Harley-Davidson. Full acceptance by this group was not extended until my first and potentially fatal accident, however. Indeed, local bikers who had only vaguely known me offered the gift of parts and assistance in reconstructing my bike and began to refer to me by my new nickname, "Doc." I sensed and was extended a new degree of acceptance after demonstrating my toughness by surviving the accident.[25]

The preoccupation with death is also reflected in subcultural mottos ("Ride to Live, Live to Ride,"), in club names ("Hell's Angels," "Satans") and insignias (the infamous "winged skull" of the Hell's Angels, the ever-present "Grim Reaper"), and in biker art and literature.[26]

The biker orientation toward death is analytically significant for several reasons. First, it represents another instance of outlaws exaggerating components of lower-class culture to produce a distinctive subcultural pattern—the lower-class preoccupation with the possibility of premature death is magnified into an actual celebration of this outcome. But the positive assessment of death can also be understood as part of a unique strategy for coming to terms with the insults and injuries of lower-class existence. By adopting a fatalistic view of one's chances for a "short and brutish" life, many lower-class individuals tacitly accept their powerlessness to control their own existence. By contrast, the bikers respond to this problem by eagerly embracing the likelihood of an early death, thereby creating an *illusion* of control over their lives. In essence, they say to the world, "We may die before our time, but it is because we're trying to!"

Bikers adopt the same approach in dealing with another problem they confront as members of lower-class culture—their poor prospects for upward mobility. While many lower-class individuals adopt an attitude of either sad resignation or overt resentment about their limited life-chances, bikers transform this dismal feature of lower-class life into a positive attribute. In the subcultural world of one-percenters, one's lack of success as defined by the dominant culture is not regarded as a source of embarrassment; rather, it is embraced as a mark of distinction. The pride that bikers take in their status as "losers" is reflected in many different subcultural forms, such as club names (the "Losers" and "Born Losers"); nicknames given to club members ("Charger Charlie the Child Molester," "Terry the Tramp," "Gut," "Dirty Ed," and "Mouldy Marvin"); and various insignia, tattoos, and other symbolic expressions of social stigma.[27] Watson's participant-observation study of the biker subculture makes explicit reference to this pattern:

> A biker who becomes economically successful or who is too legitimate is suspect. He is no longer one of them. He has succeeded in the outside and in a sense has sold out. His success alone shows his failure to subscribe to the basic values that they hold. . . . Bikers basically see themselves as losers and affect clothing, housing, and other symbols of the embittered and dangerous loser.[28]

In rounding out this analysis, we can briefly point to other critical features of the biker subculture that emerge through the amplification of lower-class culture and lifestyle patterns. One such element is the use of violence to resolve interpersonal problems. The prevalence of violence in the world of motorcycle gangs is well known to the public and extensively documented in ethnographic studies. Of special concern in the present analysis, however, is the way in which this magnified lower-class pattern is reflected in biker style. A key part of male biker fashion are accessories that function not only as articles of clothing but also as weapons—belts constructed from primary drive chains and steel-toed engineer's boots, for example. Montgomery suggests that even the trademark black Harley t-shirt worn by many bikers is designed to effect a sinister image, creating an undercurrent of impending violent behavior.[29]

An additional element of the "hard living" lifestyle prevalent among lower-class individuals is the experience of "rootlessness."[30] Once again, the ethnographic evidence reveals a lower-class pattern that is even more pronounced among bikers. Ethnographic researchers often experienced difficulties in maintaining contact with informants because of their frequent changes of residence.[31] Moreover, the institutionalization of the "clubhouse" within the biker subculture can be partly attributed to its function as a "crash pad" for club members and "mamas" who often experience periods of residential transition or homelessness.

Finally, lower-class tendencies toward political alienation and individualism are reflected in a single dominant pattern within the biker subculture. The concepts of personal freedom and autonomy are important normative principles that serve as organizing themes for a large amount of biker art and literature. These themes are expressed in terms of a narrow libertarianism focused on the types of outrageous, hedonistic, and illegal activities at the center of the biker lifestyle. As Watson notes, bikers maintain a "studied insistence that they be left alone by harassing law enforcement agencies and overregulating bureaucrats."[32] Thus, though broader political issues generate little interest among outlaw bikers, significant collective hostility accrues to social control agents that impede their search for experiential extremes.[33] Indicative of this orientation is a common biker response to government-mandated motorcycle helmets in some states—the wearing of helmets inscribed with the phrase "Fuck Helmet Laws!"

Edgework and the Criminology of Culture

We conclude this section by drawing on the data presented here to derive generalizations about the way in which bikers create symbolic resistance to cultural hegemony. Analysts of biker groups have been struck by the extremes to which members go in search of a distinction that they conceptualize as "righteousness" or "class." Although some analysts merely report this pattern as an overriding feature of the biker subculture, others have attempted to provide a theoretical explanation of the phenomenon.[34] For example, Quinn refers to Homans' deprivation-satiation principle and Blau's notion of marginal utility to conceptualize "diminishing hedonistic returns" as the dynamic governing behavioral extremes within the biker subculture.[35] A more useful theoretical explanation of the biker phenomenon, however, focuses not only on the psychodynamics of the distinguishing behavioral patterns, but also on their significance as part of a collective response to the broad structural imperatives of the U.S. political-economic system.

By combining elements of the cultural criminology perspective with the "edgework" model of risk behavior, it is possible to analyze the biker phenomenon at both the individual and collective levels.[36] In that this analysis constitutes only a part of the broader set of analytical concerns addressed in this study, we offer only a brief outline of the argument here. First, bikers' pursuit of behavioral extremes can be conceptualized as a form of "edgework," where one seeks the experiential benefits of high-risk behavior (defined in either physical or normative terms) within a broader social context of overpowering institutional constraints. According to the edgework perspective, the primary motivation for engaging in behavior that "pushes the limits" in a physical or normative sense is the seductive appeal of the experience, which produces intense feelings of spontaneity, control, spatial connectedness, and self-actualization.[37] This type of experience stands in stark contrast to the feelings of powerlessness, overdetermination, and separation that characterize behavior associated with the institutional routines of everyday life in the post-industrial order.

Although members of all social classes must contend with these institutional constraints, structural conditions that support a sense of efficacy, control, and self-determination are particularly eroded within the life-world of lower-class individuals. One response to these conditions, then, is to explore the "edge" represented by the most extreme expressions of lower-class focal concerns. Montgomery seems to speak for all bikers in acknowledging the significance of such "lifestyle edgework" in their world:

> From a One Percenter viewpoint, straight parties are boring, pretentious and restrained. Wrecking the interior of a house in winter or staggering (on foot) or careening (on motorcycle) through the woods in summer, completely stoned on whatever, may [be] deemed unwholesome to an observer from outside the subculture. As an ex-participant, however, I can assure the reader that the feeling of total abandon provides a cathartic effect which lasts for days.[38]

By relating elements of individual experience to broader social-structural forces, the edgework approach provides a more comprehensive, social-psychological explanation of the biker lifestyle pattern. But this framework is also useful for analyzing the biker phenomenon at another level. Integrating the edgework approach with a cultural criminological perspective allows us to examine the collective, subcultural dimension of motorcycle outlaws.

While the attraction of the edgework experience may motivate this type of behavior at the individual level, the collective pursuit of edge-work among the biker brotherhood ultimately produces a unique sub-cultural world. The normative and symbolic elements that demarcate a special cultural space for bikers within the broader cultural system—elements such as biker symbols, art, technology, mottos, argot, and nor-mative principles—developed as emergent products of interaction among this group of lifestyle edgeworkers. But once the subcultural reality arises in this emergent fashion, it begins to function as a unique collective strategy for resisting cultural domination.

In his ethnographic study of lower-class culture, Howell concludes that the "hard living" lifestyle represents "a way of rebelling against the life circumstances" of lower-class existence.[39] Occupying a social space in which the most extreme expressions of hard living are actively encouraged and symbolically celebrated, members of the biker subcul-ture wage a more formidable rebellion against the established norma-tive order. As discussed above, the club network offers a haven in which bikers can experience a sense of control over their lives that they are denied in mainstream culture—even if it is only the illusion of control. In their world, being a "loser" destined to die young is an aggressively pursued and normatively supported goal, not simply a socially deter-mined outcome. By embracing this subcultural orientation, bikers find a way to rebel against the social forces that determine their place in the social system.

Viewing elements of the biker subculture as forms of cultural resis-tance allows us to see this subcultural world as one type of social re-sponse to class oppression. Rather than passively accepting their fate, some pursue an individual and collective strategy to counter this op-pression. But of course social control agents in turn respond to this resistance strategy, and in so doing attempt to control cultural resis-tance through the criminalization of the subculture in which it arises.

The Making of the Menace

Institutional authorities typically respond to subcultural resistance by relying on social-control strategies designed to deal with more overt challenges to the normative or political order. Although managing cul-tural resistance differs in some important respects from the social con-trol of deviant populations or dissident political groups, the primary agents and agencies involved in the various control efforts are essentially the same. Nowhere is this illustrated more dramatically than in the case of outlaw bikers. The nature and consequences of interaction between official social-control agents and members of the biker subculture make up a critical chapter in the story we have to tell.

In relating this part of the story, we are hampered by a lack of empirical evidence on the exchanges that take place between bikers and social-control officials. Ethnographic studies of the biker subculture usually refer to the ongoing struggle between bikers and law enforcement personnel, but few of the existing accounts devote attention to the details of these exchanges. A notable exception is Hunter Thompson's ethnographic study of the Hell's Angels club. As previously indicated, Thompson was uniquely positioned to examine the role of several key social institutions in the campaign to undermine the club's organization and suppress its activities. For this reason we draw extensively on Thompson's work in this part of the analysis.

As a journalist Thompson was not guided by any particular theoretical agenda in his examination of the Hell's Angels phenomenon. However, his empirical description of the criminalization of the Hell's Angels by institutional authorities provides powerful support for the labeling theory of deviance.[40] Ironically, it was his experience and interest in journalism that led him to assemble the crucial evidence supporting this theoretical interpretation. Relying on his investigative skills as a reporter, he conducted a thorough review of stories about the Hell's Angels appearing in various national and regional newspapers and news magazines as a supplement to his participant observational data. As he attempted to reconcile news accounts with various official documents dealing with Hell's Angels' activities (i.e., police reports, commission papers), he discovered a pattern of indirect collaboration between criminal justice agencies and the media in constructing a public image of the "outlaw biker conspiracy." The story that emerges from Thompson's data constitutes a classic case of the criminalization of cultural resistance through the labeling process.

The Hollywood Connection

The Hell's Angels' subcultural world was profoundly shaped by interactions between club members, political authorities, and the media in relation to some crucial events taking place in the early to mid-1960s. But even before these events, media images of outlaw bikers played a part in the development of the subculture. Thompson's interviews with some of the founding members of the Hell's Angels revealed an important interplay between myth and reality in the original formation of the club. Hollywood supplied most of the mythology: the club name was most likely borrowed from a 1930 Jean Harlow movie about a World War I bomber squadron, entitled *Hell's Angels*. In addition, Stanley Kramer's classic *The Wild One* provided early role models for bikers in the characters portrayed by Marlon Brando and Lee Marvin.[41] Preetam Bobo, vice-president of the club during the 1950s, explained to Thompson that Kramer's 1953 movie led his loosely organized group of riders to thoroughly embrace a group identity as "wild men on motorcycles." Ironically, the movie itself was inspired by an actual historical event— the 1947 motorcycle riot in Hollister, California. Thus, the biker subculture followed a course in the early stages of its development that would be repeated in subsequent decades: media reproductions of real events produced mythological constructs that bikers internalized and elaborated in creating their own subcultural reality.[42]

The Monterey Rape and Media Frenzy

While the club continued to evolve during the 1950s, the events that transformed the Hell's Angels from an obscure group of misfits into a reputed national hoodlum network took place in California during the 1960s. In the early years of this decade, the Angels and other outlaw clubs were well-known within delimited social circles. Mainstream motorcyclists viewed them as disreputables who must be repudiated to protect the wholesome image of the sport. This repudiation eventually took the form of the American Motorcycle Association's official condemnation of outlaw groups as the "one percent" of motorcyclists that deviate from the mainstream, a designation that outlaws still proudly acknowledge with the one-percenter patch they typically wear with the club colors.

The Angels were also well-known to California law enforcement personnel in the early 1960s. The exchanges that took place between the Angels and police over minor traffic violations and other petty offenses in these years marked the beginning of the criminalization process. Although the Angels' commitment to lifestyle edgework led some club members to engage in minor criminal offenses, the overall pattern of criminal activity among the Angels was not unlike that of other lower-class males. Yet their subcultural identity and stylistic distinctiveness made them highly visible targets for police action. According to Thompson, Angels on a "run" were routinely subjected to traffic checks by the police, resulting in many citations for minor violations that would have normally been ignored. As one informant stated,

> They wrote tickets for everybody they could . . . things like seats too low, bars too high, no mirror, no hand hold for the passenger—and like always they checked us for old warrants, citations we never paid and every other goddamn thing they could think of.[43]

The primary consequence of this practice was the creation of criminal records for club members through a process of selective enforcement. While the Angels may or may not have violated the law more often than other motorcyclists, they were much more likely than their mainstream counterparts to be written up for the offenses they did commit. Thus, the pattern of criminality that emerged among the Angels in these early years was shaped as much by the social-control actions of the police as it was by the criminal proclivities of individual Angels.

Despite the Angels' complaints about ongoing police harassment, the two sides developed a form of mutual respect for one another, and they ritualized their hostile exchanges by the mid-1960s.[44] Except for the spectacle that they created on the public highways, the Angels were largely unknown to the general population during this time. Things changed rather dramatically in 1964, however, when a series of events set in motion a new turn in the criminalization spiral. The incident that launched this new chapter of the Hell's Angels story was the alleged rape of two teenage girls in Monterey, California, on Labor Day weekend of 1964.

In light of contradictory evidence, it was never completely clear whether the sexual encounter was coerced or consensual, and the formal charges lodged against the two accused Angels were eventually dropped.[45] What made this event a watershed in the Angels' rise to national prominence, however, was the response of political and law enforcement authorities and of key media sources to the incident.

Thompson documents the critical series of events in the construction of the Angels' criminal conspiracy. After extensive reporting of the incident by the regional print media, California state Senator Fred Farr publicly condemned the Hell's Angels and called for an official inquiry by the State Attorney General's office into the phenomenon of outlaw motorcycle gangs. Six months later Attorney General Thomas Lynch issued a report summarizing questionnaire data on the Angels and other outlaw clubs provided by over one hundred sheriffs, police chiefs, and district attorneys. This fifteen-page report became the catalyst for the next stage of the criminalization process.

Hunter Thompson describes the Lynch report as "colorful, interesting, heavily biased and consistently alarming—just the sort of thing to make a clanging good item for the national press." The report offered,

> plenty of mad action, senseless destruction, orgies, brawls, perversions and a strange parade of innocent victims that, even on paper and in careful police language, was enough to tax the credulity of the dullest police reporter. The demand was so heavy in newspaper and magazine circles that the Attorney General's office had to order a second printing.[46]

When a West Coast reporter for the *New York Times* filed a lengthy commentary on the Lynch report, it set off a media event that would soon become commonplace in post-war America. Media "frenzy" took over as other national publications such as *Time* and *Newsweek* struggled to outdo one another in reporting the lurid details of the outlaw biker phenomenon. In addition to reporting on the Monterey rape charges, the national press drew heavily on the Lynch report to describe the criminal history of the outlaw brotherhood and various instances of biker "invasions" of small towns, barroom brawls, and gang rapes. The combination of heavily biased police reports and the sensationalizing tendencies of the print media produced a largely fictitious account of the outlaw menace that was presented to a national audience. Hence, a new mythology emerged in the mid-1960s that, like earlier biker myths promoted by the movie industry, would have a profound impact on the future development of the biker subculture.

The construction of the outlaw conspiracy by the New York press establishment inspired responses by both law enforcement authorities and the Hell's Angels themselves that ultimately transformed the new mythology into reality. With the Angels' rise to national prominence, California law enforcement agencies redoubled their efforts to eliminate the perceived threat posed by the Angels and other outlaw groups. As with the initial police crackdown in the early 1960s, this strategy enhanced the Angels' criminal profile by ensuring that they were charged for offenses that would normally be ignored:

> The massive publicity of the Monterey rape had made [the Angels] so notorious in California that it was no longer any fun to be part of the act. Every minute on the streets was a calculated risk for any man wearing a Hell's Angels jacket. . . . At the peak of the heat a former Frisco Angel told me: "If I was fired from my job tomorrow and went back to riding with the Angels, I'd lose my driver's license within a month, be in and out of jail, go way in debt to bondsmen and be hounded by the cops until I left the area."[47]

The crackdown also placed increasing numbers of Angels in circumstances that forced them to rely on illicit activities to secure their material needs. Thompson estimated that about two-thirds of the Angels were working at the end of 1964, just before the explosion of media attention. A year later, only one-third were still employed.[48] In general, the notoriety undermined the few remaining connections the Angels had to mainstream institutions, and thus served to marginalize them further.

In the same way that the response by law enforcement agencies to the media demonization of the Angels ironically functioned to enhance their criminal status, the Angels' own responses to the media image also contributed to this outcome. A critical event in the emergence of a "deviant career," according to labeling theorists, is the internalization of an imputed identity by a social actor or actress who has been socially defined as deviant. The Hell's Angels case illustrates that this process can occur at the collective as well as the individual level. In this passage Thompson describes the events following the release of the Lynch report and the subsequent media attention:

> The whole scene changed in a flash. One day they were a gang of bums, scratching for any hard dollar . . . and twenty-four hours later they were dealing with reporters, photographers, free-lance writers and all kinds of showbiz hustlers talking big money. By the middle of 1965 they were

firmly established as all-American bogeymen. . . . Besides appearing in hundreds of wire-service newspapers and a half dozen magazines, they posed for television cameramen and answered questions on radio call-in shows. They issued statements to the press, appeared at various rallies and bargained with Hollywood narks and magazine editors. They were sought out by mystics and poets, cheered on by student rebels and invited to parties given by liberals and intellectuals. The whole thing . . . had a profound effect on the handful of Angels still wearing the colors. They developed a primadonna complex, demanding cash contributions . . . in return for photos and interviews.[49]

Confronted with the public's intense interest in their way of life, the Angels tried to conform to the media caricature that emerged in the aftermath of the Monterey rape. They responded to their newfound notoriety not only by demanding cash for interviews but also by seeking to live up to the public's expectations of them:

[Most] of the outlaws . . . are puzzled and insulted to hear that "normal people" consider them horrible. They get angry when they read about how filthy they are, but instead of shoplifting some deodorant, they strive to become even filthier. . . . This kind of exaggeration is the backbone of their style.[50]

This quotation links the earlier analysis of the evolution of the biker subculture and the present examination of the criminalization process. In the same way that the commitment to lifestyle edgework produced a distinctive subculture through the amplification of lower-class focal concerns, the tendency of bikers to actualize and exaggerate imputations of criminality by the press and police authorities helped to establish their status as a *deviant* subculture. Hence, the same force that propelled the evolution of the subculture—i.e., the exaggeration of lifestyle patterns—also gave special impetus to the dynamic process through which the Hell's Angels actually became what they were accused of being—a group of criminal misfits living on the margins of the "great society."

The Paradox of Social Control

To summarize, the central theme of the preceding analysis can be expressed most succinctly as the "paradox of social control." We have seen how the biker subculture emerged as a form of resistance to class oppression and cultural hegemony. Recognizing the dissident challenge posed by this subculture, institutional authorities responded by employing traditional social-control measures to eliminate the threat. To simply state that these measures failed is to ignore the most important fact about the history of the relationship between bikers and authorities. As demonstrated here, the attempt to control these dissidents not only failed; it produced the *antithesis* of the intended outcome. The press's campaign to identify the biker criminal conspiracy and the police crackdown created a pattern of criminal activity among bikers that would not have existed otherwise.

An even more dramatic consequence of social control efforts directed against bikers has been the explosive growth of the outlaw phenomenon. Thompson estimated that no more than eighty-five Hell's Angels resided in all of California by 1965, and no other chapters existed outside of the state before that year.[51] But in subsequent decades, Hell's Angels chapters were established in almost every state and many foreign countries. And the Hell's Angels represent just one of many clubs operating on a national level with chapters in most states. Ironically, as authorities on both the local and national levels intensified efforts to control biker groups, the outlaw identity became even more attractive to many individuals looking for alternatives to more mainstream lifestyle choices.

It must be acknowledged that our generalizations about the effect of traditional social-control strategies on cultural resistance are derived from a limited body of data, since we have been forced to rely on evidence from Thompson's case study. However, the analysis of this case is critical for understanding the broader pattern of relations between outlaw groups and social-control agencies for two reasons. First, the Angels' rise to national prominence during the mid-1960s defined perhaps the single-most important period in the history of the biker subculture. What transpired between the Angels and authorities in these years helped to shape the character of a much broader-based subcultural movement, as many other clubs sought to emulate the Hell's Angels. Secondly, the social-control strategies used against the Angels during this period were employed in later years by local and state authorities all over the country in response to a large number of biker groups. Thus, the paradoxical outcomes of social control described here were reproduced in many different times and places in the years that followed the Hell's Angels' days of infamy.

If institutionalized social-control mechanisms do not function effectively to eliminate cultural resistance and actually serve to invigorate this kind of dissident challenge, then we must look elsewhere for an explanation of how such cultural dissonance is dissipated. We now direct attention to the social control effects of institutional forces that operate in an entirely different realm—the domain of the marketplace.

The Selling of the Menace

In a recent interview, Jeffrey Bleustein, an executive vice-president of Harley-Davidson, Inc., discussed the company's prospects for developing a promising new market in Japan. Acknowledging that the strategy for penetrating the Japanese market would have to take account of the unique character of the Japanese economy and culture, Bleustein nonetheless emphasized the need to stay close to the formula that accounted for the company's phenomenal success in recent years within the U.S. market: "Our motorcycle is not a commodity like a car. It's an emotional toy. People are buying a lifestyle, the Americana image, when they buy it."[52]

In offering this view, Bleustein captures an important insight about the postmodern economy. It is ironic that one of America's oldest companies would become a model of new corporate thinking about the contemporary market. But in recognizing and responding to the market demand for a particular *lifestyle*, and understanding how their primary product articulates with this lifestyle, the executives of Harley-Davidson have moved their organization into the ranks of the most contemporary of U.S. companies. This is all the more remarkable when one considers that the company's primary product, the heavyweight motorcycle, is viewed in the industry as the least technologically advanced motorcycle currently on the market. But in the emerging postmodern economy, this inversion of "modernist" principles is not uncommon—developing new product-lines are not always driven by a commitment to progressive innovation.

The analysis now focuses on the development of a corporate strategy by Harley-Davidson, Inc., to shift from selling a manufactured product to selling a lifestyle. The strategy was not explicitly designed to take advantage of market trends in the new economy. Rather, it evolved serendipitously as key members of Harley-Davidson's managerial staff confronted the powerful subcultural phenomenon that had developed around their product. They came to see this subculture—its stylistic creations and the broader patterns of meaning embodied in them—as a source of ready-made product-lines that could be exploited by the company. Thus, they acquired a special sensitivity to the dark appeal of the biker subculture to a large segment of the general public. And in an entirely unintended fashion, they accomplished what traditional social-control agencies had failed to accomplish—the obliteration of one of the most persistent and disturbing challenges to cultural hegemony to emerge in the post-war period.

The AMF Era and the Japanese Invasion

To account for the evolution of the new corporate strategy and its so-cial-control consequences, it is necessary to describe some important strands of the company's history that are intertwined with the history of the biker subculture. Like most historical descriptions, we can pro-vide only a partial treatment of a complex story. In the present account, we chronicle portions of the corporate history that parallel the profes-sional biography of a key figure in the company's transformation—William G. Davidson, the grandson of a founding member of Harley-Davidson.

Willie G., as he is known to his colleagues and members of the biker fraternity, grew up within the corporate environment of America's pre-eminent motorcycle company, the only one of over 300 U.S. manufac-turers of motorcycles to survive beyond the 1950s. His many years of riding and racing motorcycles, coupled with work experience in various positions in the Harley-Davidson factory and a college degree in design, prepared him to enter his father's company as the head of the design department in 1963.[53] He had just settled into this position when his father's company was sold in 1968 to American Machine and Foundry (AMF), a leader in the sports-equipment business. In deciding to stay on as the head of the design department, Willie G. contributed histori-cal continuity to the company. But his greatest professional achieve-ment would come later, when he played a strategic role in preventing the company's collapse by the end of the 1970s.

With a significant infusion of new capital and the introduction of innovative manufacturing techniques, AMF was able to triple motorcycle production to 75,000 units by the mid-1970s.[54] But this dramatic increase in production led to disastrous consequences: as production went up, the quality of the product declined precipitously. The AMF-model Harleys of the 1970s became well known among motorcycle enthusiasts as inferior machines that vibrated excessively, leaked oil, and often had to be completely overhauled by the dealers before the warranty period expired.[55] As a result of these problems, an important status distinction developed within the biker subculture as the older, pre-AMF Harleys became more highly valued. While the 1970s models were still ridden by a large number of bikers, owners of the older bikes often affirmed their status superiority by referring to the newer models simply as "AMFs."

The significant quality problems of the AMF models led to a series of events that marked one of the most important eras in the company's history. At the same time that Harley-Davidson was acquiring a solid reputation for producing inferior machines, the major Japanese motorcycle manufacturers were perfecting their ability to expropriate the key stylistic components of the "Harley look." An examination of the motorcycle magazines for a ten-year period from the mid-1970s to the mid-1980s reveals a steady progression in the "cruiser" product-lines of the Japanese companies, from models that vaguely resemble Harleys to models that are virtually indistinguishable from the American machines.[56] By the early 1980s, a troubling market situation forced the upper management of AMF to reassess their decision to invest in the motorcycle business: if consumers could buy a Japanese bike that looked exactly like a Harley but offered greater reliability, better performance, and cost thousands less than the real thing, then how could Harley-Davidson possibly compete in this market? They concluded that the future was not bright for the motorcycle division of their company.

The growing Japanese domination of the motorcycle industry eventually led to a radical restructuring of Harley-Davidson in the early 1980s. As Harley's market share in its "super-heavyweight" class (850 cc and above in engine displacement) continued to decline under intense competition with the Japanese companies, AMF began looking for ways to cut its losses. When Willie G. joined with chairman Vaughn Beals, chief engineer Jeffrey Bleustein, and ten other Harley executives in proposing an $81.5 million leveraged buyout of the motorcycle division, AMF saw a way out and negotiated a deal that made Harley-Davidson a private company again on 16 June 1981.[57]

The turn-around in Harley-Davidson's fortunes was still several years away, as the company continued to lose market share through the early '80s and barely survived the loss of its chief financial lender, Citicorp, in 1984. The business journal accounts of Harley's eventual rise from the ashes emphasize the important production and managerial innovations put in place during these years, such as the "productivity triad program," based on just-in-time production, statistical process control, quality circles, and public warehousing of inventory.[58] In these accounts, production innovations led to dramatic increases in quality and lower costs, which eventually paid off in the form of much higher sales by the mid-to late-1980s. Missing from this analysis, however, is attention to the change that contributed most to Harley-Davidson's success—the decision to redefine the company's primary product. It was Willie G. who led the way in bringing about this change.

Willie G. and the Economics of Style

As the self-proclaimed "soul" of Harley-Davidson, Inc., during the last three decades, William G. Davidson has possessed a keener sense of the cultural significance of "America's motorcycle" than perhaps any other member of the company.[59] This special awareness undoubtedly arises from the unique elements of his personal biography. In addition to working almost his entire professional career for the company that bears his family name, he has been an avid motorcycle enthusiast since childhood and has always possessed a special interest in and talent for design and style. In a recent interview, he explained his decision to join the company:

> It was a golden opportunity for me. The job seemed like it would combine my artistic interests with my love for the motorcycle, and I've enjoyed every minute of it. It's a one-hundred percent involvement for me—I collect motorcycles, I ride them during my free time, I'm here during the day, and I eat, sleep, and think motorcycles.[60]

Willie G.'s professional biography also includes evidence of an unusual connection to the biker subculture. As a young man who joined

Harley-Davidson, Inc., just one year before the Hell's Angels achieved national notoriety, he was the contemporary of the first generation of outlaws who created some of the most important biker stylistic forms. Interview data also indicate that he established insider status with the subculture by cultivating the biker look. As Peter Reid notes, "He's not the only Harley executive who . . . mingles with bikers, but he's the most convincing, the one who establishes the closest rapport with riders of all sorts. And he looks the part, with full beard, black leather, and jeans."[61] In addition, he has been a regular participant in national biker events such as the Sturgis, South Dakota, and Daytona, Florida, annual runs (indeed, one of his most successful custom models, the "Sturgis," was named after that famous event). These contacts with the biker subculture were crucial precursors of a new marketing and production strategy that would begin to save the company from disaster by the end of the 1970s.

One of the first efforts to translate a subcultural creation into a marketable product was Willie G.'s version of the "chopper" design. The stylistic innovation known as the "chopped hog" evolved during the 1960s, that decade in which so many crucial developments in the biker subculture occurred. In the early 1960s, outlaws began to create distinctively styled bikes by stripping stock Harleys down to bare essentials. A stock "garbage wagon" (the term bikers use to describe the factory configuration) was typically "chopped" by removing all fairings, turn signals, mirrors, rear fender hinges, and the like to accentuate the massive V-twin engine. In a further elaboration of this motif, bikers began replacing the heavy front forks of the stock "Glide" models (Hydra Glides, Duo Glides, Electra Glides) with the lighter front-ends of the much smaller Sportster model. Willie G. created the Super Glide series in the early 1970s as the factory version of this configuration.[62] With the introduction of this highly successful model and its successors (the Low Rider, the Wide Glide, etc.), the company, for the first time, offered the public an opportunity to purchase a core symbol of subcultural resistance—an outlaw Harley. But this "hog" came with a warranty plan and a twelve-month payment schedule.

Although Willie G.'s contacts with the biker subculture had an immediate payoff in the form of the highly successful Super Glide series, it had a more important long-term consequence: it generated the critical insight that allowed him to formulate an entirely new production strategy for the company. After many years of interacting with bikers and acquiring a deep understanding of biker aesthetics, he came to fully appreciate the special feelings that bikers have for their Harleys. These machines are built from the ground up as an expression of their owner's individuality, serving as, in Hunter Thompson's words, "personal monuments." As Willie G. noted in an interview:

> Our customers really know what they want on their bikes: the kind of instrumentation, the style of bars, the cosmetics of the engine, the look of the exhaust pipes, and so on. Every little piece on a motorcycle is exposed, and it has to look just right. *It's almost like being in the fashion business.* A tube curve or the shape of a timing case cover can generate enthusiasm or be a total turnoff.[63]

Although this statement refers to the attitudes of customers, it is one of many instances in which Willie G. transmogrifies the creative ideas of bikers into the market demands of potential customers, a conceptual leap that paid off in the long run. In another interview, he acknowledged that his participation in biker rallies helped to direct his attention to the importance of custom design:

> It was during some of these very gatherings that he noticed that Harley-Davidson owners [i.e., bikers] were spending thousands of dollars on motorcycle accessories and modifications. . . . Davidson notes that meeting with customers is also "critical to understanding what we should do with the product."[64]

Just as Willie G. succeeded in bringing the "chopped hog" to the showroom floor with the Super Glide series, he also incorporated the subcultural concept of individualistic motorcycle aesthetics into the company's production plan with the Factory Custom series started in 1977.[65] The crucial role this production strategy played in keeping the company solvent has been acknowledged by company officials, even as they underestimate the long-term significance of the change. Executive vice-president Jeffrey Bleustein credits Davidson's skill with saving Harley-Davidson:

> The guy is an artistic genius. In the five year interim before we could bring the Evolution engines on stream, he performed miracles with decals and

paint. A line here and a line there and we'd have a new model. It's what enabled us to survive during those years.[66]

In suggesting that the Factory Custom concept served merely as a stopgap measure against insolvency while crucial changes in engine design were made, this statement downplays the importance of this idea in moving the company toward a redefinition of its primary product and production methods. However, many business analysts *do* emphasize the role of the custom production approach in the Harley-Davidson success story, although they do not connect the more recent incarnations of this approach to Willie G.'s pioneering efforts, or to their subcultural origination. In the language of business analysis, the notion of producing motorcycles as "personal monuments" is reified in the form of a production model focused on producing for "niche markets," by "meeting customer needs either individually or in narrowly defined market segments."[67] In this analysis, Harley-Davidson's success is attributed in large part to its use of flexible technologies and production organization, allowing it to accommodate individual customer requirements:

> Harley-Davidson's proliferation of models, accessories, and customized features together with its comparatively small output (under 40,000 bikes annually) have pushed Harley toward the much heralded goal of an "economic lot size of one."[68]

Bikers building their custom Harleys in garages and living rooms may appear to have little in common with a formal production approach designed for an "economic lot size of one," but the basic idea behind both of these productive activities is the same. And it was William G. Davidson who made the connection.

As Harley-Davidson moved from the difficult years of the mid-1980s into the years of record profits during the early 1990s, they succeeded in fully exploiting the Factory Custom approach as well as bringing additional subculturally produced motorcycle design concepts to the marketplace. Thus, after bikers began using rigid motorcycle frames ("hardtail" frames) as an expression of their disdain for safety and to create a particular aesthetic line, the company introduced the Softtail model that offered the same look but included a hidden shock for rear-end suspension. When bikers started replacing modern telescoping front forks with the old-fashioned "springer" front-ends, the company developed a new springer front-end with modern suspension capabilities and incorporated it into its Springer model. In the decade-and-a-half after Willie G. began the Factory Custom series, virtually every design innovation that emerged within the biker subculture has made its way into the Harley-Davidson product-line. The company perfected the strategy of producing custom models that have the look of outlaw Harleys, but that offer the safety features and maintenance-free characteristics demanded by non-biker, largely middle-class customers.

Motorcycle Design and Lifestyle: The Accessory Market

While the biker subculture proved to be a gold mine of motorcycle design ideas, its real potential as a source of new marketing concepts extended well beyond motorcycle customizing innovations. Company officials fully articulated the marketing and production strategy that would propel Harley-Davidson to the forefront in the postmodern economy only after they began to see the motorcycle as just one of many components of a larger package. The company now defines this package as its primary product. In Bleustein's words quoted earlier, Harley-Davidson's product is a *lifestyle*, not just a motorcycle.

By the late 1980s, Harley-Davidson had moved systematically to incorporate virtually every element of the biker subculture into its product-line, running the gamut from stylistic forms to organizational opportunities. Thus, customers looking to purchase an identity as a biker (if only a part-time identity assumed after working hours or on weekends) could find everything they needed at the local Harley-Davidson dealership. In addition to the iconic "hog," a turn-key machine virtually indistinguishable from an outlaw Harley in appearance, they could buy a biker wardrobe complete with biker boots, leather pants, and a sleeveless vest. They could find a removable tatoo to wear on the next run, purchase a wide range of goods emblazoned with one of the institutionalized Harley-Davidson logos, or buy accessory parts for further personalizing their bikes. These purchases would also entitle them to membership in the factory-sponsored club, the Harley Owners Group (H.O.G.), which organizes runs and other events for its members. What today's Harley-Davidson dealership sells, then, is a particular identity and its attendant lifestyle, with motorcycles constituting just one of the many elements that make up this identity.

Since the identity and lifestyle the company now sells originally evolved outside the corporate system, the real challenge has been to control the production and marketing of external, subcultural creations. This was accomplished through several strategic moves by Harley managers. One of the most important initiatives involved the creation of a trademark licensing program that not only secured new revenue sources, but also gave the company the power to subtly reshape its identity-relevant products for the largest clientele possible.

When the Harley-Davidson management made the decision to launch the licensing program in the early 1980s, they confronted a highly decentralized market situation, with the Harley-Davidson image being marketed by a large number of small independent vendors. In the 1960s and 1970s, these vendors served a clientele made up almost exclusively of bikers. Because of the key significance of Harleys to the biker subculture of resistance, the Harley-Davidson name and logo came to symbolize this resistance more than any other subcultural form. Hence, by displaying the Harley-Davidson name on t-shirts, wallets, and boots, or by incorporating the logo into the design of cigarette cases, window stickers, and leather jackets, the sellers of these products offered bikers a way to project a subversive image.

The company sought to modify the meaning attached to its trademark and make it more attractive to middle-class customers by establishing control over its name and logos. It accomplished this by creating a trademark licensing department in 1982 and enlisting the services of Hamilton Projects, New York, an independent licensing representative specializing in corporate licensing.[69] Thomas G. Parsons, Harley-Davidson's director of trademark licensing, clearly articulated the company's strategy in a recent interview. Lamenting the widespread unauthorized use of Harley's trademark on what he called "lousy products—coke spoons, and a lot of obscene T-shirts," he described his task as "chasing Coca-Cola as a brand."[70]

Seth Siegel, the executive vice-president for Hamilton Projects, has described the two-pronged approach his company recommended to Harley executives. The first goal was to ensure that the company would not lose the rights to its own trademark. This was achieved by instituting an enforcement program consisting of a series of sting operations for identifying and prosecuting independent vendors engaged in the unauthorized use of the trademark. Beginning in 1982, the company started sending to events like the Daytona Bike Week representatives armed with the legal authority to confiscate merchandise and issue warrants. Spandoni quotes a Harley executive who directed the initial operation: "We identified some of the major bootleggers, picked what we thought was the biggest one—the now defunct Joe's MCN, Los Angeles—and started litigation."[71] This case established the precedent needed to effectively eliminate bootleg producers. By forcing independent businesses to seek a formal licensing arrangement with Harley-Davidson, the trademark enforcement program gave the company control over accessory product-lines and secured an important new source of revenue.

Once control over the accessory market was established, the company could focus on the second major goal—using accessory goods to enhance its image. The licensing enforcement program gave Harley the power to choose which products would bear its name or logo and to issue licenses to producers of high quality goods. Spandoni describes this part of the company's strategy:

> Key to the profitability of Harley-Davidson's licensing program is the about 700 authorized franchise dealers, almost all of which allocate at least one-third of their floor space to soft goods. When the availability of bootleg products disappeared, the company took steps to satisfy dealer network demands with a steady supply of exclusive authorized, quality merchandise.[72]

With this kind of control over the accessory products, the company could now use these goods as part of the corporate marketing strategy. John Heiman, the first director of the trademark division, explains this approach:

> If the general public, not just the motorcycle buying public, becomes more familiar with the Harley name through licensed products, such as children's pajamas, the less apprehensive they become about the primary product, motorcycles. . . . If you've got a 6-year-old boy wearing Harley pajamas, sleeping on Harley sheets and bathing with Harley towels, the old man's not going to be bringing home a Suzuki.[73]

In addition to increasing the number of licenses granted in the last decade, the company also began licensing products that appeal to more affluent customers. In contrast to the pre-licensing era when the Harley trademark appeared mainly on bootleg t-shirts and drug paraphernalia, the range of official licensed products today includes wine coolers, gold jewelry, expensive leather goods, sportswear, school supplies, and even a line of men's cologne called Black Leather![74] To be sure, the company has been careful not to dilute the gritty, macho image of Harley riders too much, since this constitutes a crucial part of the identity package it wishes to sell. Thus, it has achieved a mix in the officially licensed accessory market between products that are tied to the biker persona (beer, cigarettes, edible lingerie) and more upscale accessory items such as wine coolers, gold jewelry, and men's cologne. This mix suggests to the customer that one can be a dedicated biker and also a person of privilege.

Finding the appropriate mix between products that signal seediness and danger and those that project affluence is one formula for success in the postmodern economy. Indeed, it is a formula that can inspire a cult following for one's products. Harley-Davidson represents the archetype of such an enterprise in the 1990s, as measured by such indicators as the newly opened Harley-Davidson Cafe in New York City (modeled after another postmodern institution, the Hard Rock Cafe), the increasing celebrity interest in Harleys, the emergence of a mainstream audience for "Harley poetry," the celebration of Harleys in popular music, and the like.[75] Moreover, Harley's success in establishing this cult following is increasingly recognized in the business community as a marketing strategy especially tailored for the new economy. One business publication described the lesson to be learned from Harley's recent achievements:

> To get ahead in the 1990s, a growing number of converts believe, more companies will have to learn how to think like cult marketers. This means breaking down the barriers that separate companies from consumers, and bringing consumers into the process to lead them to identify with the product.[76]

With the success of the licensing program, Harley moved on a second front to gain control of the accessory market. Just as it succeeded in bringing biker-inspired motorcycle designs into the product-line with the Super Glide and Factory Custom series, biker clothing styles were brought in-house with the creation of the Harley-Davidson Motorclothes Division. One measure of the importance of these products is the proportion of overall revenue collected by the company from this division. In 1992, on total sales of $1,105 million, $49 million of revenue came from the Motorclothes sales, a 45 percent increase over the year before.[77] Since some portion of Harley's total revenue comes from products unrelated to motorcycles, the contribution from the Motorclothes Division represents a sizable part of Harley's motorcycle business. A dealer in Orange County, California, who is typical of most dealers across the country, estimates that half of his $5 million annual business comes from sales of Harley accessories, most of which are Motorclothes products.[78] On the basis of these figures, we can conservatively estimate that no less than 25 percent of the company's total revenues can be attributed to Motorclothes sales.

Far more important than the revenue that Harley collects from its accessory lines is the company's strategic use of these items to promote its other major product, motorcycles, and the integration of all of these components into a single lifestyle package. Thus, the Motorclothes Division and Harley's licensing program serve the same essential function—both initiatives allow the company to market key elements of the biker subculture, but in forms that embody product characteristics promoted in the broader consumer market: quality, exclusivity, and high expense. That many of Harley's customers choose to invest in the clothing but not the motorcycle should come as no surprise since, in many ways, the fashion components of the package signify the biker identity more directly than does the motorcycle. Jack Sichterman, an executive at Motorclothes, recently commented on the 20 percent of his customers that do not ride motorcycles: "Some of the clothes are purely functional, but the whole life style we're talking about is more than just riding. Fashion is as important as putting gas in the gas tank."[79]

From Cult Creation to Cult Marketing

The present analysis offers an account of Harley-Davidson's rise from the ashes that differs from the story repeated so often in business publications and the popular press. Though the empirical details are the same, our interpretation of these details differs substantially from the traditional accounts. The analyses of Harley's revival appearing in such widely read business publications as *Forbes* and *Fortune* magazines, and in professional journals such as the *Sloan Management Review* and the *Journal of Business Strategy*, give primary emphasis to innovations in production and to the dramatic improvements in overall efficiency and quality of Harley's product. Thus, as already seen, the traditional account highlights such "world-class" manufacturing strategies as just-in-time inventory, the statistical operator control system, employee involvement (Quality Circles and similar management approaches), and public warehousing.[80] While these manufacturing innovations did play a role in Harley's turnaround, we contend that they were of secondary importance. More crucial to the company's success was the campaign to redefine its primary product by expropriating a distinctive subcultural identity and way of life.

The critical innovation in the company's effort to remake itself, then, was management's insightful analysis of important currents within American cultural change during the last three decades. As we have shown, one individual took the lead in orienting the company to these changes. William G. Davidson, equipped with an artist's eye and an intuitive sense of the special mystique his ancestor's creation held for a large number of people, realized the potential residing in the culture of resistance tied to Harley-Davidson motorcycles. His genius involved looking beyond aspects of the biker subculture that frightened and disgusted most people, to see the creative productions of a group seeking to carve out an exclusive cultural space for itself. Most importantly, he had the foresight to understand the appeal that these subcultural creations would have for middle-class consumers—if they could be packaged properly.

Strong support for our argument can be found in some of Harley's recent efforts to systematize the more informal approach Willie G. and other Harley representatives used to explore the biker subculture. A recent article in the *Chronicle of Higher Education*, for example, profiles two professors of marketing, John Schouten and James T. McAlexander, who followed Willie G.'s lead in organizing their formal research agenda.[81]

The explicit goal of Schouten and McAlexander's research program is to study the subculture of Harley riders. In support of the present analysis, they note that the biker subculture has generated most of the marketing ideas for Harley-Davidson, a discovery that stimulated their initial interest in bikers.[82] In the same way that Willie G. has been unusually perceptive as to the basic character of the emerging postmodern culture and economy, Schouten and McAlexander also understand that the study of contemporary marketing issues requires the use of methodological techniques particularly suited for the new economic reality, techniques more often used by students of "cultural studies":

> Studying the values, consumption interests, social structures, and rituals that unite "a bunch of guys with a common affection for Harleys . . . might look pretty homespun to anthropologists and sociologists who've been using the same methods for a long time. But as far as consumer research goes, this is pretty new."[83]

Once Schouten and McAlexander came to understand what Willie G. and his associates had achieved by "taking the creations of [the] subculture and more or less sanitizing them," they began to explore ways in which this could be accomplished more efficiently.[84] Consequently, soon after two Harley executives heard Schouten and McAlexander discuss their research at a professional meeting, the company negotiated an arrangement by which they would be compensated for sharing their research findings with Harley-Davidson management. The company's view of this arrangement was explained by Harley's director of business planning, Frank Cimermancic:

> Ethnographic research is relatively suspect in the marketing world, but "we don't have the hang-ups other companies do. . . . We get information that we feel isn't potentially colored as much as if we relied on our own employees."[85]

Harley's willingness to retain the services of these two researchers reflects management's clear understanding of how important this type of information is to the overall success of the company. As specially trained research analysts, Schouten and McAlexander possess the methodological skills to generate the kind of information that Willie G. and other Harley stylists have been seeking for several decades. Willie G. may not have regarded his interaction with the subculture as a form of participant-observational, ethnographic research, but this certainly in part characterizes his dealings with biker groups. Schouten and McAlexander simply have been more explicit about their motivations for making connections to the outlaw world.

In completing this analysis, it is important to acknowledge the insights offered by the traditional explanation of Harley's success story and to reconcile this traditional account with the framework presented here. By emphasizing the central importance of Harley's expropriation of the biker identity and lifestyle to its financial revival, we do not mean to imply that manufacturing innovations by the company played no part in its recovery. These innovations *did* contribute to Harley's improving fortunes, but not in the way suggested by the traditional account.

In the present analysis, changes in the manufacturing process that increased the quality and reliability of Harley-Davidson motorcycles are functionally equivalent to changes in the accessory product-line designed to attract middle-class customers. It is important to note that concerns about the reliability of Harleys before the 1980s never discouraged members of the biker subculture from wanting to own them. Indeed, a key element of the biker normative order was the requirement that one must actually *work* on one's Harley, not just ride it, to qualify as a "real" biker. This sentiment is captured in the often repeated subcultural statement that "I'd rather push my Harley than ride a Japanese bike."

Thus, reliability problems became a concern to the company primarily as they looked at the larger potential market of middle-class consumers. "Real" bikers may value the experience of working on their hogs, but middle-class bikers-to-be are not inclined to assume the burden of working on their motorcycles to keep them running, and most lack the skills to do so. Harley executives realized that to attract middle-class buyers, they would have to offer motorcycles that *looked* like outlaw Harleys but functioned as "turn-key" machines. Upper-middle-class professionals facing the demands of career, family life, and home mortgages can assume only a rationalized version of the biker lifestyle—one shorn of the encumbrances that interfere with one's ability to participate in the market economy. "Real" bikers, of course, have traditionally avoided this problem by shunning successful market economy participation in the first place.

Social Control and the Free Market: One Percent to Sixty Percent

Embedded in the preceding story of Harley-Davidson's impressive return to financial solvency is another story about the fate of the subculture described earlier. This counter-narrative describes the power of the marketplace to systematically destroy a subculture by opening up the unique cultural space created by its members to the transforming influences of economic forces. We have seen how Harley-Davidson, Inc., managed to expropriate almost all of the special creations of the biker subculture and in turn sell them to mainstream consumers. But we have also seen that these subcultural forms themselves originated in a collective desire to resist the institutional constraints of the dominant, mainstream social and cultural order. Thus, in the selling of the subculture, we witness a transformation of stylistic resistance into fetishized fashion.

The most obvious indication of this transformation is the subculture's separation from its class base. We have described the ontological connections between the defining elements of the subculture and dominant patterns of lower-class life, arguing that this connection is critical to understanding the meaning of biker subcultural and stylistic forms. But Harley-Davidson managed to take these forms, from motorcycle designs and clothing styles to the "club" organizational structure, and package them to attract middle-class customers. Hence, one can ride a "custom hog" without going to the trouble of building it from the ground up, can wear a pre-tattered sleeveless vest with appropriate patches without engaging in the defilement rituals signified by this garment, and can be a club member of the Harley Owners Group (H.O.G.) without incurring any special obligations to other club members. As a consequence of Harley's achievement, the population of people who now embrace the subculture's styles and organizational structures are no longer predominantly lower class, nor are they experientially connected to these forms in the way that bikers once were.

One indication of this class transformation is the emergence of the "Rich Urban Bikers" (RUBs), the newest Harley phenomenon to receive the attention of the print and electronic media. This group of Harley riders is distinguished by its postmodern temperament—its willingness to decontextualize stylistic forms so that they can be reassembled in distinctive ways—in combining the lower-class cultural resistance of the biker lifestyle with the signifiers of affluence. Thus, while thirty years ago, major media institutions like the *New York Times* introduced the Hell's Angels to the world, they now describe the growth of RUB groups and institutions:

In recent years, these "mild bunchers," as bikers who drown out the noisy angst of their midlife crises with the roars of Harley's are called, have proliferated. The Gotham City Riders roar out of Wall Street and Madison Avenue. Out of the West come the Rolex Riders, from the movie studios and talent agencies of Hollywood. . . . One of the most publicized groups is an informal gang that has formed around Jann Wenner, the publisher of *Rolling Stone* magazine, and Robert Pittman of Time Warner. In this circle, having a motorcycle-riding instructor . . . is starting to replace having a personal trainer as a status symbol.[86]

Media accounts such as this not only document the development of a cult market for Harley's products among the rich and the famous; they also describe, and play a part in, the social control of the biker subculture. As we saw earlier, the media treatment of the subculture thirty years ago worked in tandem with the broader social control campaign waged against the Hell's Angels by law enforcement agencies. The crackdown by police and the demonization of the Angels in the press only served to enhance the deviant profile of this group. By the same token, the image of bikers currently disseminated in the media has also intensified the effects of the market-driven attack on the subculture. Anyone looking for a way to express resentment as to their place at the bottom of the social order would be hard-pressed to find any hint of rebellion in the biker identity when they read newspaper accounts of the "Rolex Riders" and realize that many of the people they observe cruising around on outlaw Harleys are actually the very sorts of upwardly mobile young professionals that they quite understandably detest.

What we see in the Harley-Davidson success story, then, is an important example of the effective control of dissidence in late capitalist society. While traditional social-control strategies failed miserably as a means of dealing with the cultural resistance represented by the outlaw phenomenon, the market forces of the postmodern economy have functioned, in an entirely unintended fashion, to eliminate this resistance. In an earlier time, some lower-class individuals looked to the world of outlaw bikers as a way to respond to the degrading experience of living among the mass of unemployed and underemployed in a culture that celebrates wealth and privilege. In the face of the ongoing assault on one's dignity experienced within a lifespace marked by the dominant institutions of American society, those who joined the ranks of motorcycle outlaws created a cultural space that offered them an unusual opportunity for a certain kind of privilege and respect. But as this subcultural world has been disassembled by the free market and mixed with the cultural and economic principles of the very system that bikers sought to escape, it has ceased to function as an alternative pathway to "class" (in the biker's sense of this term). There is little honor in being a "righteous biker" when the status distinctions that emerge within the ranks of the biker fraternity mirror the broader system of stratification in American society, a system in which rich and poor stand worlds apart even as they embrace a common identity of style.

Conclusion

Our goal in this chapter has been to describe the rise and fall of a distinctively American subculture and to identify the political and economic forces that have shaped this subcultural evolution. Drawing on Herbert Marcuse's analysis of the totalizing character of late capitalist society, we have described a form of cultural resistance that was first spawned by the political economic system, next criminalized within it, and finally consumed by it. But the dynamic we have described here is, by no means, unique to outlaw bikers. The twentieth century is filled with cases of subcultural resistance that have followed the same pathway as the one-percenters. Virtually every new musical genre of this century, from jazz and rock to punk and rap, emerged as a subcultural creation of groups occupying subordinate positions within the political-economic system, only to be by turns stigmatized and appropriated. Other stylistic forms that have defined the cutting edge of artistic production or fashion design—from graffiti art to punk clothing—have also evolved from expressions of lower-class resistance into sanitized styles marketable to mainstream audiences. The marketing of biker style to middle-class Americans stands only as one of the more striking instances of the process by which the economics of style comes to dominate the politics of cultural resistance.

Notes

1. Herbert Marcuse, *One Dimensional Man* (Boston: Beacon Press, 1964).
2. Hoover's Handbook of American Business, "Harley-Davidson, Inc." (n.p., 1994), 584.

3. *Texas Monthly* 20 (July 1992).

4. Jeff Ferrell, "Towards a Critical Criminology of Culture" (Paper presented at the Annual Meeting of the Academy of Criminal Justice Sciences, Kansas City, MO, March 1993).

5. Hunter S. Thompson, *Hell's Angels: A Strange and Terrible Saga* (New York: Ballantine, 1967).

6. Craig Vetter, "Playboy Interview: Hunter Thompson," *Playboy*, November 1974, 75–90, 245–46.

7. See Randal Montgomery, "The Outlaw Motorcycle Subculture," *Canadian Journal of Criminology* 18 (1976): 332–42; Randal Montgomery, "The Outlaw Motorcycle Subculture: II," *Canadian Journal of Criminology* 19 (1977): 356–61; Mark Watson, "Outlaw Motorcyclists: An Outgrowth of Lower Class Cultural Concerns," *Deviant Behavior* 2 (1980): 31–48; Columbus B. Hooper and Jonny "Big John" Moore, "Hell on Wheels: The Outlaw Motorcycle Gangs," *Journal of American Culture* 6 (1983): 58–64; James E. Quinn, "Sex Roles and Hedonism Among Members of 'Outlaw' Motorcycle Clubs," *Deviant Behavior* 8 (1987): 47–63.

8. Because many of the key ethnographic studies used in this section were published well over twenty years ago, it is important to note that the subculture we describe here largely does not exist in the 1990s. However, the biker subculture of the 1960s and 1970s served as the primary source of product ideas for Harley-Davidson, Inc.

9. Joseph T. Howell, *Hard Living on Clay Street: Portraits of Blue Collar Families* (New York: Anchor Press, 1973); Oscar Lewis, "The Culture of Poverty," in *On Understanding Poverty: Perspectives from the Social Sciences*, ed. Daniel Patrick Moynihan (New York: Basic Books, 1968), 187–200; Walter Miller, "Lower Class Culture as a Generating Milieu of Gang Delinquency," *Journal of Social Issues* 14 (1958): 5–19.

10. Thompson, 274.

11. Quinn, 52.

12. Quinn, 51.

13. Quinn, 51–52.

14. Quinn, 55.

15. Dick Hebdige, *Subculture: The Meaning of Style* (New York: Methuen, 1979).

16. See Howell, *Hard Living*; Miller, "Lower Class."

17. Watson, 40.

18. Thompson, 148.

19. Thompson, 149.

20. Montgomery, "The Outlaw," 338.

21. Montgomery, "The Outlaw II," 358–59.

22. Montgomery, "The Outlaw," 336.

23. Watson, 41.

24. Montgomery, "The Outlaw II," 359.

25. Watson, 43.

26. Montgomery, "The Outlaw," 340. Watson, 45, noted that 40 percent of the articles in the 1977 issue of *Easyrider* were concerned with death.

27. Thompson, *Hell's Angels*; Montgomery, "The Outlaw."

28. Watson, 45.

29. Montgomery, "The Outlaw," 337.

30. Howell, 328–37.

31. Thompson, 61. Watson, 38.

32. Watson, 45.

33. See also Thompson, 313–22.

34. Watson, 43.

35. Quinn, 48.

36. Ferrell, "Towards a Critical Criminology"; Stephen Lyng, "Edgework: A Social Psychological Analysis of Voluntary Risk Taking," *American Journal of Sociology* 95 (1990): 851–86.

37. Lyng, 860–63.

38. Montgomery, "The Outlaw II," 360.

39. Howell, 355.

40. Howard S. Becker, *Outsiders: Studies in the Sociology of Deviance* (New York: The Free Press, 1963); Edwin M. Lemert, *Social Pathology: A Systematic Approach to the Theory of Sociopathic Behavior* (New York: McGraw-Hill, 1951).

41. Thompson, 85.

42. Perhaps the best example of the relationship between media constructs and the biker subculture is the influence of Peter Fonda's *Easy Rider*, released in 1967, on biker style. Among the many consequences of this very popular movie was the emergence of a national publication directed to the biker population—*Easy Rider Magazine*.

43. Thompson, 21.

44. Thompson, 12.

45. Thompson, 39.

46. Thompson, 37.

47. Thompson, 55.

48. Thompson, 73.

49. Thompson, 57–58.

50. Thompson, 65.

51. Thompson, 42. See also Gary T. Marx, "Ironies of Social Control: Authorities as Contributors to Deviance Through Escalation, Nonenforcement and Covert Facilitation," *Social Problems* 28 (1981): 221–46.

52. Barbara Holmes, "Harley's Hog Heaven," *Canadian Business* 65 (May 1992): 30.

53. "Marketer of the Month: Willie G. Davidson: Born to Ride," *Sales and Marketing Management* 143 (April 1991): 26–27.

54. Peter C. Reid, *Well Made in America: Lessons from Harley-Davidson on Being the Best* (New York: McGraw-Hill, 1990), 26.

55. One of several Harleys owned by the senior author was a seventies model "Sportster" that had been overhauled by its original owner at about 2,000 miles.

56. *Cycle* (New York: CBS Magazines, 1977–1987).

57. Reid, 214.

58. Robert M. Grant et al., "Appropriate Manufacturing Technology: A Strategy Approach," *Sloan Management Review* 33 (Fall 1991): 43–54; Michael Jenkins, "Gaining a Financial Foothold Through Public Warehousing," *Journal of Business Strategy* 13 (May–June 1992): 53–57.

59. "Marketer of the Month," 26.

60. "Marketer of the Month," 26.

61. Reid, 38.

62. Reid, 39.

63. Reid, 41, emphasis added.

64. "Marketer of the Month," 27.

65. "Marketer of the Month," 27.

66. Reid, 42–43.

67. Grant et al., 45.

68. Grant et al., 47.

69. Marie Spandoni, "Harley-Davidson Revs up to Improve Image," *Advertising Age*, 5 August 1985, 30.

70. John Marchese, "Forever Harley," *New York Times*, Sunday, 17 October 1993, sec. 9, p. 10.

71. Spandoni, 30.

72. Spandoni, 30.

73. Spandoni, 30.

74. Don Veraska, "Putting Muscle into Trademark Protection," *Advertising Age*, 9 June 1986, S12-S13.

75. Marchese, 10; Julie Schlax, "Ode to a Hog," *Forbes*, 24 December 1990, 109.

76. Jon Berry, "The Power of Cult Brands," *Adweek's Marketing Week* 33 (24 February 1992): 18–21.

77. Marchese, 10; Standard NYSE Stock Reports 61, 27 May 1994, no. 103, sec. 17.

78. Duke Hefland, "Born to Be Chic," *Los Angeles Times*, 9 September 1991, A3.

79. Marchese, 10.

80. Reid, 141–99; Grant et al., 43; Jenkins, "Gaining."

81. Peter Monaghan, "2 Professors Study the Harley Subculture," *The Chronicle of Higher Education* 39 (20 January 1993): A5.

82. Monaghan, A5.

83. Monaghan, A5.

84. Monaghan, A5.

85. Monaghan, A5.

86. Marchese, 10.

12 ◂ ◂ ◂

The World Politics of Wall Painting

JEFF FERRELL

People who live, work, and wander in cities around the U.S. increasingly encounter an urban environment decorated by street kids, alternative artists, political activists, and other unauthorized outsiders. The Chicago art collective X-Girlfriends creates a billboard featuring the iconography of Elvis, John Lennon, and Jesus, and has their billboard paint-bombed in response.[1] Near the Rocky Flats Nuclear Weapons Plant outside Denver, John Craig Freeman and Greenpeace launch Operation Greenrun II—a series of five Day-Glo billboards depicting nuclear environmental destruction.[2] In Dallas, Chicago, New York, and elsewhere, artists and activists attack alcohol and tobacco advertising not by creating billboards but by altering or destroying existing billboards aimed at minority populations. Similarly, Survival Research Laboratories founder Mark Pauline executes a series of disturbing, even threatening, "billboard pranks" in San Francisco; Z Magazine publishes a guide to billboard alteration and other forms of public "guerrilla art" aimed at countering the Columbus quincentennial; artist Robbie Conal creates "grotesquely painted" posters of religious and political leaders, which he puts up "guerrilla style, late at night, over public spaces in many cities"; and members of the artists' group Art Attack note that their public projects "fluctuate between legality and illegality. . . . In everything we do, there's some illegality in there somewhere."[3]

As city billboards and city spaces become sites for political and aesthetic activism, for the guerrilla art of social and cultural conflict, so do city walls. Considered by some artists the "mural painting capital of the world," Los Angeles has seen more than a thousand major murals go up on its walls since 1970—many of them painted by black, Latino/Latina, and women artists.[4] Latina muralist and activist Judy Baca, for example, has not only contributed important works but organized projects like "The Great Wall of Los Angeles," a monumental, ongoing collaboration among kids from diverse ethnic backgrounds.[5] Also participating in sanctioned mural projects in Los Angeles, Denver, Philadelphia, San Antonio and other cities are kids recruited from the unsanctioned hip-hop graffiti underground.[6] Growing out of the black neighborhood cultures of New York City in the early and mid-1970s, hip-hop denotes a set of alternative cultural practices that includes new forms of music (rap, sampling) and graffiti "writing." In contrast to street-gang graffiti, which is often organized around issues of territoriality and control, this hip-hop graffiti is driven by the stylistic innovations of graffiti writers who produce complex systems of street imagery and design. As this graffiti underground has spread over the past two decades to cities throughout the United States, it has quite literally changed the look of urban life. Illegal (and legal) hip-hop murals now decorate alley walls, underpasses, and other public and private city spaces across the continent.[7]

Those of us who have recently had the opportunity to take our devalued dollars out of the United States know, though, that this efflorescence of public art is hardly limited to the walls of U.S. cities. By its final years the Berlin Wall itself had been covered over with an astonishing array of images.[8] Paris walls feature a remarkable collection of elaborate, elegant stencil art—stencils of jazz players and cancan dancers, rock-throwing protesters and space travelers, zebras and spiders.[9] In Toronto, artists illicitly affix iron plaques to city walls, and bolt "book-sculptures" to telephone poles—works of street art that critique colonialism and instruct passersby in the making of Molotov cocktails.[10] London has for some years now seen aggressive billboard alteration by feminists, anarchists, and animal-rights activists, and supported an active graffiti underground.[11] Recently, London-based Pakistani artist Rasheed Araeen constructed a "Golden Verses" billboard featuring a lush oriental carpet and "foreign" calligraphy; he later produced a second work that commented on the racist graffiti the billboard quite predictably generated.[12] In Northern Ireland, Catholics paint their resistance and remembrance into heart-breaking wall murals, and Protestants and the British military respond with paint-bombs and murals of their own. Lacking access to newspaper or radio, young Palestinian militants in the occupied lands likewise use wall painting as their primary form of communication and resistance to Israeli authority.[13] In Sao Paulo, Brazilian artists participate in a modernist graffiti counterculture; in Buenos Aires, "the street communication of political ideas and messages" through wall painting and graffiti has emerged as "an accepted and structured media system."[14]

If these world-wide moments of public art are remarkable for their variety and innovation, they are also notable for the cultural connections they trace. Toronto's street sculptures, Araeen's London billboard, Northern Ireland's Catholic murals—all capture and confront the machinery of racism, colonialism, and imperialism, and in so doing move beyond the locales in which they are found to the contested relations of one culture to another. But beyond this, there exists a dynamic in world wall painting that takes us back to the streets of the United States. While visiting Prague in the summer of 1991, I came across various forms of wall painting and graffiti, including Keith Haring-style human figures and one particularly interesting wall stencil. A rearing red horse, it incorporated the following injunction, in English: "Make Graffiti!" This and other of my journeys have also confirmed what Henry Chalfant, James Prigoff, and others had begun to document by the mid-1980s: hip-hop graffiti, the graffiti of the urban underclass in the U.S., has taken hold beyond the borders of the United States. Chalfant and Prigoff photographed stylish, sophisticated hip-hop graffiti murals—and discovered active hip-hop graffiti subcultures—in London, Amsterdam, Paris, Copenhagen, Vienna, and other large and small cities throughout Europe and beyond. More recently, researchers have begun to document the spread of hip-hop graffiti to Mexico and Central America—often the result of the deportation efforts of the U.S. Immigration and Naturalization Service.[15] My own recent research into European hip-hop graffiti verifies the tremendous scope and vitality of world hip-hop wall painting. In Amsterdam, London, Frankfurt, and other major cities—but also in smaller cities and towns throughout Great Britain, the Netherlands, and Germany—innumerable murals decorate school buildings, apartment houses, bridge abutments, walkways, and especially the walls in and around train stations and subway platforms. And while the many murals certainly incorporate individual innovations and the shared aesthetics of the local subcultures, they also reproduce with remarkable precision the stylistic conventions of U.S. hip-hop graffiti.

This interplay of cultural resources locates world wall painting directly inside issues of cultural diffusion and cultural imperialism. As wall painters around the world appropriate the language, imagery, and style of cultural production elsewhere—and especially the innovations of hip-hop graffiti writers and other U.S. artists—they at the same time participate in the politics of world culture. In some cases those engaged in this process idolize and mythologize their counterparts elsewhere, utilizing not only the work of alternative artists but the products of the mainstream culture industries in the United States and other "developed" countries. In other cases the process is less one of canonization than of confrontation, as street artists memorialize resistance to cultural imperialism and political domination. In whatever form, though, the production of wall painting and street art worldwide interlocks with broader relationships of world politics and power.

Significantly, world wall painting also goes on within the political dynamics of crime and criminalization. The remarkable expansion of hip-hop graffiti throughout the United States has been shadowed by increasingly aggressive "wars on graffiti" in cities across the country. Coordinated by groups like the National Graffiti Information Network—an organization of political and corporate elites that disseminates information, develops legislation, engineers "sting" operations, and pressures those who support graffiti-style art—these campaigns work to criminalize hip-hop and other graffiti forms. Working with political leaders, judges, and police officials on new strategies of enforcement and control, and with local and national media on strategies of "moral panic," the anti-graffiti campaigns mirror the "wars" on drugs, gangs, and other late capitalist demons.[16] Outside the United States, street artists also face the power of local and national authorities. Some work within political systems that define their wall painting as a direct threat to state authority, and therefore confront the possibility of violent state reprisals.[17] Others operate in political and cultural climates that condemn their appropriation of foreign imagery and style as a sort of treasonous betrayal of national identity. In Paris, for example, political leaders, security agencies, and local newspapers debate the merits and dangers of graffiti. The debate, though, centers not on the wall stencils described earlier but around the fact that France's culture minister, Jack Lang, a man who "has long tried to shield France from incursions by American culture," has recently embraced "graffiti writers [as] the artists of hip hop culture."[18] To examine graffiti around the world—with its elaborate intersections of cross-cultural style, political resistance, and criminalization—is therefore to inquire into the world politics of wall painting.

Case Studies in Wall Painting, Politics, and Law

Two contemporary cases begin to get at this politics of street painting, revealing the situated dynamics of local wall art and also the intersituational interplay of cross-cultural politics that gives the art its meaning. First, as Joel Sheesley and Wayne Bragg have documented, Nicaraguan national hero Augusto Sandino has maintained a remarkable, ongoing presence in contemporary Nicaraguan life through the multitude of Sandino images that decorate Nicaragua's streets.[19] This contemporary Nicaraguan street iconography has recalled, and reproduced, Sandino's passionate resistance to outside domination in the 1920s and 1930s; the images of Sandino on public walls have contributed to an ongoing historical battle, to a continuity of resistance. As such, the images, and the painting of them, have constituted active participation in an evolving national and international conflict, rather than mere memories or reflections of earlier altercations.

Prior to the overthrow of Somoza in 1979, for example, Nicaraguans illegally painted Sandino images and Sandinista slogans as signs of protest and resistance; in the apt phrase of Omar Cabezas, they engaged in "la insurreccion de las parades"—the insurrection of the walls. These insurrectionary images "gave voice to people who had no voice and gave a medium to ideas that otherwise could not appear."[20] After the overthrow this wall painting continued but took on the character of a collective, public discussion about political progress, social change, and other issues—with the image of Sandino often used to signify popular solidarity and resistance to continued U.S. aggression. During 1984—the fiftieth anniversary of Sandino's assassination—his street images took on additional, commemorative meanings.

Since the election of Violeta Chamorro in 1990 Sandino street images and other Sandinista murals have come under attack, and in the process have acquired still other permutations of legal, political, and cultural meaning. Before leaving power, the Sandinista government passed Law 90, which declared many murals historical treasures to be preserved. Despite this, "maintenance workers" employed by the new government have painted over many Sandino images and Sandinista murals—at times with paint donated by a U.S.-based paint company. This mural obliteration campaign—part of a larger campaign to erase Sandinista symbols and ideas from Nicaraguan culture—has in turn led to "pitched battles" between muralists and armed "goons," new forms of graffiti in response, and ongoing public criticism and debate.[21]

If the meaning of Sandino street images and murals has continued to emerge out of large-scale political conflict and change, it has also taken shape within specific social and cultural moments of production. The message carried by a particular Sandino image depends in part on other images that are painted along with it: revolutionary figures, machetes and rifles, laurel branches, and a dove of peace. Moreover, long before the recent obliteration campaign, Sandino images were caught up in the interplay of street politics and thus often carried commentary added after the painting of the image, or after subsequent alterations that communicated condemnation or endorsement. Street images of Sandino have in this way participated in an ongoing, "informal medium of communication in Nicaragua"; as Sheesley and Bragg say, "One gets the feeling in Managua that the news is erupting on the walls. And the messages are always changing."[22]

The specific manner in which Sandino's image has been reproduced on Nicaraguan walls carries its own meaning as well. Like the Parisian images of jazz players and space travelers, many Sandino street images have been produced from hand-cut stencils. Whether the products of individuals, or organized groups like the Juventud Sandinista (Sandinista Youth) or CPC (Popular Center for Culture), these stenciled images of Sandino embody a variety of meanings that other images do not. To begin with, stencil images ride the boundary between the professional, machine aesthetic of endless reproducibility and the hand-made aesthetic of personal innovation. Although many of the stenciled Sandino images have been the products of organized groups, the images are most often designed by nonprofessional artists within the groups, and are because of this "striking in their variation" and "informality."[23] These stenciled images therefore capture nicely the dialectic between organization and spontaneity, between a regularized iconography and an irregular process of production. And in this way they reproduce not only Sandino's image, but the complex meaning of his resistance. Sandino's guerrilla war against U.S. intervention succeeded to the extent that it blended organization and innovation, predictability and particularity; contemporary street stencils of Sandino reinvent this dialectic. Of course, under Somoza (and perhaps Chamorro) the actual process of street stenciling Sandino images also recalls earlier forms of resistance. As a simple and portable means of image reproduction, stenciling provides the safety of quickness and relative anonymity within a hostile legal and political climate, as well as the practical mechanism for creating a collective style of protest and resistance to it.[24]

John Bushnell moves across the globe to examine a similar flowering of graffiti in Moscow and other formerly Soviet cities over the past fifteen years.[25] Bushnell traces the development of contemporary urban graffiti in the Soviet Union from its origins in the late 1970s activities of soccer team fan gangs, or "fanaty." These organized fanaty groups painted their favorite soccer team's logo on city walls, altered or defaced competing logos, and in so doing evolved identifiable symbolic and linguistic codes for writing and responding to graffiti. Soon this impetus toward graffiti writing, and the writing codes themselves, were taken up by others. Kids immersed in the rock-and-roll underground began to write Western band names and declarations of band loyalty; fans of heavy metal rock music formed distinct groups—the "metallisty"—and started writing a unique logo, "HMR" (for "Heavy Metal Rock"), along with lists of Western bands.[26] Pacifists, punks, and other members of a well-organized counterculture—as well as their countercultural enemies like neo-fascists ("fashisty") and the working-class vigilante "Liubery"—also adapted the argot and style of fan gang graffiti by the early to mid-1980s. And at the same time, a remarkable graffiti collection was emerging in a Moscow stairwell: graffiti devoted to the writer Mikhail Bulgakov and his novel *The Master and Margarita*.

Like Sandino graffiti in Nicaragua, these new forms of Soviet graffiti must be understood as something more than mere "representations" of cultural and subcultural activities. The writing of illegal graffiti, and in turn the increasing public presence of graffiti images, helped shape and define the subcultures themselves. Early on, fanaty gangs grew largely through their graffiti; fanaty graffiti served as a "declaration of existence," which "spread a message . . . elicited imitative behavior" and ultimately "helped to organize and demark the gang subculture." As graffiti writing spread to other groups, it likewise provided organizing codes and symbols: the HMR logo for metallisty, the circled-A anarchy symbol for punks, the four-pronged peace symbol for pacifists. As Bushnell concludes in regard to the larger Soviet urban youth subculture of which these groups are a part:

> The history of the subculture in most respects is coterminus with the history of Soviet public graffiti, because graffiti have played a crucial role in generating, defining, and sustaining the subculture. And we can read in the graffiti many of the subculture's social and cultural attributes. As argot, the graffiti express a cultural program and distance the subculture from adult society.[27]

Bushnell's conclusions about a Soviet urban youth subculture that incorporates the particular subcultures of metallisty, punks, pacifists, and others points to a second characteristic of this emerging graffiti: it provided a socio-linguistic structure through which subcultural groups could carry on a sort of collective conversation beyond their borders. Certainly within particular subcultures the graffiti furnished both the medium and the motivation for exchanges of ideas and the public assignment of status. In part because of its common origins in fanaty graffiti, though, this graffiti also incorporated conventions of public discourse that transcended its use by any one group. For some subcultural groups, this shared graffiti created common ground, and for some of their members, the possibility of movement between one group and another. But even those subcultures that stood against each other, which battled one another on the level of ideology and style, were also joined by their graffiti—that is, by the medium through which their conflicts were conducted. Thus, despite their differences, "the writers of the graffiti constitute a sharply demarked linguistic community . . . a community sharing a language of cultural opposition," which "constitutes the Soviet urban youth subculture."[28]

To see in this subcultural graffiti "a language of cultural opposition" is to recognize it as part of a larger stylistic assault that Soviet youth launched on the calcified Soviet legal and political hierarchy and on the drab society it engineered. As Soviet youth subcultures begin to write and organize around graffiti, they at the same time developed a broad politics of stylistic resistance. As a medium of definition and communication, Soviet subcultural graffiti interwove with dress codes, hair styles, band names and affiliations, public presentations of self, and other stylistic decisions to construct distinct subcultural identities. Thus, Bushnell argues, the Soviet youth subculture evolved a set of symbols that constituted "a challenge to the dominant verities and values of society." In one case, punks and pacifists painted "Punki" and a pacifist logo on a headquarters of Komsomol, the official Soviet youth agency. But beyond this sort of focused confrontation, the sheer volume and audacity of Soviet youth style, as embodied in graffiti and other forms, challenged the official facade of Soviet society. If the Soviet hierarchy could promulgate the equation of "blank walls, orderly society," then the emergence of subcultural graffiti could proclaim "the kinds of unregulated, spontaneous activities that were taking place" underneath the official order.[29]

As subcultural graffiti and style announced a playful undermining of the Soviet state's legal and political authority, they also helped shape resistance to this authority. The Soviet rock-and-roll underground constructed an alternative aesthetic for Soviet youth, provided networks of informal organization and, moreover, generated a thriving and illegal underground economy. Amateur and semi-professional bands, unofficial band tours, black-market musical instruments and tapes—all created a subterranean world of relative autonomy and influence. The graffiti devoted to Bulgakov and his *The Master and Margarita* had a similar effect. As this graffiti began to accumulate in a stairwell associated with the novel, it not only expressed "a carnivalesque assault on dogma and authority" but began to build a certain social momentum. More graffiti drew more young Bulgakov admirers, who left still more graffiti and who demanded that a nearby apartment be converted to a Bulgakov museum. The building manager, city officials, and other authorities of course refused; but eventually, the apartment was abandoned, admirers moved in, and an official Bulgakov museum evolved. Bushnell concludes that "the Bulgakov fans who four years earlier had broached the idea of creating a museum had triumphed completely, due in no small part to the impact of the graffiti themselves. The graffiti not only expressed opinion, they organized it." And, when these sorts of popular actions spread under Gorbachev, "the subculture led the way: in 1988 most political graffiti either included countercultural labels . . . or appeared at or near countercultural tusovki [hangouts]."[30]

Significantly, the essential language of this subcultural graffiti, and thus the essential language of opposition and resistance for Soviet youth, was English. Soviet youth subcultures have picked up English words and phrases from Western band names, rock lyrics, and other sources, and Soviet kids pepper their speech and writing with English. As a member of the Russian rock band Aquarium said to me, when I apologized for visiting Leningrad but not speaking Russian, "If the Beatles had been Russian, you would speak Russian!"[31] Beyond this casual use, Soviet youth incorporated English in their graffiti in such a way as to construct a "cultural boundary" between themselves and the larger Soviet culture. Pacifists and punks carefully wrote their graffiti in English. Within the graffiti of fan gangs, rock and heavy metal aficionados, and even the Liubery, English was likewise the "language of exaltation," the linguistic medium for elevating status and style beyond that which the Russian language could convey. In developing a new linguistic practice—an emergent, sometimes jumbled form of "Soviet graffiti English"—Soviet youth at the same time created a language of cultural opposition that subverted Soviet language and culture and set the young apart from it.[32]

Official Soviet commentators, of course, regularly dismissed such developments as corruptions of Soviet life by pernicious Western influences. Many progressives in the West may be tempted to agree, viewing this as a classic case of Western cultural imperialism. But the social and cultural dynamics are not so simple; they reflect less monolithic cultural imposition than subtle, ambiguous, and ironic processes of cultural appropriation and change. To see how Soviet youth subcultures adopted and adapted Western symbols and identities, and the English language itself, is not to deny the awesome, intrusive power of Western culture industries but rather to affirm the creative cultural prowess of Soviet kids. Like Nicaraguan street painters and U.S. graffiti artists, Soviet graffiti writers are not passive victims of their own society's mass culture or of cultures imported from abroad; especially when working within active subcultures, they are able to reshape outside cultural products as they incorporate them into their daily lives.

This reworking of cultural imperialism into an oppositional counterculture—this reshaping of imported mass culture into local popular culture—reminds us also that cultural materials and practices must be examined not in the abstract but in the specific social circumstances of their production and use. The various meanings of the Beatles, Augusto Sandino, and other cultural constructions evolve in the contexts of everyday life. Such cultural products carry a complex capacity, an ambiguous potential, for stagnation and liberation, both in the countries of their origin and in those to which they may be imported. This ambiguity also embodies an instructive irony. As Soviet youth culture shows, the very products of cultural imperialism—the identities and styles that dominate world markets and world culture—can be used by their recipients to repudiate and undermine domination domestically. Especially in the case of Soviet youth, who encountered Western language and music through an underground cultural and economic system rather than through market saturation and aggressive advertising campaigns, foreign cultural products could become stylish levers for prying loose an oppressive social order.[33]

World Wall Painting and Cultural Criminology

Hip-hop graffiti artists in the U.S. and abroad; wall painters in Northern Ireland, the Gaza Strip, and other contested lands; Nicaraguan Sandino muralists; kids inventing new forms of graffiti from inside the underground youth cultures of the Soviet Union—all reveal the remarkable range of informal, illegal wall painting worldwide. But as we survey this rich range of illicit public art, we are confronted time and again with the same dilemma: world wall painting hopelessly and inexorably confounds the categories of art, culture, crime, and politics. Street painters from Managua to Moscow demonstrate that illegal wall painting worldwide can no more be conveniently categorized alongside other forms of artistic production than it can simply be subsumed under headings of cultural imperialism, vandalism, or juvenile delinquency. It is all of these, and more. Illegal wall painting exists at the intersection of art and crime, at the crossroads of cultural production, political resistance, and criminalization. Though wall painters worldwide draw on a plethora of folk art and art world traditions, and in some cases benefit from training or participation in legitimate art worlds, the illegality of their art alters the lived experience and lived politics of their artistic production.[34] And though wall painters worldwide are often apprehended, categorized—and dismissed—by legal and political authorities as nothing more than juvenile delinquents, vandals, or mindless destroyers of public and private property, they clearly are something more; their motivations, politics, and style give distinctive texture and shape to their criminality.

Moreover, wall painting around the world reveals that the very categories of art, culture, politics, and crime do not represent discrete arenas of lived experience but rather moments intertwined along a changing continuum of marginality and resistance. In Northern Ireland, Catholic mural painting draws on evocative cultural symbols to commemorate prison hunger strikers and other past victims of legal injustice; but these murals in turn incur the wrath of the British military and the RUC, which respond with paint-bombs and, in one case, the killing of a sixteen-year-old youth, gunned down while painting slogans on a Belfast wall.[35] In Nicaragua, street painters move in and out of illegality and danger as they challenge Somoza, ridicule ongoing U.S. imperialism, and commemorate popular victories past and present. When their works are in turn obliterated under the Chamorro government, the legality of painting over the murals now becomes an issue. Soviet graffiti artists utilize Western symbols, styles, and language to carve out cultural space, to shape alternative youth subcultures, inside the Soviet Union; but in so doing they also function to undermine the turgid legal and political authority of the Soviet state and to harbinger new social and cultural arrangements. Hip-hop graffiti artists in the U.S. confront a social and political order that increasingly criminalizes their everyday lives, invent in response an elaborate alternative culture, and see this culture carried not only into the galleries and collections of the mainstream art world but to artistic undergrounds in Europe and beyond. At the same time, though, aggressive anti-graffiti campaigns in the United States increasingly criminalize hip-hop graffiti, lead to the arrest of more and more graffiti artists, and promote public understandings of hip-hop graffiti as indistinguishable from street-gang activity and other forms of everyday criminality.[36]

The world politics of wall painting—the worldwide production of street painting as a form of cultural identification and political resistance, the appropriation and reinvention of cultural and cross-cultural materials in this painting, and the criminalization of this process by those it threatens—can therefore only be understood from within a perspective that critically synthesizes cultural and criminological analysis. Critical criminological analysis can reveal the legal and political structures that stand in opposition to wall painting, the evolution of particular statutes and enforcement strategies within these structures, the broader process by which wall painting and wall painters are criminalized, and the various ways in which wall painters resist these legal controls. Critical cultural analysis can in turn explore issues ranging from the shared aesthetics of wall painting subcultures to the representational and symbolic dynamics of anti-wall-painting media campaigns. Synthesized within a cultural criminology, these two approaches can begin to get at the aesthetic assumptions of legal authorities as well as wall painters, the subtle interplay between legal control strategies and symbolic resistance, the ironic relationship between criminalization and increased subcultural visibility, and other lived interconnections between the culture and crime of wall painting.

As such a cultural criminology explores the confluence of cultural and criminal processes in illegal wall painting, it can also tackle the tangled politics of cross-cultural appropriation, confrontation, and criminalization. While the murals of Northern Ireland and Nicaragua expose and confront outside political domination, for example, the hip-hop murals of Europe and Central America and the "graffiti English" of Russian youth subcultures expose other less imperial strands of cross-cultural communication. And in each of these cases, it is not only the wall painting itself but the reactions of legal and political authorities to it that are shaped by issues of cultural integrity and cultural imposition. Along with exploring broad cross-cultural currents, a cultural criminology can also expose the smaller, situated structures of symbolism and perception that surround wall painting. What, for example, are the day-to-day meanings of wall painting and other forms of illicit public resistance for the street artists and activists who create them, for the passersby who encounter them, and for the agents of legal control sent out against them?

The social and cultural dynamics of world wall painting highlight two further dimensions of interest for any cultural criminology. First, as illegal wall painting again demonstrates, the intersections of culture and crime seem most often to be occupied by a particular social group: the young. The street stencils of Nicaraguan Juventud Sandinista members, the wall painting among the subcultures of Soviet youth, the pervasive graffiti of young hip-hop writers in the U.S. and beyond—all remind us that kids and their subcultures form aesthetic communities that survive in the changing margins between artistry and authority, innovation and criminalization.

Second, the politics of world wall painting make clear that, for young painters and old authorities alike, style once again matters. When street painters around the world confront those in power with the elaborate and illegal symbolism of their work, they do not engage in some generic criminality; they engage in particular "crimes of style." At the same time, the responses of those in power are shaped by their own stylistic imperatives, by an "aesthetics of authority" that defines for them the beauty and desirability of official public art and clean, orderly urban environments.[37] The conflict between illicit wall painters and legal authorities worldwide incorporates issues of age, power, and resistance, but also, inevitably, the issue of style. As I have written elsewhere,

> Contemporary graffiti . . . raises again the question raised by the Paris barricades of 1871 and 1968, by pachucos, pachucas and low riders, and by street kids and street fighters: who owns the streets? As always, answers to this question form not only around politics, economics, and ethnicity, but aesthetics. The battle for the streets is a battle for property and space, but also for meaning, appearance, and perception. It is a battle over style.[38]

But issues of style, perception, power, and resistance surface, of course, not only in the streets and in the illegally painted wall murals that decorate them. They in fact run throughout the subject matter of cultural criminology: through the gallery photographs of Robert Mapplethorpe, the popular songs of the Sex Pistols, Ice-T, and 2 Live Crew, and the daily lives of gays, lesbians, punks, performance artists, low riders, bikers, gangbangers, and other outsiders of the world who operate, like wall painters, somewhere between culture and crime.

Notes

An earlier version of this chapter was published in the journal *Social Justice* (1993), and is reprinted here by permission.

1. "On the Line," *The Progressive* 56, July 1992, 13.

2. Lucy Lippard, "Sniper's Nest: Post No Bills," *Z Magazine* 4 (October 1991): 58–60.

3. *Re/Search #11: Pranks!* (San Francisco: Re/Search Publications, 1987); "How to '92: Model Actions for a Post-Columbian World: Media Activism," *Z Magazine* 5 (March 1992): 12–31; Joan Hugo, "Smoke Screen Censorship," *New Art Examiner* 18 (November 1990): 56; Robbie Conal, *Art Attack: The Midnight Politics of a Guerrilla Artist* (New York: HarperCollins, 1992); Anne Barclay Morgan, "Interview: Alberto Gaitan and Lynn McCary," *Art Papers* 18 (January/February 1994): 21–22. Informal and illegal public art covers a remarkable range of issues and techniques. For example, activists involved in the child abuse/"false memory" controversy recently painted slogans on newspaper boxes in San Francisco; see John Chapman, "False Memory Syndrome," *Z Magazine* 7 (June 1994): 2–3. And on Interstate 80 along the edge of the Great Salt Lake in Utah, I have observed mile after mile of names, messages, and designs—not painted on signs or walls, but formed by travelers who have arranged flat black rocks in the shallow water.

4. Eva Cockcroft, "Writing on the Wall," *New Art Examiner* 19 (November 1991): 20.

5. Lucy Lippard, *Get the Message? A Decade of Art for Social Change* (New York: E. P. Dutton, 1984); Paul Von Blum, "Women Political Artists in Los Angeles: Judy Baca's Public Art," *Z Magazine* 4 (October 1991): 70–74.

6. Kathy Lowry, "Painting the Town," *Texas Monthly* 20 (May 1992): 76, 80, 82, 84.

7. Craig Castleman, *Getting Up: Subway Graffiti in New York* (Cambridge: M.I.T. Press, 1982); Martha Cooper and Henry Chalfant, *Subway Art* (London: Thames and Hudson, 1984); Steven Hager, *Hip Hop: The Illustrated History of Break Dancing, Rap Music, and Graffiti* (New York: St. Martin's, 1984); Henry Chalfant and James Prigoff, *Spraycan Art* (London: Thames and Hudson, 1987); Susan Stewart, "Ceci Tuera Cela: Graffiti as Crime and Art," in *Life After Postmodernism*, ed. John Fekete (New York: St. Martin's, 1987): 161–80; Richard Lachmann, "Graffiti as Career and Ideology," *American Journal of Sociology* 94 (1988): 229–50; Devon Brewer and Marc Miller, "Bombing and Burning," *Deviant Behavior* 11 (1990): 345–69; Jeff Ferrell, *Crimes of Style: Urban Graffiti and the Politics of Criminality* (New York: Garland, 1993); Ivor Miller, "Piecing: The Dynamics of Style," *Calligraphy Review* 11 (1994): 20–33; Jeff Ferrell, "Urban Graffiti: Crime, Control, and Resistance," *Youth and Society* 26 (forthcoming).

8. Hermann Waldenburg, *The Berlin Wall* (New York: Abbeville, 1990).

9. Joerg Huber, *Paris Graffiti* (New York: Thames and Hudson, 1986).

10. Phil Kummel, "Beyond Performance and Permanence," *Border/Lines* 22 (1991): 10–12. Lucy Lippard documents a similar project in New York City; see Lucy Lippard, "Sniper's Nest: Anti-Amnesia," *Z Magazine* 5 (December 1992): 63–66. See also Bruce Wright, "Art in the Public Realm," *Public Art Review* 2 (1990): 16, on the politics of public art.

11. Jill Posener, *Spray It Loud* (London: Pandora Press, 1982); Chalfant and Prigoff, *Spraycan Art*.

12. Lippard, "Post No Bills."

13. Bill Rolston, *Politics and Painting: Murals and Conflict in Northern Ireland* (London: Associated University Presses, 1991); Chris Hedges, "To Read All About It, Palestinians Scan the Walls," *New York Times*, 24 January 1994, 12B. On a recent trip to Northern Ireland, one of my students confirmed that the British military had continued to alter Catholic murals so as to remove or reverse offending messages. Jewish women artists have also collaborated with Palestinians to create Palestinian independence murals; see "Break the Silence Mural Project National Tour 1993," *Z Magazine* 6 (January 1993): back cover.

14. *Brazilian Dreams* (San Francisco: BACAT, 1990, video); Lyman Chaffee, "Political Graffiti and Wall Painting in Greater Buenos Aires: An Alternative Communication System," *Studies in Latin American Popular Culture* 8 (1989): 37; see Lyman Chafee, *Political Protest and Street Art* (Westport, CT: Greenwood, 1993). See also the entire issue of *Border/Lines* 27 (1993), "Special Issue on Latin America," on graffiti, youth, politics, and style in Latin America.

15. Chalfant and Prigoff, *Spraycan Art*; Patricia Brett, "Flourishing Graffiti Art Leads to Credit at Parisian 'Worker's University,' " *The Chronicle of Higher Education* 37 (1991): A34; Sebastian Rotella, "Border Lines," *Los Angeles Times*, 20 March 1994, A3, A26; Luis J. Rodriguez, "Los Angeles' Gang Culture Arrives in El Salvador, Courtesy of the INS," *Los Angeles Times*, 8 May 1994, M2.

16. Stanley Cohen, *Folk Devils and Moral Panics* (London: MacGibbon and Kee, 1972); Ferrell, *Crimes of Style*.

17. See, for example, Julio Cortazar, "Graffiti," in *We Love Glenda So Much and Other Tales*, ed. Julio Cortazar (New York: Knopf, 1983), 33–38.

18. Alan Riding, "Parisians on Graffiti: Is It Vandalism or Art?" *New York Times*, 6 February 1992, A6.

19. Joel Sheesley and Wayne Bragg, *Sandino in the Streets* (Bloomington: Indiana University Press, 1991).

20. Sheesley and Bragg, xxii.

21. David Kunzle, "The Mural Death Squads of Nicaragua," *Z Magazine* 6 (April 1993): 62–66. See also Betty La Duke, *Companeras: Women, Art, and Social Change in Latin America* (San Francisco: City Lights, 1985), on the politics of women's art in Nicaragua and other Latin American countries.

22. Sheesley and Bragg, xxi, xxv.

23. Sheesley and Bragg, xxiv.

24. Street stenciling also plays off an official, even authoritarian, aesthetic of clean, repetitive imagery, and thus gives a new twist to Benjamin's classic concept of "the work of art in the age of mechanical reproduction"; see Walter Benjamin, "The Work of Art in the Age of Mechanical Reproduction," in Walter

Benjamin, *Illuminations*, ed. Hannah Arendt (New York: Harcourt, Brace, and World, 1968), 219–53. For more on the aesthetics and politics of stenciling, see, for example, Jean-Christophe Bailly's introduction to Huber, *Paris Graffiti*; David Robinson, *Soho Walls: Beyond Graffiti* (New York: Thames and Hudson, 1990); Ferrell, *Crimes of Style*, 79–80, 98; and the discussion of John Fekner's work in Lippard, *Get the Message?* Sheesley and Bragg, 52, also include a photograph of a young boy with a Sandino image drawn or tattooed on his biceps. As this photograph reminds us, both wall painting and tattooing can be understood as forms of popular or folk art; see Clinton R. Sanders, *Customizing the Body: The Art and Culture of Tattooing* (Philadelphia: Temple, 1989).

25. John Bushnell, *Moscow Graffiti: Language and Subculture* (Boston: Unwin Hyman, 1990).

26. For more on Soviet/Russian rock-and-roll and popular music, see, for example, Thomas Cushman, "Rich Rastas and Communist Rockers," *Journal of Popular Culture* 25 (1991): 17–61; and Pedro Ramet and Serbei Zamascikov, "The Soviet Rock Scene," *Journal of Popular Culture* 24 (1990): 149–74. For an update on Moscow gangs, see Fiona Fleck, "Moscow Gets Western Import: Gangs," *Rocky Mountain News (Reuter)*, 7 October 1992, 4.

27. Bushnell, 40, 41, 59, 215–16.

28. Bushnell, 163, 164, 222.

29. Bushnell, 223, 22; see 231–32.

30. Bushnell, 181, 192, 226.

31. Bushnell's "A Postscript on Art and Life," in *Moscow Graffiti*, captures this same sense of cultural dissemination. Bushnell also discusses a remarkable stairwell full of graffiti devoted to Boris Grebenshchikov, the leader of the Soviet/Russian rock band Aquarium. As my visit in 1986 confirmed, this stairwell display in Grebenshchikov's apartment building approached the subcultural power and scope of the Bulgakov collection. See Bushnell, 237–41, 98–103.

32. Bushnell, 53, 89, 103, 160.

33. See also the insightful discussion of these issues in Reebee Garofalo, *Rockin' the Boat: Mass Music and Mass Movements* (Boston: South End Press, 1992), 1–7; and John Fiske, "An Interview with John Fiske," *Border/Lines* 20/21 (1991): 4–7, on the remaking of mass culture into popular culture. To the extent that the new (world) order in Russia has replaced Soviet domination with that of "free" markets and McDonald's, of course, a further historical irony has unfolded. And in this sense, a 1990s McDonald's hamburger and a 1970s bootleg Beatles tape, while both products of Western culture, must certainly incorporate different dimensions of power, control, and lived meaning for the Russians who consume them.

34. See Howard S. Becker, *Art Worlds* (Berkeley: University of California Press, 1982). See also, for example, Ferrell, *Crimes of Style*; Rolston, *Politics and*

Painting; and Sheesley and Bragg, *Sandino*, on the participation of illegal wall painters in art worlds and art world/folk art traditions. Wall painters also regularly report that a distinctive "adrenaline rush" develops from the intersection of illegality and artistry in the practice of their craft, and that this "rush" distances their experience from that of other artists; see, for example, Ferrell, *Crimes of Style*, and Ferrell, "Urban Graffiti."

35. Rolston, 102–3.
36. See Ferrell, *Crimes of Style*; Ferrell, "Urban Graffiti."
37. See Ferrell, *Crimes of Style*; Ferrell, "Urban Graffiti."
38. Ferrell, *Crimes of Style*, 186.

PART FOUR . . .
CONCLUSIONS AND PROSPECTS

13 ◦ ◦ ◦
Toward a Cultural Criminology

JEFF FERRELL AND CLINTON R. SANDERS

By placement and intention, this final essay serves to summarize the essays collected here while drawing together some of the many issues and themes that have emerged. More importantly, it also points beyond the essays in this volume. It serves as a prospectus for an emerging cultural criminology, a speculation as to the trajectory such a criminology might take, and therefore an exploration of issues and themes not necessarily found in this collection. Our intention, both in the collection as a whole and in this essay, is not so much to define cultural criminology narrowly as to establish a series of starting points, and to invite other scholars and scholarship into this process.

That this final essay should be characterized more by speculation and invitation than by closure and definition seems entirely appropriate to this new cultural criminology. To begin with, cultural criminology is an orientation in its infancy, just being born out of the cross-fertilization of criminology, cultural and media studies, critical theory, and other approaches that we will discuss. For cultural criminology, the future remains to be written. Moreover, cultural criminology incorporates not only these approaches, but postmodern, feminist, and other perspectives as well—perspectives that critique totalizing tendencies and promote openness to a plurality of viewpoints. Both by its stage of development and its intellectual heritage, then, cultural criminology constitutes less a closed analytic system than an open road into the study of culture, crime, and their interconnections.

This openness, and the continual opening up, of cultural criminology pervades the following discussions of theory, methodology, and substantive directions. As will be seen, cultural criminology incorporates an array of theoretical orientations, points to methodologies that can create a variety of culturally situated criminological accounts, and provides new insights into a wide range of substantive areas. In that these theoretical, methodological, and substantive orientations overlap and interweave, they together create still other possibilities for new understandings of culture and crime.

The Road So Far

The various essays collected here have shown that shared symbolism and mediated meaning, subcultural style and collective imagery, define the nature of crime, criminality, and social control not only for criminals engaged in the daily enterprise of criminality but for everyone caught up in the larger social process of constructing and perceiving crime and control. The interactionist tradition in criminology has taught us that, to understand crime and deviance, we must take notice of all those involved in episodes of deviance or criminality—not only those labeled criminal, but co-conspirators, control agents, friends and neighbors, judges and juries, moral entrepreneurs, and others.[1] In the essays collected here we have begun to see that, as we examine all involved, we must look also at those cultural forces that link them, at the many lines of meaning and perception in which they are collectively entangled.[2]

To paraphrase Durkheim, we see that shared symbolism and meaning constitute the social adhesive, the collective consciousness, that holds together both criminality and attempts to construct and control it.[3] Thus it is not only criminals and cops, but public attitudes and perceptions, media dynamics, and the subtleties of subcultural style that constitute the appropriate subject matter of a cultural criminology. Moreover, a cultural criminology must not only account for these specific cultural phenomena but expose their manifold interconnections. That is, it must examine these intersecting lines of social discourse and cultural meaning holistically—as components in a complex process by which crime and control come to have meaning for all involved.

If cops, criminals, and "the public" begin to understand the meaning and reality of crime and social control by way of elaborate, elegant systems of symbols and signs, then a cultural criminology must be able to recognize the symbols and signs and make sense of the systems. In other words, it must be geared toward paying close attention both to the nuances of popular cultures and criminal subcultures, and to the broader patterns of meaning and control that these nuances trace. Cultural criminology must account precisely not only for the gritty images and recurring moral motifs of contemporary "real life" cop shows, for example, but also for the broader role of these shows in constructing public fears and perceptions, legitimating police power, and setting agendas for crime control. It must be able to describe the situated, subcultural meanings of shaved heads, oversized clothing, and secret language, and also the ongoing process by which these subcultural symbols flow from and, in turn, circulate back through mediated channels of news reporting, advertising, and consumption. Cultural criminology must take careful notice of the symbolic universe created by barred windows, gated streets, security signs, and other nuances of contemporary urban life, as well as the broader patterns of social control, social inequality, and fear of crime that these everyday markers trace.[4]

In these examples we again see the collective nature of crime and crime control—and the myriad ways in which this collectivity incorporates dimensions of shared symbolism and meaning. With varying degrees of power and influence, criminals, control agents, and the many producers of mediated images and situated symbols, all participate in the collective construction of crime and control. Thus, in the day-to-day experience of social life, cultural and criminal processes endlessly collide. For minority gang members and white-power skinheads, probation officers and motorcycle riders, television producers, film viewers, and newspaper readers, "culture" and "crime" exist less as discrete phenomena to be perceived and experienced than as processes interwoven along continua of political power, social stigma and marginality, and style.

Given this, criminologists must likewise interweave the categories of "culture" and "crime" in their work. If we wish to understand the social meaning of crime and control, we cannot maintain the type of dichotomy that sorts some situations and experiences into the category of "culture" and others into "crime." As this collection shows, mediated images of drug violence and serial killers, the internal dynamics and social control of criminal subcultures, and a plethora of other identities and events hardly lend themselves to such dichotomous categorization. Instead, we must continue to develop a synthetic approach—a cultural criminology—whose integration of cultural and criminological analyses parallels the intersection of cultural and criminal practices in everyday life.

But what intellectual traditions and theoretical orientations contribute to this integrated understanding of culture and crime? What methods address both particularities of symbolism and style and larger patterns of mediated meaning? And what substantive areas, beyond those addressed in this collection, might profitably be examined through the lens of cultural criminology?

Theoretical Trajectories

First, a warning and disclaimer: What follows under this heading is not meant to be a comprehensive "overview" of the theoretical orientations that make up cultural criminology. As throughout this final essay, and throughout this collection as a whole, we strive here to be speculative, not exhaustive. We are interested neither in crafting a theoretical pedigree for cultural criminology, nor in drawing up firm theoretical guidelines for its future. We wish only to trace a few of the theoretical threads that have to this point been woven into cultural criminology and to suggest some general tendencies that this form of theoretical work may take.

That being said, it is clear that the interactionist tradition in criminology and sociology constitutes one of cultural criminology's starting points. The essays in this collection explore the process by which the multitude of interactions involving criminals, control agents, media producers, media consumers, and others collectively construct the meaning of crime and crime control for all involved. Many of these essays also investigate the sorts of collective associations, activities, and perceptions that emerge within criminal subcultures, and between these subcultures and other social groups and institutions. As seen earlier, and in "Style Matters" and other essays, these works perhaps contribute to the interactionist understanding of crime by exploring and expanding the "symbolic" in "symbolic interaction." In examining media channels and images, subcultural styles, musical lyrics, and other symbolic components essential to the construction of crime and criminalization, these essays stand firmly within interactionist traditions in sociology and criminology, while relocating these traditions within emerging intersections of culture and crime. To the extent that they take this sort of analysis into the worlds of media institutions and collective perception, they also draw on, and contribute to, constructionist approaches to understanding the emergence of crime, deviance, and social problems.[5]

Cultural criminology's concern with exploring subcultural styles, media dynamics, and other symbolic dimensions of crime and crime control in turn manifests a concern with exploring the politics of crime and crime control, and the cultural channels through which these politics are played out. That is, cultural criminology is not only inherently interactionist but essentially critical as well. Drawing on critical perspectives in criminology and sociology, cultural criminology examines media texts and images as components in the perpetuation and expansion of both legal authority and "official" perceptions of crime; explores subcultural styles as products not only of criminal associations but of criminalization itself, and resistance to it; and most broadly, looks critically at the role of cultural practices in ongoing social conflicts over crime, crime control, state power, and legal authority.

Significantly, cultural criminology's critical edge is honed on a variety of radical or progressive perspectives. The essays in this volume, for instance, draw on anarchist, neo-Marxist, feminist, and other critiques of legal domination and social injustice. While these perspectives are represented here to varying degrees—or at times are simply assumed or implied—they all help shape the wide-ranging critical analysis embedded in cultural criminology. As we will discuss subsequently, this volume suffers, for example, from an overemphasis on male crime and criminalization, and in that sense fails to take heed of feminist critiques of criminology's traditional gender myopia. However, feminist insights as to the situated politics of personal experience and everyday criminality, emerging feminist understandings of methodology, and other feminist reconceptualizations of both crime and criminology pervade this volume and the cultural criminology it attempts to create. In this sense cultural criminology remains feminist even in those moments where its subject matter remains decidedly male.

In critically examining the symbolic interactions that surround and construct crime and criminality, cultural criminology, of course, relies upon and expands the field of cultural studies. As many of the essays here make obvious, the classic works in the British cultural studies/ Birmingham School tradition—many of which themselves focused on the interplay of crime, deviance, juvenile delinquency, youth subcultures, and media processes—have been particularly influential.[6] In their attention to cultural detail and dynamics and to the everyday politics of both mediated images and subcultural styles, these works set the tone for a cultural criminology. But newer developments in cultural studies—in France, the U.S., Great Britain, and elsewhere—have also contributed to the sort of analysis developed here. When, for example, Grossberg, Nelson, and Treichler utilize in their definitive edited work, *Cultural Studies*, categories like "The Politics of Aesthetics," "Popular Culture and Its Audiences," and "Ethnography and Cultural Studies," they anticipate the categories within which cultural criminology operates.[7] And in that regard, a further parallel can be noted. Recently a review essay on Grossberg, Nelson, and Treichler's *Cultural Studies* claimed to expose cultural studies' "hidden agenda": to serve as a postmodern permutation of earlier progressive orientations, designed to critically examine the role of cultural dynamics in struggles over meaning, authority, and power.[8] But, of course, this "agenda" was never "hidden" at all (except to those too blind to see it). It has framed the emergence of cultural studies, and it likewise shapes the development of cultural criminology here.

To speak of cultural studies, and by extension cultural criminology, as a "postmodern permutation" points to postmodernism as the final theoretical thread woven into cultural criminology. Among the modernist hierarchical assumptions that postmodernism undermines is the notion that form must be stripped away so as to get at the meaningful kernel of content. In place of this dualistic hierarchy, postmodernism proposes that form is content, that style is substance, that meaning resides on the surface of things, in presentation and representation.[9] Postmodern analysis therefore emphasizes that contemporary authority—and indeed contemporary social order—is constructed out of an endless interplay of images, out of the hyper-real politics of representation and identity. This orientation, in turn, suggests that contemporary legal authority rests on media operations and symbolic crusades, that crime and criminality incorporate subtleties of style and representa-

tional meaning, and that the discussions collected in this volume therefore contribute to criminological analysis. As Barak notes in his essay
here, this orientation also points to constitutive criminology and newsmaking criminology—criminologies that, in various ways, attempt to
create and disseminate alternative cultural representations of crime
and justice—as components of any critical, activist cultural criminology.[10] Cultural criminology as represented in this volume thus speaks
directly to certain critiques of labeling and constructionist analysis.[11] It
points the way beyond detached analysis to a "criminology of peacemaking" directed at exposing and altering oppressive social arrangements.

Postmodernism not only establishes a context for cultural criminology but sets the tone for it. In opening new lines of substantive and
theoretical inquiry, postmodernism (and cultural studies) have generated a collective enthusiasm for research into the forms of "cultural
trash" once discarded from legitimate scholarly inquiry. In decentering
(and dismantling) the stern rationality that has guided such inquiry,
postmodernism has likewise introduced a certain playfulness into contemporary scholarship, a willingness both to have fun with the research
process and to make fun of those legal, political, and intellectual authorities who would constrain it.[12] As we hope is obvious by now, cultural criminology shares this sense of enthusiastic engagement with its
subjects of study as well as with the politics of its subject matter. Mediated images of drug violence, serial murder, and surveillance; subtleties
of skinhead and biker styles; the aesthetics of gang members and graffiti writers—all of these warrant serious research and analysis. But
given the depths of meaning, beauty, horror, and power they carry, they
also warrant a methodological intensity and analytic exuberance that
transcend the abstract turgidity and dry statistical mastication of much
mainstream criminology.[13]

Cultural criminology, then, incorporates a wide range of theoretical
orientations—interactionist, constructionist, critical, feminist, cultural
studies, postmodern, constitutive, and newsmaking—in its attempt to
understand the confluence of culture and crime in contemporary life.
Cultural criminology can be seen, therefore, as a synthetic approach, a
criminology that blends and reworks existing sociological and criminological approaches into a new theoretical amalgam. Within this larger
theoretical synthesis, cultural criminology seems particularly well

suited for bridging the dualisms of agency and structure, self and society. The terrain of cultural criminology—mediated debates over the criminogenic effects of media images on individuals; interplays of subcultural styles, media texts, and legal authority; traces of political conflict and symbolic resistance in the everyday interactions of control agents and criminals—shows that agency and structure, self and society exist not as separate spheres but as social strands so tightly interwoven in the construction of crime and control as to be indistinguishable one from the other. In investigating this terrain, then, cultural criminology is compelled to move toward what Cohen has called "a structurally and politically informed version of labeling theory," and what Melossi has similarly described as a sort of "grounded labeling theory," which synthesizes interactionist, critical, and other macro- and micro-criminological approaches.[14]

But, in the postmodern spirit of fractured authority and exploded meta-narratives, cultural criminology may serve best by engaging, rather than synthesizing, the many criminologies on which it draws. The plethora of contemporary, alternative criminologies—of which cultural criminology now becomes another—perhaps constitutes, from a modernist perspective, a paradigmatic crisis in criminology. From a postmodern perspective, though, they represent instead a sign of intellectual vitality, an opening up of the field to voices previously unheard. Our goal here is not, therefore, to synthesize or subsume these criminologies under a unified cultural criminology but to encourage critical conversation among them, to invite them into a collective exploration of culture and crime. As we have already noted, this sense of open and eclectic inquiry defines cultural criminology as a whole, and it defines the methodological possibilities that emerge within it.

Methods of Cultural Criminology: Bits of Broken Glass

The qualitative methods, and Participant Observation used in the research, and the ethnographic format of the presentation were dictated by the nature of my interest in "the cultural." These techniques are suited to record this level and have a sensitivity to meanings and values as well as an ability to represent and interpret symbolic articulations, practices and forms of cultural production.

—*Willis,* Learning to Labor[15]

Wedding oneself to a particular theory, perspective, or method of knowing is like relying on a single sense to describe a garden of flowers.

—*Kappeler, Blumberg, and Potter,* The Mythology of Crime and Criminal Justice[16]

What might be the methodology of an approach that seeks to locate the social reality of crime both in the daily operations of the mass media and in the stylish dynamics of criminal subcultures? To put it differently: How does an approach that argues that we must pay attention to representation, style, and situated meaning in criminality go about doing so?

As a starting point, we can recall anarchist philosopher of science Paul Feyerabend's methodological injunction: "The only principle that does not inhibit progress is: *anything goes.*"[17] In other words, rather than seeking a single best method of research, or evaluating methods one against the other, cultural criminology embraces a plurality of methodological possibilities. As Feyerabend would be the first to point out, though, this methodological tolerance constitutes, at the same time, a broad intolerance for certain traditional methodological assumptions. If, for example, conventionally popular methods like survey research and quantitative analysis are to be part of cultural criminology's methodological mix, they must be dislodged from the frameworks of epistemic and scientific authority in which they are now encased. As techniques designed to generate objective, quantifiable, comparative data, survey methods are of little use to cultural criminology; their illusions of precise objectivity mask an inherent and imposed imprecision, an inability (and an unwillingness) to explore the particular meanings of legal authority, situated symbolism, and interpersonal style in the lived experiences of everyday criminality.[18] To the extent that such methods come wrapped both in modernist notions of objectivity and truth and in layers of rationality and arithmetic, they contribute more to systems of intellectual and political domination than to grounded understandings of culture and crime. In imposing exterior, authoritative categories of meaning, they systematically miss the meanings that develop inside the identities and events that cultural criminology wishes to study.

Such methods need not be discarded, though. They potentially can be of use if recontextualized within cultural criminology. If surveys of public opinion about crime, or statistical analyses of crime and victimization rates, are reconceptualized as imperfect human constructions rather than as measures of that presumed to be objectively real, they can suggest patterns of meaning and perception within which various groups make sense of crime. As these approaches are utilized within other methodologies more attentive to situated structure and meaning, they can also provide initial sketches, if not final measures, of cultural and criminal dynamics.[19] To utilize conventional methodologies in this way is, of course, not only to recontextualize them, but to stand them on their heads. Where such methodologies once contributed to the epistemic authority of criminology, they now operate so as to sketch the situated epistemology of criminal processes and events. Where these methodologies once perpetuated the myth of objective knowledge accumulating toward certainty and truth, they now operate only as particular strategies useful within particular cultural contexts.

What remains when we abandon myths of objectively abstract knowledge and scientific truth about culture and crime—when we demystify old methodologies and realize we are only giving up what we never had? What remains is the ethnographic case study. Feminist criminologists, qualitative sociologists and criminologists, and others emphasize the necessity of *ethnographic immersion* in the cultural and experiential realities of particular criminal events.[20] In that crime and criminalization incorporate a series of cultural identities, embody subtleties of symbolism and meaning, and emerge out of the symbolic interaction of media sources, legal authorities, and others, we must have methodologies that get us as close to the (inter)action as possible. The nuances of criminal style and conversation, the shades of meaning surrounding brands of athletic shoes or particular motorcyle accessories, and the collective reasoning behind and within criminal events are surely more subtle than any survey or statistical summary can catch. Ethnographic methods, on the other hand, can begin to unravel the phenomenological foreground of criminality. In this context, Daly and Chesney-Lind point out that feminist criminologists remain uncomfortable with making "global claims" and instead "seek to understand crime at close range"; Caulfield and Wonders list "participant-observation, ethnographies, life histories, interpretive methodologies, and other similar techniques . . . employed by feminist researchers in order to reveal parts of the social world that remain hidden by more traditional techniques."[21]

In the same way that these methods put richness and texture ahead of abstraction and generalizability, they also embody Feyerabend's notion that "anything goes," for the case study in cultural criminology is designed to cover a broad sweep of criminological ground rather than to conform to one standard. Detailed ethnographic studies can serve as "notes from underground"—that is, as reports on the otherwise inaccessible cultural dynamics of criminal subcultures or criminal events.[22] But these techniques can also be used to explore specific instances of moral entrepreneurship and mediated criminalization and to make sense of the particular meanings that these mediated events take on in the lives of criminals and non-criminals alike.[23] Further, as Caulfield and Wonders emphasize, case studies can develop not only as examinations of particular events, but they can also reveal the ongoing social and cultural dynamics by which the meaning of law, crime, and criminality is constructed.[24] Case studies in cultural criminology must be able to capture the emergent meanings of crime as the style codes of criminal subcultures evolve and new mediated panics over criminality are manufactured.

Within cultural criminology, then, rather than creating an objective, authoritative representation of a self-contained reality, the ethnographer engages with social groups and social processes to construct an inherently incomplete, but ideally elegant and persuasive, account of cultural and criminal dynamics.[25] Moreover, for cultural criminology the case study itself exists less in the service of abstract theorizing about culture and crime than for its own sake. As cultural ethnographer Dick Hebdige has said, "If I have a preference at all, then, it is that obdurate English preference for the particular, for the thing itself . . . [thus] the old saw about sledgehammers and walnuts. My only hope is that . . . the walnut proves so tough, so recalcitrant, it shatters the sledgehammer."[26] As with the theoretical and substantive dimensions of cultural criminology, the preferred methodology is particularistic, decentralized, and inclusive. It is designed to generate a plethora of insights and understandings rather than "reliable" results or a single, unified, and authoritative theory of culture and crime.

The methodological trajectory of cultural criminology points, therefore, toward a plurality of ethnographic studies attentive to the manifold interconnections between culture and crime. At its best this methodology produces various, elegant accounts of the large- and small-scale cultural dynamics embedded in everyday crime and criminality; it generates an informal federation of information and ideas, a series of scholarly dots loosely connected into the shape of cultural criminology. Cultural criminologists would at their best thus create, as did the Chicago sociologists of the past, "an array of brilliant monographs that combined journalistic acumen with sophisticated sociological insight," and would link this array within broad criminological sensitivities to meaning, style, and representation.[27] Cultural criminology makes room for a rich variety of studies, each offering situationally "truthful" accounts that can perhaps accumulate toward broader understandings of culture and crime. This is the goal toward which this initial, diverse collection of essays in cultural criminology is directed. Cultural criminology as conceived and represented here recognizes that, in the ongoing process of attending to culture and crime, alternative accounts sparkle like bits of broken glass.[28]

Emerging Categories of Inquiry

The essays collected here have exposed a variety of social circumstances in which cultural and criminal processes interweave. As bits of broken glass, these essays reflect a remarkable range of substantive interests and analytic styles. But rather than exhausting cultural criminology's possibilities, this collection points toward the rich field of issues in culture and crime yet to be explored.

Media

As the essays here have shown, media images are constructions, rather than reflections, of reality. Basic to this mediated field of images are representations of crime, deviance, and related forms of insubordination. It is no longer possible to retain the quaint, linear view of a world in which criminal acts and other objective happenings occur, are then observed and reported by the news media, and are finally transformed into quasi-factual stories or offered as fictionalized representations for the entertainment of the public audience. Instead, the most viable model is one in which media presentations, real-life events, personal perceptions, public policies, and individual actions spiral about each other in a complex, mutually affecting, and ever-changing structure of inter-relationships.

In their presentation of crime and criminality, the news media in particular construct and offer up a commercial product composed of decontextualized quasi-facts that become contemporary morality plays. Here we are shown those who threaten the public welfare, what causes them to behave so badly, the consequences of their misbehavior, and what must be done for the forces of conventional good to regain control and effectively protect the endangered citizenry and the social order. The dominant image is of a war—a battle between minorities and whites, young people and adults, the poor and the middle class, drug users and straights. Salvation, in turn, can only come from providing police, courts, prisons, and other agencies of conventional control with the resources they require.

Depending largely upon official sources for the materials from which they construct images of crime and criminality, of perpetrators and victims, the media act as public relations vehicles for agents of social control. The essays here by Sanders and Lyon (chap. 2), Brownstein (chap. 3), and Barak (chap. 7) stress that the acts of criminality offered, and the crime waves generated through the repetitive reconstruction of these acts, precipitate moral panics that, in turn, are reacted to by criminal justice agencies intent on enhancing their legitimacy by ostensibly being responsive to public concerns and appearing effective in protecting the public order.

One theoretical consequence of this orientation toward the roots and impacts of media representations of crime is an enhanced and expanded view of labeling theory. While retaining the basic focus of labeling—that deviance is not a characteristic of particular behaviors but, instead, is located in social reactions to actual or presumed behaviors—we can move toward an understanding of labeling as part of a larger cultural dynamic. Media presentations have impact upon labeling and social reaction at an interpersonal level by shaping the macrocultural processes that provide the context for immediate social interactions. Attention is focused on the labeling, reaction, and consequent response of group and organizational-scale "acting units" as media organizations represent the character of selected groups (minorities, drug users, young people) and their misbehaviors, whereupon control agencies and other interest groups devise responses premised on these mediated representations.[29]

The labeling perspective on crime and deviance is further extended by cultural criminology through its focus on style and symbolism within deviant and criminal subcultures. Permanent body alterations, distinctive clothing, uniquely meaningful hand gestures, and other subcultural symbolic elements are directly connected to, and help fix, the socially constructed deviant or criminal identities of those who belong or profess allegiance to insubordinate groups. As voluntarily assumed symbols of stigmatized status, these symbols both set members apart from conventional society and are used by control agents and others to identify the unconventional, and thereby aid in targeting societal reactions. However, as these components of subcultural style are discovered and disseminated by the media, they are rapidly diffused into the larger cultural system and adopted as elements of fashion by otherwise conventional members of the society, for whom they often present a relatively safe means of being "a little bit bad." This recasting and watering down of subcultural style, in turn, prompts a consistent process of street-level rejection of past symbols and subsequent innovation in the search for new and more effectively menacing stigma identifiers.[30]

This complex interplay among the activities of media organizations, constructed media images, deviant and criminal styles, public perceptions, and the responses of agencies of social control spotlights the necessity of employing an expanded repertoire of methodological tools. While critical content analyses of media messages of the kind offered by Brownstein, Tunnell, and others in this volume will continue to be necessary and instructive, cultural criminology must move beyond content to focus on groups and interactions. Rich insights can best be gained by examining the meanings that media texts take on in criminal and non-criminal social and cultural settings. This goal requires a renewed emphasis on ethnographic studies of identifiable subcultural groups, organizations of policy and control, media workers, and other key players in the media-public-criminal subculture nexus. The products of these studies, ideally, will lead not only to a more firmly grounded understanding of the interplay between media messages and cultural dynamics but also, as Barak emphasizes in his discussion, to a further exposition of the intimate connections between the apparatus of cultural production and powerful agents of social and legal control.

Pleasure, Escape, and Skin

When we find people engaged in criminal(ized) endeavors because these activities generate participatory pleasure, cheap fun, or erotic excitement rather than providing economic gain, we are likely glimpsing phenomena that intertwine criminal and cultural dynamics and therefore fall within the purview of cultural criminology. Tunnell has explored the "criminal calculus" by which armed robbers, burglars, and others decide to engage in their crimes.[31] Here, we highlight what we might call the "criminal pleasures" or "criminal erotics" that draw individuals and groups into criminality. In distinguishing himself from a more obedient boy, one of the "lads" in Willis's study of British working-class juvenile delinquency reported:

> Well . . . we've been through all life's pleasures and all its fucking displeasures, we've been drinking, we've been fighting, we've known frustration, sex, fucking hatred, love and all this lark, yet he's known none of it. . . . He's not known so many of the emotions as we've had to experience, and he's got it all yet to come.[32]

Kids likewise steal particular makes and models of automobiles that they see as providing the most stylish and pleasurable "joyrides"; others carefully modify their cars in accordance with the stylistic codes of illegal street "cruising."[33] Kids and others are often pulled into shoplifting not by economic necessity but by commodified desire for consumer goods; and as seen earlier, those who possess illegal weapons often value their aesthetic symbolism as much as their deadly force. Those caught up in the world of illegal graffiti actually lose money on their criminality, but they persist because of the stylish pleasures they share there. And for consumers of illegal pornography or illegal drugs, clients of prostitutes, and others, the negative economic calculus and potential dangers of the situation are similarly overridden by its positive criminal pleasures.

Moreover, within these and other sorts of criminality, the "adrenaline rush" of illicit pleasure and excitement that participants experience exists not as an unpleasant price to be paid for economic gain, nor as an unintended byproduct of fleeing or avoiding apprehension, but often as an end in itself. Graffiti writers, for example, consistently report that their experience is defined by the adrenaline rush that results from exercising their artistry in illegal and dangerous settings.[34] Other kids regularly recount the intense pleasure and excitement that accompanies their participation in everyday criminality.[35] And even some of Tunnell's property criminals report that stealing is "a high, now, I mean it's exhilarating. . . . I get off going through doors."[36] Clearly, the lust for kicks, the titillating pleasures of the moment, drive these and other criminal activities as surely as they do more conventional, non-criminal(ized) cultural or recreational activities like participation in music, sports, dance, and sex.[37] What is gained by these criminal and non-criminal activities alike is not necessarily material wealth or physical advantage, but a wealth of pleasure and excitement.

To make sense of these types of criminal events, then, we need a criminology that incorporates understandings of humor and pleasure, excitement and desire, entertainment and emotion, and the entanglement of these human experiences in and around the sensuality of the human body. That is, we need a cultural criminology that accounts for crime in terms not only of its social and legal consequences but also its entertainment value—its construction as pleasure and fun—for those involved in it. Riemer notes that

> deviant behavior as a fun activity has been consistently ignored in the work of social scientists. Rarely has deviance been considered a spontaneous, "just for the hell of it" activity, in which the participants engage simply for the pleasure it provides.[38]

With its foundations in cultural studies and interactionist perspectives on situated style and meaning, feminist notions of personal conduct and identity as political, and postmodernism's attentiveness to the often ignored dynamics of everyday culture and entertainment, cultural criminology can begin to unravel the threads of pleasure that run through various forms of criminality.

In attempting to sort out the pleasurable dynamics of criminality we see again the importance of paying attention to the particulars of crime, of developing both theoretical and methodological approaches that can take us inside the specific experiences of criminal activity. Clearly, stealing a television to sell to a fence differs from stealing a sports jacket to fulfill one's desire for that symbolically luminous object. Stealing a

sporty car for a joyride differs from stealing a car in order to systematically strip and sell the parts, though they may seem the same if we only
glimpse their shadows in resulting rates of car theft. Painting graffiti
for the adrenaline rush of illicit artistry may be categorized in police
reports as "vandalism" or "destruction of private property" and may
surface in cumulative crime rates as such, but it is clearly not the same
act of vandalism as scrawling racist slogans, desecrating graveyards, or
smashing windows (though all may incorporate specifically pleasurable
dimensions for those involved).[39] In each case, we as criminologists
must situate ourselves as close to the action as possible. We must catch
a taste of whatever pleasure and excitement are present if we are to
understand and distinguish between these forms of criminality. As cultural criminologists we must develop a form of *criminological verstehen*
that can lead to at least partial entry into the lived experiences—and
lived pleasures—of criminality.[40]

If this focus on criminality as situated pleasure and excitement returns us to cultural criminology's roots in interactionist, feminist, and
postmodern approaches, and in ethnographic research methods, it returns us to its foundation in critical criminology as well. For these criminal pleasures in turn expose structures of political and economic power
and inequality, as they are organized, like many non-criminal activities
in late capitalist society, around consumption, socially constructed desire, and interpersonal domination. In this sense shoplifting shares
common ground with larger patterns of perpetually conspicuous consumption; the production and enjoyment of hard-core pornography incorporates the broader pornographic presentation of female sexuality
in the culture at large; and the use of illegal drugs flourishes within a
society itself addicted to the sorry tension between individual excess
and social control.

The politics of criminal pleasure, though, incorporate more possibilities than the simple reproduction of larger social structures. The various
pleasures associated with crime and deviance capture, in odd mixes
and twisted configurations, the complex politics by which individuals
and groups reproduce—but also reinvent and resist—the constraints
of consumption, social class, gender, and sexuality under which they
operate. Feminists and others, for example, debate the personal and
social meanings of pornography, its complex potential for both sexual
domination and liberation, and the extent to which its production and

use should be criminalized.[41] Similarly, feminists and other scholars have argued for some time that we must consider rape not as a crime of passion but as one of domination and power, and in so doing have developed an essential corrective to the inexcusable public confusion of rape with consensual sex. At the same time, though, if we are to understand and confront sexual assault, we must ask: what sorts of pleasures are interwoven with this domination, such that rapists are themselves able to confound sexual assault and sexual arousal? In turn, what does this experiential confusion reveal to us as criminologists—both about the act of rape and about larger patterns of sexual inequality and domination—that a neat bifurcation of "passion" and "power" does not? Paying attention to the various pleasures of crime—however distasteful—can begin to define not only its phenomenological foreground but its complex political underpinnings as well.[42]

If we take the body and its pleasures to be a locus of political meaning, a site of both political repression and liberation, we can see that criminal pleasures also incorporate forms of political resistance and escape.[43] Graffiti writers, for example, enjoy writing graffiti not only for the appreciation of other writers but also as a move against the spatial and cultural controls that limit their lives in contemporary urban environments, and against those urban authorities who campaign to stop them. Ironically, the aggressive campaigns to publicize and criminalize graffiti in turn *enhance* the intensely pleasurable adrenaline rush of graffiti writing, and thus further shape graffiti writing as pleasurable resistance.[44] In this light we can see that the pleasures of other seemingly "pointless" or "escapist" crimes committed by both kids and adults—joyriding, cruising, riding with motorcycle gangs, using and abusing alcohol and other drugs, "wilding"—may carry deeper political meanings as well. To categorize such crimes as escapist is often to dismiss them as forms of false escape, as a running away from "real" problems and "real" solutions because of immaturity or a need for immediate gratification. But for their participants, these crimes may represent a real, if badly flawed, escape from powerlessness and domination, in the moments of daily life. If the pleasures such crimes convey do in fact carve out a temporary escape from daily domination, if they take their participants for a moment outside the maddening noise of the quotidian hum, then aren't such escapes real for them on the level of everyday experience? This sort of analysis—from inside the lived dynamics and lived pleasures of everyday crime—can perhaps better explain the prevalence and attraction of such crime than can popular psycho/physiological notions of "addiction" or "low self-esteem."

Once again, though, the politics of criminal pleasure are hardly simple. These illicit pleasures often cost their participants time and money, draw them away from more socially acceptable activities, and entangle them in legal control and institutional labeling. Because of this, they may well help trap participants in the very situations they wish to escape. Like the subcultural styles discussed earlier in this collection, these criminal pleasures may constitute both a response to powerlessness or inequality and a factor in their perpetuation.[45] But while this type of legal/political analysis is critically important for understanding cycles of crime and criminalization, and the reproduction of social inequalities through these cycles, it is not enough by itself. If we are to make sense of crime, we must recognize not only the long-term effects, but also the immediate lived experience and situated meanings, of criminal pleasures.

Moreover, what would we propose that the poor, ethnic minorities, "Generation X" kids, and others do in place of shoplifting, drinking, and dealing and taking drugs, if they are to "make it" in an increasingly mean-spirited, unequal, and unjust social order?[46] Do we really believe that, given today's social and economic arrangements, postponing pleasure, staying sober and "honest"—in the barrio, the hood, or behind the fast food service line—is a ticket out, a solution? If so, sociologists might well remind us that we are blaming the victim, proposing individualistic solutions to social problems. Those trapped in the ghetto or in minimum wage jobs might point out that we not only want them to inhabit an increasingly bleak future, but to do so clean and sober. Thus the awful suspicion arises that drinking heavily, dealing drugs, shoplifting, or otherwise seeking out criminal pleasures are "rational" responses to a bankrupt future—rational not in the sense of abstract calculation, but of the situated rationality of lived experience and day-to-day endurance. Perhaps these "senseless" forms of sensual criminality can best be understood as neither escape nor entrapment but as echoes of a senselessly unjust world, as forms of fatalism that reflect not individual pathology but social decay.

Kushner speaks of a "socialism of the skin" in reference to lesbian and gay politics of pleasure and desire, the systematic repression of pleasure and desire under regimes of political and sexual authority, and the dream of a social world in which these human sensualities are restored.[47] Here we propose, similarly, a *criminology of the skin*, a criminology that understands and analyzes everyday criminality on the level of pleasure and desire and explores the complex process by which criminal pleasures reproduce, redefine, and resist larger patterns of power, authority, and domination. For pornographers and graffiti writers, drug users and joyriders, the politics of criminality skip across the surface of the skin, and across the many moments of illicit pleasure and sensual excitement that their criminality exudes.[48]

Ellipses

Beyond the issues explored in the essays collected here, and beyond the issues just sketched in this final essay, stretch innumerable intersections of culture and crime. By way of highlighting, once again, the emergent and speculative nature of this new cultural criminology, we here note briefly a few of these intersections—some glimpsed now and again throughout this collection, others not at all. These brief discussions can perhaps best be seen as a series of ellipses that both signify some of the issues omitted from the present discussion and at the same time trail off into the possible futures of cultural criminology. . . .

Youth. The essays collected here imply that, if we are to make sense of the specific pleasures kids find in criminality, and the larger category of "juvenile delinquency" as well, we must understand "youth" less as a temporal moment than as a *culturally constructed* category of collective experience. Certainly "youth" in late capitalist society constitutes a socially produced category of experience shaped by legal and political powerlessness, exclusion from and exploitation by labor markets, and other factors. But as the essays included here begin to show, "youth" also constitutes a category of cultural experience, a relatively distinct constellation of styles, images, and identities. It is the coincidence of these social and cultural forces that begins to explain the involvement of kids in particular forms of deviance and criminality as well as the ongoing criminalization of youthful activities.[49]

Rather than simply noting the well-recognized correlation of youth and crime, cultural criminology can help in deconstructing the social and cultural politics of this correlation. Sociologists have long recognized social class, ethnicity, and gender as the holy trinity of societal inequalities that construct differences in identity, achievement—and participation in and victimization by crime. Here we would add a fourth category, age—though, again, less in chronological than in sociological terms. As scholars working within the British cultural studies tradition and elsewhere have shown, those with the least social status and power are often left to define themselves and their resistance to the powerful by using that over which they do retain some control—that is, by personal and collective symbolism and style.[50] It is little wonder then that young people consistently develop distinctive subcultural styles designed to symbolically register social difference and encode cultural disobedience. It is also not surprising that kids caught not only within inequalities of age, but also of poverty and ethnic minority status, develop extremisms of style that dwarf those of other kids and mystify and trouble adults, the affluent, and the powerful.

As the essays by Ferrell, Miller, Hamm, Lyng, and others in this volume have shown, these youthful styles come to symbolize, for legal authorities and others, the criminally deviant nature of youthful activities and associations. Ways of walking and talking, styles of dress and transportation, configurations of music and dance, all take on not only subcultural meaning but larger social meanings as well. This process of negotiated meaning goes on, of course, not only between kids and agents of legal control, but also within the realm of media dynamics and orchestrated sensationalism. Young people and their subcultures are susceptible to the sort of "moral panic" on which the mass media thrive and are vulnerable to being publicly reconstructed as "folk devils" responsible for a host of social and criminal ills. Issues of gangs, graffiti, youth violence, curfews, and the like—all take on meaning through their symbolic construction in an ideological system that consistently lays public blame on the least powerful among us.

In constructing their subcultural identities, young people borrow from and reconstruct the mediated symbols and identities that wash over them. As part of an ongoing cultural process, media institutions, commercial interests, and legal and political powers, in turn, reappropriate kids' symbolic universes, in some cases for sale back to them, in others for demonization and criminalization. Thus, it is not simply "youth" as a chronological category that correlates with crime, but youth as a category of political contestation and collective cultural experience. And in this sense, youth constitutes not only a locus of criminality but a central intersection of culture and crime as well.

"Bad Boys" and Beyond.   If we reconceptualize "youth," "crime," and related phenomena as cultural categories, we must reconceptualize them as gendered ones as well. That is, we must move beyond the usual "bad boys" approach to crime and delinquency that pays attention to the criminal activities and criminal subcultures of young males while either ignoring or marginalizing those of younger and older women alike. Certainly this volume itself serves too much as a sort of home for wayward boys; especially in its consideration of subculture and style, it focuses on the young males who populate the world of bikers, skinheads, minority gang members, and graffiti writers. It helps reproduce, unfortunately, what Daly and Chesney-Lind have characterized as criminology's "traditional focus on low-income boy's delinquency and men's street crime," or worse, what Heidensohn terms the "delinquent machismo tradition in criminology."[51] Yet, as a variety of studies have shown, women and girls also participate in gang activities, graffiti writing, prostitution, and various other criminal endeavors.[52] And these studies also show that the cultural dynamics of these worlds define for their female members the experience of criminality.

Thus, we need not only to "get our hands dirty and to plunge more deeply into the social worlds of girls and women," but to plunge into their *cultural* worlds as well.[53] That is, we need to develop not only a better criminology of girls and women but also a better and more attentive cultural criminology.

Similarly, we need a cultural criminology that can understand the criminal worlds of lesbians and gays, and especially the ongoing criminalization of gay and lesbian life. Largely in response to their social marginalization and criminalization, members of gay and lesbian subcultures have developed elaborately stylish codes of personal conduct and presentation of self—style codes that define not only much of the experience of queer life but many of the more progressive edges of straight life as well. But, following the dynamic we have seen often in this volume, it is these very codes of marginality that are in turn seized on by moral entrepreneurs, religious reactionaries, legal authorities, and others in their efforts to further criminalize lesbian and gay life. The attempt to suppress the homoerotic photography of Robert Mapplethorpe and the works of other queer artists, the distortion and exploitation of queer style and eroticism in anti-gay political campaigns, and the larger attempt to deny lesbians and gays legal and political rights on the basis of "lifestyle" reveal that it is the culture as much as the sexuality of gay and lesbian life that constitutes the locus of criminalization. Thus, in the same way that "queer theory" now must become a part of sociological theory, "queer criminology" must be part of any cultural criminology that sets out to explore in depth the politics of culture and crime.[54]

Certainly, young, straight males account for the majority of crime and criminal violence that pervade our social and cultural arrangements; and it is increasingly clear that this criminality is not an aberration from, but rather a predictable outcome of, straight male gender roles and expectations.[55] As the essays by Tunnell, Epstein, Hamm, and others in this volume show, however, this correlation should lead us to an exploration of the mediated images, subcultures, and styles through which this violent criminality is shaped and expressed, rather than to some sort of biological reductionism. This correlation of young, straight males and crime must not become, in turn, an excuse for ignoring those forms of crime and culture that fall outside its boundaries. If the criminality and criminalization of women and girls, lesbians and gays tend to be overshadowed by the coincidence of masculinity and crime, we must develop a cultural criminology that highlights these alternative processes and the gendered politics within which they occur.

Art, Authority, and Crime. Beyond exposing the cultural dimensions of crime and criminalization within the lives of girls and boys, lesbians and gays, and others, cultural criminology seems particularly well suited for exploring those moments when artistic and aesthetic dimensions of social life intersect with crime, criminalization, and social control. As seen in this volume, phenomena as diverse as contemporary urban graffiti, punk and skinhead music, and gay and lesbian art all exist at this intersection, as do many other moments of social and cultural existence. Within the confines of prison walls and prison life, for example, the shared culture, folklore, and artistic production of prisoners shape the contours of everyday life and craft various forms of resistance to this life as well. From the shared symbolism of prison tattoos to the slippery linguistic codes designed to evade the grasp of prison authorities, from the "envelope art" of Latino/Latina prisoners in the U.S. to the republican art that has emerged in the prisons of Northern

Ireland, the culture of imprisonment embodies the lived politics of the prison.[56]

If we are to understand crime, criminalization, and social control, it is not only the aesthetics of criminals and prisoners that merit our attention. We must also consider the "aesthetics of authority"—that is, the dimensions of aesthetics, style, and meaning built into the operations of social control.[57] Clearly, the panoptic structures and spaces of the modern prison and the postmodern city, the secured shopping malls, gated communities, and "belligerent lawns" of contemporary urban and suburban life, operate as environments of direct physical control. But these also function as symbolic environments, as a series of signs and codes that communicate the aesthetic and political imperatives of their builders and managers to those they would criminalize and control.[58] We cannot make sense of legal and political authority, nor of the responses of those in authority to graffiti writing, gang stylings, gay art, vagrancy, trespass, street cruising, and a host of other criminalized activities, if we do not explore authorities' own notions of beauty, style, and meaning, and the practices through which they build these notions into structures of social and legal control.[59]

A cultural criminology that integrates understandings of both cultural and criminal processes is also uniquely equipped to investigate the criminal dynamics that emerge inside more conventional worlds of art, music, and literature. Within mainstream art worlds, for example, crimes of art theft and art forgery, and legal efforts to control them, embody subtle, shared determinations of aesthetic quality, artistic authenticity, and cultural value.[60] Within the world of popular music, legal battles over "sampling" (the reuse and recontextualization of older bits of music or sound within contemporary songs) manifest a similar dynamic, with legal decisions often intertwined with aesthetic considerations of musical quality and originality. And within the worlds of commercial literature and film, cultural criminology can investigate legal actions involving plagiarism, copyright violation, and the like, and also the ways in which crime fiction, classic and contemporary film noir, and other texts produce and reproduce larger understandings of crime and control.[61]

There is, of course, more. Our intention in this volume has not been to exhaust the possibilities of cultural criminology, but quite the opposite: to imagine the shape that cultural criminology might take, to explore some of its dimensions, and to invite further speculation and participation. This open stance is dictated, in turn, not only by the emergent nature of cultural criminology but by the emergent nature of its subject matter. As public perceptions and fears of crime take on greater and greater political significance; as mediated channels structure more and more of social life and shared meaning, in part through a steady stream of crime and crime control images; as criminal subcultures and styles evolve out of, and in resistance to, these processes, cultural criminology must itself remain an unfinished project, open to the many and emerging intersections of culture and crime in everyday life.

Notes

1. See Howard S. Becker, *Outsiders: Studies in the Sociology of Deviance* (New York: The Free Press, 1963), 183–84.

2. See Jeff Ferrell, "The Brotherhood of Timber Workers and the Culture of Conflict," *Journal of Folklore Research* 28 (1991): 163–77.

3. See Emile Durkheim, *The Elementary Forms of Religious Life* (Glencoe, IL: The Free Press, 1947).

4. See, for example, Mike Davis, *City of Quartz* (New York: Vintage, 1992); Jeff Ferrell, "Urban Graffiti: Crime, Control, and Resistance," *Youth and Society* 26: (forthcoming).

5. On interactionist sociology and criminology see, of course, Becker, *Outsiders*. On constructionist approaches, see, for example, William Gamson, "A Constructionist Approach to Mass Media and Public Opinion," *Symbolic Interaction* 11 (1988): 161–74; Joel Best, ed., *Images of Issues* (Hawthorne, NY: Aldine de Gruyter, 1989); Malcolm Spector and John Kitsuse, *Constructing Social Problems* (Hawthorne, NY: Aldine de Gruyter, 1987); Victor Kappeler, Mark Blumberg, and Gary Potter, *The Mythology of Crime and Criminal Justice* (Prospect Heights, IL: Waveland, 1993).

6. See Paul Willis, *Learning to Labor* (New York: Columbia University Press, 1977); Stuart Cosgrove, "The Zoot-Suit and Style Warfare," *Radical America* 18 (1984): 38–51; and similarly, Stanley Cohen, *Folk Devils and Moral Panics* (London: MacGibbon and Kee, 1972).

7. Lawrence Grossberg, Cary Nelson, and Paula Treichler, eds., *Cultural Studies* (New York: Routledge, 1992), 20–21.

8. Steven Jay Sherwood, Philip Smith, and Jeffrey Alexander, "The British Are Coming . . . Again! The Hidden Agenda of 'Cultural Studies,' " *Contemporary Sociology* 22 (1993): 370–75.

9. See, for example, Jean Baudrillard, *Jean Baudrillard: Selected Writings*, ed. Mark Poster (Oxford: Polity Press, 1988); William Bogard, "Closing Down the Social: Baudrillard's Challenge to Contemporary Sociology," *Sociological Theory* 8 (1990): 1–15; Dick Hebdige, *Subculture: The Meaning of Style* (London: Methuen, 1979); Dick Hebdige, *Hiding in the Light* (London: Routledge, 1988).

10. On constitutive criminology, see Stuart Henry and Dragan Milovanovic, "Constitutive Criminology: The Maturation of Critical Theory," *Criminology* 29 (1991): 293–315; Stuart Henry and Dragan Milovanovic, "The Constitution of Constitutive Criminology: A Postmodern Approach to Criminological Theory," in *The Futures of Criminology*, ed. David Nelken (London: Sage, 1994), 110–33. On newsmaking criminology, see Gregg Barak, "Newsmaking Criminology: Reflections on the Media, Intellectuals, and Crime," *Justice Quarterly* 5 (1988): 565–87; Gregg Barak, *Media, Process, and the Social Construction of Crime* (New York: Garland, 1994).

11. See Alexander Liazos, "The Poverty of the Sociology of Deviance: Nuts, Sluts, and Perverts," *Social Problems* 20 (1972): 102–20, and Joel Best, Afterword, *Images of Issues*, 243–53.

12. See Jeff Ferrell, *Crimes of Style: Urban Graffiti and the Politics of Criminality* (New York: Garland, 1993), 159–97, on "making fun of authority" as a postmodern political strategy.

13. For more on postmodern and other alternatives to traditional criminology, see, for example, Martin D. Schwartz, "The Undercutting Edge of Criminology," *The Critical Criminologist* 1 (1989): 1–2, 5; Martin D. Schwartz and David O. Friedrichs, "Postmodern Thought and Criminological Discontent: New Metaphors for Understanding Violence," *Criminology* 32 (1994): 221–46.

14. Stanley Cohen, *Against Criminology* (New Brunswick, NJ: Transaction, 1988): 68; Dario Melossi, "Overcoming the Crisis in Critical Criminology: Toward a Grounded Labeling Theory," *Criminology* 23 (1985): 193–208.

15. Willis, 3; see Stuart Hall and Tony Jefferson, eds., *Resistance Through Rituals* (London: Hutchinson, 1976).

16. Kappeler, Blumberg, and Potter, 19.

17. Paul Feyerabend, *Against Method* (London: Verso, 1975), 23; emphasis in original.

18. See Gilbert Geiss, "The Case Study Method in Sociological Criminology," in *A Case for the Case Study*, ed. Joe Feagin, Anthony Orum, and Gideon Sjoberg (Chapel Hill: University of North Carolina Press, 1991), 201–2; Paul Atkinson, *The Ethnographic Imagination: Textual Constructions of Reality* (London and New York: Routledge, 1990); Yvonna Lincoln and Egon Guba, *Naturalistic Inquiry* (Beverly Hills: Sage, 1985).

19. See, for example, Mark Hamm, *American Skinheads: The Criminology and Control of Hate Crime* (Westport, CT: Praeger, 1993), as well as his essay in this collection (chap. 9).

20. Among feminist criminologists, see, for example, Kathleen Daly and Meda Chesney-Lind, "Feminism and Criminology," *Justice Quarterly* 5 (1988): 497–535; Susan Caulfield and Nancy Wonders, "Gender and Justice: Feminist Contributions to Criminology," in *Varieties of Criminology*, ed. Gregg Barak (Westport, CT: Praeger, 1994), 213–29. Among qualitative criminologists and sociologists, see, for example, Joe Feagin, Anthony Orum, and Gideon Sjoberg, eds., *A Case for the Case Study*; George McCall, *Observing the Law* (New York: The Free Press, 1978); Geiss, "Case Study"; Michael Burawoy et al., *Ethnography Unbound* (Berkeley: University of California Press, 1991); Lyn Lofland, "Fighting the Good Fight—Again," *Contemporary Sociology* 22 (1993): 1–3; John Hagan, "Structural and Cultural Disinvestment and the New Ethnographies of Poverty and Crime," *Contemporary Sociology* 22 (1993): 327–32; Jack Katz, *Seductions of Crime* (New York: Basic Books, 1988); Hamm, *Skinheads*; Clinton R. Sanders, *Customizing the Body: The Art and Culture of Tattooing* (Philadelphia: Temple, 1989); Jeff Ferrell, "Making Sense of Crime," *Social Justice* 19 (1992): 110–23; Ferrell, *Crimes*; Felix Padilla, *The Gang as an American Enterprise* (New Brunswick, NJ: Rutgers, 1992); Joan W. Moore, *Homeboys* (Philadelphia: Temple, 1978); John M. Hagedorn, *People and Folks* (Chicago: Lake View Press, 1988); Anne Campbell, *The Girls in the Gang*, 2d ed. (Oxford: Basil Blackwell, 1991); William Sanders, *Gangbangs and Drive-bys* (Hawthorne, NY: Aldine de Gruyter, 1994).

21. Daly and Chesney-Lind, 517–18; Caulfield and Wonders, "Gender," 223; see Geiss, "Case Study." As with cultural criminology's theoretical underpinnings, the methods of cultural criminology are thus "feminist" in their epistemological assumptions, their rejection of abstraction and universality, and their attention to the lived texture of culture and crime, whatever the gender of those who employ them or those they are designed to study.

22. See, for example, Ned Polsky, *Hustlers, Beats and Others* (Garden City, NY: Doubleday, 1969); Katz, *Seductions*; Hamm, *Skinheads*; Ferrell, *Crimes*; Luis J. Rodriguez, *Always Running: La Vida Loca, Gang Days in L.A.* (Willimantic, CT: Curbstone, 1993); John Hagedorn, "Homeboys, Dope Fiends, Legits, and New Jacks," *Criminology* 32 (1994): 197–219.

23. See, for example, Richard Bolton, ed., *Culture Wars* (New York: New Press, 1992).

24. Caulfield and Wonders, "Gender," 223–25.

25. See, for example, Patricia Ticineto Clough, *The End(s) of Ethnography* (Newbury Park, CA: Sage, 1992); Andrea Press, "Feminist Methodology? A Reassessment," *Contemporary Sociology* 22 (1993): 23–29; David Snow and Calvin Morrill, "Reflections on Anthropology's Ethnographic Crisis of Faith," *Contemporary Sociology* 22 (1993): 8–11.

26. Hebdige, *Hiding*, 12.

27. Geiss, 205.

28. As Feagin, Orum, and Sjoberg, *A Case*, demonstrate, this methodology of attentiveness and immersion would, if widely adopted, require a wholesale reconceptualization of a criminology that now runs on both quantitative analysis and the quick quantity of journal articles produced.

29. See Howard S. Becker, "Labelling Theory Reconsidered," in *Deviance and Social Control*, ed. Paul Rock and Mary McIntosh (London: Tavistock, 1974), 41–66.

30. For recent examples of this, see Donna Gaines, *Teenage Wasteland: Suburbia's Dead End Kids* (New York: Pantheon, 1991); Sarah Thornton, "Moral Panic, the Media and British Rave Culture," in *Microphone Fiends: Youth Music and Youth Culture*, ed. Andrew Ross and Tricia Rose (New York: Routledge, 1994), 176–92; and Wayne Wooden, *Renegade Kids, Suburban Outlaws* (Belmont, CA: Wadsworth, 1995).

31. Kenneth D. Tunnell, *Choosing Crime: The Criminal Calculus of Property Offenders* (Chicago: Nelson-Hall, 1992).

32. Willis, 16; see also 14–16.

33. See, for example, Jack Kerouac's accounts of Neal Cassady's car stealing in *On the Road* (New York: New American Library, 1955).

34. See Ferrell, *Crimes*; Ferrell, "Urban Graffiti."

35. See, for example, Mike Presdee, "Young People, Culture, and the Construction of Crime: Doing Wrong versus Doing Crime," in *Varieties of Criminology*, ed. Gregg Barak (Westport, CT: Praeger, 1994), 179–87.

36. Tunnell, *Choosing*, 45. See also Stephen Lyng, "Edgework: A Social Psychological Analysis of Voluntary Risk Taking," *American Journal of Sociology* 95 (1990): 851–86; and Pat O'Malley and Stephen Mugford, "Crime, Excitement, and Modernity," in *Varieties of Criminology*, 189–211.

37. See Lyng, "Edgework."

38. Jeffrey Riemer, "Deviance as Fun," in *Constructions of Deviance*, ed. Patricia Adler and Peter Adler (Belmont, CA: Wadsworth, 1994), 21.

39. See Vernon Allen and David Greenberger, "An Aesthetic Theory of Vandalism," *Crime and Delinquency* 24 (1978), 309–21; Hamm, *Skinheads*.

40. See Katz, *Seductions*; Ferrell, *Crimes*; Mark S. Hamm and Jeff Ferrell, "Rap, Cops, and Crime," *ACJS Today* 13 (1994): 1, 3, 29.

41. See, for example, Laura Kipnis, "(Male) Desire and (Female) Disgust: Reading *Hustler*," in *Cultural Studies*, 373–91; Sallie Tisdale, "Talk Dirty to Me," *Utne Reader* 58 (July/August 1993): 65–70.

42. See Katz, *Seductions*; John Fiske, "An Interview with John Fiske," *Border/Lines* 20/21 (1991): 4–7; John Fiske, "Cultural Studies and the Culture of Everyday Life," in *Cultural Studies*, 154–65. Thus, as does Hebdige, *Hiding*, 18, we here "want to challenge the distinction between 'pleasure' and 'politics' . . . and to pose instead another concept: the politics of pleasure."

43. See Michel Foucault, *The Use of Pleasure* (New York: Pantheon, 1985); also James Miller, *The Passion of Michel Foucault* (New York: Simon and Schuster, 1993).

44. See Ferrell, *Crimes*; Ferrell, "Making Sense"; Ferrell, "Urban Graffiti." Clearly, for kids the pleasures of many other criminal and noncriminal activities likewise derive at least in part from their (often symbolic) resistance to the constraints of adult authority.

45. See, for example, Willis, *Learning*; and similarly, William Thompson, "Hanging Tongues: A Sociological Encounter with the Assembly Line," *Qualitative Sociology* 6 (1983): 215–37.

46. See, for example, Hagan, "Structural and Cultural."

47. Tony Kushner, "A Socialism of the Skin," *The Nation* 259 (4 July 1994): 9–14.

48. The pleasure and danger that are central to the politics of skin are strikingly apparent in the contemporary phenomena of tattooing and other forms of permanent body alteration. In addition to being aesthetic practices, branding, scarification, piercing, and tattooing within certain subcultural situations are key modes of "voluntary stigmatization" by which group members symbolically set themselves off from "ordinary citizens." These alterations also act as powerful "marks of affiliation," demonstrating inclusion within, and commitment to, the group and the insubordination around which its culture is centered. Constantly on the look-out for enticingly exotic material, the media have increasingly focused on permanent body modification, first as a deviant practice, and then—as media-generated attention increased the diffusion of the practice into the realm of popular culture—as a semi-acceptable element of contemporary fashion. This diffusion and cooptation, in turn, diminished the political impact of body alteration as deviance was transformed into a marginally legitimate commercial product that no longer offered young people an effective way of annoying adults, or the "bad" a means of symbolically thumbing their noses at the "good." See Sanders, *Customizing*; James Myers, "Nonmainstream Body Modification: Genital Piercing, Branding, Burning, and Cutting," *Journal of Contemporary Ethnography* 21 (1992): 267–306.

49. See, for example, Anthony Platt, "The Triumph of Benevolence: The Origins of the Juvenile Justice System in the United States," in *Criminal Justice in America*, ed. Richard Quinney (Boston: Little, Brown, 1974), 362–83; Presdee, "Young People."

50. See, for example, Hebdige, *Subculture*; Willis, *Learning*; Hall and Jefferson, *Resistance Through Rituals*; James Scott, *Weapons of the Weak: Everyday Forms of Peasant Resistance* (New Haven: Yale, 1985); James Scott, *Domination and the Arts of Resistance* (New Haven: Yale, 1990). See also Gaines, *Teenage Wasteland*.

51. Daly and Chesney-Lind, 514; Heidensohn as quoted in Daly and Ches-

ney-Lind, 519. See also Angela McRobbie, "Settling Accounts with Subcultures: A Feminist Critique," *Screen Education* 34 (1980): 37–49; Angela McRobbie, *Feminism and Youth Culture* (Boston: Unwin Hyman, 1991).

52. Among the many studies, see, for example, Campbell, *Girls*; Joan W. Moore, *Going Down to the Barrio: Homeboys and Homegirls in Change* (Philadelphia: Temple, 1991); Jody Miller, " 'Your Life Is on the Line Every Night You're on the Streets': Victimization and Resistance Among Street Prostitutes," *Humanity and Society* 17 (1993): 422–46; Adrian Nicole LeBlanc, "While Manny's Locked Up," *New York Times Magazine*, 14 August 1994, 26–33, 46, 49, 53; Kerry Carrington, "Girls and Graffiti," *Cultural Studies* 3 (1989): 89–100.

53. Daly and Chesney-Lind, 519.

54. See, for example, Steven Seidman, "Symposium: Queer Theory/Sociology: A Dialogue," *Sociological Theory* 12 (1994): 166–77, and the other essays included in this symposium. See also Jeff Ferrell, "Criminalizing Popular Culture," in *Criminal Justice and Popular Culture*, ed. Donna Hale and Frankie Bailey (forthcoming).

55. See, for example, James W. Messerschmidt, *Masculinities and Crime* (Lanham, MD: Rowman and Littlefield, 1993).

56. See Inez Cordozo-Freeman (with Eugene Delorme), *The Joint: Language and Culture in a Maximum Security Prison* (Springfield, IL: Thomas, 1984); *Artpaper* 12 (1992), "Prison Envelope Art: Imagery in Motion," 16–17; Bill Rolston, *Politics and Painting* (London: Associated University Presses, 1991), 74–75.

57. Ferrell, *Crimes*.

58. Davis, *City*, 249; see Michel Foucault, *Discipline and Punish: The Birth of the Prison* (New York: Pantheon, 1977); Miller, *Passion*; Ferrell, *Crimes*; Ferrell, "Urban Graffiti."

59. Similarly, if we wish to understand the role of the police as agents of legal control, we must continue to explore the culture/subculture of policing and its aesthetic: the heavy and often hurtful stylings of police on the street, the shared and secretive values of police social worlds, and other factors.

60. On art worlds, see Howard S. Becker, *Art Worlds* (Berkeley: University of California Press, 1982); on art world crime, see, for example, John Conklin, *Art Crime* (Westport, CT: Praeger, 1994).

61. See, for example, David Glover and Cora Kaplan, "Guns in the House of Culture? Crime Fiction and the Politics of the Popular," in *Cultural Studies*, 213–26.

References

Print Media

Abbott, Karen. "Dress Code." *Rocky Mountain News*, 2 November 1993, 8D, 10D.

Agnew, Robert. "Foundations for a General Strain Theory of Crime and Delinquency." *Criminology* 30 (1992): 47–86.

Alder, Christine. "Gender Bias in Juvenile Diversion." *Crime and Delinquency* 30 (1984): 400–414.

Allen, Vernon, and David Greenberger. "An Aesthetic Theory of Vandalism." *Crime and Delinquency* 24 (1978): 309–21.

American Civil Liberties Union. "The Arts Censorship Project." Pamphlet. New York: ACLU, 1992.

Anderson, Elijah. *Streetwise: Race, Class, and Change in an Urban Community.* Chicago: University of Chicago Press, 1990.

Anderson, Sean, and Gregory J. Howard. "Crime, Criminal Justice, and Popular Culture." *Journal of Criminal Justice Education* 5 (1994): 123–31.

Arguello, Tony. "Doing the Right Thing Sparks Controversy." *El Semanario (The Denver Post)*, 14 April 1994, 1, 19.

"Arizona Teen Chewed Out in School for Wearing 'The Penguin' T-shirt." *Rocky Mountain News*, 12 November 1992, 41.

Aronowitz, Alexis A. "Germany's Xenophobic Violence: Criminal Justice and Social Responses." In *Hate Crime: International Perspectives on Causes and Control,* edited by Mark S. Hamm, 37–70. Cincinnati: Academy of Criminal Justice Sciences/Anderson, 1994.

Arons, Stephen, and Ethan Katsh. "How TV Cops Flout the Law." *Saturday Review* 4 (19 March 1977): 11–18.

Artis, Bob. *Bluegrass.* New York: Hawthorn Books, 1975.

Arts Censorship Project Newsletter. "Attacks on Rap Music Continue as Paris and ACLU Launch Affirmative Free-Music Campaign." New York: ACLU, Winter 1993.

Atkins, Robert. "A Censorship Time Line." *The Art Journal* (Fall 1991): 33–37.

Atkinson, Paul. *The Ethnographic Imagination: Textual Constructions of Reality*. London: Routledge, 1990.

Attinger, Joelle. "The Decline of New York." *Time*, 17 September 1989, 38.

Austin, James, and Aaron D. McVey. "The 1989 NCCD Prison Population Forecast: The Impact of the War on Drugs." *NCCD Focus* (1989).

Baez, Joan. *And a Voice to Sing With: A Memoir*. New York: Summit Books, 1987.

Bailey, Karen. "Schools Target Gang Colors." *Rocky Mountain News*, 10 October 1990, 8, 11.

Barak, Gregg. *Gimme Shelter: A Social History of Homelessness in Contemporary America*. New York: Praeger, 1991.

———. "Newsmaking Criminology: Reflections on the Media, Intellectuals, and Crime." *Justice Quarterly* 5 (1988): 565–87.

———, ed. *Media, Process, and the Social Construction of Crime: Studies in Newsmaking Criminology*. New York: Garland, 1994.

Barrile, L. "Television and Attitudes about Crime." Ph.D. diss., Boston College, 1980.

Bartels, Lynn. "It Was a Night of Bad Tricks." *Rocky Mountain News*, 2 November 1994, 5A, 6A.

———. "Teen Nabbed in Sports Jacket Sting." *Rocky Mountain News*, 9 December 1993, 4A.

Baudrillard Jean. *Jean Baudrillard: Selected Writings*. Edited by Mark Poster. Oxford: Polity Press, 1988.

Becker, Howard S., *Art Worlds*. Berkeley: University of California Press, 1982.

———. "Labelling Theory Reconsidered." In *Deviance and Social Control*, edited by Paul Rock and Mary McIntosh, 41–66. London: Tavistock, 1974.

———. *Outsiders: Studies in the Sociology of Deviance*. New York: The Free Press, 1963.

———. *Sociological Work*. Chicago: Aldine, 1970.

Becker, Howard S., and Michal McCall, eds. *Symbolic Interaction and Cultural Studies*. Chicago: University of Chicago Press, 1990.

Belenko, Steven. "The Impact of Drug Offenders on the Criminal Justice System." In *Drugs, Crime, and the Criminal Justice System*, edited by Ralph A. Weisheit, 27–78. Cincinnati: Anderson Press, 1990.

Benedict, Helen. *Virgin or Vamp: How the Press Covers Sex Crimes*. New York: Oxford University Press, 1992.

Benjamin, Walter. "The Work of Art in the Age of Mechanical Reproduction." In *Illuminations*, edited by Hannah Arendt, 219–53. New York: Harcourt, Brace, and World, 1968.

Bennett, H. Stith, and Jeff Ferrell. "Music Videos and Epistemic Socialization." *Youth & Society* 18 (1987): 344–62.

Berger, Peter L., and Thomas Luckman. *The Social Construction of Reality*. Garden City, NY: Doubleday and Company, 1966.

Berman, Ronald. *How Television Sees Its Audience*. Beverly Hills, CA: Sage, 1987.

Berry, G. I. "Multicultural Role Portrayals on Television as a Social Psychological Issue." In *Television as a Social Issue*, edited by Stuart Oskamp, 88–102. Newbury Park, CA: Sage, 1988.

Berry, Jon. "The Power of Cult Brands." *Adweek's Marketing Week* 33 (24 February 1992): 18–21.

Best, Joel, ed. *Images of Issues: Typifying Contemporary Social Problems*. Hawthorne, NY: Aldine de Gruyter, 1989.

Binder, Amy. "Constructing Racial Rhetoric: Media Depictions of Harm in Heavy Metal and Rap Music." *American Sociological Review* 58 (1993): 753–67.

Bing, Leon. *Do or Die*. New York: Harperperennial, 1991.

Bjerregaard, Beth, and Carolyn Smith. "Patterns of Male and Female Gang Membership." Working Paper No. 13. Albany: Rochester Youth Development Study, 1992.

Blackwood, Roy E. "The Content of News Photos: Roles Portrayed by Men and Women." *Journalism Quarterly* 60 (1983): 710–14.

Blalock, Hubert M., Jr. *Social Statistics*. New York: McGraw-Hill, 1960.

Von Blum, Paul. "Women Political Artists in Los Angeles: Judy Baca's Pubilc Art." *Z Magazine* 4 (October 1991): 70–74.

Blumer, Herbert. "The Crowd, the Public and the Mass." In *New Outline of the Principles of Sociology*, edited by Alfred M. Lee, 178–98. New York: Barnes and Noble, 1939.

Bogard, William. "Closing Down the Social: Baudrillard's Challenge to Contemporary Sociology." *Sociological Theory* 8 (1990): 1–15.

Bolton, Richard. "The Cultural Contradictions of Conservatism." *New Art Examiner* 17 (June 1990): 24–29, 72.

———, ed. *Culture Wars*. New York: New Press, 1992.

"Boy Gets Jersey Back." *Rocky Mountain News*, 8 June 1994, 29A.

"Boy Robbed of Jacket." *Rocky Mountain News*, 30 November 1993, 15A.

"Boys Robbed of Jacket, Cap." *Rocky Mountain News*, 11 April 1994, 15A.

Brake, Mike. *Comparative Youth Culture*. London: Routledge and Keagan Paul, 1985.

———. *The Sociology of Youth Culture and Youth Subcultures*. London: Routledge and Kegan Paul, 1980.

"Break the Silence Mural Project National Tour 1993." *Z Magazine* 6 (January 1993): back cover.

Brennan, Charlie. "Company May Put Anti-Crime Patch on Jackets." *Rocky Mountain News*, 10 December 1993, 20A.

———. "Death Played Muse for Carl Banks." *Rocky Mountain News*, 7 November 1993, 15A.

———. "Give Gang Culture a Wide Berth, Open Door Director Advises." *Rocky Mountain News*, 14 December 1993, 28A.

————. "Sportsfan Stores Pushing 'No Gangs, No Drugs' Patches." *Rocky Mountain News,* 4 December 1993, 4A.

Brett, Patricia. "Flourishing Graffiti Art Leads to Credit at Parisian 'Worker's University.' " *The Chronicle of Higher Education* 37 (1991): A34.

Brewer, Devon, and Marc Miller. "Bombing and Burning." *Deviant Behavior* 11 (1990): 345–69.

Broder, David. *Behind the Front Page—A Candid Look at How the News Is Made.* New York: Simon and Schuster, 1987.

Bronski, Michael. "It's Not the Flesh, It's the Flowers: The 'Art Wars' Rage On." *Radical America* 23 (1989): 47–55.

Brownstein, Henry H. "Demilitarization of the War on Drugs: Toward an Alternative Drug Strategy." In *The Great Issues of Drug Policy,* edited by Arnold S. Trebach and Kevin B. Zeese, 114–22. Washington, D.C.: Drug Policy Foundation, 1990.

————. "The Social Construction of Public Policy: A Case for Participation by Researchers." *Sociological Practice Review* 2 (1991): 132–40.

Brownstein, Henry H., Hari R. Shiledar Baxi, Paul J. Goldstein, and Patrick J. Ryan. "The Relationship of Drugs, Drug Trafficking, and Drug Traffickers to Homicide." *Journal of Crime and Justice* 15 (1992): 25–44.

Burawoy, Michael, et al. *Ethnography Unbound.* Berkeley: University of California Press, 1991.

Burchill, Julie, and Tony Parsons. *The Boy Looked at Johnny.* London: Pluto Press, 1978.

Bushnell, John. *Moscow Graffiti: Language and Subculture.* Boston: Unwin Hyman, 1990.

"CAC, Barrie Win in Court." *New Art Examiner* 18 (November 1990): 13.

Cameron, Deborah, and Elizabeth Frazer. *A Lust to Kill.* Oxford: Basil Blackwell, 1987.

Campbell, Anne. *The Girls in the Gang.* New York: Basil Blackwell, 1984.

————. *The Girls in the Gang.* 2d ed. Oxford: Basil Blackwell, 1991.

Campbell, Richard, and Jimmie L. Reeves. "Covering the Homeless: The Joyce Brown Story." *Critical Studies in Mass Communications* 6 (1989): 21–42.

Cantwell, Robert. *Bluegrass Breakdown: The Making of the Old Southern Sound.* Urbana: University of Illinois Press, 1984.

Caputi, Jane. *The Age of Sex Crime.* Bowling Green, OH: Popular Press, 1987.

————. "The New Founding Fathers: The Lore and Lure of the Serial Killer in Contemporary Culture." *Journal of American Culture* 13 (1990): 1–12.

Carnahan, Ann. "Teen Names Pal as Kid Who Killed for Jacket." *Rocky Mountain News,* 9 September 1994, 4A, 6A.

Carrington, Kerry. "Girls and Graffiti." *Cultural Studies* 3 (1989): 89–100.

Cash, Wilbur Joseph. *The Mind of the South.* New York: Random House, 1941.

Castleman, Craig. *Getting Up: Subway Graffiti in New York.* Cambridge, MA: MIT Press, 1982.

Caulfield, Susan, and Nancy Wonders. "Gender and Justice: Feminist Contributions to Criminology." In *Varieties of Criminology,* edited by Gregg Barak, 213–29. Westport, CT: Praeger, 1994.

———. "Personal AND Political: Violence Against Women and the Role of the State." In *Political Crime in Contemporary America: A Critical Approach,* edited by Kenneth Tunnell, 79–100. New York: Garland, 1993.

Centers for Disease Control, "Homicide among Young Black Males—United States, 1978–1987." *Morbidity and Mortality Weekly Report* 39 (7 December 1990). Atlanta: Centers for Disease Control, 870–72.

Chaffee, Lyman. "Political Graffiti and Wall Painting in Greater Buenos Aires: An Alternative Communication System." *Studies in Latin American Popular Culture* 8 (1989): 37–60.

———. *Political Protest and Street Art.* Westport, CT: Greenwood, 1993.

Chalfant, Henry, and James Prigoff. *Spraycan Art.* London: Thames and Hudson, 1987.

Chambers, Iain. *Popular Culture: The Metropolitan Experience.* London: Methuen, 1986.

Chambliss, William J. Foreword to *American Skinheads: The Criminology and Control of Hate Crime,* by Mark S. Hamm. Westport, CT: Praeger, 1993.

———. The Saints and the Roughnecks." In *Down to Earth Sociology.* 6th ed. Edited by James Henslin, 263–77. New York: The Free Press, 1991.

Chancellor, John, and Walter R. Mears. *The News Business.* New York: Harper and Row, 1983.

Chapman, John. "False Memory Syndrome." *Z Magazine* 7 (June 1994): 2–3.

Chesney-Lind, Meda. "Girls, Gangs and Violence: Anatomy of a Backlash." *Humanity and Society* 17 (1993): 321–44.

Chevigny, Paul. "Other Rodney Kings?: Let's Make It a Federal Case." *The Nation* 257 (23 March 1992): 370–72.

Chibnall, Steve. *Law-and-Order News.* London: Tavistock, 1977.

Child, Francis J. *The English and Scottish Popular Ballads.* Vol. 5. New York: Dover, 1965.

Christgau, Robert. *Any Old Way You Choose It.* Baltimore: Penguin, 1973.

Christie, Nils. *Crime Control as Industry.* London: Routledge, 1993.

Cirino, Robert. *Don't Blame the People.* New York: Vintage, 1972.

Clarke, Alan. " 'This Is Not the Boy Scouts': Television Police Series and the Definitions of Law and Order." In *Popular Culture and Social Relations,* edited by Tony Bennett, Colin Mercer, and Janet Woollacott, 219–32. Philadelphia: Open University, 1986.

Clarke, John. "Style." In *Resistance Through Rituals,* edited by Stuart Hall and Tony Jefferson, 175–91. London: Hutchinson, 1976.

Claster, Daniel S. *Bad Guys and Good Guys: Moral Polarization and Crime*. Westport, CT: Greenwood Press, 1992.

Cleaver, Eldridge. *Soul on Ice*. New York: McGraw-Hill, 1967.

Clough, Patricia Ticineto. *The End(s) of Ethnography*. Newbury Park, CA: Sage, 1992.

Cloward, Richard, and Lloyd Ohlin. *Delinquency and Opportunity: A Theory of Delinquent Gangs*. New York: The Free Press, 1960.

Cockcroft, Eva. "Writing on the Wall." *New Art Examiner* 19 (November 1991): 20.

Cohen, Albert. *Delinquent Boys: The Culture of the Gang*. New York: The Free Press, 1955.

Cohen, Stanley. *Against Criminology*. New Brunswick, NJ: Transaction, 1988.

———. *Folk Devils and Moral Panics*. London: MacGibbon and Kee, 1972.

Cohen, Stanley, and Jock Young, eds. *The Manufacture of News: Deviance, Social Problems, and the Mass Media*. London: Constable, 1981.

———. *The Manufacture of News: A Reader*. Beverly Hills, CA: Sage, 1973.

Collier, Peter, and David Horowitz. *Destructive Generation: Second Thoughts About the Sixties*. New York: Summit Books, 1989.

Conal, Robbie. *Art Attack: The Midnight Politics of a Guerrilla Artist*. New York: HarperCollins, 1992.

Conklin, John. *Art Crime*. Westport, CT: Praeger, 1994.

Cooper, Martha, and Henry Chalfant. *Subway Art*. London: Thames and Hudson, 1984.

"Cops Bait Jacket Thieves." *Rocky Mountain News*, 1 December 1993, 31A.

Cordozo-Freeman, Inez, with Eugene Delorme. *The Joint: Language and Culture in a Maximum Security Prison*. Springfield, IL: Thomas, 1984.

Cortazar, Julio. "Graffiti." In *We Love Glenda So Much and Other Tales*, edited by Julio Cortazar, 33–38. New York: Knopf, 1983.

Cosgrove, Stuart. "The Zoot-Suit and Style Warfare." *Radical America* 18 (1984): 38–51.

Couch, Carl J. *Social Processes and Relationships*. Dix Hills, NY: General Hall, 1989.

Cox, Terry C., and Kenneth D. Tunnell. "Competency to Stand Trial or the Trivial Pursuit of Justice." In *Homicide: The Victim-Offender Connection*, edited by Anna Wilson, 415–40. Cincinnati, OH: Anderson, 1993.

Crew, B. Keith. "Acting Like Cops: The Social Reality of Crime and Law on TV Police Dramas." In *Marginal Conventions: Popular Culture, Mass Media, and Social Deviance*, edited by Clinton R. Sanders, 131–43. Bowling Green, OH: The Popular Press, 1990.

Crockett, Art, ed. *Serial Murderers*. New York: Windsor, 1990.

Crosby, David, and Carl Gottlieb. *Long Time Gone: The Autobiography of David Crosby*. New York: Doubleday, 1988.

Csikszentmihalyi, Mihaly, and Eugene Rochberg-Halton. *The Meaning of Things*. New York: Cambridge University Press, 1981.

Culligan, Joseph T. *When in Doubt Check Him Out*. Miami: Hallmark Press, 1993.

Cuomo, Mario M. "Message to the Legislature." Albany, 1987.

———. "Message to the Legislature." Albany, 1989.

Currie, Elliott. *Reckoning: Drugs, the Cities, and the American Future*. New York: Hill and Wang, 1993.

Curtis, Lynn. *Violence, Race, and Culture*. Lexington, MA: Heath, 1975.

Curtis, Lynne A. "The National Drug Strategy and Inner City Policy." Testimony before the Select Committee on Narcotics Abuse and Control, U.S. House of Representatives, 15 November 1989.

Cushman, Thomas. "Rich Rastas and Communist Rockers." *Journal of Popular Culture* 25 (1991): 17–61.

Cycle. New York: CBS Magazines, 1977–1987.

Daly, Kathleen, and Meda Chesney-Lind. "Feminism and Criminology." *Justice Quarterly* 5 (1988): 497–535.

Dancis, Bruce. "Safety-Pins and Class Struggle: Punk Rock and the Left." *Socialist Review* 8 (1978): 58–83.

Davis, F. James. "Crime News in Colorado Newspapers." *American Journal of Sociology* 57 (1952): 325–30.

Davis, Fred. *Fashion, Culture, and Identity*. Chicago: University of Chicago Press, 1992.

Davis, Mike. *City of Quartz*. New York: Vintage, 1992.

Davis, Murray. *What's So Funny?* Chicago: University of Chicago Press, 1993.

Davis, Stephen. *Hammer of the Gods: The Led Zeppelin Saga*. New York: Ballantine Books, 1985.

Dawtrey, Adam, and Jeffrey Jolson-Colburn. "Scotland Yard Confiscates Rap Album." *Rocky Mountain News (The Hollywood Reporter)*, 7 June 1991, 111.

Delio, Michelle. "Robt. Williams: Esthetician of the Preposterous." *Art?Alternatives* 1 (April 1992): 33, 45.

Denisoff, R. Serge. *Sing a Song of Social Significance*. Bowling Green, OH: Bowling Green University Press, 1972.

Denisoff, R. Serge, and Mark H. Levin. "The Popular Protest Song: The Case of 'Eve of Destruction.' " *Public Opinion Quarterly* 35 (1971): 117–22.

Denzin, Norman K. *Symbolic Interaction and Cultural Studies: The Politics of Interpretation*. Cambridge, MA: Blackwell, 1992.

Dickson, Grierson. *Murder by Numbers*. London: Robert Hale, 1958.

Van Dijk, Teun Adrianus. *Racism and the Press*. London: Routledge, 1991.

Division of Criminal Justice Services. "Crime and Justice Annual Report." Albany: Division of Criminal Justice Services, 1988.

———. "Crime and Justice Trends in New York State: 1985–89." *Office of Justice Systems Analysis Bulletin*. Albany: Division of Criminal Justice Services, 1990.

———. "Uniform Crime Reporting—Index Offenses Reported—Final Counts for 1989." *Office of Justice Systems Analysis Bulletin*. Albany: Division of Criminal Justice Services, 1990.

Dominick, Joseph. "Crime and Law Enforcement in the Mass Media." In *Deviance and Mass Media*, edited by Charles Winick, 105–28. Beverly Hills: Sage, 1978.

"Do the Rights Thing." *Entertainment Weekly*, 30 March 1990, 38–39.

"Drug Violence Undermining Queens Hopes." *The New York Times*, 21 April 1988, B1.

Dubin, Steven. *Arresting Images: Impolitic Art and Uncivil Actions*. London: Routledge, 1992.

Duran, Marlys. "Teens Behind Bars." *Rocky Mountain News*, 6 March 1994, 22A, 32A.

Durkheim, Emile. *The Division of Labor in Society*. New York: The Free Press, 1984.

———. *The Elementary Forms of Religious Life*. Glencoe, IL: The Free Press, 1947.

Eco, Umberto. *Apocalypse Postponed*. Bloomington: Indiana University Press, 1994.

Egger, Steven. *Serial Murder: An Elusive Phenomenon*. New York: Praeger, 1990.

Milton S. Eisenhower Foundation. "Youth Investment and Community Resurrection—Street Lessons on Drugs and Crime for the Nineties, Final Report." Milton S. Eisenhower Foundation, 1990.

Ensslin, John. "Coat Bandits Terrorize Denver-Area Youths." *Rocky Mountain News*, 14 February 1993, 8.

———. "Mom Had No Idea of Trouble She Was Buying." *Rocky Mountain News*, 14 February 1993, 8.

———. "3 Arrested as Elitch's Fights Gangs." *Rocky Mountain News*, 27 May 1991, 6.

Erbesen, Wayne. *Backpocket Bluegrass Songbook*. New York: Pembroke Music, 1981.

Ericson, Richard. "Mass Media, Crime, Law, and Justice: An Institutional Approach." *The British Journal of Criminology* 31 (1991): 219–49.

Falco, Malthea. *Winning the Drug War—A National Strategy*. New York: Priority Press, 1989.

Feagin, Joe, Anthony Orum, and Gideon Sjoberg, eds. *A Case for the Case Study*. Chapel Hill: University of North Carolina Press, 1991.

Fedler, Fred, and Deane Jordan. "How Emphasis on People Affects Coverage of Crime." *Journalism Quarterly* 59 (1982): 474–78.

Ferrell, Jeff. "The Brotherhood of Timber Workers and the Culture of Conflict." *Journal of Folklore Research* 28 (1991): 163–77.

———. *Crimes of Style: Urban Graffiti and the Politics of Criminality*. New York: Garland, 1993.

————. "Criminalizing Popular Culture." In *Criminal Justice and Popular Culture*, edited by Donna Hale and Frankie Baily (forthcoming).

————. "Making Sense of Crime: A Review Essay on Jack Katz's *Seductions of Crime*." *Social Justice* 19 (1992): 110–23.

————. "Towards a Critical Criminology of Culture." Paper presented at the Annual Meeting of the Academy of Criminal Justice Sciences, Kansas City, MO, March 1993.

————. "Urban Graffiti: Crime, Control, and Resistance." *Youth and Society* 26 (forthcoming).

Feyerabend, Paul. *Against Method*. London: Verso, 1975.

Finestone, Harold. "Cats, Kicks, and Color." In *The Other Side: Perspectives on Deviance*, edited by Howard S. Becker, 281–97. New York: The Free Press, 1964.

Finkelman, Paul. "In War Civil Liberties Is the Second Casualty: The War on Drugs and the Bill of Rights." Paper presented at the Annual Meeting of the American Society of Criminology, Baltimore, MD, 1990.

Fishman, Mark. "Crime Waves as Ideology." *Social Problems* 25 (1978): 530–43.

————. *Manufacturing the News*. Austin: University of Texas Press, 1980.

————. "Police News: Constructing an Image of Crime." *Urban Life* 9 (1981): 371–94.

Fiske, John. "Cultural Studies and the Culture of Everyday Life." In *Cultural Studies*, edited by Lawrence Grossberg, Cary Nelson, and Paula Treichler, 154–65. New York: Routledge, 1992.

————. "An Interview with John Fiske." *Border/Lines* 20/21 (1991): 4–7.

Fleck, Fiona. "Moscow Gets Western Import: Gangs." *Rocky Mountain News (Reuter)*, 7 October 1992, 4.

Fletcher, Connie. *What Cops Know*. New York: Simon and Schuster, 1990.

Flippo, Chet. "The History of Rolling Stone: Part III." *Popular Music & Society* 3 (1974): 281–98.

Foucault, Michel. *Discipline and Punish: The Birth of the Prison*. New York: Pantheon, 1977.

————. *The Use of Pleasure*. New York: Pantheon, 1985.

Fox, James G. "The New Right and Social Justice: Implications for the Prisoners' Movement." *Crime and Social Justice* 20 (1983): 63–75.

Fox, Kathryn. "Real Punks and Pretenders: The Social Organization of a Counterculture." *Journal of Contemporary Ethnography* 16 (1987): 344–70.

Frith, Simon. *The Sociology of Rock*. London: Constable, 1978.

Gaines, Donna. *Teenage Wasteland: Suburbia's Dead End Kids*. New York: Pantheon, 1991.

Gamson, William. "A Constructionist Approach to Mass Media and Public Opinion." *Symbolic Interaction* 11 (1988): 161–74.

"Gang Attack: Unusual for Its Viciousness." *New York Times*, 25 April 1989, B1, B11.

"Gang Manual." Santa Rosa, CA: National Law Enforcement Institute, 1991.

Gans, Herbert J. *Deciding What's News—A Study of CBS Evening News, NBC Nightly News, Newsweek, and Time*. New York: Pantheon, 1979.

———. *Deciding What's News—A Study of CBS Evening News, NBC Nightly News, Newsweek, and Time*. New York: Vintage Books, 1980.

———. *Popular Culture and High Culture*. New York: Basic Books, 1974.

Garofalo, Reebee. *Rockin' the Boat: Mass Music and Mass Movements*. Boston: South End Press, 1992.

Gastil, Raymond D. "Violence, Crime, and Punishment." In *Encyclopedia of Southern Culture*, edited by Charles R. Wilson and William Ferris, 1473–76. Chapel Hill: University of North Carolina, 1989.

Geiss, Gilbert. "The Case Study Method in Sociological Criminology." In *A Case for the Case Study*, edited by Joe Feagin, Anthony Orum, and Gideon Sjoberg, 200–223. Chapel Hill: University of North Carolina Press, 1991.

Gerbner, George. "The Dynamics of Cultural Resistance." In *Hearth and Home: Images of Women in the Mass Media*, edited by Gaye Tuchman, Arlene Kaplan Daniels, and James Benet, 46–50. New York: Oxford, 1978.

Gerbner, George, Larry Gross, Nancy Signorielli, Marilyn Jackson-Beeck, and Suzanne Jeffries-Fox. "Cultural Indicators: Violence Profile No. 9." *Journal of Communication* 28 (1978): 176–207.

Gerbner, George, Larry Gross, Nancy Signorielli, Marilyn Jackson-Beeck, and Michael Morgan. "The Demonstration of Power: Violence Profile No. 10." *Journal of Communication* 29 (1979): 177–96.

Gerbner, George, Larry Gross, Nancy Signorielli, and Michael Morgan. "Charting the Mainstream: Television's Contributions to Political Orientations." *Journal of Communication* 32 (1982): 100–127.

———. "The Mainstreaming of America: Violence Profile No. 11." *Journal of Communication* 30 (1980): 10–29.

Giddens, Anthony. *The Constitution of Society: Outline of the Theory of Structuration*. Oxford: Polity Press, 1984.

Gilroy, Paul. *There Ain't No Black in the Union Jack: The Cultural Politics of Race and Nation*. Chicago: University of Chicago Press, 1991.

Gitlin, Todd. *The Whole World is Watching*. Berkeley: University of California Press, 1980.

Glionna, John. "Pals in the Posse." *Los Angeles Times*, 28 February 1993, B1, B3.

Glover, David, and Cora Kaplan. "Guns in the House of Culture? Crime Fiction and the Politics of the Popular." In *Cultural Studies*, edited by Lawrence Grossberg, Cary Nelson, and Paula Treichler, 213–26. New York: Routledge, 1992.

Goffman, Erving. *Gender Advertisements*. Cambridge, MA: Harvard University Press, 1979.

Goldstein, Paul J. *Prostitution and Drugs*. Lexington, MA: Lexington Books, 1979.

Goldstein, Paul J., Henry H. Brownstein, and Patrick J. Ryan. "Drug-Related Homicide in New York: 1984 and 1988." *Crime and Delinquency* 38 (1992): 459–76.

Goldstein, Paul J., Henry H. Brownstein, Patrick J. Ryan, and Patricia A. Bellucci. "Crack and Homicide in New York City, 1988: A Conceptually Based Event Analysis." *Contemporary Drug Problems* 16 (1989): 651–87.

Goode, Erich, and Nachman Ben-Yehuda. *Moral Panics*. Cambridge, MA: Blackwell, 1994.

Gore, Tipper. *Raising PG Kids in an X-Rated Society*. Nashville: Abingdon, 1987.

Gormley, W. T. "An Evaluation of the FCC's Cross Ownership Policy." *Policy Analysis* 6 (1980): 61–83.

Governor's Office of Employee Relations. "Crackdown on Crack." *GOER News* 2 (1986): 16.

———. "Crack—The Deadliest Cocaine of All." *GOER News* 2 (1986): 11–12.

Graber, Doris Appel. *Crime News and the Public*. New York: Praeger, 1980.

Grant, Robert M., R. Krishnan, Abraham B. Shani, and Ron Baer. "Appropriate Manufacturing Technology: A Strategy Approach." *Sloan Management Review* 33 (Fall 1991): 43–54.

Green, Archie. "Hillbilly Music: Source and Symbol." *Journal of American Folklore* 78 (1968): 204–28.

Greenberg, David. "Delinquency and the Age Structure of Society." *Contemporary Crises* 1 (1977): 189–223.

Greenberg, Jonathan. "All About Crime." *New York*, 3 September 1990, 20–32.

Grogan, Emmett. *Ringolevio: A Life Played for Keeps*. Boston: Little, Brown, 1972.

Grossberg, Lawrence, Cary Nelson, and Paula Treichler, eds. *Cultural Studies*. New York: Routledge, 1992.

Gutierrez, Hector. "T-shirts Make a Cultural Statement." *Rocky Mountain News*, 3 May 1993, 26A.

———. "Young and Proud Hispanics Wear Their Hearts on Their T's." *Rocky Mountain News (Las Noticias)*, 5 September 1993, 4N.

Hagan, John. "Structural and Cultural Disinvestment and the New Ethnographies of Poverty and Crime." *Contemporary Sociology* 22 (1993): 327–32.

Hagedorn, John M. "Gangs, Neighborhoods and Public Policy." *Social Problems* 38 (1991): 529–42.

———. "Homeboys, Dope Fiends, Legits, and New Jacks." *Criminology* 32 (1994): 197–219.

———. *People and Folks: Gang, Crime and the Underclass in a Rustbelt City*. Chicago: Lake View Press, 1988.

Hager, Steven. *Hip Hop: The Illustrated History of Break Dancing, Rap Music, and Graffiti*. New York: St. Martin's, 1984.

Hall, Stuart. *The Hard Road to Renewal: Thatcherism and the Crisis of the Left*. New York: Verso, 1988.

———. "What Is This 'Black' in Black Popular Culture?" *Social Justice* 20 (1993): 104–14.

Hall, Stuart, and Tony Jefferson, eds. *Resistance Through Rituals: Youth Subcultures in Post-War Britain*. London: Hutchinson, 1976.

Hall, Stuart, Chas Critcher, Tony Jefferson, John Clarke, and Brian Roberts. *Policing the Crisis: Mugging, the State, and Law and Order*. London: Macmillan, 1978.

Hamm, Mark S. *American Skinheads: The Criminology and Control of Hate Crime*. Westport, CT: Praeger, 1993.

———. "Conceptualizing Hate Crime in a Global Context." In *Hate Crime: International Perspectives on Causes and Control*, edited by Mark S. Hamm, 173–94. Cincinnati: Academy of Criminal Justice Sciences/Anderson, 1994.

———. "Doing Criminology Like It Matters: A Review Essay on Jeff Ferrell's *Crimes of Style*." *Social Justice* 20 (1993): 203–10.

Hamm, Mark S., and Jeff Ferrell. "Rap, Cops, and Crime: Clarifying the 'Cop Killer' Controversy." *ACJS Today* 13 (1994): 1, 3, 29.

Hartman, Paul G., and Charles Husband. *Racism and Mass Media*. London: Davis Poynter, 1974.

Hauge, Michael. *Writing Screenplays That Sell*. New York: McGraw-Hill, 1988.

Hebdige, Dick. *Hiding in the Light*. London: Routledge, 1988.

———. *Subculture: The Meaning of Style*. London: Methuen, 1979.

Hedges, Chris. "To Read All About It, Palestinians Scan the Walls." *New York Times*, 24 January 1994, 12B.

Hefland, Duke. "Born to Be Chic." *Los Angeles Times*, 9 September 1991, A3.

Heitmeyer, Wilhelm. "Hostility and Violence Against Foreigners in Germany." In *Racist Violence in Europe*, edited by Tore Bjorgo and Rob Witte, 17–28. New York: St. Martin's Press, 1993.

"He'll Put Bullet Holes in Your Clothes." *Rocky Mountain News*, 19 July 1994, 96A.

Henry, Stuart, and Dragan Milovanovic. "The Constitution of Constitutive Criminology: A Postmodern Approach to Criminological Theory." In *The Futures of Criminology*, edited by David Nelken, 110–33. London: Sage, 1994.

———. "Constitutive Criminology: The Maturation of Critical Theory." *Criminology* 29 (1991): 293–315.

Henry, Tricia. *Break All Rules! Punk Rock and the Making of a Style*. Ann Arbor: UMI Research Press, 1989.

Hernandez, Romel, and Dean Krakel. "Teens, Guns and Violence in the Suburbs." *Rocky Mountain News*, 23 May 1993, 5A–6A, 8A–12A; 24 May 1993, 8A–11A.

Herrick, Thaddeus. "Sociologist Says Gang Culture Saturating Society, Los Angeles Not To Blame for Denver's Ills." *Rocky Mountain News*, 24 October 1993, 10A.

Hickey, Eric. *Serial Murderers and Their Victims*. Pacific Grove: Brooks/Cole, 1991.

Hill, Fred. *Grass Roots: Illustrated History of Bluegrass and Mountain Music*. Rutland, VT: Academy Books, 1980.

Hofstadter, Richard. "Reflections on Violence in the U.S." In *American Violence*, edited by Richard Hofstadter and Michael Wallace, 3–43. New York: Vintage, 1970.

Holden, David. "Pop Go the Censors." *Index on Censorship* 22 (1993): 11–14.

Holmes, Barbara. "Harley's Hog Heaven." *Canadian Business* 65 (May 1992): 30–31.

Holmes, Ronald, and James De Burger. *Serial Murder*. Newbury Park, CA: Sage Publications, 1988.

hooks, bell. *Black Looks: Race and Representation*. Boston: South End Press, 1992.

———. "My 'Style' Ain't No Fashion." *Z Magazine* 5 (May 1992): 27–29.

Hooper, Columbus B., and Jonny "Big John" Moore. "Hell on Wheels: The Outlaw Motorcycle Gangs." *Journal of American Culture* 6 (1983): 58–64.

Hoover's Handbook of American Business. "Harley Davidson, Inc." N.p., 1994.

"How to '92: Model Actions for a Post-Columbian World: Media Activism." *Z Magazine* 5 (March 1992): 12–31.

Howell, Joseph T. *Hard Living on Clay Street: Portraits of Blue Collar Families*. New York: Anchor Press, 1973.

Huber, Joerg. *Paris Graffiti*. New York: Thames and Hudson, 1986.

Hugo, Joan. "Smoke Screen Censorship." *New Art Examiner* 18 (November 1990): 56.

Hunt, Alan. "The Big Fear: Law Confronts Postmodernism." *McGill Law Journal* 35 (1990): 507–40.

Hutchinson, Ray. "Blazon Nouveau: Gang Graffiti in the Barrios of Los Angeles and Chicago." In *Gangs: The Origins and Impact of Contemporary Youth Gangs in the United States*, edited by Scott Cummings and Daniel Monti, 137–71. Albany: State University of New York Press, 1993.

"Investigating Street Gangs for the Street Police Officer." Burbank: Burbank Police Department, n.d.

Irwin, John. *Prisons in Turmoil*. Boston: Little, Brown, 1980.

Jackson, Devon. "Serial Killers and the People Who Love Them." *The Village Voice* (22 March 1994): 26–32.

Jackson, Pamela Irving. "Crime, Youth Gangs and Urban Transition: The Social Dislocations of Postindustrial Economic Development." *Justice Quarterly* 8 (1991): 379–96.

Jackson, Patrick. "In Search of Gangs and Social Policy: A Literature Review." Unpublished manuscript, University of Missouri, 1988.

Jackson, Robert K., and Wesley D. McBride. *Understanding Street Gangs*. Costa Mesa, CA: Custom Publishing Company, 1985.

Jankowski, Martin Sanchez. *Islands in the Streets: Gangs and American Urban Society*. Berkeley: University of California Press, 1991.

Jenkins, Michael. "Gaining a Financial Foothold Through Public Warehousing." *Journal of Business Strategy* 13 (May–June 1992): 53–57.

Jenkins, Philip. " 'The Ice Age': The Social Construction of a Drug Panic." *Justice Quarterly* 11 (1994): 7–31.

———. *Intimate Enemies: Moral Panics in Contemporary Great Britain*. Hawthorne, NY: Aldine de Gruyter, 1992.

———. *Using Murder: The Social Construction of Serial Homicide*. Hawthorne, NY: Aldine de Gruyter, 1994.

Jensen, Eric. "International Nazi Cooperation: A Terrorist-Oriented Network." In *Racist Violence in Europe*, edited by Tore Bjorgo and Rob Witte, 80–95. New York: St. Martin's Press, 1993.

Johns, Christina. *State Power, Ideology, and the War on Drugs: Nothing Succeeds Like Failure*. New York: Praeger, 1992.

Joint Committee on New York Drug Law Evaluation. "The Nation's Toughest Drug Law: Evaluating the New York Experience, Final Report." New York: The Association of the Bar of New York, 1977.

Kappeler, Victor, Mark Blumberg, and Gary Potter. *The Mythology of Crime and Criminal Justice*. Prospect Heights, IL: Waveland, 1993.

Katz, Jack. *Seductions of Crime: Moral and Sensual Attractions in Doing Evil*. New York: Basic Books, 1988.

———. "What Makes Crime 'News'?" *Media, Culture, and Society* 9 (1987): 47–75.

Kelley, Robin D. G. "Know the Ledge." *The Nation* 258 (14 March 1994): 350–55.

Kerouac, Jack. *On the Road*. New York: New American Library, 1955.

Kingsman, Caroline. "High Theory . . . No Culture: Decolonizing Canadian Subcultural Studies." Unpublished manuscript, Carlton University, Ottawa, Ontario, n.d.

Kipnis, Laura. "(Male) Desire and (Female) Disgust: Reading *Hustler*." In *Cultural Studies*, edited by Lawrence Grossberg, Cary Nelson, and Paula Treichler, 373–91. New York: Routledge, 1992.

Kizer, Elizabeth J. "Protest Song Lyrics as Rhetoric." *Popular Music & Society* 9 (1983): 3–11.

Kleiman, Mark A. R. *Marijuana—Costs of Abuse, Costs of Control*. New York: Greenwood Press, 1989.

Klein, Malcolm W. *The American Street Gang: Its Nature, Prevalence and Control.* New York: Oxford University Press, forthcoming.

———. "Attempting Gang Control by Suppression: The Misuse of Deterrence Principles." *Studies on Crime and Crime Prevention: Annual Review* (1993): 88–111.

Klein, Malcolm W., and Cheryl L. Maxson. "Street Gang Violence." In *Violent Crime, Violent Criminals,* edited by Neil Weiner and Marvin Wolfgang, 198–231. Newbury Park, CA: Sage, 1988.

Klingler, David. "Demeanor or Crime? Why 'Hostile' Citizens Are More Likely to Be Arrested." *Criminology* 32 (1994): 475–93.

Koch, Tom. *The News as Myth—Fact and Context in Journalism.* New York: Greenwood Press, 1990.

Krisberg, Barry, Ira M. Schwartz, Paul Litsky, and James Austin. "The Watershed of Juvenile Justice Reform." *Crime & Delinquency* 32 (1986): 5–38.

Kummel, Phil. "Beyond Performance and Permanence." *Border/Lines* 22 (1991): 10–12.

Kunzle, David. "The Mural Death Squads of Nicaragua." *Z Magazine* 6 (April 1993): 62–66.

Kushner, Tony. "A Socialism of the Skin." *The Nation* 259 (4 July 1994): 9–14.

LACE, *Surveillance.* Los Angeles: LACE, 1984.

Lachmann, Richard. "Graffiti as Career and Ideology." *American Journal of Sociology* 94 (1988): 299–50.

La Duke, Betty. *Companeras: Women, Art, and Social Change in Latin America.* San Francisco: City Lights, 1985.

LaFree, Gary D. *Rape and Criminal Justice: The Social Construction of Sexual Assault.* Belmont, CA: Wadsworth, 1989.

Lamont. Michele, and Marcel Fournier. *Cultivating Differences: Symbolic Boundaries and the Making of Inequality.* Chicago: University of Chicago Press, 1992.

Laudon, Kenneth C. *Dossier Society.* New York: Columbia University Press, 1986.

Leapoldt, LeRoy. "Please, No Black Jerseys." *Rocky Mountain News,* 22 March 1992, 56.

LeBlanc, Adrian Nicole. "While Manny's Locked Up." *New York Times Magazine,* 14 August 1994, 26–33, 46, 49, 53.

Lee, Alfred McClung. *The Daily Newspaper in America—The Evolution of a Social Instrument.* New York: Octagon Books, 1973.

———. *Sociology for People—Toward a Caring Profession.* Syracuse, NY: Syracuse University Press, 1988.

———. *Sociology for Whom?* New York: Oxford University Press, 1978.

Lee, Alfred McClung, and Elizabeth Briant Lee. *The Fine Art of Propaganda—A Study of Father Coughlin's Speeches.* New York: Harcourt, Brace and Company, 1939.

Lefever, Ernest W. *Television and National Defense: An Analysis of News.* Washington, D.C.: Brookings Institution, 1976.

Lemert, Edwin M. *Social Pathology: A Systematic Approach to the Theory of Sociopathic Behavior.* New York: McGraw-Hill, 1951.

Levin, Jack, and James Alan Fox. *Mass Murder: America's Growing Menace.* New York: Plenum Press, 1985.

Lévi-Strauss, Claude. *The Elementary Structures of Kinship.* London: Eyre & Spottiswood, 1969.

Lewis, Oscar. "The Culture of Poverty." In *On Understanding Poverty: Perspectives from the Social Sciences,* edited by Daniel Patrick Moynihan, 187–200. New York: Basic Books, 1968.

Liazos, Alexander. "The Poverty of the Sociology of Deviance: Nuts, Sluts, and Perverts." *Social Problems* 20 (1972): 102–20.

Lichter, Linda S., and Robert S. Lichter. *Prime Time Crime.* Washington, D.C.: The Media Institute, 1983.

Lichter, Linda S., Robert S. Lichter, and Daniel Amundson. "The New York News Media and the Central Park Rape." New York: Center for Media and Public Affairs, 1989.

Lichter, Robert S., Stanley Rothman, and Linda S. Lichter. *The Media Elite.* Bethesda, MD: Adler and Adler, 1986.

Lincoln, Yvonna, and Egon Guba. *Naturalistic Inquiry.* Beverly Hills: Sage, 1985.

Lindsay, Sue. "Ruling Tromps on Racism in Drug Arrests." *Rocky Mountain News,* 11 November 1993, 48A.

Lippard, Lucy. *Get the Message? A Decade of Art for Social Change.* New York: E. P. Dutton, 1984.

———. "Sniper's Nest: Anti-Amnesia." *Z Magazine* 5 (December 1992): 63–66.

———. "Sniper's Nest: Post No Bills." *Z Magazine* 4 (October 1991): 58–60.

Lofland, Lyn. "Fighting the Good Fight—Again." *Contemporary Sociology* 22 (1993): 1–3.

Los Angeles City Attorney Gang Prosecution Section. "Civil Gang Abatement: A Community Based Policing Tool." Los Angeles: Office of the Los Angeles City Attorney, 1992.

Lowry, Kathy. "Painting the Town." *Texas Monthly* 20 (May 1992): 76, 80, 82, 84.

Lunde, Donald. *Murder and Madness.* San Francisco: San Francisco Book Company, 1976.

Lundman, Richard. "Demeanor or Crime? The Midwest City Police-Citizen Encounters Study." *Criminology* 32 (1994): 631–56.

Lydon, John. *Rotten: No Irish, No Blacks, No Dogs.* New York: St. Martin's Press, 1994.

Lyman, David. "Post-Mapplethorpe Blues in Cincinnati." *New Art Examiner* 18 (January 1991): 56.

Lyman, Stanford M. "From Matrimony to Malaise: Men and Women in American Film 1930–1980." *International Journal of Politics, Culture and Society* (1987): 73–100.

Lyng, Stephen. "Edgework: A Social Psychological Analysis of Voluntary Risk Taking." *American Journal of Sociology* 95 (1990): 851–86.

Lyon, Eleanor. "Deserving Victims: The Moral Assessment of Victims of Crime." Paper presented at the annual meeting of the Society for the Study of Social Problems, Miami, FL, August 1993.

———. "Media, Murder and Mayhem: Violence on Network Television." In *Marginal Conventions: Popular Culture, Mass Media and Social Deviance*, edited by Clinton R. Sanders, 144–54. Bowling Green, OH: The Popular Press, 1990.

———. "Services to Families of Homicide Victims." Report submitted to the Connecticut Commission on Victim Services, 1987.

MacArthur, John R. *Second Front: Censorship and Propaganda in the Gulf War*. New York: Hill and Wang, 1992.

McCall, George. *Observing the Law*. New York: The Free Press, 1978.

McCracken, Grant. *Culture and Consumption*. Bloomington: Indiana University Press, 1988.

McDermott, Catherine. *Street Style: British Design in the 80s*. New York: Rizzoli, 1987.

McDonald, James R. "Politics Revisited: Metatextual Implications of Rock and Roll Criticism." *Youth & Society* 19 (1988): 485–504.

McQuail, Denis. *Media Performance: Mass Communication and the Public Interest*. London: Sage Publications, 1992.

McRobbie, Angela. *Feminism and Youth Culture*. Boston: Unwin Hyman, 1991.

———. "Settling Accounts with Subcultures: A Feminist Critique." *Screen Education* 34 (1980): 37–49.

Majors, Richard, and Janet Mancini Billson. *Cool Pose: The Dilemmas of Black Manhood in America*. New York: Lexington, 1992.

"Mall Outlaws Backward Caps." *Rocky Mountain News*, 8 January 1994, 39A.

Malone, Bill C. "Music." In *Encyclopedia of Southern Culture*, edited by Charles R. Wilson and William Ferris, 985–92. Chapel Hill: University of North Carolina Press, 1989.

———. *Southern Music, American Music*. Lexington: University Press of Kentucky, 1979.

Mannheimer, Steven. "Cincinnati Joins the Censorship Circus." *New Art Examiner* 17 (June 1990): 33–35.

Marchese, John. "Forever Harley." *New York Times*, Sunday, 17 October 1993, sec. 9, p 10.

Marcuse, Herbert. *One Dimensional Man*. Boston: Beacon Press, 1964.

"Marketer of the Month: Willie G. Davidson: Born to Ride." *Sales and Marketing Management* 143 (April 1991): 26–27.

Markman, Ronald, and Dominick Bosco. *Alone with The Devil.* New York: Bantam Books, 1989.

Marks, A. "Television Exposure, Fear of Crime and Concern about Serious Illness." Ph.D. diss., Northwestern University, 1987.

Markson, Stephen. "Claims-making, Quasi-theories, and the Social Construction of the Rock 'n' Roll Menace." In *Marginal Conventions: Popular Culture, Mass Media, and Social Deviance,* edited by Clinton R. Sanders, 29–40. Bowling Green, OH: The Popular Press, 1990.

Marx, Gary T. "Ironies of Social Control: Authorities as Contributors to Deviance Through Escalation, Nonenforcement and Covert Facilitation." *Social Problems* 28 (1981): 221–46.

———. *Windows into the Soul: Surveillance and Society in an Age of High Technology.* ASA-Duke University Jensen Lectures, forthcoming.

Massing, Michael. "Crack's Destructive Sprint across America." *New York Times Magazine,* 1 October 1989, 38–41, 52–58.

Mauer, Marc. "Men in American Prisons: Trends, Causes, and Issues." *Men's Studies Review* 9 (1993): 10–12.

Mayer, Martin. *Making News.* Garden City, NY: Doubleday and Company, 1987.

Melossi, Dario. "Overcoming the Crisis in Critical Criminology: Toward a Grounded Labeling Theory." *Criminology* 23 (1985): 193–208.

Menninger, Karl. *The Crime of Punishment.* New York: Viking, 1966.

Messerschmidt, James W. *Masculinities and Crime: Critique and Reconceptualization of Theory.* Lanham, MD: Rowman and Littlefield, 1993.

Messner, Steven F. "Television Violence and Violent Crime: An Aggregate Analysis." *Social Problems* 33 (1986): 218–35.

Meyer, David, and William Hoynes. " 'Shannon's Deal': Competing Images of the Legal System on Primetime Television." *Journal of Popular Culture* 27 (1994): 31–42.

Mieczkowski, Tom. "Crack Distribution in Detroit." *Contemporary Drug Problems* 17 (1990): 9–29.

Miller, Daniel. *Material Culture and Mass Consumption.* Oxford: Basil Blackwell, 1987.

Miller, Ivor. "Piecing: The Dynamics of Style." *Calligraphy Review* 11 (1994): 20–33.

Miller, James. *The Passion of Michel Foucault.* New York: Simon and Schuster, 1993.

Miller, Jody. " 'Your Life Is on the Line Every Night You're on the Streets': Victimization and Resistance Among Street Prostitutes." *Humanity and Society* 17 (1993): 422–46.

Miller, Mark. "A Failed 'Test Case': Washington's Drug War." *Newsweek,* 29 January 1990, 28–29.

Miller, S. H. "The Content of News Photos: Women and Men's Roles." *Journalism Quarterly* 52 (1975): 70–75.

Miller, Walter. "Lower Class Culture as a Generating Milieu of Gang Delinquency." *Journal of Social Issues* 14 (1958): 5–19.

Milovanovic, Dragan. *Postmodern Law and Disorder: Pyschoanalytic Semiotics, Chaos and Juridic Exegeses.* Liverpool: Deborah Charles Publications, 1992.

Moehringer, J. R. "Killers Wanted Boy's Jacket." *Rocky Mountain News,* 3 December 1993, 5A.

Moers, Gigi. *How and Why Lovers Cheat and What You Can Do About It.* New York: Shapolsky Press, 1992.

Molina, Alexander A. "California's Anti-Gang Street Terrorism Enforcement and Prevention Act: One Step Forward, Two Steps Back?" *Southwestern University Law Review* 22 (1993): 457–81.

Monaco, Richard, and Bill Burt. *The Dracula Syndrome.* New York: Avon Books, 1993.

Monaghan, Peter. "2 Professors Study the Harley Subculture." *The Chronicle of Higher Education* 39 (20 January 1993): A5.

Montgomery, Randal. "The Outlaw Motorcycle Subculture." *Canadian Journal of Criminology* 18 (1976): 332–42.

———. "The Outlaw Motorcycle Subculture: II." *Canadian Journal of Criminology* 19 (1977): 356–61.

Moore, Jack B. *Skinheads Shaved for Battle: A Cultural History of American Skinheads.* Bowling Green: Bowling Green State University Press, 1993.

Moore, Joan W. *Going Down to the Barrio: Homeboys and Homegirls in Change.* Philadelphia: Temple, 1991.

———. *Homeboys.* Philadelphia: Temple, 1978.

———. "Isolation and Stigmatization in the Development of an Underclass: The Case of Chicano Gangs in East Los Angeles." *Social Problems* 33 (1985): 1–12.

Morgan, Anne Barclay. "Interview: Alberto Gaitan and Lynn McCary." *Art Papers* 18 (January/February 1994): 21–22.

Mukerji, Chandra, and Michael Schudson. "Introduction: Rethinking Popular Culture." In *Rethinking Popular Culture: Contemporary Perspectives in Cultural Studies,* edited by Chandra Mukerji and Michael Schudson, 1–61. Berkeley: University of California Press, 1991.

Munro-Bjorklund, Vicky. "Popular Cultural Images of Criminals and Convicts Since Attica." *Social Justice* 18 (1991): 48–70.

Myers, James. "Nonmainstream Body Modification: Genital Piercing, Branding, Burning, and Cutting." *Journal of Contemporary Ethnography* 21 (1992): 267–306.

Nadelmann, Ethan A. "Drug Prohibition in the United States: Costs, Consequences, and Alternatives." *Science* 245 (1989): 939–47.

———. "U.S. Drug Policy: A Bad Export." *Foreign Policy* 70 (1988): 83–108.

Nash, Jay Robert, and Stanley Ralph Ross, eds. *The Motion Picture Guide Vols. 1–12 and Annual Editions.* Chicago: Cinebooks, 1985–1992.

Needleman, Bert, and Norman Weiner. "Heroes and Villains in Art." *Society* 14 (1976): 35–39.

Nehring, Neil. *Flowers in the Dustbin: Culture, Anarchy, and Postwar England.* Ann Arbor: University of Michigan Press, 1993.

Newman, Graeme. "Popular Culture and Criminal Justice: A Preliminary Analysis." *Journal of Criminal Justice* 18 (1990): 261–74.

Newton, Michael. *Hunting Humans: The Encyclopedia of Serial Killers.* Vol. 2. New York: Avon Books, 1990.

Norris, Joel. *Serial Killers: The Growing Menace.* New York: Doubleday, 1988.

Nurco, David, Timothy Kinlok, and Thomas Hanlon. "The Drugs-Crime Connection." In *Handbook of Drug Control in the United States,* edited by James Inciardi, 71–90. Westport, CT: Greenwood, 1991.

Office of the Attorney General. "Drug Trafficking—A Report to the President of the United States." Washington, D.C.: U.S. Department of Justice, 1989.

Office of National Drug Control Policy. "National Drug Control Strategy." Washington, D.C.: Executive Office of the President, 1989.

———. "National Drug Control Strategy." Washington, D.C.: Executive Office of the President, 1990.

———. "National Drug Control Strategy." Washington, D.C.: Executive Office of the President, 1992.

O'Malley, Pat, and Stephen Mugford. "Crime, Excitement and Modernity." In *Varieties of Criminology: Readings from a Dynamic Discipline,* edited by Gregg Barak, 189–211. Westport, CT: Praeger, 1994.

"On the Line." *The Progressive* 56 (July 1992): 13.

Operation Safe Streets Street Gang Detail. "Los Angeles Style: A Street Gang Manual of the Los Angeles County Sheriff's Department." Los Angeles: Sheriff's Department, County of Los Angeles, 1992.

"Opium Dens for the Crack Era." *New York Times,* 18 May 1986, 38.

Ostrowski, James. "Thinking About Drug Legalization." *Policy Analysis, Cato Institute* 121 (1989).

Padilla, Felix. *The Gang as an American Enterprise.* New Brunswick, NJ: Rutgers University Press, 1992.

Paletz, David, and Robert Entman. *Media, Power, and Politics.* New York: The Free Press, 1981.

Pearson, Anthony. "The Grateful Dead Phenomenon: An Ethnomethodological Approach." *Youth & Society* 18 (1987): 418–32.

Pepinsky, Harold, and Richard Quinney, eds. *Criminology as Peacemaking.* Bloomington: Indiana Univeresity Press, 1991.

Peterson, Ruth D., and William C. Bailey. "Murder and Capital Punishment in the United States: The Question of Deterrence." In *Criminal Law in Action,* edited by William J. Chambliss, 435–48. New York: Wiley, 1984.

Phillips, David. "Airplane Accidents, Murder, and the Mass Media: Towards a Theory of Imitation and Suggestion." *Social Forces* 58 (1980): 1001–24.

Phillips, David, and Lundie Carstensen. "The Effects of Suicide Stories on Various Demographic Groups 1968–1985." In *The Media and Criminal Justice Policy,* edited by Ray Surette, 63–72. Springfield, IL: Thomas, 1990.

Plasketes, George M., and Julie Grace Plasketes. "From Woodstock Nation to Pepsi Generation: Reflections on Rock Culture and the State of Music, 1969–Present." *Popular Music and Society* 11 (1987): 25–52.

Platt, Anthony. "The Triumph of Benevolence: The Origins of the Juvenile Justice System in the United States." In *Criminal Justice in America,* edited by Richard Quinney, 362–83. Boston: Little, Brown, 1974.

Plaza, Tina. " 'Let's See Some Papers': In El Paso, Looking Latin Is a Crime." *The Progressive* 57 (1993): 18, 23.

"Police Look to Stop 'Cop Killer.' " *Rocky Mountain News,* 18 June 1992, 86.

Polsky, Ned. *Hustlers, Beats, and Others.* Garden City, NY: Anchor, 1969.

Pooley, Eric. "Fighting Back Against Crack." *New York,* 23 January 1989, 32.

Posener, Jill. *Spray It Loud.* London: Pandora Press, 1982.

Presdee, Mike. "Young People, Culture, and the Construction of Crime: Doing Wrong versus Doing Crime." In *Varieties of Criminology,* edited by Gregg Barak, 179–87. Westport, CT: Praeger, 1994.

Press, Andrea. "Feminist Methodology: A Reassessment." *Contemporary Sociology* 22 (1993): 23–29.

Price, Steven D. *Old as the Hills: The Story of Bluegrass Music.* New York: Viking Press, 1975.

Prinsky, Lorraine E., and Jill Leslie Rosenbaum. " 'LEER-ICS' or Lyrics: Teenage Impressions of Rock 'n' Roll." *Youth & Scoiety* 18 (1987): 384–97.

"Prison Envelope Art: Imagery in Motion." *Artpaper* 12 (1992): 16–17.

Puller, Lewis B., Jr. *Fortunate Son: The Autobiography of Lewis B. Puller Jr.* New York: Bantam Books, 1991.

Quinn, James E. "Sex Roles and Hedonism Among Members of 'Outlaw' Motorcycle Clubs." *Deviant Behavior* 8 (1987): 47–63.

Quintanilla, Michael. "War of the Walls." *Los Angeles Times,* 14 July 1993, E1.

Ramet, Pedro, and Serbei Zamascikov. "The Soviet Rock Scene." *Journal of Popular Culture* 24 (1990): 149–74.

Rapping, Elayne. "Tabloid TV and Social Reality." *The Progressive* (August 1992): 35–37.

"Record Year for Killings Jolts Officials in New York." *New York Times,* 31 December 1990, B1.

Reid, Peter C. *Well Made in America: Lessons from Harley-Davidson on Being the Best.* New York: McGraw-Hill, 1990.

Reinarman, Craig. "The Social Construction of Drug Scares." In *Constructions of Deviance,* edited by Patricia Adler and Peter Adler, 92–104. Belmont, CA: Wadsworth, 1994.

Reinarman, Craig, and Harry G. Levine. "Crack in Context: Politics and the Media in the Making of a Drug Scare." *Contemporary Drug Problems* 16 (1989): 535–78.

Reiner, Ira. "Gangs, Crime and Violence in Los Angeles: Findings and Proposals from the District Attorney's Office." Los Angeles: District Attorney, County of Los Angeles, 1992.

Re/Search #11: Pranks! San Francisco: Re/Search Publications, 1987.

Ressler, Robert, and Tom Shachtman. *Whoever Fights Monsters.* New York: St. Martin's Press, 1992.

Riding, Alan. "Parisians on Graffiti: Is It Vandalism or Art?" *New York Times,* 6 February 1992, A6.

Riemer, Jeffrey. "Deviance as Fun." In *Constructions of Deviance,* edited by Patricia Adler and Peter Adler, 21–25. Belmont, CA: Wadsworth, 1994.

Ritzer, George. *Frontiers of Social Theory: The New Syntheses.* New York: Columbia, 1990.

Roberg, Roy, and Jack Kuykendall. *Police and Society.* Belmont, CA: Wadsworth Publishing Company, 1993.

Robinson, David. *Soho Walls: Beyond Graffiti.* New York: Thames and Hudson, 1990.

Rodnitzky, Jerome. "The Decline of Contemporary Protest Music." *Popular Music & Society* 1 (1971): 44–50.

———. *Minstrels of the Dawn: The Folk Protest Singer as Cultural Hero.* Chicago: Nelson-Hall, 1976.

Rodriquez, Luis J. *Always Running: La Vida Loca, Gang Days in L.A.* Willimantic, CT: Curbstone, 1993.

———. "Los Angeles' Gang Culture Arrives in El Salvador, Courtesy of the INS." *Los Angeles Times,* 8 May 1994, M2.

Rolling Stone, 1 March 1984.

Rolston, Bill. *Politics and Painting: Murals and Conflict in Northern Ireland.* London: Associated University Presses, 1991.

Rosenberg, Neil V. "Bluegrass." In *Encyclopedia of Southern Culture,* edited by Charles R. Wilson and William Ferris, 993–94. Chapel Hill: University of North Carolina Press, 1989.

———. *Bluegrass: A History.* Urbana: University of Illinois Press, 1985.

Ross, Richard, and Marjorie Cohen. "New York Trends in Felony Drug Offense Processing." Albany: Division of Criminal Justice Services, 1988.

Rotella, Sebastian. "Border Lines." *Los Angeles Times,* 20 March 1994, A3, A26.

Rule, James B. "1984—The Ingredients of Totalitarianism." In *1984 Revisited: Totalitarianism in Our Century,* edited by Irving Howe, 166–79. New York: Harper and Row, 1983.

Ryan, Patrick J. "The Relationship of Drugs, Drug Trafficking, and Drug Traffickers to Homicide." *Journal of Crime and Justice* 15 (1992): 25–44.

Sanchez-Tranquilino, Marcos, and John Tagg. "The Pachuco's Flayed Hide: Mobility, Identity, and Buenas Garras." In *Cultural Studies,* edited by Lawrence Grossberg, Cary Nelson, and Paula Treichler, 556–70. New York: Routledge, 1992.

Sanders, Clinton R. *Customizing the Body: The Art and Culture of Tattooing.* Philadelphia: Temple, 1989.

———. "Marks of Mischief: Becoming and Being Tattooed." In *Constructions of Deviance,* edited by Patricia Adler and Peter Adler, 511–29. Belmont, CA: Wadsworth, 1994.

———, ed. *Marginal Conventions: Popular Culture, Mass Media, and Social Deviance.* Bowling Green, OH: The Popular Press, 1990.

Sanders, William. *Gangbangs and Drive-bys: Grounded Culture and Juvenile Gang Violence.* Hawthorne, NY: Aldine de Gruyter, 1994.

Santoro, Gene. "How 2 B Nasty." *The Nation* 251 (2 July 1990): 4–5.

Saunders, Michael. " 'Gangsta' Rap: Rising with a Bullet." *Rocky Mountain News (The Boston Globe),* 27 October 1993, 24D.

Scanlon, Bill. " 'Harassing' of Youths Gets Hearing." *Rocky Mountain News,* 23 August 1993, 16A.

Schattenberg, Gus. "Social Control Functions of Mass Media Depictions of Crime." *Sociological Inquiry* 51 (1981): 71–77.

Scheingold, Stuart A. *The Politics of Law and Order: Street Crime and Public Policy.* New York: Longman, 1984.

———. *The Politics of Street Crime: Criminal Process and Cultural Obsession.* Philadelphia: Temple University Press, 1991.

Schiller, Dan. *Objectivity and the News—The Public and the Rise of Commercial Journalism.* Philadelphia: University of Pennsylvania Press, 1981.

Schlax, Julie. "Ode to a Hog." *Forbes,* 24 December 1990, 109.

Schmidt, Michael. *The New Reich: Violent Extremism in Unified Germany and Beyond.* New York: Pantheon Books, 1993.

Schneider, Andrew, and Mary Pat Flaherty. " 'Profile' Stops Called the New Racism." *Rocky Mountain News (The Pittsburgh Press),* 12 August 1991, 4, 20, 22.

Schur, Edwin. *Narcotic Addiction in Britain and America—The Impact of Public Policy.* Bloomington: Indiana University Press, 1962.

Schutz, Alfred. *Collected Papers I—The Problem of Reality,* edited by Maurice Natanson. The Hague: Martinus Nijhoff, 1962.

Schwartz, Martin D. "The Undercutting Edge of Criminology." *Critical Criminologist* 1 (1989): 1–2, 5.

Schwartz, Martin D., and David O. Friedrichs. "Postmodern Thought and Criminological Discontent: New Metaphors for Understanding Violence." *Criminology* 32 (1994): 221–46.

Schwendinger, Herman, and Julia Schwendinger. *Adolescent Subcultures and Delinquency*. New York: Praeger, 1985.

Scott, James. *Domination and the Arts of Resistance*. New Haven: Yale, 1990.

———. *Weapons of the Weak: Everyday Forms of Peasant Resistance*. New Haven: Yale, 1985.

Seidman, Steven. "Symposium: Queer Theory/Sociology: A Dialogue." *Sociological Theory* 12 (1994): 166–77.

Seltzer, Mark. "Serial Killers." *Differences* 5 (1993): 92–129.

Shaheen, Jack, Joseph Ostroy, Bernadette Wimberley, Dario Scuka, and Cavan Hoque. "Media Coverage of the Middle East: Perception and Foreign Policy." *Annals of the American Academy of Political and Social Science* 482 (1985): 160–73.

Shain, R. E., and K. Higgens. "Middle-Class Delinquents and Popular Music: A Pilot Study." *Popular Music & Society* 2 (1972): 23–42.

Shapiro, Bruce. "The Art Cops." *The Nation* 251 (9 July 1990): 40–57.

Shapiro, Mark. "Voorhees' Last Stand." *Fangoria* (August 1993): 125.

Sharp, Cecil, and Maud Karpeles. *English Folk Songs from the Southern Appalachians*. London: Oxford University Press, 1932.

Sheehan, Neil. *A Bright Shining Lie: John Paul Vann and America in Vietnam*. New York: Viking, 1988.

Sheesley, Joel, and Wayne Bragg. *Sandino in the Streets*. Bloomington: Indiana University Press, 1991.

Shelley, Joseph, and Cindy Ashkins. "Crime, Crime News, and Crime Views." *Public Opinion Quarterly* 45 (1989): 492–501.

Sherizen, Sanford. "Social Construction of Crime News: All the News Fitted to Print." In *Deviance and Mass Media*, edited by Charles Winick, 203–24. Beverly Hills, CA: Sage, 1978.

Sherman, Lawrence W., Leslie Steele, Deborah Laufersweiler, Nancy Hoffer, and Sherry A. Julian. "Stray Bullets and 'Mushrooms': Random Shootings of Bystanders in Four Cities, 1977–1988." *Journal of Quantitative Criminology* 5 (1989): 297–316.

Sherwood, Steven Jay, Philip Smith, and Jeffrey Alexander. "The British Are Coming . . . Again! The Hidden Agenda of 'Cultural Studies.' " *Contemporary Sociology* 22 (1993): 370–75.

Shoemaker, Donald. "Facial Stereotypes of Deviants and Judgements of Guilt or Innocence." *Social Forces* 51 (1973): 427–33.

"Shop Owner Takes Rap on Rap Album." *Rocky Mountain News*, 4 October 1990, 2.

Signorielli, Nancy, and Michael Morgan, eds. *Cultivation Analysis*. Newbury Park, CA: Sage, 1990.

Sklar, Holly. "Young and Guilty by Stereotype." *Z Magazine* 6 (July/August 1993): 52–61.

Skolnick, Jerome, and James J. Fyfe. *Above the Law: Police and the Excessive Use of Force*. New York: The Free Press, 1993.

Smith, Joan. *Misogynies: Reflections on Myths and Malice*. New York: Fawcett Columbine, 1989.

Smith, Laquita Bowen. "Kente Cloth Is a Symbol of African Heritage, Pride." *Rocky Mountain News (Scripps Howard)*, 9 June 1994, 90.

Snow, David, and Calvin Morrill. "Reflections on Anthropology's Ethnographic Crisis of Faith." *Contemporary Sociology* 22 (1993): 8–11.

Solomon, Michael, and Basil Englis. "Reality Engineering: Blurring the Boundaries Between Commercial Signification and Popular Culture." *Journal of Current Issues and Research in Advertising* (forthcoming).

Spandoni, Marie. "Harley-Davidson Revs up to Improve Image." *Advertising Age*, 5 August 1985, 30.

"Special Issue on Latin America." *Border/Lines* 27 (1993).

Spector, Malcolm, and John Kitsuse. *Constructing Social Problems*. Hawthorne, NY: Aldine de Gruyter, 1987.

Spergel, Irving A., and G. David Curry. "The National Youth Gang Survey: A Research and Development Process." In *The Gang Intervention Handbook*, edited by Arnold P. Goldstein and C. Ronald Huff, 359–400. Champaign, IL: Research Press, 1993.

Spitz, Bob. *Dylan: A Biography*. New York: McGraw-Hill, 1989.

"Sports Jacket Theft Reported." *Rocky Mountain News*, 25 October 1994, 22A.

Standard NYSE Stock Reports 61 (no. 103, sec. 17). 27 May 1994.

Statewide Anti-Drug Abuse Council. "State of New York Anti-Drug Abuse Strategy Report." Albany: The Governor's Statewide Anti-Drug Abuse Council, 1989.

Stevens, Howard, and Mary Stevens. "Chained Beauties for the Prowling Sex Monster!" In *Serial Murderers*, edited by Art Crockett, 397–411. New York: Windsor Publishing Corporation, 1990.

Stewart, Susan. "Ceci Tuera Cela: Graffiti as Crime and Art." In *Life After Postmodernism*, edited by John Fekete, 161–80. New York: St. Martin's, 1987.

Stone, Gregory P. "Appearance and the Self." In *Social Psychology Through Symbolic Interaction*, edited by Gregory P. Stone and Harvey A. Farberman, 394–414. Waltham, MA: Xerox College Publishing, 1970.

Strossen, Nadine. "Academic and Artistic Freedom." *Academe* 78 (November/December 1992): 8–15.

Sudnow, David. "Normal Crimes: Sociological Features of the Penal Code in a Public Defender Office." *Social Problems* 12 (1965): 255–76.

Sullivan, Mercer. *"Getting Paid": Youth Crime and Work in the Inner City.* Ithaca: Cornell, 1989.

Surette, Ray. "Criminal Justice Policy and the Media." In *The Media and Criminal Justice Policy: Recent Research and Social Effects*, edited by Ray Surette, 3–17. Springfield, IL: Thomas, 1990.

———. *Media, Crime and Criminal Justice: Images and Realities.* Pacific Grove, CA: Brooks/Cole, 1992.

———, ed. *The Media and Criminal Justice Policy: Recent Research and Social Effects.* Springfield, IL: Thomas, 1990.

Sutherland, Edwin, and Donald Cressey. *Criminology.* 10th ed. Philadelphia: Lippincott, 1978.

Swickard, Joe. "Computer Programs Help Flesh Out Likely Mass-Killer Types." *Hartford Courant*, 27 October 1988, F1, F3.

"Teen Arrested in Jacket Theft." *Rocky Mountain News*, 24 November 1993, 23A.

"Teen Trio Beaten by Gang." *Rocky Mountain News*, 31 October 1994, 12A.

Texas Monthly 20 (July 1992).

"Thieves Get 2 Sport Jackets." *Rocky Mountain News*, 17 November 1993, 23A.

Thompson, Hunter S. *Hell's Angels: A Strange and Terrible Saga.* New York: Ballantine, 1967.

Thompson, William. "Hanging Tongues: A Sociological Encounter with the Assembly Line." *Qualitative Sociology* 6 (1983): 215–37.

Thornton, Sarah. "Moral Panic, the Media and British Rave Culture." In *Microphone Fiends: Youth Music and Youth Culture*, edited by Andrew Ross and Tricia Rose, 176–92. New York: Routledge, 1994.

Tisdale, Sallie. "Talk Dirty to Me." *Utne Reader* 58 (July/August 1993): 65–70.

Tomlinson, Alan, ed. *Consumption, Identity, and Style: Marketing, Meanings, and the Packaging of Pleasure.* London: Routledge, 1990.

Tomsho, Robert. "Dowdy Work Duds Make Fashion Statement." *Rocky Mountain News (Wall Street Journal)*, 15 May 1993, 46A.

Traum, Happy. *Bluegrass Guitar.* New York: Oak Publications, 1974.

Trebach, Arnold S. *The Heroin Solution.* New Haven: Yale University Press, 1982.

Tribe, Ivan M. "The Hillbilly versus the City: Urban Images in Country Music." *JEMF Quarterly* 10 (1974): 41–51.

Triplett, Ruth. "The Conflict Perspective, Symbolic Interactionism, and the Status Characteristic Hypothesis." *Justice Quarterly* 10 (1993): 541–58.

Tuchman, Gaye. *Making News.* New York: The Free Press, 1978.

Tucker, Karl. "Rock into the Future." In *Rock of Ages: The Rolling Stone History of Rock and Roll*, edited by Ed Ward et al., 614. Englewood Cliffs, NJ: Rolling Stone/ Prentice-Hall, 1986.

Tunnell, Kenneth D. *Choosing Crime: The Criminal Calculus of Property Offenders.* Chicago: Nelson-Hall, 1992.

———. "Film at Eleven: Recent Developments in the Commodification of Crime." *Sociological Spectrum* 12 (1992): 293–313.

Turner, Ralph H., and Samuel Surace. "Zoot-Suiters and Mexicans: Symbols in Crowd Behavior." *American Journal of Sociology* 62 (1956): 14–20.

Twitchell, James. *Preposterous Violence.* Oxford: Oxford University Press, 1989.

"2,000 Christian Conservatives Cheer Anti-Abortion Speech." *Rocky Mountain News,* 12 September 1993, 34A.

Vance, Carole. "The War on Culture." *Art in America* 77 (1989): 39–43.

Veraska, Don. "Putting Muscle into Trademark Protection." *Advertising Age,* 9 June 1986, S12–S13.

Vetter, Craig. "Playboy Interview: Hunter Thompson." *Playboy* (November 1974): 75–90, 245–46.

Vigil, James Diego. *Barrio Gangs: Street Life and Identity in Southern California.* Austin: University of Texas Press, 1988.

Villela, Minnerly Lucia, and Richard Markin. "A Star Wars As Myth: A Fourth Hope?" *Frontiers* 5 (1987): 17–24.

Waldenburg, Hermann. *The Berlin Wall.* New York: Abbeyville Press, 1990.

Waldman, Steve. "Stylin': Gangs and Good Kids: It's Getting Harder and Harder to Tell Them Apart." *Up the Creek,* 23–29 April 1993, 8–9.

Walker, Martin. *Powers of the Press—Twelve of the World's Influential Newspapers.* New York: The Pilgrim Press, 1983.

Warner, Priscilla. "Fantastic Outsiders: Villains and Deviants in Animated Cartoons." In *Marginal Conventions: Popular Culture, Mass Media, and Social Deviance,* edited by Clinton R. Sanders, 117–30. Bowling Green, OH: The Popular Press, 1990.

Watney, Simon. *Policing Desire: Pornography, AIDS and the Media.* Minneapolis: University of Minnesota Press, 1987.

Watson, Mark. "Outlaw Motorcyclists: An Outgrowth of Lower Class Cultural Concerns." *Deviant Behavior* 2 (1980): 31–48.

Weber, Brian. "Cruisers Lose on West 38th." *Rocky Mountain News,* 23 April 1992, 7A.

Weisheit, Ralph A. "Civil War on Drugs." In *Drugs, Crime, and the Criminal Justice System,* edited by Ralph A. Weisheit, 1–10. Cincinnati: Anderson, 1990.

Wernick, Peter. *Bluegrass Songbook.* New York: Oak Publications, 1976.

Werthman, Carl, and Irving Piliavin. "Gang Members and Police." In *The Sociology of Juvenile Delinquency,* edited by Ronald Berger, 358–66. Chicago: Nelson-Hall, 1991.

Wilkins, Leslie. *Consumerist Criminology.* New York: Academic Press, 1985.

———. "Information and the Definition of Deviance." In *The Manufacture of*

News, edited by Stanley Cohen and Jock Young, 22–27. Beverly Hills, CA: Sage, 1973.

Willis, Paul. *Learning to Labor*. New York: Columbia University Press, 1977.

Winfree, L. Thomas, Jr., Kathy Fuller, Teresa Vigil, and G. Larry Mays. "The Definition and Measurement of 'Gang Status': Policy Implications for Juvenile Justice." *Juvenile and Family Court Journal* (1992): 29–37.

Winick, Charles, and M. Winick. "Courtroom Drama on Television." *Journal of Communication* 24 (1974): 67–73.

Wisotsky, Steven. *Breaking the Impasse in the War on Drugs*. New York: Greenwood Press, 1986.

Wolfe, Charles. "Bluegrass Touches: An Interview with Bill Monroe." *Old Time Music* 16 (1975): 6–12.

———. *Kentucky Country: Folk and Country Music of Kentucky*. Lexington: University Press of Kentucky, 1982.

———. *Tennessee Strings*. Knoxville: University of Tennessee Press, 1977.

Wolfe, Thomas. *You Can't Go Home Again*. New York: Harper & Brothers, 1940.

Wolfgang, Marvin E., and Franco Ferracuti. *The Subculture of Violence: Towards an Integrated Theory in Criminology*. Beverly Hills, CA: Sage, 1982.

Wolfgang, Marvin E., and Marc Riedel. "Race, Judicial Discretion, and the Death Penalty." In *Criminal Law in Action*, edited by William J. Chambliss, 449–61. New York: Wiley, 1984.

Wooden, Wayne. *Renegade Kids, Suburban Outlaws*. Belmont, CA: Wadsworth, 1995.

Wright, Bruce. "Art in the Public Realm." *Public Art Review* 2 (1990): 16.

Wright, Steven. *Meditations in Green*. New York: Bantam Books, 1983.

Young, Jock. "The Amplification of Drug Use." In *The Manufacture of News*, edited by Stanley Cohen and Jock Young, 50–59. Beverly Hills, CA: Sage, 1973.

———. "Mass Media, Drugs, and Deviance." In *Deviance and Social Control*, edited by Paul Rock and Mary McIntosh, 229–59. London: Tavistock, 1974.

"Youths Steal Team Jackets." *Rocky Mountain News*, 10 November 1993, 27A.

Zuckerman, E. "The Year of the Cop." *Rolling Stone* 23 (1977): 57–63.

Non-Print Media

Brazilian Dreams. San Francisco: BACAT, 1990. Video.

Lowe, Nick. "(I Love the Sound of) Breaking Glass." On Nick Lowe, *Basher: The Best of Nick Lowe*, 1984.

Contributors

Gregg Barak is professor and head of the Department of Sociology, Anthropology, and Criminology at Eastern Michigan University. He is the author of numerous articles, two books, and three anthologies. His book *Gimme Shelter: A Social History of Homelessness in Contemporary America* was selected by *Choice* for its List of Outstanding Academic Titles for 1991. His latest books include *Varieties of Criminology: Readings from a Dynamic Discipline* and *Media, Process, and the Social Construction of Crime: Studies in Newsmaking Criminology*, both published in 1994.

Mitchell L. Bracey, Jr., is a second-year graduate student in the Department of Sociology and Anthropology at Virginia Commonwealth University. He received his undergraduate degree in sociology in 1993 at VCU and earned a MS degree in sociology in May 1995. He entered a doctoral program in sociology in the fall of 1995. His present interests include deviant behavior, criminology, religious movements, and race relations.

Henry H. Brownstein is the chief of the Bureau of Statistical Services at the New York State Division of Criminal Justice Services. He is responsible for the production of official crime and criminal justice statistics in New York. For the past decade he has also been co-principal investigator for a series of studies of drugs and violence conducted jointly with National Development and Research Institutes, Inc. He earned his Ph.D. in sociology from Temple University in 1977.

Su C. Epstein continues to investigate issues of culture, crime, and the sociology of the strange and obscure. She is currently an assistant professor at Gallaudet University.

Jeff Ferrell is associate professor of criminal justice at Northern Arizona University. His research on crime and delinquency, popular culture, workers' culture, and social and labor history has appeared in journals ranging from *Social Justice* and *Labor History* to *Youth and Society*, the *Journal of Popular Culture*, the *Journal of Criminal Justice and Popular Culture*, and the *Journal of Folklore Research*, and in a variety of edited collections. He is the author of *Crimes of Style: Urban Graffiti and the Politics of Criminality*.

Mark S. Hamm is a professor of criminology at Indiana State University. He has published numerous studies exploring such topics as prisoner rehabilitation, romantic violence, and state-organized crime. He is the author of *American Skinheads: The Criminology and Control of Hate Crime*, winner of the Frederic Milton Thrasher Award; *Hate Crime: International Perspectives on Causes and Control*; and *The Abandoned Ones: The Imprisonment and Uprising of the Mariel Boat People*.

Stephen Lyng is an associate professor of sociology at Virginia Commonwealth University. He is the author of a monograph entitled *Holistic Health and Biomedical Medicine: A Countersystem Analysis* and has published articles on voluntary risk taking, social movements, and health care planning. He is presently rebuilding a 1950 FL model Harley-Davidson and continues his recuperation from injuries suffered in a serious motorcycle accident.

Eleanor Lyon has been a research associate in the Research and Planning division of the Village for Families & Children, Inc., of Hartford, Connecticut, for over eleven years. Her work there has focused on family violence and criminal justice policy research, supported primarily by federal and state grants and contracts. She is currently directing a statewide evaluation of sentencing alternatives to incarceration and co-conducting research for the state's Task Force on Minority Fairness. She is also an adjunct professor of sociology at the University of Connecticut.

Gary T. Marx is professor emeritus, M.I.T., professor and chair of the Sociology Department at the University of Colorado at Boulder, and director of the Center for the Social Study of Information Technology. He has published extensively in leading sociology, criminology, and law journals. He is the author of *Protest and Prejudice*, *Collective Behavior and*

Social Movements (with Doug McAdam) and *Undercover: Police Surveillance in America,* winner of the Outstanding Book Award from the Academy of Criminal Justice Sciences and other awards.

Jody A. Miller is currently working toward her Ph.D. in sociology at the University of Southern California. She is editor, with Malcolm W. Klein and Cheryl L. Maxson, of *The Modern Gang Reader.* Articles based on her research on street prostitution appear in the *Journal of Contemporary Ethnography, Deviant Behavior,* and *Humanity & Society.* Her dissertation research is on female gang participation.

Clinton R. Sanders is professor of sociology at the University of Connecticut. He is the author of *Customizing the Body: The Art and Culture of Tattooing* and the editor of *Marginal Conventions: Popular Culture, Mass Media and Social Deviance.* His current research is directed at exploring the development and maintenance of social relationships between people and companion animals. His book *Regarding Animals: Investigating Human Relationships with Other Species* (with Arnold Arluke) is forthcoming.

Kenneth D. Tunnell is an associate professor of criminal justice at Eastern Kentucky University. He has published in a variety of periodicals such as *Justice Quarterly, Sociological Spectrum,* and the *Journal of Popular Culture.* His books include *Choosing Crime, Political Crime in Contemporary America,* and the forthcoming text with Jeffrey Ian Ross, *The Dynamics of Political Crime.* His ongoing research interests include qualitative approaches to understanding crime and justice and the political economy of crime and punishment.

Index